Robert Ryder
The Acoustical Unconscious

Interdisciplinary German Cultural Studies

Edited by
Irene Kacandes

Volume 32

Robert Ryder

The Acoustical Unconscious

From Walter Benjamin to Alexander Kluge

DE GRUYTER

ISBN 978-3-11-135687-7
e-ISBN (PDF) 978-3-11-073300-6
e-ISBN (EPUB) 978-3-11-073302-0
ISSN 1861-8030

Library of Congress Control Number: 2021950241

Bibliographic information published by the Deutsche Nationalbibliothek
The Deutsche Nationalbibliothek lists this publication in the Deutsche Nationalbibliografie;
detailed bibliographic data are available on the Internet at http://dnb.dnb.de.

© 2023 Walter de Gruyter GmbH, Berlin/Boston
This volume is text- and page-identical with the hardback published in 2022.
Cover image: mtv2020/iStock/Getty Images Plus
Typesetting: Integra Software Services Pvt. Ltd.
Printing and binding: CPI books GmbH, Leck

www.degruyter.com

―――

dedicated to

mom

&

Lulu

Acknowledgements

It is impossible to thank everyone who has aided or abetted in whole or in part to this book, which is both quite old and relatively new. That said, it is easy to begin with the singular scholar, colleague, and friend whose influence can be found on every page, who gave me the chance long ago to present in Santa Barbara in his stead, and who has been a source of knowledge, insight, wisdom, and inspiration since I first arrived at Northwestern: Sam Weber. I would also like to thank Michael Levine, who has since the beginning been a fount of insight and encouragement for this project, as well as the late Edward Branigan, who was also present in Santa Barbara and who encouraged me to publish my first article on the topic in *The New Review of Film and Television Studies*.

The arguments that I have since developed in the following pages have profited from many conversations and invited lectures at various institutions over many years. I would first and foremost express my sincere gratitude to the incredibly supportive and intellectual community at Northwestern University, both then and now, and especially to all my colleagues and friends during graduate school in the German department and Comparative Literature Program. I also feel very fortunate to have been able to share and discuss my work with friends, colleagues and mentors both in the Chicagoland area and abroad. What follows only begins to thank those who have been sympathetic to my project, who read or heard various versions and provided precious feedback, and helped me at one point or another along the way: Peter Fenves, Jörg Kreienbrock, Rainer Rumold, Linda Austern, Berthold Hoeckner, David Wellbery, Tom Gunning, Sara Hall, Imke Meyer, Heidi Schlipphacke, Peter Szendy, Thomas Schestag, Doris Bachmann-Medick, Hubertus Büschel, Alexandra M. Stewart, Florence Feiereisen, Mary Helen Dupree, Adrian Daub, Elisabeth Krimmer and Marcel Krings. I am also grateful to the anonymous readers of the book's earlier renditions, who gave me much to consider, and a special thanks to Julie Beth Napolin, whose in-depth reading and stimulating suggestions at the end of this long process were as refreshing as they were reassuring.

I cannot thank enough the incredibly supportive and efficient team of scholars and editors at De Gruyter who have made this book possible, including Myrto Aspioti, who as acquisitions editor was the first to reach out to me; Irene Kacandes, who enthusiastically agreed to add this book to her series and whose honesty, patience and professionalism were everything I could have hoped for; and Stella Dietrich, who as project editor made the path to the book's present format as smooth as could be. The manuscript would not have been nearly as polished without Connie Tappy's keen attention to detail and extraordinary editorial skills, and many thanks also to Becca Cain for her incredibly useful and user-friendly index.

Finally, I wish to thank my family and circles of friends both near and far, who would still think the world of me had I never published this book, but who share my joy in its completion. In particular, I wish to express my gratitude to Peter Jaros and Bishupal Limbu, who accompanied me along the long journey and kept me going in more ways than I could ever say, and to Paul North, whose boundless friendship above all helped to see me through. To my parents-in-laws, Bill and Jane, I owe an enormous debt of gratitude for always being ready to share with the work and joys of parenting. I could never have imagined even studying in the USA without my parents' unwavering faith in me and would never have pursued this winding path into academia if it was not for my mother instilling in me her love of literature, music and life. And finally, my wife Becky provided just the right blend of urging, understanding and encouragement required to bring this project to its completion. No words can thank her for the ways she aided me in this endeavor.

Elements of the first and third section of Chapter One appeared in article form as "Walter Benjamin's Shell-Shock: Sounding the Acoustical Unconscious" in *The New Review of Film and Television Studies* 5.2 (2007): 135–155, which have been reprinted here with express permission of the Taylor & Francis Group. I am also thankful to the editors of the special section of *The Goethe Yearbook* 25 (2018): 55–76, who have kindly permitted me to reprint much of my interpretation of Tieck's story in Chapter Two from my earlier article, "Of Barks and Birdsong: Listening in on the Forgotten in Tieck's *Der blonde Eckbert*." Finally, sections two and three of Chapter Four was originally published in *Germany in the Loud Twentieth-Century* (2012) and appear here slightly modified and with the kind permission of Oxford University Press.

Contents

Acknowledgements —— VII

List of Abbreviations —— XI

Introduction: Hearing Otherwise —— 1

1 Walter Benjamin's Shell-Shock: Sounding the Acoustical Unconscious —— 28
    1.1 Characteristics of An Acoustical Unconscious —— 29
    1.2 All Ears: Benjamin's Telephone —— 41
    1.3 The Acoustical Un-conch-ious —— 50

2 Of Birds and Barks: Listening in on the Forgotten in Freud, Benjamin, and Tieck —— 66
    2.1 Freud's trompe l'oreille —— 71
    2.2 The Signorelli-Strohmian Strain —— 78
    2.3 The Bark of the Forgotten —— 86
    2.4 Waldeinsamkeit – Wiederhörbarkeit —— 94

3 Voices Carry: Benjamin and Arnheim on Radio —— 102
    3.1 Materiality and Expression in Arnheim's (Radio) Art —— 108
    3.2 Arnheim's Art of Not Listening —— 117
    3.3 The Gesticulating Voice in Benjamin —— 127
    3.4 Per Sona and Rustling Papers in *The Cold Heart* —— 134
    3.5 Mickey and Kasperl —— 140

4 Glimpsing the World through Our Ears: Günter Eich and the Acoustical Unconscious —— 155
    4.1 "Dichterisch wohnet der Eich": Eich and Heidegger —— 158
    4.2 Awakening in *Dreams* to Eich's Soundscapes —— 167
    4.3 Eich's *poisons de l'öuie* —— 172
    4.4 Eich's Echoes: *Sabeth* —— 178
    4.5 The Word in its Transformation: *The Year Lazertis* —— 185

5 Clatter in Kracauer and Kluge: Politicizing the Acoustical Unconscious —— 192
    5.1 Something like an "Acoustic Unconscious" —— 195
    5.2 Kluge's Fantasy in Film —— 202

5.3	"An Observation on Walter Benjamin" by Kluge —— 207	
5.4	Movement, Music and Film in *Cinema Stories* —— 210	
5.5	New Sound Perspectives and the Dissolution of *Götterdämmerung* —— 216	
5.6	Fantasy in *Die Macht der Gefühle* and *Die Patriotin* —— 223	

Conclusion: Toward a Genealogy of the Acoustical Unconscious —— 239

Works Cited —— 249

Index —— 261

List of Abbreviations

Unless otherwise noted, all references to Walter Benjamin's work will refer first to the *Gesammelte Schriften*, then to the *Werke und Nachlass*, if available, and finally to the *Selected Writings*. The first number will be the volume number, followed by the page number.

AP	*Arcades Project*, Walter Benjamin.
CS	*Cinema Stories*, Alexander Kluge.
GA	*Gesamtausgabe*, Martin Heidegger.
GS	*Gesammelte Schriften*, Walter Benjamin.
GesW	*Gesammelte Werke*, Günter Eich.
GvK	*Geschichten vom Kino*, Alexander Kluge.
GW	*Gesammelte Werke*, Sigmund Freud.
OGT	*Origin of the German Trauerspiel*, Walter Benjamin.
ÖuE	*Öffentlichkeit und Erfahrung. Zur Organisationsanalyse von bürgerlicher und proletarischer Öffentlichkeit*, Alexander Kluge and Oskar Negt.
PLT	*Poetry Language Thought*, Martin Heidegger.
PSE	*Public Sphere and Experience: Toward an Analysis of the Bourgeois and Proletarian Public Sphere*, Alexander Kluge and Oskar Negt.
SE	*The Standard Edition of the Complete Psychological Works of Sigmund Freud*, Sigmund Freud.
s.v.	*sub verbo*, under the word
SW	*Selected Writings of Walter Benjamin*, Walter Benjamin.
WuN	*Werke und Nachlass: Kritische Gesamtausgabe*, Walter Benjamin.

Introduction: Hearing Otherwise

In a short text entitled "The Lamp" ("Zur Lampe," 1933), Walter Benjamin for the first time sketches out thoughts that would soon lead him to a theory of mimesis, which becomes more thoroughly formulated in two other, more well-known texts from the same year, "On the Mimetic Faculty" ("Über das mimetische Vermögen") and "Doctrine of the Similar" ("Lehre vom Ähnlichen"). But in "The Lamp" Benjamin compares two objects, a gas lamp and a conch shell, to the point where these otherwise disparate objects begin to lose their distinction. When he finally picks up the shell and puts it to his ear, Benjamin begins to describe what he hears and, more importantly, what he does not:

> Now the nineteenth century is empty. It lies there like a large, dead, cold seashell (*Muschel*). I pick it up and hold it up to my ear. What do I hear? I do not hear the noise of field artillery or of Offenbach's gala music; nor do I hear the factory sirens or the cry that goes up at midday on the stock exchange – not even the din of soldiers on parade or the long-drawn-out whistle on the train. I can of course imagine all these things [*Vorstellen kann ich mir das alles wohl*]. But what I hear when I put the shell up to my ear is an other [*ist ein anderes*].[1]

What follows is a descriptive list of singular sounds from his childhood home, like the fall of anthracite into the stove or the clinking of the lampshade when carried from room to room. Since the descriptions of these singular sounds are subjected to a more thorough analysis in Chapter One, I will refrain from further discussing them here. But at the end of the passage above, what is clearly distinguished are sounds that are readily representable and those that constitute "a something other." Other than what? One of the more obvious explanations is that this "something other" diverges from what might otherwise be associated with something called "the nineteenth century." Against the generalities of Offenbach's music or the sounds of artillery, which are more easily representable to what might be called a collective sonic imagination, Benjamin is listening for the singularity of his own childhood memories in order to disrupt the conventional meaning of what the nineteenth century sounds like. Such a disruption of conventions is a motif that runs throughout Benjamin's work: already in his habilitation, *Origin of the German Trauerspiel* (*Ursprung des deutschen Trauerspiels*, 1928), not only does Benjamin begin his discussion

---

[1] Walter Benjamin, *Gesammelte Schriften* (Frankfurt a.M.: Suhrkamp, 1972) (hereafter, *GS*), 7:793; Walter Benjamin, *Selected Writings*, ed. Michael W. Jennings, Marcus Bullock, Howard Eiland, and Gary Smith, trans. Rodney Livingstone and Edmund Jephcott (Cambridge: Harvard University Press, 1996–2003) (hereafter, *SW*), 2:692.

of allegory in opposition to the common (mis)understanding of the term, but he goes on to define allegory as always pointing to something other than what it ostensibly designates: allegory "signifies precisely the nonbeing [*das Nicht-Sein*] of that which it represents [*vorstellt*]."[2] Benjamin's discussion of allegory is a similar disruption of conventional meaning and expectation, with the same recourse to the "other" – in this case, the nonbeing – of representation. This may also be why Benjamin avoided neologisms: because they are created to signify exactly that which they are intended to represent, their intention is too direct. Instead of inventing words that signify directly, even if unconventionally, what they represent, Benjamin would rather re-inscribe a term's previous meanings, as he does with allegory, by rummaging through "the historical memory of language" to recover what has been collectively forgotten in the very establishment of its more conventional meaning.[3]

A major part of the present study is devoted to emphasizing the acoustical variant of this process found throughout Benjamin's work. Already in the "Epistemo-Critical Preface" to his *Trauerspiel* book, for instance, he writes how ideas are given "not so much in a primal language [*Ursprache*] as in a primal hearing [*Urvernehmen*]," through which "words possess the nobility of their naming power undiminished by the signification necessary to knowledge [*erkennende Bedeutung*]."[4] Beyond their recognizable and cognitive meaning, words have a "noble" relation to names that, instead of being derivative of an originary language, are given as long as one adopts a certain receptivity or *Urvernehmen*, which Samuel Weber rightly translates as "originary listening."[5] This mode of

---

[2] Benjamin, *GS* 1:406; Walter Benjamin, *Origin of the German Trauerspiel*, trans. Howard Eiland (Cambridge: Harvard University Press, 2019) (hereafter, *OGT*), 255.

[3] Samuel Weber makes a similar point about Benjamin's avoidance of creating neologisms in his introduction of *Benjamin's – abilities*: "by introducing new words, [neologisms] ignore the historical memory of language. Rather than investing words, Benjamin's discussion, and his writing practice, advocates the reinscribing of established terms so that they part company with themselves – which is to say, with their previous identities" (Samuel Weber, *Benjamin's – abilities* [Cambridge: Harvard University Press, 2008], 9–10).

[4] Benjamin, *GS* 1:216; *OGT* 13.

[5] While the term *Urvernehmen* is rendered by John Osborne in his 1977 translation of the *Trauerspiel* book as "primoridal form of perception" (Benjamin, *The Origin of German Tragic Drama*, trans. John Osborne [London: New Left Books, 1977], 36), Eiland translates it in his new translation as "primal hearing" (Benjamin, *OGT* 13). Like Eiland, a number of scholars have emphasized the acoustic dimension of the German word. In *Wild, Unforgettable Philosophy*, Monad Rrenban acknowledges its connection to a "primordial hearing": such "hearing is the theological basis of philosophy. Impelled by hearing the sound without spatial correlate, this theology is a ceaseless movement in, beyond, and between layers of meaning" (Monad Rrenban, *Wild, Unforgettable Philosophy in Early Works of Walter Benjamin* [Lanham, MD: Lexington Books, 2004], 100). Dag

listening is fundamental to the task of philosophy for Benjamin, a task that entails a certain remembrance:

> It is the concern of the philosopher, through staging [*durch Darstellung*],[6] to reestablish in its primacy the symbolic character of the word [. . .]. Since philosophy may not presume to speak in tones of revelation, this can happen only through a remembering that goes back first of all to originary listening [*durch ein aufs Urvernehmen allererst zuruckgehendes Erinnern*] [translation modified].[7]

While it is difficult to bridge Benjamin's theoretical reflections in the preface of the *Trauerspiel* book to "The Lamp" fragment with which I began, one could say that Benjamin "stages" an act of originary listening when he picks up the conch shell: it becomes a conduit through which words are separated from their identifiable or "cognitive" meaning, from that which is representable (*vorstellbar*) and made perceptible or audible (*vernehmbar*). While Benjamin picks up the conch shell to listen in on those singular, unconventional sounds of the nineteenth century that have been long-forgotten in the vast mnemonic soundscape of his childhood, he is simultaneously enacting this mode of originary listening that remembers these words' noble relation to names. It is no coincidence that for Benjamin the nineteenth century *is* the shell, which is itself an unconventional, even kitchy vessel to house an entire century.[8] As an already unexpected receptacle of the forgotten, it also mimics Proust's madeleine or Kafka's animals, as Benjamin describes them.[9] But above all, this shell is the medium through which certain sounds, which could not otherwise be made representable to thought, are nevertheless heard once again, as if for the first time. Benjamin's shell allows him to listen and thereby remember otherwise. Benjamin's shell, I

Petersson describes *Urvernehmen* as "the tonal potentiality of the word, which may actualize a remnant of the creative language before the fall" (Dag Petersson, *The Art of Reconciliation: Photography and the Conception of Dialectics in Benjamin, Hegel, and Derrida* [Hampshire: Palgrave, 2013], 125). I follow Weber's translation, "originary listening," which "in turn entails *remembrance*. Through such remembering words are 'once again' given the ability 'to reassert their rights to name'" (Weber, *Benjamin's -abilities*, 9).

6 Throughout *Benjamin's -abilites*, Weber emphasizes the importance of translating Benjamin's use of *Darstellung* differently from representation: Benjamin's "'ideas,' for instance, become 'monads,' which in turn are defined through their character as 'presentation' or 'exposition' – *Darstellung* – a term that Benjamin understands more in its chemical sense, that of *recombination*, than its traditional meaning of *representation*" (Weber, *Benjamin's -abilities*, 303). I return to Benjamin's ideas and *Darstellung* in Chapter Three.

7 Benjamin, *GS* 1:216–217; *OGT* 13.

8 I will return to the shell as *etui* and kitsch near the end of Chapter One, especially in relation to Benjamin's "Some Remarks on Folk Art."

9 Benjamin, *GS* 2:430; *SW* 2:810.

would argue, is a kind of allegorical hearing aid for the acoustical unconscious, allowing him and by extension his readers, to hear otherwise.

If the conch shell in Benjamin's work is the primary sound figure that, through its staging, promotes a mode of "originary listening" that hears otherwise, a similar mode of hearing can be found in the final passage of Derrida's *Speech and Phenomena* (*La voix et le phénomène*, 1967). In a rather cryptic way, Derrida is introducing différance as a concept that must be thought beyond the metaphysics and history of presence. Very little in this passage seems to have anything to do with sound, and so may strike the reader as an arbitrary comparison to Benjamin's autobiographical reflection about sounds emitting from a conch shell in 1933. And yet their aim seems to be one and the same: in the following passage Derrida is calling for another mode of understanding beyond representational knowledge and conventional systems of meaning. He does so by employing certain key words that, like Benjamin's *Urvernehmen* above, have acoustic connotations that gesture towards what might be called a hearing otherwise:

> For that which "begins," then, "beyond" absolute knowledge, *unheard-of* thoughts [*pensées inouïes*] are required that are sought for across the memory of old signs. As long as we ask if the concept of différance should be conceived on the basis of presence or antecedent to it, it remains one of these old signs [. . .]. It is necessary that it be heard/understood this way and otherwise [*Il faut l'entendre ainsi et autrement*]. Otherwise, that is to say, in the openness of an unheard-of question that opens neither upon knowledge nor upon nonknowledge like a knowledge to come. In the openness of this question *we no longer know*. [. . .] Such a question will be legitimately heard/understood as *wanting-to-say nothing* [*sera légitimement entendue comme* ne voulant rien dire], as no longer belonging to the system of meaning [*vouloir-dire*] [emphasis original].[10]

The two words Derrida uses in this passage that are relevant for our purposes are "entendre," which, depending on the context, is typically translated as either to hear or to understand, and "inouïe." The latter word, like its English counterpart, "unheard-of," also has multiple meanings: apart from its literal definition of something not heard at all, it more often refers to something unprecedented, in the sense of something out of the ordinary, even unacceptable, as in the example: "from the first he broke out into unheard-of extravagance."[11]

---

10 Jacques Derrida, *La voix et le phénomène* (Paris: Presses universitaires de France, 1967), 115–116; *Speech and Phenomena*, trans. David B. Allison (Evanston, IL: Northwestern University Press, 1973), 103. Subsequent references will first give the original French pagination, then the English.
11 From F. W. Farrar, *Darkness and Dawn*, 1.15:125, cited under "unheard-of," *Oxford English Dictionary*, 2nd ed. (Oxford: Oxford University Press, 1989).

These latter definitions reflect a break from conventional meaning, from the historically or socially codified. Moreover, Derrida's own use of it in the phrase, "dans l'ouverture d'une question inouïe" (*in the openness of an unheard-of question*), gestures less toward something like an "open-ended question" than toward a certain open *response*, a response or stance toward something that does not fit into existing (and therefore conventional) expectations and structures of knowledge. In the openness of this responsive stance, our ears remain open to the unprecedented and even unacceptable.

The second word, "entendre," should also be considered in terms of the unconventional, and specifically to unconventional modes of meaning, not simply because it can also be translated as "to understand." The word can be traced back to a few passages in *Speech and Phenomena* in which Derrida reads Husserl's distinction between interpretation (*Deutung*) and meaning (*Bedeutung*) in section five of the *Logical Investigations* (*Logische Untersuchungen*, 1901). While highlighting Husserl's entanglement between expression and intention, Derrida writes that if

> expression is always inhabited and animated by a meaning (*bedeuten*), as *wanting* to say [vouloir *dire*], this is because, for Husserl, the *Deutung*, the interpretation or understanding/hearing [*l'entente*] of the *Bedeutung* can never take place outside oral discourse (*Rede*). Only such discourse is subject to a *Deutung*, which is never primarily reading, but listening [*écoute*].[12]

Although Derrida is not explicit, the two French verbs *entendre* (to hear) and *écouter* (to listen) seem to be reserved for *Bedeutung* and *Deutung* respectively. *Bedeutung*, often translated into English as "meaning," is closely associated in Husserl with expression (*Ausdruck*), in that an expression always embodies meaning. The term *Deutung*, on the other hand, is defined as the interpretative act of indicative communication, such as the interpretation of gestures or facial expressions. In the passage above Derrida adds to Husserl's distinction an aural difference: we only *listen* to latent expressions while we *hear* that which is meant via oral expression. Of course, the philosophical distinction between these modes of acoustic perception must also inevitably overlap: only by listening to the indicative *Deutung* do we come to hear and therefore understand expressive meaning (*Bedeutung*). In another passage a few pages later, Derrida is even more explicit:

> This interpretation (*Deutung*) makes a latent expression *heard* [*entendre*], brings a meaning (*bedeuten*) out from what was still held back. Nonexpressive signs mean (*bedeuten*) only in the degree to which they can be made to say what was murmuring in them [*ce qui

---

12 Derrida, *voix*, 36; *Speech*, 33–34.

se murmurait en eux], in a stammering attempt [*dans une sorte de bredouillement*]. Gestures mean something only insofar as we can listen to them [*les écouter*], interpret them (*deuten*).¹³

Interpretive listening is what "makes a latent expression *heard*," seeking a way to hear a certain kind of meaning in nonexpressive signs, which for Husserl is not possible. Like the singular sounds emitting from Benjamin's conch shell, meaning *murmurs* for Derrida in gestures and facial expressions: only by "listening" to these indicative modes of communication can one "hear" meaning in these otherwise nonexpressive signs. In the context of this revaluation of Husserl's entanglement with meaning and interpretation, we may return to the end of *Speech and Phenomena*: to hear otherwise would thus include the possibility of hearing a certain kind of meaning in the nonexpressive sign, to listen in on the murmur of meaning that is concerned with neither conventional systems of knowledge nor historical modes of representation. Hearing otherwise involves being receptive to unconventional meaning via the nonexpressive and to that unheard-of question in which, as Derrida emphasizes in italics, *"we no longer know."*¹⁴

The question that arises from this comparison, and which is pertinent to this study in particular, may be formulated as follows: when dealing with the effort to problematize historically codified, if not petrified, conventional expectations and meanings, might such an effort be made more amenable when it is framed in terms of the acoustical rather than the visual or "cognitive"? Are

---

13 Derrida, *voix*, 38; *Speech*, 36.
14 Although it falls out of the purview of this introduction, Benjamin also challenges Husserl's distinction between meaning and interpretation in a series of logico-linguistic studies from around 1916. See in particular "The Judgment of Designation" in Benjamin, *GS* 6:9–10. Peter Fenves, in the introduction to his *Messianic Reduction*, describes Benjamin's alteration of Husserl's entanglement with meaning and interpretation as follows: "In place of the opposition between expression and indication, Benjamin introduces a distinction between 'judgments of predication' and 'judgments of designation': only in the case of the former can one speak of meaning, properly speaking, whereas in cases of designation, there is merely 'inauthentic meaning [uneigentliche Bedeutung].' Whenever a term is said to mean something, its meaning is categorially different from the meaning of a term that means something in the absence of any stipulation of what it is supposed to mean. This 'something' that a properly meaningful term means is, however, first and foremost meaning pure and simple. For this reason, the term in question cannot properly be called a 'term' but is in a certain sense indeterminate, which is to say, infinite in its own particular way" (Peter Fenves, *Messianic Reduction: Walter Benjamin and the Shape of Time* [Stanford, CA: Stanford University Press, 2010], 10). Like Derrida, Benjamin was thus also searching for an alternative mode of meaning beyond the Husserlian *Bedeutung*. For an extended reading of Benjamin's transformation of the distinctions with which *Logical Investigations* begins, see especially the second chapter of *Messianic Reduction*.

conventional meanings and systems of knowledge more susceptible to alteration insofar as they are acoustical and not visual? Much of this study's encounter with and interpretation of the acoustical unconscious goes in the direction of redefining what "knowledge" involves. Of course, the concept of the unconscious already introduces a new way of knowing already at work in Freud. But even before embarking on the difficult task of (re)defining knowledge with respect to the acoustical unconscious, it is important in these opening remarks to point out the way both Benjamin and Derrida are already employing terms like *Urvernehmen* and *entendre autrement* in their own theoretical work in order to undermine conventional modes of representation and meaning. Neither critic is simply relegating this mode of receptivity to the "acoustic" realm; to do so would be antithetical to the multivalent modes of knowledge and meaning they are both seeking to accentuate and practice in these very passages. What both Benjamin's *Urvernehmen* and Derrida's *entendre* have in common is precisely this multivalence: as we have seen, *vernehmen* in German can mean to both "listen" and "perceive," while *entendre* in French can be translated as to "hear" as well as to "understand." Both Benjamin and Derrida recognize the importance of – and practice the art of – remaining open to the particular indeterminacy of a word's meanings. Just as *inouïe* has multiple meanings, *différance* is "immediately and irreducibly multivalent," rich with *pensées inouïes*. To extrapolate Benjamin's image of the conch shell above, one could say that when Derrida picks up the word "difference" and puts it to his ear, what he hears "ist ein anderes," a différance.¹⁵ When attempting to problematize conventional modes of representation and meaning, both Benjamin and Derrida tend to employ words that revolve around the acoustical more so than the visual, in part, one might

---

15 My reasons for maintaining these words' relevance to the sonic in Derrida's final paragraph of *Speech and Phenomena* are not merely strategic. Although Derrida's deconstructive strategy has often been criticized for being inapplicable to music and the sonorous domain in general, he is nevertheless adamant that "the a of différance [. . .] is not heard [*ne s'entend pas*]; it remains silent, secret, and discreet, like a tomb" (Derrida, *Speech*, 132). As paradoxical as it may sound, it is precisely this inaudible difference between the two phonemes that opens one up to hearing it otherwise: "The difference between the two phonemes, which enables them to exist and to operate, is inaudible. The inaudible opens the two present phonemes to hearing [*L'inaudible ouvre à l'entente les deux phonèmes présents*], as they present themselves. [. . .] The difference that brings out phonemes and lets them be heard and understood [*et les donne à entendre*] itself remains inaudible" (Derrida, *Speech*, 133). Derrida proposes here a certain mode of hearing generated only through that which cannot be heard, which echoes the notion of "*unheard-of* thoughts" at the end of *Speech and Phenomena*: Derrida italicizes *inouïe* in the passage to emphasize its relation not only to the unprecedented and unacceptable but also to the unheard, that such a thought gives itself to hearing precisely by being unheard (of).

say, because the ear is more susceptible to the dismantling, however brief, of conventional modes of representation, meaning and knowledge than the eye. This is not to say that their theories of language are fundamentally acroamatic, only that a certain dimension of their reflections on language, and therefore by extension their modes of analysis, is acroamatic in nature, which is typically attributed to neither Benjamin nor Derrida.

∴

In an oft-cited interview with Peter Brunette and David Wells, Jacques Derrida admits that what he does with words

> is to make them explode so that the nonverbal appears in the verbal. [. . .] And if I love words it is also because of their ability to escape their proper form, whether they interest me as visible things, letters representing the spatial visibility of the word, or as something musical or audible [. . .] [it] probably has something to do with a non-discursive sonority, although I don't know whether I would call it musical.[16]

Derrida's reference to "a non-discursive sonority" of words as they escape their proper form is what Benjamin, I would argue, was similarly interested in and sought out in his autobiographical writings, especially but not exclusively in *Berlin Childhood around 1900* (*Berliner Kindheit um 1900*, 1932–1934, revised 1938) and *Berlin Chronicle* (*Berliner Chronik*, 1932). Both Benjamin and Derrida gesture in their own way toward a "non-discursive sonority" of language that apparently has as little to do with music as it does with representation or meaning, knowledge or nonknowledge. But it nevertheless requires a certain mode of listening in on language: in order to hear its non-discursive sonority, one must be able to hear something other than conventional modes of representation or meaning. One must be able to hear otherwise.

In this book I am first and foremost interested in how poets and critics attuned to the "non-discursive sonority" of language read, and how such reading involves a certain mode of listening, because I am convinced that one cannot think the acoustical unconscious without recourse to language's non-discursive sonority. In other words, the acoustical unconscious involves a certain mode of reading, one that would take into consideration a word's sonority at least as much as its signification. But like its optical counterpart in Benjamin's work, the acoustical unconscious can also – and as some would argue, should primarily – be thought in terms of technological media that record and transmit sounds, music, the spoken word, and so forth. As Miriam Hansen once wrote of

---

16 Peter Brunette and David Wells, *Screen/Play: Derrida and Film Theory* (Princeton, NJ: Princeton University Press, 1989), 20–21.

the optical unconscious, Benjamin requires either film or the photograph to think the optical unconscious.[17] In like manner, sound media from the gramophone and telephone to radio and sound film should also allow one "to think" the acoustical unconscious.

These two ways of defining a Benjaminian acoustical unconscious – as both a mode of reading attuned to the non-discursive sonority of language and a dependence on acoustic media for it to be thought – may at first appear incompatible. Naturally questions arise: what then is the difference between reading words and just being able to hear them on the telephone or loudspeaker? Must we be *listening* to a voice or music in order to think the acoustical unconscious, or is it just as relevant when simply *reading* about singular experiences with an acoustic medium like a conch shell or telephone? After all, in the shell scene above, Benjamin is recording with words the memory of an experience of hearing, writing down what he thought he heard. I would argue that the acoustical unconscious, at least as I derive it from Benjamin's work, bridges both interpretive modalities. Like the optical unconscious, the acoustical unconscious can help us think, through media like sound film, radio, the telephone, etc., the way in which we hear voices and music in previously unheard-of ways. But it may be equally applicable to a text that, while not specifically broadcasted or recorded via an acoustic medium, nevertheless refers to sounds or music heard via an acoustic medium. One example would be Benjamin's description of his use of the shell, which I examine in more detail in Chapter One; another would be the echoing sounds "heard" by Bertha and Eckbert in Tieck's fantastical tale, "Der blonde Eckbert" ("Eckbert the Fair" [hereafter, "Eckbert"]), which comprises a significant portion of Chapter Two.

While there is bound to be friction between these two modes of thinking the acoustical unconscious, the challenge I propose is nevertheless to think them simultaneously. Because when taken together, they illustrate first and foremost the term's relationship to and distinction from the optical unconscious: while a technological medium may still be required to think the acoustical unconscious, the latter nevertheless involves a complex relationship to phonetic and linguistic phenomena to which the optical unconscious has no recourse. Just as importantly, these two elements of the acoustical unconscious are by no means mutually exclusive: its second quality (its technological dependency)

---

17 Miriam Hansen, "Benjamin and Cinema: Not a One-Way Street," in *Benjamin's Ghosts: Interventions in Contemporary Literary and Cultural Theory*, ed. Gerhard Richter (Stanford, CA: Stanford University Press, 2002), 68. This technological reliance of a specifically Benjaminian acoustical unconscious is examined more closely in Chapter One.

typically amplifies and makes more potentially analyzable the first (its relationship to language). Whereas poets and certain authors have long used language to play with the dissociation between semantic and paronymic modes of words and phrases, acoustic media such as the telephone, radio or sound film tend to heighten this capacity of listening to the non-discursive sonority of language. In the simplest of terms but without, I hope, sounding too reductive, I am interested in how acoustic media tend to modify and amplify the ways in which we already "hear otherwise."

Another way to think these two modalities together is to think of the acoustical unconscious as a concept in Benjamin's strict sense of *Begriff*. In her posthumous book, *Cinema and Experience*, Hansen writes that, while she thinks "there is still purchase to Benjamin's claim, we should bear in mind that the optical unconscious is obviously not a philosophical concept but rather an experimental metaphor and, like all complex tropes, has multiple and shifting meanings."[18] While I agree with Hansen that, like the optical unconscious, the acoustical unconscious similarly has multiple and shifting meanings, it is unclear what she means by "experimental metaphor." Instead, I propose to read the acoustical unconscious according to what Benjamin meant by "concept": unlike the way we typically think of concepts – as establishing sameness between phenomena so that they can be subsumed under what might be called a category or common denominator – the main role of the concept for Benjamin is to sustain what makes phenomena separate and distinguishable from each other.[19] While this may sound counterintuitive, it is crucial when considering any one of Benjamin's concepts, including a concept like the "optical unconscious" or the "dialectical image." In the "Epistemo-Critical Preface" to his *Trauerspiel* book, Benjamin maps out the correlation between phenomena, concepts, and ideas. Their correlation is extremely complex, and this is not the place to go into it in detail, except to say that the concept plays a mediating role between phenomena and the idea.[20] One way it does this is by preparing the phenomenon for conceptual use by "decomposing – today we might even say 'deconstructing' – the preexisting empirical organization" of the phenomenon such that it is able "to *part company with* itself. The phenomenon, determined as a 'thing,' is decomposed into its 'thing-like elements,' which have the

---

18 Miriam Hansen, *Cinema and Experience* (Berkeley: University of California Press, 2012), 156.
19 This, moreover, is why Hansen rejects calling the "optical unconscious" a "philosophical concept": because like Benjamin, she rejects the function of a concept that subsumes phenomena under a single heading.
20 See Weber's introduction to *Benjamin's -abilities*, esp. 7–10.

potential, the ability, to recombine into something else" (emphasis original).[21] A Benjaminian concept thus helps us think how empirical phenomena, decomposed into their "thing-like elements," can enter into constellations with each other that do not to establish sameness but maintain their distinctiveness and non-synthesis. Such a conceptual "rearrangement" is described by Weber as at best a "challenge, since what results is a configuration that can never be fully self-present, for such a presence would reduce the uniqueness – *das Einmalige* – by treating it as though it were identically or essentially repeatable *as the same*" (emphasis original).[22] This is the challenge referred to above with regard to the two modalities of the acoustical unconscious: to think of its relation to linguistic phenomena and acoustic media simultaneously without subsuming them as identical or the same, i.e., grouping them conceptually while maintaining their non-synthesis. This is also why the readings that constitute every chapter of this study are themselves singular and unique: they focus on what might best be called dialectical sound figures, that is, attempts at redeeming singular sense phenomena that make legible an "intensive temporality" and a certain knowability that bypass or surpass convention, putative meanings and the establishment of sameness.[23] The acoustical unconscious as a specifically Benjaminian concept thus names a space of convergence of disparate phenomena, a blending of conscious and unconscious knowing, in which singular sound figures present the intensive and potentially redemptive time and place of this knowing.

∴

Despite having spent many years on the topic, the term "acoustical unconscious" is not my own.[24] Furthermore, over the last fifteen years it has taken on

---

21 Weber, *Benjamin's -abilities*, 7–8.
22 Weber, *Benjamin's -abilities*, 9.
23 In order to avoid a major detour to Benjamin's concept of the "dialectical image," I only wish to emphasize how it too already implies non-synthesis: it "disappears in appearing, takes leave in arriving" (Weber, *Benjamins -abilities*, 52), and perhaps most importantly involves a curious relation to time, in that time offers itself up not linearly but "intensively," that is to say, as a leap out of any sense of a continuum or out of that which can be measured, and into the discontinuous and proleptic. For Benjamin, the concept is that which allows the dialectical image not only to emerge but to become an instrument of knowledge. See Tamara Tagliacozzo's reading of the correlation between concept, idea, and the dialectical image from Benjamin's *Ursprung des deutschen Trauerspiels* (esp. Benjamin, *GS* 1:215–216; *OGT* 11–14) in *Experience and Infinite Task: Knowledge, Language and Messianism in the Philosophy of Walter Benjamin* (Lanham, MD: Rowman & Littlefield, 2018). See also Werner Hamacher, "Intensive Sprache," in *Übersetzen: Walter Benjamin*, by Christiaan L. Hart Nibbrig (Frankfurt am Main: Suhrkamp, 2001), 174–235.
24 The first appearance of the acoustical unconscious I am aware of is found in Kevis Goodman's *Georgic Modernity and British Romanticism: Poetry and the Mediation of History* (Cambridge:

a number of different and, in some cases radically disparate, definitions in scholarship. Problems already begin with the terminology used. While the term "unconscious" appears consistent throughout scholars exploring this idea, there is little agreement on the first term: some refer to "acoustic unconscious" while I and others have consistently referred to the slight variant, the "acoustical unconscious." Benjamin of course never refers specifically to either, but my preference for the "acoustical unconscious" over "acoustic," "sonic" or "auditory" derives in part from translations of his optical unconscious. In German, "optisch" can be translated as both optic and optical, but Benjamin scholars usually agree on translating "das optische Unbewußte" as the opti*cal* unconscious. Moreover, a debate between members of the Acoustical Society of America in the 1950s over the title of their association, as either the Acoustic or Acousti*cal* Society of America, also informs the way I distinguish between these two terms.[25]

And yet, scholars have also referred to the "sonic unconscious" and "auditory unconscious."[26] It is as if we have all agreed on the family name of this

---

Cambridge University Press, 2004). Goodman uses the term to describe how euphemistic language in Wordsworth's *Excursion* tends toward "a deliberate attempt to introduce within the written poem an 'acoustical unconscious,' a reverberation that tends in the opposite direction, toward dysphemistic knowledge" (Goodman, *Georgic Modernity*, 139). While it remains unclear how this can be called unconscious, Goodman's interpretation of the acoustical unconscious as a mode of *reading* helped confirm my interest in the same, albeit more in terms of Walter Benjamin's reflections on language.

25 Frederick Vinton Hunt, a pioneer in the field of acoustic engineering and Harvard professor from 1928 to shortly before his death in 1972, submitted a letter to the editor of *The Journal of the Acoustical Society of America* in 1955 in which he distinguished between the two terms: "*acoustic* is used when the term being qualified designates something that has the properties, dimensions, or physical characteristics associated with sound waves." Such terms might include "impedance, inertance, load (radiation field), output (sound power), energy, wave, medium, signal, conduit," and so on. *Acoustical* for Hunt thus qualifies terms that are *not* specifically associated with the physical properties of sound waves, such as "society, method, engineer, school, glossary, symbol, problem, measurement, point of view, end-use, device." (See F. V. Hunt, "Acoustical vs Acoustical," *The Journal of the Acoustical Society of America* 27, no. 5 [1955]; published online 29 June 2005, https://doi.org/10.1121/1.1908102.) While there is nothing wrong with the term, "acoustic unconscious," it would, following Hunt's distinction, imply more the physical properties of sounds, whereas the acousti*cal* unconscious is more apt to the way I am employing it in this study.

26 Emily McArthur uses the "auditory unconscious" to explore a way to think "an emancipatory way of hearing" fostered specifically by new technologies. See Emily McArthur, "The iPhone *Erfahrung*: Siri, the Auditory Unconscious and Walter Benjamin's 'Aura,'" in *Design, Mediation and the Posthuman*, ed. Dennis M. Weiss, Amy D. Propen, and Colbey Emmerson Reid (Lanham, MD: Lexington Books, 2014), 113–128. And Christoph Cox, who emphasizes a

conceptual creature, the "unconscious" – which as we will see already means something different to Benjamin than to Freud – but have yet to fix its *Eigenname* or "proper name." Again, Benjamin is relevant here because a name, like any term, is never reducible to any identifiable semantic concept. The same can be said for the word, "sound," and sound studies more generally. The question "what *is* the acoustical unconscious?" will turn out to be about as difficult to answer as Jonathan Sterne admitting the impossibility of unifying the scattered histories of sound in *The Audible Past*:

> without some kind of overarching, shared sensibility about what constitutes *the history of sound, sound culture,* or *sound studies*, piecing together a history of sound from the bewildering array of stories about speech, music, technology, and other sound-related practices has all the promise and appeal of piecing together a pane of shattered glass. We know that the parts line up somehow, we know that they can connect, but we are unsure of how they actually link together [emphasis original].²⁷

Whether intended or not, Sterne's shattered glass metaphor is reminiscent of Walter Benjamin's image of the mosaic in the opening pages of the "Epistemo-Critical Preface" of his *Origin of the German Trauerspiel*: "Just as the majesty of mosaics remains intact when they are disassembled into capricious bits, so philosophical observation fears no dissipation of momentum. Both come together out of the singular and disparate; [. . .] The value of thought-fragments [*Denkbruchstücken*] is all the more decisive the less they are immediately capable of measuring themselves by an underlying conception."²⁸ For Benjamin, the image of the mosaic stands in for – or more precisely, simultaneously contributes to while making more semantically indeterminate – philosophy or history in its proper distortion, a distortion that must be sustained in order for truth to be conceived of as an explosion of all meaning, as a "non-integrative dialectics of explosive convergence or coincidence."²⁹ The concept of an acoustical unconscious is already a kind of mini-mosaic: it converges two terms that, beyond their individual connotations, tend to distort more than inform each other, in all senses of the term "distortion." The hope is to tune into and sustain their proper distortion. Put another way, while answering the question, "what is the acoustical unconscious?" will be complex and multifaceted, this does not

---

unique mode of auditory perception which he links back to Leibniz's *petits perceptions*, appears to use "sonic" and "auditory" unconscious interchangeably in his article "Sound Art and the Sonic Unconscious," *Organised Sound* 14, no. 1 (2009): 19–26.

27 Jonathan Sterne, *The Audible Past: Cultural Origins of Sound Reproduction* (Durham, NC: Duke University Press, 2003), 4–5.
28 Benjamin, *GS* 1:208; *OGT* 3.
29 Weber, *Benjamin's -abilities*, 49.

mean that it should not be posed. The various ways in which "the" acoustical unconscious – even its determinate article should be interrogated – and its variants have already been interpreted in recent scholarship only confirms the concept's malleability and shifting meanings.

Without denying the significance of other new and exciting scholarship on the topic, I wish to highlight three scholars from different disciplines who have all taken up the acoustical unconscious in their own way: Miriam Hansen, Viet Erlmann, and Julie Beth Napolin. While the latter two scholars explicitly address the concept and its myriad implications, Hansen only mentions it in passing. And yet, given her towering influence in film studies and the way she made the work of Siegfried Kracauer and Walter Benjamin accessible to North American film scholars throughout her career, her almost parenthetical reference to "a kind of 'acoustic unconscious'" is worth examining in some detail. In the last chapter of her posthumous book, *Cinema and Experience* (2012), Hansen appends a new footnote to what she calls Kracauer's "remarkably prescient chapter on 'dialogue and sound'" in *Theory of Film: The Redemption of Physical Reality* (1960):

> Kracauer's reflections on film sound gesture toward something like an 'acoustic unconscious' and foreground experimental uses of sound ("anonymous noises," multi-lingual speech, etc.) from Fritz Lang to René Claire and G. W. Pabst. They also describe hypothetical practices that were to be realized in different ways by the French and German New Waves (Godard, Kluge), New Hollywood during the 1960s and 1970s (Altman, Coppola), and the "New Talkies" of the 1980s (Duras, Rainer).[30]

This is the only reference to an acoustic unconscious in *Cinema and Experience*, and indeed throughout all of Hansen's work on Kracauer or Benjamin, leaving the term tantalizingly cryptic. And yet it is clear that for Hansen the term has more to do with film than the written word. Hansen was certainly inspired by Benjamin's optical unconscious, to which she dedicates an entire chapter section. But in the passage above, Hansen not only refers to Kracauer's own emphasis on the materiality of the image in cinema and to the materiality of the "sound-image" in particular, but also suggests that an acoustic unconscious would "foreground experimental uses of sound," meaning unconventional, or previously unheard-of uses of sound in film. Comparing Hansen's reference to "something like an 'acoustic unconscious'" in Kracauer's work with a more Benjaminian approach pursued here is challenging, in part because of Kracauer and Benjamin's different approaches to and emphasis on "materiality."[31] At the

---

30 Hansen, *Cinema and Experience*, 261, 352–353.
31 See the first section of Chapter Five for a more extended discussion of Kracauer's use of the term "materiality."

same time, it raises the unavoidable question of the "materiality" of sound, for if the acoustical unconscious pursued in this book implies the influence of a word's "non-discursive sonority" in conjunction with or against its putative meaning, such a mode of listening would necessarily pay close attention to phonemes and their echoes, that is, to the "material" of language. The exploration of an acoustical unconscious via Kracauer's *Theory of Film* may thus help bridge the conceptual divide between a language-based acoustical unconscious and its applicability to hearing a voice over the radio or sounds and music in film.

The two other scholars I wish to highlight grapple much more explicitly with the notion of the acoustical unconscious, and via the work of Walter Benjamin in particular. As such, both Erlmann and Napolin emphasize dimensions of the concept that both resonate with the way I explore it in this study while also already pointing to productive extrapolations beyond it. While he originally refers to the acoustic unconscious in a chapter of his earlier book, *Reason and Resonance* (2010), Erlmann acknowledges in a more recent article, "'Acoustic Space' – Marshall McLuhan Defended Against Himself" (2016), that "Benjamin goes one step beyond psychophysiology." Because Erlmann's rendering of the "acoustic-unconscious" (the hyphen is his own) follows a number of Benjamin's quotations that I retrace in Chapter One, it suffices to say that Erlmann is convinced that Benjamin's "'now of the auditory' is not simply that of 'sound,' but that of sound as structure, language, and meaning":

> Or, more precisely, Benjamin's "realm of acoustics" does not consist of audible sounds per se as much as it encompasses successive stages of "soundness and "unsoundness." Of sounds being undone and reassembling [. . .] the acoustic unconscious for Benjamin shelters a secret code whose key has been lost and whose meaning must be retrieved through a form of redoubling, through painstaking deciphering, decoding, and "reading."[32]

Erlmann is convinced here, as am I, that the acoustical unconscious has less to do with "sounds per se" than with "sound as structure, language, and meaning," and therefore with the "soundness" of/as "reading," which certainly seems to gesture toward that non-discursive sonority of language I describe above. Erlmann further believes that a Benjaminian acoustical unconscious "cannot be grasped as part of an auditory field. Nor is it about hearing."[33] But he nevertheless ends his reflections on the acoustical unconscious with a curious return to sound:

---

[32] Veit Erlmann, "'Acoustic Space' – Marshall McLuhan Defended Against Himself," *The Senses & Society* 11, no. 1 (2016): 41–42.
[33] Erlmann, "'Acoustic Space,'" 42.

> The acoustic-unconscious rather is an assemblage, a nexus that undercuts the coordinates of space and time. It is close to what Lyotard calls the *matrix*, a space that does not know any structure, language or fixed oppositions – such between visual and auditory. The acoustic-unconscious, then, is not another form of the unconscious or an anti-optical unconscious, but an unconscious-as-sound.[34]

Erlmann's emphasis on the peculiar assemblage that makes up the "acoustic-unconscious" is particularly useful in the context of this study, since space and time are indeed up for grabs in much of what follows.[35]

Finally, Julie Beth Napolin advances the notion of the acoustical unconscious of the written word by taking up William Faulkner's "propagative technique of working with voices and sonorities."[36] In her article, Napolin traces not-yet heard sounds and other "circumambient echoes" in Faulkner's writing in order to outline how their resonance exceeds the boundaries of memory, experience and the individual. In a succinct passage in which she reads Benjamin's references to sound in "News of a Death" (1932–1934), Napolin concludes that there are "sounds that while ignored or misapprehended have not gone unrecorded by the perceiver," subsequently defining the acoustical unconscious as follows:

> The acoustical unconscious is not a site of storage: it is a site, without location and with object, of material transfiguration. There are acts of listening that are deferred because they are partial; they stand in relation to an object that cannot be registered, only overtonally recorded. [. . .] The physical and dialectical features of an acoustical unconscious turn upon residual listening, but in advance of listening as a personal event.[37]

Napolin's emphasis of "material transfiguration" echoes Kracauer's focus on the materiality of sound-images and Hansen's call for "a kind of 'acoustic unconscious.'" But by focusing not on film but on Faulkner, and specifically his unique narrative ear and the echoic effects of his writing, Napolin is to my

---

34 Erlmann, "'Acoustic Space,'" 42.
35 Equally important is the notion of an unconscious as matrix that does not distinguish between the visual and auditory, nor between any other sense perception. But if there is no differentiation of sense perception, then why discuss the unconscious as "acoustic-unconscious"? What does "sound" mean in Erlmann's last formulation, "an unconscious-as-sound," especially if we append to it "sound as structure, language, and meaning" but not to sounds per se? These and other questions concerning Erlmann's specific formulations and approach to Benjamin would require a more in-depth reading that goes beyond the purview of this introductory survey. When applicable, I will compare and/or contrast Erlmann's reading of the acoustical unconscious in his article with my own.
36 Julie Beth Napolin, "The Fact of Resonance: An Acoustics of Determination in Faulkner and Benjamin," *symploke* 23, no. 1–2 (2015): 172.
37 Napolin, "Fact of Resonance," 179–180.

knowledge the first to expand convincingly the possibility of "socially unconscious sounds" and their relation to what might be called a collective acoustical unconscious, an exciting line of inquiry that the present study only gestures toward.

This brief but by no means exhaustive survey illustrates the myriad ways in which the concept has developed in scholarship from numerous disciplines – from musicology and philosophy to film, media and literary studies – over the last fifteen years. One can already assess, especially in the recent work of both Erlmann and Napolin, that the acoustical unconscious is becoming ever more securely tied to Walter Benjamin's curious "realm of acoustics," which is then used as a touchstone for further interpretive discussions of various acoustic phenomena, whether in the written work of Faulkner or McLuhan, or to address issues from sound film theory to recent natural language processing technology. All of which illustrate the extent to which this term's use has proven, in its short life, to be neither stable nor unproductive. The malleability of the acoustical unconscious as a term is once again reminiscent of the way Jonathan Sterne describes how "sound" is defined by various scholars interested in sound studies: raising more questions than answers, Sterne argues not for a necessary ambiguity of the term, but rather for the necessity of scholars to take a stand on what sound means because 1) "sound" can never be defined once and for all; and because 2) however one defines it, a scholar's definition of sound will have "direct consequences for what gets studied in terms of what counts as the fundamental phenomenon under investigation and the very definition of context" (8). Sterne's advice suggests that the problem of defining "sound" is not necessarily a problem of meaning, but a problem of use. In a similar vein, the way the acoustical unconscious has already been picked up and employed by various scholars reveals less any single, representative meaning of the concept and more the singular perspective(s) and analyses of the critics themselves. In this way, its various interpretations take on particular nuances that reveal less the term's own putative or fixed meaning and more the singular perspective of the critic who utilizes it for their own purposes. I am of course no exception, since the chapters that follow are informed by my own training in German critical and literary theory from the early twentieth century, in comparative literature and media studies. I also cannot underestimate the importance of music in my life and the extent to which I have always been intrigued by the sounds and music in all that I read and watch. Others in their own fields will of course approach (and already have approached) the "acoustical unconscious" in new and fascinating ways. This does not mean that the pursuit of thinking the acoustical unconscious is hopelessly singular or indeterminate. Rather, it illustrates the concept's plasticity or "resonance" with scholars from myriad disciplines who have begun to shape and mold it. Again, the purpose here is not fully to fix the term or its origins – as if that were possible or even desirable – but rather to explore its various resonances across disciplines and, in the process, find some common threads.

Just as Hansen, Erlmann and Napolin all emphasize various elements of the acoustical unconscious, the present study explores and is organized around a number of dimensions that I have singled out as constitutive of the concept. In the most general terms, one can say that the acoustical unconscious has a mnemonic, technological, linguistic, psychological, collective and political dimension. None of these can be entirely disentangled from each other, but together they provide the varying emphases that distinguish the interpretive discussions contained in the following chapters. The challenge that this book proposes is thus to imagine an acoustical unconscious that is applicable to multiple media while equally constitutive of the various dimensions listed above. As Benjamin does with the conch shell, I too have raised the concept of the acoustical unconscious to my ear and have asked, what do I hear?

∴

The pursuit of defining what is the acoustical unconscious seems only to multiply exponentially the problems already inherent in the two words "acoustical" and "unconscious," which are themselves nearly impossible to define. As mentioned earlier, the combination of these two words engenders a certain distortion, which is to say, a kind of distortion that points well beyond the limits of either term's own amorphous definitions. Furthermore, the acoustical unconscious immediately raises problems concerning theories of perception and knowledge. How is it, we might ask, that we hear something "unconsciously"? Can we say definitively that "unconscious hearing" is a mode of perception? Or perhaps the acoustical unconscious has nothing to do with the way *we* hear or listen to things (or with "hearing per se," as Erlmann writes), but is nevertheless intrinsic to the aural realm itself. But if that were the case, how might the aural field – the world of sonic phenomena like car horns, sirens, voices, bird song, music – have an unconscious "of its own"?[38]

When I embarked many years ago on the search for an acoustical unconscious, my first inclination was to look for its critical origins in the work of either Sigmund Freud or Theodor Adorno. However, neither thinker inquires specifically into the relevance of an acoustical unconscious: in the realm of psychology, neither Freud nor Jung explicitly realized the implications of an unconscious

---

[38] This line of questioning is expressed in like manner by Rosalind E. Krauss in *The Optical Unconscious* (Cambridge: MIT Press, 1993).

acoustics,[39] and Freudian psychology has seldom been reconciled with this omission.[40] Even Theodor Adorno, the preeminent scholar of music and its relation to philosophy and media of the mid-twentieth century, was disdainful of tracing affinities between acoustical perception and what he called a "symbolism of the unconscious" ("Rückblickend auf den Surrealismus," 1963), which explains at least in part his earlier rebuke of Walter Benjamin's famous artwork essay in "On the Fetish-Character in Music" ("Über den Fetischcharakter in der Musik," 1938).[41]

Another way I had originally thought to enter into a discussion of the acoustical unconscious was by way of the visual counterpart: Benjamin's optical unconscious. In the context of the present study, the first steps on the royal road to the acoustical unconscious are taken alongside Benjamin's concept of the optical unconscious, which he applied to both photography and film. In Chapter One I argue that Benjamin's optical unconscious can offer insight into the analysis of acoustical media, but I also suggest that Benjamin was already gesturing toward an acoustical variant of the optical unconscious in his autobiographical works, most notably in *Berlin Childhood around 1900* and *Berlin Chronicle*, without explicitly referring to it as such. What develops from reading specific characteristics of Benjamin's optical unconscious alongside his own autobiographical work is a specifically Benjaminian acoustical unconscious, by which I mean an acoustical unconscious that considers not only Benjamin's

---

39 See R. Murray Schafer, "Open Ears," in *Auditory Culture Reader*, ed. Michael Bull and Les Back (New York: Berg, 2003), 32.
40 For an extended analysis of Freud's notion of sound, see Edith Lecourt's *Freud et l'univers sonore: le tic-tac du désir* (Paris: L'Harmattan, 1992). Also, since at least Lacan, numerous scholars have attempted to reconcile Freud's work with a theory of the voice. See especially chapter six of Mladen Dolar's *A Voice and Nothing More* (Cambridge: MIT Press, 2006).
41 Adorno's original 1927 submission for his *Habilitation*, which he later withdrew in place of his Kierkegaard book, was entitled "On the Concept of the Unconscious in the Transcendental Doctrine of the Soul." Andrew Bowie writes how, at the end of this withdrawn *Habilitation*, Adorno changes from a predominantly positivistic approach that attempts to discover theoretical grounds for "scientific" psychology to a social critique that reveals irrationalist theories of the unconscious as fundamentally ideological: Adorno "maintains that the very popularity of irrationalist theories of the unconscious in a world which is ever more economically rationalised indicates that the aim of such theories 'is to complete what is lacking in reality' [. . .], and that they thereby function as ideology" (Andrew Bowie, *From Romanticism to Critical Theory: The Philosophy of German Literary Theory* [New York: Routledge, 1996], 250). This sheds light on why Adorno remains circumspect of Benjamin's use of the unconscious in his Baudelaire essay, as well as why Adorno never pursued any notion of an acoustical unconscious. For more on Adorno's withdrawn *Habilitation* and its impact on his later work, see Bowie, *From Romanticism to Critical Theory*, esp. 249–251.

theory of media and reproducibility but also his reflections on language and scattered references to sound in his notes and autobiographical work.

Already underlying Benjamin's notion of the optical unconscious is a very different way of thinking about the unconscious than the way Freud used the term, which has far-reaching implications for a Benjaminian acoustical unconscious. In *Optical Unconscious* (1993), Rosalind E. Krauss correctly points out that, "for Freud, a sentence like Benjamin's 'The camera introduces us to unconscious optics as does psychoanalysis to unconscious impulses,' from the 'Work of Art' essay, would simply be incomprehensible."[42] The first two chapters thus necessarily take into account the different ways in which Benjamin conceived of the unconscious, not simply in terms of the camera and the optical unconscious but equally in terms of awakening and forgetting.

Before examining Benjamin's decidedly Proustian account of the unconscious, both the optical and acoustical unconscious must also be reconciled with Benjamin's theory of perception. Benjamin is of course careful not to resign his optical unconscious simply to what can or cannot be seen, or as Napolin concisely writes, it is "not how one perceives 'more' from or 'closer' to an object of perception."[43] We should also not forget the influence of Leibniz's theory of apperception on Benjamin, especially when considering the optical unconscious. In the artwork essay, Benjamin also explicitly compares Freud's *Psychopathology of Everyday Life* (*Psychopathologie des Alltagslebens*, 1901) when he writes that "a similar deepening of apperception throughout the entire spectrum of optical – and now also acoustic – impressions (*Merkwelt*) has been accomplished in film."[44] We will return often to this key sentence. But it is already clear that, in Benjamin's precise phrasing, film does not deepen our means of "perception" but rather our "apperception," and that it does so not throughout the entire breadth of the visually perceptual world (*Wahrnehmungswelt*), but throughout the entire spectrum of the optical *Merkwelt* – a term misleadingly rendered in the English translation as "impressions."[45] While one may define "impression" as the physical pressure upon something "so as to leave a mark,"[46] it erases the "world" of Benjamin's word, *Merk-welt*, and with it the idea of a world of marks or markings; in short, a

---

42 Krauss, *Optical Unconscious*, 179.
43 Napolin, "Fact of Resonance," 181.
44 Benjamin, *GS* 1:498 [Walter Benjamin, *Werke und Nachlass: Kritische Gesamtausgabe* (Frankfurt a.M.: Suhrkamp, 2008–) (hereafter, *WuN*), 16:239]; *SW* 4:265.
45 My thanks to Samuel Weber for pointing out this crucial difference between *Merkwelt* and *Wahrnehmungswelt* and its repercussions.
46 "Impression," *Oxford English Dictionary*, 2nd ed. (Oxford: Oxford University Press, 1989) (hereafter, *OED*), s.v.

world of signs. Such a "mark-world" helps to define Benjamin's use of the unconscious in terms of optics and acoustics: if the unconscious is related less to perception as such and more to a world of amorphous marks and signs, it must be distinguishable from any unified perception of things. The perceiving of signs is not simply being "conscious" of them, but involves a unifying process that is both the prerequisite for and the result of *self*-consciousness, which is precisely what the unconscious does not offer. In other words, whereas the perception of signs or marks always already involves a self that, from a fixed position, puts those marks "in place," both the optical and acoustical unconscious involve for Benjamin a mode of consciousness *without* any fixed place of perceiving visual and acoustical marks and signs. Such marks must therefore constantly be re-marked, which in turn resituates the marker, that is, the "perceiver" who has no fixed point-of-view or point-of-audition. These constant re-markings not only point toward the logic of iterability as explored by Derrida in his own reformulating of the term "unconscious," but also necessarily generate an indeterminate, displaced self.[47] Defined in Proustian terms, this is the "consciousness of the body" during the distinct experience of awakening; in Freud, it is the consciousness of night dreams that is incapable of postulating a unified subject. Whereas the optical unconscious can be defined as the index for an optics without a "seeing" self, the acoustical unconscious would similarly involve an acoustical *Merkwelt* in the absence of any self-contained, localizable or identifiable "hearing" self. In this way, both are strictly demarcated from empirical notions of perception, and are instead related to what

---

47 Throughout his work, Derrida was not so much reticent of Freud's unconscious as he was highly suspicious of it: not only does "the concept of a (conscious or unconscious) subject necessarily refer to the concept of substance – and thus of presence," but Derrida also suggests we "ought perhaps to read Freud the way Heidegger read Kant; like the *cogito*, the unconscious no doubt is timeless only from the standpoint of a certain vulgar conception of time" (see Derrida's chapter "Freud and the Scene of Writing" in Jacques Derrida, *Writing and Difference*, trans. Alan Bass [Chicago, University of Chicago Press, 1978], 229, 215, respectively). With the unconscious being bound to both the metaphysics of presence and a "vulgar conception of time," it is no wonder why Derrida sought an alternative to the unconscious by replacing and radicalizing it with trace-related terminology throughout his career. That he relates the logic of the unconscious to iterability specifically in one of his last published texts illustrates the extent to which even Derrida always felt the need to qualify the term. Iterability makes no claim to presence, since it refers to the structural possibility of iteration; it refers not to that which can be identified by the repetition of the same, but to the multiplicity of that which seems to occur even once, because even "this one time is in itself divided or multiplied in advance by its structure of repeatability" (Derrida, cited by Weber, *Benjamin's -abilities*, 6). In this way, the unconscious for Derrida no longer describes an inerasable trace or a timelessness where "nothing ends, nothing happens, nothing is forgotten," but an unconscious that is always on the move, always already divided and multiple.

might be called, following Rosalind Krauss, preconditions for the very *emergence* of the perceptual object to vision and audition.[48]

Another problem involves distinguishing between hearing and sight, which necessarily leads to distinctions between the acoustical and optical unconscious, despite some of their terminological and structural congruities. Perhaps the most striking characteristic that distinguishes the acoustical unconscious from its optical counterpart is its complex relationship to phonetic and linguistic phenomena. This is not to say that hearing words and the sounds they are comprised of is necessarily the purview of the acoustical unconscious since, as we have just observed with Benjamin's own appropriation of the unconscious, "hearing" as an empirical mode of perception is already what is being undermined. Furthermore, although the acoustical unconscious may necessarily involve the repetition of words and their phonemes, it should also be distinguished from linguistics and its subfields, phonetics and phonology. The reason for this is again due to its connection to that peculiar "unconscious" à la Benjamin: whereas the study of phonetics and phonology deal respectively with the physical properties of sounds and how they are patterned to encode meaning in spoken human language, the acoustical unconscious, working in the *absence* of any internal principle of unification, tends to break down a word's meaning, working to amplify its non-discursive sonority. Instead of encoding meaning, the acoustical unconscious tends rather to disperse meaning amidst a flurry of phonemes. One might even go so far as to say that the acoustical unconscious, with its emphasis on sonic heterogeneity and indeterminacy, does not simply disperse meaning into so many sound particles, but dispenses with the human from spoken language, if by "human" we mean a unified and homogeneous essence of "man," itself a correlative of self-consciousness. Perhaps this is why the sounds of animals and nature, but also that "other nature" of technology, come back again and again throughout the following chapters.

A third distinction to be made – one in which notions of language and the human are equally pertinent – between the optical unconscious and its acoustical

---

[48] Krauss's own argument against empirical vision in *The Optical Unconscious* is as follows: "Empirical vision must be canceled, in favor of something understood as the precondition for the very emergence of the perceptual object to vision" (Krauss, *Optical Unconscious*, 15). And while she is not quite as explicit about the marks of a *Merkwelt* as I am above, she nevertheless suggests a painterly mark with similar connections to the unconscious as those described above: "the drip pictures [of Jackson Pollock] can still be seen to retain the cutting edge of an indexical mark, one that slices the works lose [sic] from their purported verticality, by dropping them, visually, to the floor. It is a mark, as well, that cuts itself away from any intentional matrix to achieve its own isolation as "clue," the simultaneity of the visual present already thus fissured by time" (Krauss, *Optical Unconscious*, 308).

variant is the latter's applicability to the voice, and to a non-discursive voice in particular. With the voice, Derrida's reflections on the non-discursive sonority of language explored earlier becomes even more significant. The non-discursive voice of radio in particular becomes the central concern in Chapters Three and Four, in which the wireless transmission of the voice raises major issues about how one listens to the tone and timbre of a voice in relation to the language spoken. If one of the characteristics of the acoustical unconscious is the corruption or contagion of a "listening subject" with the sonic marks around it,[49] then we may turn to the difference between voice and sound as one way to think of this contagion, which is amplified in radio. Just as the acoustical unconscious involves a word's detachment from its meaning through its multiple sound parts, it also dissociates and displaces the voice as it is commonly understood – namely, as unified and expressive – allowing the sounds of the voice to emerge, sounds that are much more difficult to characterize or attribute to a single identity, whether human or nonhuman. In other words, instead of attempting to understand the voice as such, it is necessary to consider what Benjamin, in "Reflections on Radio" ("Reflexionen zum Rundfunk," 1931), calls the bearing or comportment of the voice (*das Benehmen der Stimme*) – that is, the non-discursive sounds, tones and timbres that disrupt and multiply the notion of any single, unified voice. Benjamin's curious insistence on the relation of this non-discursive, radiophonic voice to language is a good starting point for thinking the acoustical unconscious in radio.

---

49 In his influential book *Listening Subjects*, David Schwarz distinguishes between two "registers of listening" that he calls a fantasy thing and a fantasy space: "Listening as a fantasy thing is produced when attributes of a structure represented in music are described and related to one another. Listening as a fantasy space is produced when music-theoretical, music-historical, cultural, psychoanalytic, or personal thresholds are crossed and enunciated" (David Schwartz, *Listening Subjects: Music, Psychoanalysis, Culture* [Durham, NC: Duke University Press, 1997], 3–4). Of these two modes, "listening as fantasy space" seems most applicable to the acoustical unconscious, since Schwarz lists its attributes as potentially "heterogeneous, fragmented, coordinated, culture specific, and personally specific" (Schwartz, *Listening Subjects*, 4). At the same time, the subject still appears relatively intact in Schwarz's description, even in terms of what he calls the "sonorous envelope." For instance, when describing the relation of music to fantasy space, Schwarz writes: "Music represents the sonorous envelope as a fantasy *space* when attributes of a thing are related to other conventional registers *in which the subject finds him/herself*" (emphasis mine; Schwartz, *Listening Subjects*, 8). Schwarz is still able to identify a subject that "finds" itself, which suggests unification and closure, of the "sonorous envelope" if necessary. The acoustical unconscious, on the other hand, tends towards a subject's involvement, displacement, indeterminacy and openness. A more critical examination of Schwarz's vocabulary, moreover, would have to address specifically his notions of "space" and "threshold," especially in relation to the German words, *Raum* and *Schwelle*.

A final distinction that this study addresses between the optical and acoustical unconscious returns us to film. Because film is one of the mediums through which Benjamin originally defined the optical unconscious, the implications of an acoustical unconscious in film appear entirely appropriate on the one hand, and particularly difficult to isolate on the other. Instead of attending to the voice, Chapter Five listens for ways in which the acoustical unconscious is attributable to the sounds and music in film. Recall Benjamin's notion that, with the coming of sound film, a deepening of apperception throughout the whole range of the acoustical *Merkwelt* has been made possible. Of course, the notion of "silent film" and its European counterpart, "mute cinema" (*der Stummfilm, cinéma muet*), has long been regarded as a misnomer,[50] suggesting that the acoustical unconscious may not necessarily be bound to the technological innovations of the so-called "sound film." In other words, with the rattling of the first film projector, an acoustical unconscious of film can be thought. Alexander Kluge is deeply committed to an overarching principle of cinema that is closely tied to his thoughts concerning both music and early cinema. Moreover, Kluge directly addresses Benjamin's optical unconscious while simultaneously developing what he calls "sound perspectives" that push sound material to the verge of disintegration, thereby opening up "new qualities within it."[51] In examining how he appropriates and reorganizes previous music and sound material in order to give them new meaning beyond their otherwise fixed historical contexts, it is also possible to interpret Kluge as politicizing the acoustical unconscious. For when that which is usually reserved as the unique, "other nature" of the camera becomes instrumentalized to help restore – Kluge's word is to "emancipate" – the repressed reality of an alternative history of class struggle, the stakes of film's optical and acoustical unconscious change dramatically.

Kluge is of course not alone in politicizing the unconscious. When situating the acoustical unconscious among late twentieth-century theories of the unconscious and non-oedipal psychologies more generally, it is useful to recall Deleuze and Guattari's famous definition of the unconscious: it "poses no problem

---

50 Film director Robert Bresson once remarked that "there was never a mute cinema" (cited by Michel Chion, *The Voice in Cinema*, trans. Claudia Gorbman [New York: Columbia University Press, 1999], 7), and Béla Balázs wrote at the threshold of sound film that "silence has meaning only when it could also be loud" (Béla Balázs, *Der Geist des Films* [Frankfurt a.M.: Suhrkamp, 2001], 121).

51 See Alexander Kluge, "Ein imaginärer Opernführer," in *Jahrbuch der Hamburgischen Staatsoper 1984–1988* (Hamburg: Intendanz der Hamburgischen Staatsoper, 1988). The English citation is taken from Alexander Kluge, "Kluge on Opera, Film, and Feelings," ed. Miriam Hansen, trans. Miriam Hansen and Sara S. Poor, *New German Critique* 49 (Winter 1990): 89–138; here, 136.

of meaning, solely problems of use,"[52] which is echoed by Sterne's reflections on the term, "sound." But when the idea of the unconscious is reformulated beyond its psychological, subjective roots and in terms of function, it very quickly becomes a politically motivated function. Frederic Jameson's influential project, *The Political Unconscious* (1981), introduced how a repressed history of class struggle can be made conscious through literary and cultural analysis. More influenced by Jameson than Benjamin,[53] Rosalind Krauss transfers Jameson's project into the field of art history with her own version of the optical unconscious, making the concept relevant as that which describes a certain politically-charged and historically-determined way of "seeing" modern works of art. The final chapter of this present study focuses on Kluge's written and filmic work as an exemplary case for how the acoustical unconscious can be politicized in like manner.

At first glance, the chapters in this book might appear to be rather arbitrary "case studies" that subsequently "apply" the notion of the acoustical unconscious pursued in Chapter One. But I wish to highlight at least two reasons for why this book should not be read in this manner. Chapter One combines elements of the optical unconscious in the artwork essay with reflections on and references to sound in Benjamin's autobiographical works with the aim of outlining how the concept of an acoustical unconscious might be thought in terms of Benjamin's work. But Chapter One should not be read as "uncovering" an implicit notion of the acoustical unconscious that was "latent" or always already there to be discovered, which I have been careful to avoid throughout the study. For such a reading would already presuppose the conventional structure of the unconscious, i.e., as something latent or concealed that subsequently comes to light. This would be, following Derrida's reading of Freud's unconscious, the "vulgar" way of thinking the acoustical unconscious in Benjamin's work, by relying on the conventional dichotomy of presence and absence. Just as Derrida reworks the notion of the unconscious as always being on the move, divided and multiple, I would similarly attribute the nature of the acoustical

---

[52] Gilles Deleuze and Félix Guattari, *Anti-Oedipus: Capitalism and Schizophrenia*, trans. Robert Hurley, Mark Seem, and Helen R. Lane (Minneapolis: University of Minnesota Press, 1983), 129.
[53] The last sentence to chapter one of *The Optical Unconscious* reads as follows: "And so this book will be called *The Optical Unconscious*. Does the title rhyme with *The Political Unconscious*? It's a rhyme that's intended" (Krauss, *Optical Unconscious*, 27). As opposed to the rhyming relationship to Jameson's project, Krauss situates her own use of the optical unconscious "at an angle to Benjamin's. If it can be spoken of at all as externalized within the visual field, this is because a group of disparate artists have so constructed it there, constructing it as a projection of the way that human vision can be thought to be less than a master of all it surveys, in conflict as it is with what is internal to the organism that houses it" (Krauss, *Optical Unconscious*, 179–180).

unconscious as never fixed, stable, or "latent." Rather, when we go looking for it, as it were, we are confronted by something like an unfulfilled trace that demands being returned to somewhere else, to both before and later.[54] This more accurately describes what I attempt to accomplish in Chapter One while also reflecting the methodology behind subsequent chapters.

Second, while every chapter was written with a particular goal in mind – thinking the acoustical unconscious in terms of the written word (Chapter Two), radio (Chapter Three and Chapter Four) and film (Chapter Five) – they all nevertheless relate back to Benjamin. For instance, Ludwig Tieck's "Eckbert," which is subjected to close analysis in Chapter Two, was routinely referred to by Benjamin, who once admitted it was his *locus classicus* of his theory of forgetting and who nearly wrote an essay on Tieck's story instead of his now famous Baudelaire piece. Benjamin was also actively writing for and about radio, making the radiophonic voice and how words are articulated in Chapters Three and Four relevant to any examination of a specifically Benjaminian acoustical unconscious. Finally, Kluge makes repeated references to both Adorno and Benjamin throughout his work, at one point reflecting explicitly on Benjamin's optical unconscious. Kluge emphasizes, not unproblematically, an "emancipatory" approach to Benjamin's work as a whole that nevertheless heightens the possibility of a political dimension when determining the elements of an acoustical unconscious as it relates to film. By exploring the "applicability" of a specifically Benjaminian acoustical unconscious in the German radio plays of Günter Eich in the 1950s and in the written texts and films of Alexander Kluge from the 1970s to some of his most recent work, Chapters Four and Five should not be read as an attempt to follow any fixed chronological history of the acoustical unconscious in twentieth-century German media. Nor should the choice of examining the work of Eich and Kluge necessarily calibrate the acoustical unconscious towards a fundamental modernist orientation, whereby an artist is entrusted with the task of wrenching or tearing the listener's habits of perception out of their ossified, conventionalized and ultimately falsified norms. Rather, all chapters should be read as singular instances within different media that nevertheless echo the struggle to redefine self and knowledge by hearing otherwise.

To this end, the concept of the acoustical unconscious should be characterized not simply by its apparent intermediality, in that it crosses multiple media like the written word, radio and film, but equally by its *intra*mediality, by which I mean the different ways and times in which it becomes applicable due

---

54 I want to thank Julie Beth Napolin for helping me emphasize and formulate this point.

to the evolving language *within* a specific medium or evolving technology. Such intramediality can be reduced neither to Marshal McLuhan's "the medium is the message" nor to Krauss's interpretation of the Benjaminian optical unconscious as being somehow "externalized within the visual field."[55] Rather the acoustical unconscious retains the singularity of each medium that is reflected in the same way Benjamin conceives of the camera's "other nature," which will become central to my inquiry in Chapter One: the camera is "'other' above all in the sense that a space [*Raum*] interwoven with human consciousness gives way to a space interwoven with the unconscious."[56] Only in this singular way – by paying attention to the details of that "other nature" of each medium in question and the interweaving and mutable spaces of consciousnesses within and about it – can the acoustical unconscious retain its essential inter- and intramedial, historical and cultural plasticity.

---

55 Krauss, *Optical Unconscious*, 179.
56 Benjamin, *GS* 1:500 [*WuN* 16:240]; *SW* 4:265.

1 Walter Benjamin's Shell-Shock: Sounding the Acoustical Unconscious

In both the photography essay and the artwork essay, Benjamin introduces the notion of the optical unconscious but does not explicitly propose an acoustical variant. As has been frequently remarked, Benjamin was most often concerned with visual stimuli and typically favored visual images in particular, such as mosaics and constellations. While it can be argued whether Benjamin's use of visual metaphors further explicates or problematizes his theoretical claims, it is incontrovertible that Benjamin rarely used examples taken from the acoustic realm.[1] This chapter examines a number of passages in Benjamin's work, including the *déjà vu* fragment at the end of *Berlin Chronicle* and the telephone and shell scenes in *Berlin Childhood around 1900* that refer to sounds and the acoustic realm more generally, so as to trace a concept of the acoustical unconscious that is closely tied to Benjamin's theory of language. My claim here is that, while he never explicitly theorizes it, Benjamin gestures toward an acoustical counterpart to the optical unconscious in his work, one that is as applicable to acoustic (and acoustic-visual) media as it is to written texts.

The first part of this chapter develops an acoustical unconscious that finds some comparison to the optical unconscious, which for Benjamin is relevant to both film and photography. But instead of exploring the ways in which an acoustical unconscious is relevant to specific acoustic media, such as the gramophone, radio and sound film – reserved for later chapters in this book – the last two sections of this chapter examine a few of Benjamin's autobiographical reflections that together suggest a mode of reading that attunes to the nondiscursive sonority of language that Derrida refers to when discussing what interests him about words.[2] Another way to describe this mode of reading, one that reflects the metaphorical image of the conch shell so central to this chapter and the book as a whole, is that it involves being attuned to the mnemonic

---

[1] There has been growing interest in Benjamin's scattered references to hearing, music, tone and the acoustic realm more generally. A notable early example is Gerhard Richter's chapter on "Benjamin's Ear" in *Walter Benjamin and the Corpus of Autobiography* (Detroit: Wayne State University Press, 2000). More recent scholarship includes the articles by Erlmann, Napolin, and McArthur cited in the Introduction, as well as the collection of German essays edited by Tobias Robert Klein and Asmus Trautsch: *Klang und Musik bei Walter Benjamin* (Munich: Wilhelm Fink, 2013).

[2] I am referring to Derrida's interview with Peter Brunette and David Wells, which I cite near the beginning of the Introduction.

resonance chamber of language: how the sounds of words and syllables resonate with, reassemble or disfigure each other, thereby disassembling their meaning while generating paronymic associations built around how those words and phrases might be heard, or might have been heard as a child. As is well known, Benjamin refers to a number of phonetic transmogrifications in *Berlin Childhood*, such as hearing "Mark-Thalle" in the word "Markthalle," deriving "Näh-Frau" from the words "gnädige Frau," or one of the mishearings central to this chapter: the "Muhme Rehlen" as "Mummerehlen."[3] In one of his last letters to Adorno, Benjamin attempts to defend his use of the term "unconscious," by way of Proust's example of the madeleine: for Benjamin, the child's first taste of the madeleine "no doubt becomes unconscious to the extent that the taste [*Geschmack*] becomes more familiar."[4] The same could be said of these transmogrified words: the first "taste" of a word, however misconstrued, becomes unconscious to the extent that its putative, conventional meaning becomes ever more familiar. In *Berlin Childhood*, it is as if Benjamin wishes to return to those long-forgotten misheard words and phrases, seeking to rediscover his first encounter with them, to hear and produce them again, as if for the first time.

1.1 Characteristics of An Acoustical Unconscious

In the artwork essay, Benjamin makes almost no reference to sound or acoustics. This is strange since by 1935, the year of the essay's first publication, sound film was already well-established. Lutz Koepnick writes that Benjamin's silence on sound in the artwork essay makes his argument lack "critical tools

---

[3] For the "Markthalle" as "Mark Thalle," see Walter Benjamin, *Gesammelte Schriften* (Frankfurt a.M.: Suhrkamp, 1972) (hereafter, *GS*), 7:402 [Walter Benjamin, *Werke und Nachlass: Kritische Gesamtausgabe* (Frankfurt a.M.: Suhrkamp, 2008–) (hereafter, *WuN*), 11.1:291]; Walter Benjamin, *Selected Writings*, ed. Michael W. Jennings, Marcus Bullock, Howard Eiland, and Gary Smith, trans. Rodney Livingstone and Edmund Jephcott (Cambridge: Harvard University Press, 1996–2003) (hereafter, *SW*), 3:360. For the "gnädige Frau" example, see Benjamin, *GS* 7:425 [*WuN* 11.1:313–14]. The latter, which is found in "The Sewing Box" fragment, is not translated in the *Selected Writings*. See especially Eli Friedlander's and Asmus Trautsch's contributions in *Klang und Musik bei Walter Benjamin*: Eli Friedlander, "Farben und Laute in der *Berliner Kindheit um neunzehnhundert*," in *Klang und Musik bei Walter Benjamin*, ed. Tobias Robert Klein and Asmus Trautsch, 54–67 (Munich: Wilhelm Fink, 2013; Asmus Trautsch, "Die abgelauschte Stadt und der Rhythmus des Glücks," in *Klang und Musik bei Walter Benjamin*, ed. Tobias Robert Klein and Asmus Trautsch, 17–46 (Munich: Wilhelm Fink, 2013).

[4] This critical exchange between Adorno and Benjamin will be discussed in more detail in the telephone section of the present chapter.

for understanding the ways in which Nazi cinema coordinated emotion and engineered assent."[5] While this is no doubt true, such an analysis of Nazi techniques would certainly have necessarily led Benjamin to emphasize some of the more negative implications of cinema. Perhaps this is why subsequent versions of the artwork essay reflect Benjamin's growing concern for the use of cinema as a vehicle for Fascist ideology.[6] Yet Benjamin continued even at the end of 1938 to sustain a relatively positive approach, despite knowing that this stance might inevitably weaken his argument and limit the "historical plasticity" of his essay.[7]

In the third version of the artwork essay, Benjamin introduces the optical unconscious with a new paragraph in section thirteen that expands on the comparison made in all of his previous versions between the optical unconscious and Freud's "impulse-driven unconscious" (*Triebhaft-Unbewußte*).[8] In this paragraph,

---

[5] Lutz Koepnick, "Benjamin's Silence," in *Sound Matters: Essays on the Acoustics of Modern German Culture*, ed. Nora M. Alter and Lutz Koepnick (New York: Berghahn Books, 2004), 128.

[6] Benjamin's growing concern about the fascist acquisition of revolutionary innovations can already be found in the first version of the artwork essay, which is the relegated in subsequent versions to a footnote (see Benjamin, *GS* 7:378 [*WuN* 16:132]; *SW* 3:130). Miriam Hansen argues that Benjamin's concern for this is what lead him to forego the figure of Mickey Mouse, give up on the term "innervation," and significantly diminish the mnemotechnical dimensions earlier ascribed to the notion of the unconscious (Miriam Hansen, "Of Mice and Ducks: Benjamin and Adorno on Disney," *South Atlantic Quarterly* 92, no. 1 [Winter 1993], 71; see also Miriam Hansen, *Cinema and Experience* [Berkeley: University of California Press, 2012], 161–62). See also my contribution of the term, "Innervation," in *Fueling Culture: 101 Words for Energy and Environment*, ed. Jennifer Wenzel, Patricia Yaeger, and Imre Szeman (New York: Fordham University Press, 2017), 202–205.

[7] Benjamin famously communicates all this in a letter to Adorno on December 9, 1938: "In my piece, I tried to articulate the positive moments of this upheaval as clearly as you have done for the negative ones. I thus see a strength in your work where there was a weakness in mine. Your analysis of the psychological types generated by industry, and your account of how they are generated, is most successful. Had I paid more attention to this aspect of the matter, my essay would have gained something in historical plasticity [*größere historische Plastizität*]." See Theodor Adorno and Walter Benjamin, *Briefwechsel 1928–1940* (Frankfurt a.M.: Suhrkamp, 1995), 384; Benjamin, *SW* 4:110–111.

[8] It should be noted that Harvard's *Selected Writings* include only two translations of the Artwork essay, which they label the Second Version (1936) and Third Version (1939), respectively. The new *Werke und Nachlass* edition (volume 16, published in 2012), dedicated entirely to the Artwork essay, includes five versions, the fourth being Benjamin's version in French. Harvard's Second Version corresponds to *Werke und Nachlass*'s third version, while Harvard's Third Version is *Werke und Nachlass*'s fifth. For ease of my readers who have access only to the two English translations, I have limited my references to the two versions in Harvard's *Selected Writings*, but include all references in German first to the *Gesammelte Schriften* and then to the *Werke und Nachlass* in square brackets.

however, Benjamin refers specifically to Freud's *Psychopathology of Everyday Life*, further elaborating the comparison as follows:

> [Freud's *On the Psychopathology of Everyday Life*] isolated and made analyzable things which had previously floated unnoticed on the broad stream of the perceived [*Strom des Wahrgenommenen*]. A similar deepening of apperception throughout the entire range of the optical – and now also the acoustical – sensorium [*Merkwelt*] has been accomplished by film [translation modified].[9]

"[U]nd nun auch der akustischen": this new reference to acoustics in the 1938 version of the essay, despite being almost parenthetical in nature, is perhaps one of the reasons why Benjamin had to defend his artwork essay in a letter to Adorno,[10] since it certainly seems to suggest that the whole breadth of the acoustical *Merkwelt* is now also potentially receptive to heightened analyzability, at least through film. This passing reference to acoustics is, if not explicit confirmation, then at least textual justification for an "acoustical unconscious," one that would be based not on the same, but on similar qualities as its optical counterpart.

Pinning down the unique characteristics of the optical unconscious, however, is no easy task. Much work has already been done in Benjamin scholarship to define the theoretical scope of Benjamin's optical unconscious, perhaps most notably by Miriam Hansen. But even in her posthumous work, *Cinema and Experience*, under the subheading where she condenses her thoughts on the optical unconscious, Hansen is hesitant to define the term once and for all.[11] Moreover, Hansen begins her reading of the optical unconscious by thinking of it in terms of Benjamin's mimetic faculty: the optical unconscious "adds a psychoanalytic dimension to the anthropological, language-philosophical, and mystical underpinnings of the mimetic faculty. With the optical unconscious, one might say, the mimetic faculty has migrated into the visual media and their aesthetic possibilities."[12] According to this view, the optical unconscious becomes Benjamin's "optico-psychoanalytic" derivation of his own more general but no less idiosyncratic notion of mimesis, most famously outlined in "On the Mimetic Faculty" and "Doctrine of the Similar." And yet, I would argue the optical unconscious is both more specific and more complex than a simple

---

9 Benjamin, *GS* 1:498 [*WuN* 16:239]; *SW* 4:265.
10 For a more detailed account of Adorno and Benjamin's debate in relation to sound film and analyzability, see the first section of my article "Shell-Shock: Sounding the Acoustical Unconscious," *The New Review of Film and Television Studies* 5, no. 2 (August 2007): 135–155. The present chapter derives partly from this earlier article.
11 I define the acoustical unconscious as a specifically Benjaminian concept near the middle of the Introduction.
12 Hansen, *Cinema and Experience*, 155.

"visual" extrapolation of Benjamin's mimetic faculty. The same can be said of the acoustical unconscious, in that it cannot simply be an extension of the optical unconscious. Examining specific qualities of the optical unconscious, not all of which are tied to the visual realm, will nevertheless help us to compare similar characteristics that may be attributable to the acoustical unconscious. There are at least three.

Hansen remarks in an earlier article that Benjamin requires either film or the photograph *to think* the optical unconscious.[13] Film in particular, with its unique technological effects like slow motion and enlargement, allows details to be isolated and therefore made analyzable; hence Benjamin's own reference in the artwork essay to how we "are generally familiar with the movement of picking up a cigarette lighter or a spoon, but know almost nothing of what really goes on between hand and metal, and still less how this varies with the different moods in which we find ourselves" (translation modified).[14] Assuming that the optical unconscious requires such a technical medium as film or photography, the acoustical unconscious – and this would be its first criterion – must also require some technological medium or prosthesis in order for it to be thought. Of course, there are a number of acoustic media to choose from, including the telephone, gramophone, radio and sound film. All of these have, to varying degrees, the capacity to transmit and record isolated sound "events," which theoretically allow them to be "repeated" and subsequently analyzed.

But before turning to any one technological medium that exemplifies an increase in acoustic analyzability, a few more distinguishing features of the optical unconscious need to be examined in order to help constitute some of the dimensions of an acoustical variant. Again, in the third version of the artwork essay, section thirteen, Benjamin adds a new reference to Rudolf Arnheim's description of slow motion. Benjamin cites Arnheim's *Film as Art* (*Film als Kunst*, 1932) on how slow motion

> might, for instance, serve [artistic purposes by slowing] down natural movements grotesquely; but it can also create new movements [*neue Bewegungen*], which do not appear as the retarding of natural movements but have a curious gliding, floating, otherworldly [*überirdische*] characteristic of their own [translation modified].[15]

---

13 Miriam Hansen, "Benjamin and Cinema: Not a One-Way Street," in *Benjamin's Ghosts: Interventions in Contemporary Literary and Cultural Theory*, ed. Gerhard Richter (Stanford, CA: Stanford University Press, 2002), 68.
14 Benjamin, *GS* 1:500 [*WuN* 16:240]; *SW* 4:266.
15 Benjamin, *GS* 1:500 [*WuN* 16:240]; *SW* 4:266. The full passage is found in Rudolph Arnheim, *Film as Art* (Berkeley: University of California Press 1960), 116–117, or in the original German: Rudolph Arnheim, *Film als Kunst* (Berlin: Rowohlt, 1932), 138. It should be noted however that

Crucial for Benjamin is the way Arnheim describes slow motion as not merely slowing down the natural world, but also offering for the first time the possibility of seeing new movements wholly other to this world, indeed other-"earthly" (*überirdisch*). From here Benjamin points out how these new, otherworldly movements could not have been previously observed by the naked eye, suggesting that the "optical" in film relates less to the eye than to the camera. Benjamin's famous formulation directly follows: "Clearly, it is an other nature [*eine andere Natur*] that speaks to the camera than to the eye."[16] Let me dwell on this key sentence, which is originally found in the photography essay and is repeated without alteration in every version of the artwork essay. First, it is important to emphasize that this nature is *other* than the nature we as humans are accustomed to. It is easy to miss – and thereby dismiss – the importance of this other nature when reading the Harvard English translation: "*another* nature speaks to the camera." Instead, I translate the phrase as "an other nature" to emphasize its otherness; it is "other" in the same way that, as in the Arnheim quote, slow motion is "other"-worldly.

Secondly, it is no accident that Benjamin describes this other nature as "speaking [*spricht*]" to the camera, however odd this may sound. We typically think of the camera as "capturing" a unique moment: it is the camera that does the acting upon the world, pulling or taking the world in or framing it, so to speak. But in Benjamin's formulation, the relation of the camera to its nature is flipped: its nature, otherwise inaccessible to us without the camera, is not acted upon but rather *speaks to* the camera. Not only is the relation between the camera and this other nature fundamentally linguistic, the camera is the recipient of this otherworldly *Natursprache*. In order to begin to understand how a camera might be receptive to something like a language of nature, it is important to return to Benjamin's early essay, *On Language as Such and on the Language of Man* (1916), in which he proposes that the languages of painting and sculpture are equally founded on and translate the language of things (*Dingsprache*) in nature. Benjamin is careful to note that he is concerned "with nameless, nonacoustic languages [*unakustische Sprachen*], languages issuing from matter."[17] And yet, to further illustrate how all languages of artistic form should be thought in connection to their appropriate *Natursprachen*, he writes: "An example that is obvious because it belongs to the acoustic sphere is the

---

the English translation in *Selected Writings* strangely omits the third characteristic, "otherworldly," around which the present analysis revolves.
16 Benjamin, *GS* 1:500; *SW* 4:265.
17 Benjamin, *GS* 1:156; *SW* 1:73.

kinship between song and the language of birds."[18] While he makes no reference to cinema in his language essay, these remarks nevertheless help explain how in the artwork essay an "other" nature "speaks" to the camera: just as there is a *Natursprache* that is both tied to and translated by the languages of artistic form, a unique nature-language speaks to the camera. It is a nonacoustic language, to be sure, but it is a language to which the camera is nevertheless receptive in ways that our naked eye simply cannot be.[19]

How might this be applicable to the acoustical unconscious? In a similar way, the acoustical unconscious– and this would be its second characteristic – would also have to be affiliated with a nature *other* than the one that "speaks" to the naked ear, which brings us back to the notion of hearing otherwise. Just as slow-motion in film produces new movements never before seen, so too the slowing down or speeding up of a recorded voice would create new, literally unheard-of voices that are as otherworldly as the floating image of a figure in slow motion. Such might be the "other" nature of the microphone, a nature accessible only by means of a receptive acoustical apparatus capable of recording and producing such an effect during playback.

A third and by far the most complex characteristic of the optical unconscious that is transferrable to the acoustical unconscious involves its curious mode of temporality. Again, as Hansen puts it, "the notion of the optical unconscious involves a distinct and heightened temporality – a temporality that inevitably implies and implicates the beholder."[20] Returning briefly for a moment to Benjamin's citation of Arnheim on slow motion above, one can see this in the German word *Zeitlupe,* or literally "time-magnifier":[21] slow-motion puts prescription

---

18 Benjamin, *GS* 1:156; *SW* 1:73.
19 One might also hear in Benjamin's formulation an echo of Johann Wilhelm Ritter's distinction between tone and light: "But tone itself is *light,* which must already belong to another sense than to the *eye* [*das ohnehin einem anderen Sinne, als dem* Auge, *gehören mußte*], because the eye does *not* see light, but rather only *mediates* that of light = of tone" (Johann Wilhelm Ritter, *Fragmente aus dem Nachlasse eines jungen Physikers* [Leipzig: Kiepenhauer Verlag, 1984], 275). This fascinating discussion of light, tone and the mediating eye in Ritter's text should be read as informing Benjamin's own thoughts on the other nature that speaks to the camera than to the eye. I will return to this curious indistinction between light and tone in the final section of this chapter.
20 Hansen, "Benjamin and Cinema," 66.
21 The English cognate of *Lupe* also maintains the reference to sight and spying (as in "loophole"). But one should not overlook its other – and in English at least – more prominent use: of loop as "a doubling or return into itself [. . .] so as to leave an aperture between its parts" ("loop," *Oxford English Dictionary*, 2nd ed. [Oxford: Oxford University Press, 1989], s.v.). This double sense of "loop" as both peering through an aperture and returning into or back to itself is not only central to the concerns of this chapter – it conveniently returns us to the shape of a

glasses on time, allowing the beholder to see minute movements that would otherwise not be accessible in real-time. Hansen's remark, however, does not simply refer to the effects of slow motion, but more to what Benjamin calls those "tiny sparks of contingency [*Zufall*]" in a photograph or film that indicate an inconspicuous "spot" or site wherein the optical unconscious can be (re)discovered. This is where the notion of isolated details becomes most relevant to Benjamin's reflections in the artwork essay: isolating these moments does not merely "reactualize a lost prior vision; rather [the optical unconscious] makes us see 'images that we have never seen *before* we remember them.'"[22] In other words, the photographic or filmic accident mobilizes for Benjamin an unconscious optical past that is only remembered, or that only comes to consciousness *after* we see it for the first time.[23] This is similar to the phenomenon of déjà vu: we have the distinct feeling of "having seen this before," but only after we see it for the first time. This sense, furthermore, is what "implicates the beholder": the long-forgotten moment, buried deep in the beholder's own supposed "unconscious," erupts in a flash of recognition, and with it the uncanny notion that we had somehow already foreseen this; that is to say, we had already seen it, but didn't see it coming.

It is perhaps no accident then that Benjamin suggests in the *Berlin Chronicle* an alternative to the déjà vu: that the metaphor "most appropriate to the process [of déjà vu] should not rather be taken from the realm of acoustics."[24] Benjamin's justification for this rather surprising claim[25] utilizes similar vocabulary found in the artwork essay used precisely to describe the optical unconscious. Only here at the very end of *Berlin Chronicle*, he attributes them to the acoustical realm:

Hörmuschel – but also bridges the relationship between the aperture of a medium and technology's own inherent reproducibility. In this way, both senses should be maintained simultaneously.

22 Hansen, citing Benjamin, "Benjamin and Cinema," 67.

23 In *Cinema and Experience*, Hansen illustrates this point by referring to Benjamin's account of the portrait of the photographer Dauthendey and his fiancée, who slashes her wrists after giving birth to her sixth child. See Hansen, *Cinema and Experience*, esp. 107, 157.

24 Benjamin, *GS* 6:518 [*WuN* 11.1:77]; *SW* 2:634.

25 One reason why Benjamin thought that the metaphor of acoustics would be more appropriate than optics is because of the phenomenon of the echo. The echo has arguably no equivalent in the realm of vision, except perhaps in terms of allegorical objects. On echo in Benjamin, see especially Bettine Menke, "'However One Calls Into the Forest . . .': Echoes of Translation," in *Walter Benjamin and Romanticism*, ed. Andrew E. Benjamin and Beatrice Hanssen (New York: Continuum, 2002), 83–97, and Rainer Nägele, *Echoes of Translation: Reading Between Texts* (Baltimore: Johns Hopkins University Press, 1997). In the Muhmerehlen section that follows, I suggest that another possible reason why Benjamin chooses the "realm of acoustics" as his preferential metaphor for the déjà vu is its surroundability.

> One ought to speak of events that reach us like an echo awakened by a call, a sound that seems to have been heard somewhere in the darkness of a past life. Accordingly, if we are not mistaken, the shock with which moments step into [*treten*] consciousness as if already lived usually strikes us in the form of a sound.[26]

Although Benjamin is describing here an acoustical correlate to the déjà vu – what might be called the *déjà entendu*[27] – this passage is the clearest evidence in Benjamin's work, beyond his oblique reference to the acoustic sphere in the artwork essay, that supports the notion of an acoustical unconscious. A closer reading reveals that the call or sound echoed must have at some point faded into the darkness of a life that has already passed, but the shock of its occurrence – and precisely the shock of its occurrence *as* recurrence – enters or, translated literally, steps into (*treten*) consciousness. Now, compare this passage with the one in the artwork essay, where Benjamin describes the contours of the optical unconscious. In the third version, the following passage comes directly on the heels of his citation of Arnheim on slow motion:

> Clearly, it is an other nature that speaks to the camera than to the eye. Other above all in the sense that, there where space is interwoven with human consciousness, a space interwoven with the unconscious steps in [*tritt*] [translation modified].[28]

Just as Benjamin's déjà entendu in *Berlin Chronicle* involves an echo that steps into the light of consciousness out from the darkness of a life seemingly passed by, the other nature of the camera involves a similar process whereby a space interwoven with the unconscious "steps into" a space interwoven with consciousness. If nothing else, this psycho-spatial parallel clearly illustrates the extent to which Benjamin is adapting his own notion of the optical unconscious in terms of the acoustical realm. It should be remembered that the *Berlin Chronicle* was written and compiled during his stay in Ibiza in the spring of 1932, just a year after completing his essay on photography, wherein Benjamin first outlines his idea of the optical unconscious.

---

26 Benjamin, *GS* 6:518 [*WuN* 11.1:77–78]; *SW* 2:634.
27 In a highly informative study on the déjà vu, Alan Brown notes that, although "the physical setting is the most common eliciting factor with déjà vu, spoken words are oft-noted triggers to déjà vu illusions" (Alan S. Brown, *The Déjà Vu Experience* [New York: Psychology Press, 2004], 189). Of the scientific explanations that he examines (dual processing, neurological, memory, and double perception), only the first two can account for both visually- and auditorily-based déjà vu experiences. Nevertheless, he encourages further research to extend "the memory and double perception interpretations to the realm of auditory processing" (Brown, *Déjà Vu*, 189).
28 Benjamin, *GS* 1:500 [*WuN* 16:240]; *SW* 4:266.

Let us turn briefly now to that photography essay in order to examine one other temporal characteristic of the optical unconscious that further confirms Benjamin's adaptation of it into the realm of acoustics: its relationship to the future. In "Little History of Photography" ("Kleine Geschichte der Fotografie," 1931), Benjamin makes an interesting, albeit somewhat cryptic, reference to the future. The oft-cited sentence is as follows:

> No matter how artful the photographer, no matter how carefully posed his subject, the beholder feels an irresistible urge to search such a picture for the tiny spark of contingency [*Zufall*], of the here and now, with which reality has (so to speak) seared the character of the image, to find the inconspicuous spot where in the thusness [*Sosein*] of that long-forgotten moment the future nests so eloquently that we, looking back, may rediscover it.[29]

The strange idea of the future nesting in the "thusness" of that long-forgotten moment might again be explained in terms of the déjà vu: with its occurrence as recurrence comes the notion that somehow the future was already predicted long ago; with the arrival of that precise moment, glance or alignment, it is as if we are living that long-predicted future in the present now, unexpectedly and involuntarily. Howard Caygill accurately describes this concept of the future according to Benjamin as "the future subsist[ing] in the present as a contingency which, if realized, will retrospectively change the present."[30] Like the déjà vu, the optical unconscious allows for the "possibility of creating an openness to the future,"[31] but an openness that is experienced only in the present and via an unexpected and involuntary detour through the past, wherein "the future nests so eloquently."

It is not surprising, then, to see how the future also plays a role in Benjamin's description of the acoustical variant of the déjà vu in the *Berlin Chronicle*, written only a year later:

> It is a word, a tapping, or a rustling that is endowed with the magic power to transport us into the cool tomb of long ago, from the vault of which the present seems to return only as an echo. But has the counterpart [*Gegenbild*] of this entranced removal ever been investigated – the shock with which we come across a gesture or a word the way we suddenly find in our house a forgotten glove or reticule? And just as they let us infer that a stranger had been there, so there are words or gestures from which we infer that invisible foreign entity, the future, that forgot them with us [translation modified].[32]

---

29 Benjamin, *GS* 2:371. This translation is taken from Hansen's version of the passage in her essay "Benjamin and Cinema," 67.
30 Howard Caygill, *Walter Benjamin: The Colour of Experience* (New York: Routledge, 1998), 94.
31 Caygill, *Colour of Experience*, 94.
32 Benjamin, *GS* 6:518 [*WuN* 11.1:78]; *SW* 2:634–635.

Benjamin's description of a lost glove and an invisible stranger makes it all the more difficult to assess why exactly he refers here to the future. The word itself is placed in the sentence between two commas, appearing in a gap, seemingly as an after-thought, almost forgotten. But it is at the heart of the sentence itself. One thing is clear: we have no control over what was left behind or forgotten in our house of memory. But what is not so evident is why Benjamin equates these long-lost words, gestures or sounds with the future, and what precisely the relationship is between them.[33] The clue comes in the form of the counter-image or *Gegenbild*: as opposed to the magical power of the word or knock that bans us to what once was, making the present simply the reverberation of a distant echo, Benjamin is looking to reorient this reverberation away from the past and toward the direction to what will be, that is to say, to a deeply forgotten future that revitalizes the present rather than freezes it in the icy crypt of the Once (*das Einst*, which even sounds like *Eis*). Interpreted this way, the word, gesture, knock or rustling opens the present to remnants of the future lost in the folds of a distant and otherwise inaccessible past. This is a strange, paradoxical

---

[33] The various English translations only serve to confuse matters. Gerhard Richter translates the passage as follows: "And just like these [lost gloves or reticules] lead us to infer the former presence of a strange woman or strangeness [*eine Fremde*], there are also words or gestures that permit us to infer that invisible strange woman or strangeness, the future which she or it forgot in the house" (Richter, *Corpus of Autobiography*, 173). Edmund Jephcott's translation in the *Selected Writings* manages to keep the syntax intact, but with it another meaning emerges: "And just as they cause us to surmise that a stranger has been there, there are words or gestures from which we infer this invisible stranger, the future, who left them in our keeping" (Benjamin, *SW* 2:635). In Richter's translation, the future is what was left behind, while in Jephcott's translation it appears that the future is the invisible stranger that leaves the words behind. Which one is right? The confusion arises from the very ambiguous pronoun, "sie" in the last phrase of the original sentence: ". . . die Zukunft, welche sie bei uns vergaß." The "sie" could refer either to *eine Fremde* (this is Richter's reading), in which case it (she) would be the subject and singular; or it may refer to those lost words and gestures (Jephcott's reading), in which case "sie" would be the object and plural. By looking closer at the structure of the analogy, it appears that, just as the lost gloves point to the former presence of *a* strange female (eine *Fremde*), so the words and gestures point to *that* invisible foreign entity (jene *unsichtbare Fremde*), which is not the female just referred to, but rather the future set off by commas. In other words, the word *jene* misleads readers to refer back to *eine Fremde* when in fact it should refer, fittingly enough, *forward to* "the future." A translation that best reflects this reading would be roughly the following: "And just as [the gloves] let us infer a stranger had been there, so are there words and gestures from which we infer that invisible foreign entity, the future, which forgot them with us." The consequence of this interpretation is significant: instead of being fixed to a time beyond the present, the future, as Benjamin describes it, is an entity that freely roams into the past, leaving remnants of its foreignness behind, to be rediscovered in moments of déjà vu.

future indeed, but a future that is nevertheless reminiscent of what was described in the photography essay: as nesting so eloquently in a long-forgotten moment. Between the temporal disjunction affiliated with the optical unconscious in "Little History of Photography" and the echoing déjà vu at the end of *Berlin Chronicle*, Benjamin's reflections on the future are virtually indistinguishable. The only difference is between the optical and the acoustical spheres. That, and his choice of which one to publish: while he refers to the notion of the optical unconscious in his photography essay and every version of the artwork essay, he leaves the idea of an acoustical déjà vu almost entirely unheard, relegating it to a metaphor at the end of *Berlin Chronicle*.

This raises a specific linguistic issue, since as a figure of speech, how can a metaphor be one of the central tenets of a concept like the acoustical unconscious? To repeat Benjamin's own words: "the *metaphor* [emphasis mine] appropriate to the process [of déjà vu] would not be far better taken from the realm of acoustics."[34] One way to answer this question is to say that the acoustical unconscious is constitutive of temporal characteristics best elucidated by Benjamin's own metaphor of the déjà entendu. Another way to answer this question would be to follow what Miriam Hansen wrote of Benjamin's optical unconscious: it is "obviously not a philosophical concept but rather an experimental *metaphor* [emphasis mine] and, like all complex tropes, has multiple and shifting meanings."[35] But what does Hansen mean by "experimental metaphor" exactly? It is certainly true that the acoustical unconscious has "multiple and shifting meanings," but labeling it as a metaphor seems reductive. Instead, I prefer to think the acoustical unconscious not as an "experimental metaphor" but as a concept in the strict Benjaminian sense as described in the Introduction: a grouping of disparate phenomena that allows for the emergence of a dialectical image, through which time is not linear but "intensive," that is, discontinuous, immeasurable and proleptic. This intensive notion of time is precisely what

---

34 Benjamin, *GS* 6:518 [*WuN* 11.1:77]; *SW* 2:634.
35 Hansen, *Cinema and Experience*, 156. Like Hansen with the optical unconscious, Napolin also recognizes the metaphorical element of Benjamin's acoustical déjà vu, insisting that it must remain open to both its material and figural dimensions: "The fold between matter and metaphor is obdurate: these events affect us 'like' an echo, yet they are also awakened 'by' a sound. Here [. . .] it is difficult to discern whether the acoustical component is material or figural, belonging to their fold. This fold is introduced by what has not happened in a full or complete way, what remains without positive knowledge. The fold designates what is not fully recoverable through narrative, as if sounds were its shard" (Julie Beth Napolin, "The Fact of Resonance: An Acoustics of Determination in Faulkner and Benjamin," *symploke* 23, no. 1–2 [2015]: 180–181).

Benjamin gestures toward in the passage above on the echo and the "counter-image" at the end of *Berlin Chronicle*.

To summarize, three attributes for a heightened awareness of the optical unconscious have been examined. The first is the necessity of a technical apparatus, like a camera or microphone, for the optical or acoustical unconscious to be thought, respectively. The second is the other nature that *speaks* to said apparatus, and with it the details that the naked eye or ear could not otherwise perceive on their own; details, furthermore, which could be isolated and subsequently analyzed. Finally, a third characteristic involves an enigmatic contingency and heightened temporality that folds the future into the past.[36] One might argue, as Hansen does, that even this third quality, while remaining intact in the photography essay, seems to fall away from Benjamin's own description of the optical unconscious in the final version of the artwork essay. At the same time, it is the only characteristic of the optical unconscious in Benjamin's work that finds an explicitly acoustical correlate in the form of the acoustical déjà vu at the end of *Berlin Chronicle*.

The next two sections seek to amplify the importance of Benjamin's telephone and shell scenes in *Berlin Childhood around 1900* by interpreting them as two exemplary stagings of the acoustical unconscious. Both "shell" and "telephone receiver" are referred to in German with the same word, "Muschel," or more specifically, "Hörmuschel" (ear piece or literally, "hearing shell"). But in the short "Telephone" section of *Berlin Childhood*, Benjamin remembers how as a child he used to have to tear off (*abreißen*) the two receivers from the wall, thrust his head between them and in so doing was ruthlessly delivered over (*gnadenlos ausgeliefert*) to the voice that spoke. In contrast, Benjamin writes in the "Mummerehlen" section how he picks up a conch shell in, holds it to his ear and asks reflectively: "What do I hear?"[37] Whereas with the telephone he loses any sense of control, pointing to a state of uncontrollability that disrupts any sense of self, place and time, Benjamin appears fully in control with the shell,

---

[36] It would also be necessary to consider a fourth element of the optical unconscious, one that, according to Hansen, Benjamin also relinquishes in the final version of the artwork essay: its possibility of being transindividual and collective. This is a tantalizing notion that would generate political implications for the acoustical unconscious as much as it does for Benjamin's optical unconscious. The remainder of this chapter, however, remains both within the confines of Benjamin's references to the acoustic and at the level of the singular rather than the collective. For a suggestive reading of "socially unconscious sounds whose dialectic exceeds personal memory," see Napolin, "Fact of Resonance," 171–186.

[37] Benjamin, *GS* 7:417 [*WuN* 11.1:539]; *SW* 3:392. As I will later explain, there are at least three versions of the "Mummerehlen" section, due in part to Benjamin's revision of *Berlin Childhood around 1900* in 1938. The present references are to the final version.

being able to differentiate between what he does not hear and those singular sounds from his childhood that he would otherwise not be able to hear again. But in both cases, he is propelled via sound to another place and time. As such, Benjamin's staging of the telephone and shell illustrate the experiential spectrum of acoustic othering, foreground his specific use of concept of the unconscious, and highlight the correlation of the acoustical unconscious to memory and language.

1.2 All Ears: Benjamin's Telephone

One of the most revealing scenes in *Berlin Childhood around 1900* in which Benjamin puts an object to his ear occurs in the piece, "Das Telephon."[38] As Gerhard Richter puts it, "when it comes to a thing such as the telephone, an object that Benjamin [. . .] strategically calls his 'twin,' the textual imbrication of thingliness, thinking, selfhood and critique even functions as one of the primal scenes of his entire autobiographical corpus."[39] It is not lost on Richter that, for any scene to be "primal" in Benjamin's ouvre, the "scene" in question can never be singular or fixed but is always on the move, always in transition, always already doubled or in the act of doubling. The curious doubling, changing nature of the telephone is referenced throughout the section, starting with the

---

38 The *Werke und Nachlass* edition includes three versions of *Berlin Childhood around 1900*, each one including a slight variation of same "Telephone" piece. The Harvard *Selected Writings* translates only the final, 1938 version (Benjamin, *SW* 3:349–350). Unless I state otherwise, my German reference will also be to Benjamin's 1938 edition (Benjamin, *GS* 7:390–391 [*WuN* 11.1:507–509]). The telephone also appears in a short passage in *Berlin Chronicle*, where the telephone is described as a "truly infernal machine" when it rang during his parents' afternoon nap between two and four (Benjamin, *GS* 6:498 [*WuN* 11.1:51]; *SW* 2:619).

39 See Gerhard Richter's *Inheriting Walter Benjamin* (London: Bloomsbury, 2016), especially chapter three, "Benjamin's Ear: *Berlin Chronicle*," 71. No other critic has approached this fragment so thoroughly as Richter does in this chapter. In *Aberrations of Mourning*, Laurence Rickels focuses less on Benjamin's text and more on the telephone's birth and the "umbilical chord" it provides, suggesting that, along with psychology, the telephone "introduces the nuclear family as we know it, forever disbanded and bonded through the phone, forever keeping in *tele-touch*" (Laurence A. Rickels, *Aberrations of Mourning* [Minneapolis: University of Minnesota Press, 2011], 108). And given the breadth of Avital Ronell's *The Telephone Book*, it is surprising to see Benjamin's telephone fragment relegated to a brief reference in her introduction: "Take Benjamin's hand, if you will, when he, resounding Bell, names the telephone after an absent brother ('mein Zwillingsbruder'). The telephone of the Berlin childhood performed the rescue missions from a depleted solitude" (Avital Ronell, *The Telephone Book: Technology, Schizophrenia, Electric Speech* [Lincoln: University of Nebraska Press, 1989], 6–7).

opening sentence that is nearly impossible to translate. The following translation is at best awkward, but it emphasizes two elements: Benjamin's double use of the verb "liegen" in the sentence, and his repeated use of the impersonal "es" pronoun, both of which are lost in the official English translation:

> Whether it [es] lies with the construction [Bau] of the apparatus or with that of memory [Erinnerung] – what is certain is that the noises of the first telephone conversations, upon reverberation, lie differently [anders] in the ears from those of today. It were [Es waren] nocturnal noises."[40]

The first thing to recognize is Benjamin's curious use of the impersonal "es" pronoun. In both instances, the "es" decidedly does not refer to the telephone, despite the neuter gender of "*das* Telefon." Rather, both uses of "es" have a curious relation to the noises of the first telephone, noises heard in the dark. As such, the impersonal singularity of "it" becomes pluralized in the second, much shorter sentence: "Es waren Nachtgeräusche."[41] From the outset then, Benjamin's use of the impersonal "es" already proposes an "it" that is other than the telephone, an "it" that is also plural and lies somewhere between the apparatus's mechanical construction and Benjamin's memory, itself a mneumonic construct he is attempting to reconstruct on the page.

In order to recognize the importance of the double use of the verb, "liegen," I wish to return, in a round-about way, to some of the attributes of the acoustical unconscious described in the previous section and reflect on why they are relevant here. Clearly the need for a technical apparatus in order to think the acoustical unconscious appears to be fulfilled: Benjamin is describing the telephone as one such acoustic device. The second attribute, involving an other nature that speaks to the camera, also appears relevant: the night noises of the earliest telephone conversations echo otherwise (*anders*) in his ears from those of today. As such, these "other" sounds point to an other nature of the telephone. Benjamin's description of them, moreover, is equally reminiscent of the

---

40 Benjamin, *GS* 7:390 [*WuN* 11.1:507]; *SW* 3:349.
41 Richter also points to the "surprising conjunction 'or'" in the opening sentence of "Telephone" (Richter, *Inheriting Walter Benjamin*, 179). Along with his reading of "two-ling," of the "one who is two" (Richter, *Inheriting Walter Benjamin*, 182), Richter emphasizes the importance of pluralization for Benjamin's autobiographical self: "Recognizing the other would thus not mean, as it often does today in the so-called struggles for recognition and the politics of identity, to identify and affirm others as stable selves and self-identical others. On the contrary, to affirm and recognize the other would mean for the self to acknowledge precisely those moments when the other is no longer itself but assumes a multitude of guises and forms, that is, becomes pluralized in its ability to become similar to other persons and objects" (Richter, *Inheriting Walter Benjamin*, 184).

way he once described the notion of the unconscious to Adorno. When Adorno voiced his concern over the use of the term "unconscious" in the Baudelaire essay, Benjamin wrote the following:

> I do not think that, in order to give forgetting its fair due, one needs to call into question the notion of *mémoire involontaire*. The childhood experience of the taste [*Erfahrung des Geschmacks*] of the madeleine, which returns involuntarily to Proust's memory one day [*wieder ins Gedächtnis tritt*], was indeed unconscious. But his first bite into his first madeleine would not have been. (Savoring [*Kosten*] is a conscious act). Yet this tasting [*Schmecken*] no doubt becomes unconscious to the extent that the taste [*Geschmack*] becomes more familiar. The "tasting again" [*Wiederschmecken*] by the grown man is, of course, conscious [translation modified].[42]

Neither we nor Adorno could have asked for a clearer explanation of the unconscious according to Benjamin, especially as it relates to Proust's madeleine, or what might be called the gustatory unconscious. By explaining the "unconscious" via Proust and not Freud, Benjamin posits a notion of the unconscious not limited strictly to psychoanalytic, i.e., mental structures, but one that necessarily includes sense perception and the physiological, which goes a long way to explain why Benjamin develops a notion of the "optical" unconscious in the first place. For Benjamin, what returns involuntarily to memory is the singular childhood experience of tasting the madeleine as a child, which was conscious at the time of first tasting but which has "no doubt [become] unconscious to the extent that the taste [*Geschmack*] becomes more familiar." The process of generalizing the taste through habit and familiarity is the same process that transforms the first bite into an unconscious *Schmecken*. By nominalizing the verb, "the tasting" (*das Schmecken*), Benjamin implies not simply a taste that occurred once in the past and is now complete. Rather, "das Schmecken" is best translated in the gerund form of the verb, "the tasting," in part to differentiate it from "das Geschmack" (the taste), but more importantly because its gerund suggests that the experience is ongoing and unfinished. For Samuel Weber, the gerund is crucial in the work of Benjamin:

> Why the gerund? Because the gerund, and the present participle from which it is derived (as its nominal form), entail a form of "presence" that involves both participation and partiality. Like Benjamin's origin, the present participle is never complete, always returning, but forever unfinished. And it is "present" only with respect to the instance of its enunciation.[43]

---

42 Adorno and Benjamin, *Briefwechsel*, 425–426; Benjamin, *SW* 4:413.
43 Samuel Weber, *Benjamin's -abilities* (Cambridge: Harvard University Press, 2008), 171. In this passage, Weber discusses Benjamin's reflections on awakening in the *Arcades Project*, which is structurally similar to the way in which the first bite of the madeleine is awakened to consciousness. In both cases, Benjamin's model is Proust. Awakening in the Proustian and

This is why *das Schmecken*, which Benjamin states is "indeed unconscious," returns instantly and involuntarily to the grown man as a *Wiederschmecken*, interrupting the familiarity of the habitualized *Geschmack*.

This same construct is evident in the beginning sentence of "The Telephone": "it is certain that the noises of the first telephone conversations echo (*im Nachhall*) differently in my ear (*anders in den Ohren liegen*) from those of today."[44] The sounds in their very echo amount to the *Wiederhören* of those first telephone conversations, the reverberations of which are "very other" than those which have since become familiar. The distinction between childhood experiences that have become unconscious and their sudden and involuntary conscious return to the adult is paramount in Benjamin's description of both the madeleine and telephone. The phrase "in den Ohren liegen" not only repeats the verb, *liegen*, from the first phrase, thereby staging that very return, but also means a kind of curious, even incessant repetition: between people, the phrase means to pester or badger someone. In the case of sounds, they seem to "lie" around, forever incomplete, reverberating in our ears. The hearing again of those first telephone calls thus exemplifies the notion of iteration: one could say that their "Wieder-hören," which parallels Benjamin's description of the madeleine's *Wiederschmecken*, is a return to those first "hearings" that are "very other" in their reverberations.

The mneumonic construct described here – a returning to first tastings or first hearings that have since been buried under the ossified taste of the madeleine or the repeated telephone conversations of today – is not unrelated to a passage in the artwork essay in which Benjamin reflects on what film allows us to do: he writes how we "are generally familiar (*geläufig*) with the movement of picking up a cigarette lighter or a spoon, but know almost nothing of what really plays out between hand and metal (*was sich zwischen Hand und Metall dabei eigentlich abspielt*), and still less how this varies with the different moods in which we find ourselves."[45] Further on in "The Telephone" section, Benjamin similarly explores what was "really playing out" when he first picked up those telephone receivers, along with the particular mood in which he found himself:

> When, having mastered my senses with great effort (*meiner Sinne mit Mühe mächtig*), I arrived to quell the uproar [of the telephone] after prolonged fumbling through the gloomy corridor, I tore off (*abriß*) the two receivers, which were heavy as dumbbells,

---

Benjaminian sense will become even more central in the reading of Tieck's "Der blonde Eckbert" ("Eckbert the Fair") in the following chapter.
44 Benjamin, *GS* 7:390 [*WuN* 11.1:507]; *SW* 3:349.
45 Benjamin, *GS* 1:500 [*WuN* 16:241]; *SW* 4:266.

pressed my head between them, and was inexorably delivered over (*gnadenlos ausgeliefert*) to the voice that now spoke. There was nothing that diminished the uncanny violence (*die unheimliche Gewalt*) with which it invaded me.[46]

The excerpt begins with a slight variation on the common figure of speech, to "no longer be in control of one's senses" (*seiner [fünf] Sinne nicht mehr mächtig sein*), which is closely related to being unconscious or passed out (*ohnmächtig*). Benjamin is thus already describing a scene in which he must go to great lengths just to maintain control of his senses; he must pass through the passage without passing out. The scene above can furthermore be read as a pathway toward the unconscious in at least two ways. First, it can be interpreted similarly to what the camera allows us to do in the artwork essay above: just as the camera offers us new knowledge about what really happens between hand and metal, Benjamin describes with the telephone what he experienced when his hands picked up the two telephone receivers. Important also is his reference to the various moods "that we find ourselves in" (*in denen wir uns befinden*), a phrase curiously truncated in the Harvard translation of the artwork essay.[47] Both the camera and the telephone impose upon us certain moods or states (*Verfassungen*) that we may become aware of but have no control over. Hence Benjamin's recollection of how he was delivered mercilessly over to the telephonic voice with nothing to diminish the uncanny violence that would invade him.[48]

This leads to the second way the telephone scene above should be read in terms of the unconscious. When analyzing the role of the telephone in the work of Freud and Kafka, Laurence Rickels writes in *Aberrations of Mourning*: "Freud

---

46 Benjamin, *GS* 4:243 [*WuN* 11.1:439]; *SW* 3:350.
47 "We are familiar with the movement of picking up a cigarette lighter or a spoon, but know almost nothing of what really goes on between hand and metal, and still less how this varies with different moods" (Benjamin, *GS* 1:500 [*WuN* 16:241]; *SW* 4:266).
48 In "Telefonie und Literatur," Bernhard Siegert compares this passage with Kafka's descriptions of the telephone to argue that it has a direct impact on the nervous system. Moreover, the telephonic voice is despotic because it fragments the subject and passes control speech and action over to another will or perverse desire (Bernhard Siegert, "Hold me in your arms, Ma Bell. Telefonie und Literatur," in *Telefonie und Gesellschaft. Beiträge zu einer Soziologie des Telefons*, ed. Ulrich Lange and Klaus Beck [Berlin: Spiess, 1989], 337). One should add to this argument Benjamin's own description of its violence as uncanny (*unheimlich*), a term he uses sparingly but which resonates with the shell scene in the following section. See also Anthony Enn's "Telepathie – Telefon – Terror. Ausweitung und Verstümmelungen des Körpers," in *Hörstürze: Akustik und Gewalt im 20. Jahrhundert*, ed. N. Gess, F. Schreiner, and M. Schulz (Würzburg: Königshausen & Neumann, 2005), 89–112, and Kata Gellen's section, "The Telephonic Acousmêtre in *The Castle*," in *Kafka and Noise: The Discovery of Cinematic Sound in Literary Modernism* (Northwestern University Press, 2019), 163–171.

argues that there is no *no* in the unconscious: instead, things are more or less cathected – *besetzt*. According to both Freud and Kafka, there is no *no* on the phone."[49] While it is surprising that Rickels does not include Benjamin alongside Freud and Kafka, the analogy of the telephone to the unconscious is certainly nothing new. Its history begins with Freud's own comparison of transference to a telephonic exchange between two unconsciousnesses and, if one were to follow Avital Ronell's interpretation, perhaps ends with Derrida and Lacan's notes on the constitution of the subject via a certain external locus of the Other:

> This relation – of a constituting impurity or alterity, the constituting non-presence – compellingly resembles what Freud in Derrida's sense called the unconscious: "A certain alterity – to which Freud gives the metaphysical name of the unconscious – is definitively exempt from every process of interpretation by means of which we would call upon it to show itself in person." This is not a hidden, virtual or potential self-presence but an apparatus that sends out delegates, representatives, proxies, phony messages, and obscene calls taken but not essentially put through, often missing their mark. Perhaps that is the end of the analogy referring the unconscious to the telephone, unless both were generally to be understood as that which is inside the subject but which can only be realized in a dimension of outside, that is to say, says Lacan of the one, "in that locus of the Other in which alone it may assume its status."[50]

Whether or not this is the end of the analogy between the unconscious and the telephone, what remains is a curious encounter, be it between two unconsciousnesses (Freud) or between the self and a "certain alterity" (Derrida, Lacan). Like the encounter between hand and metal, or between the camera and the eye, where "a space interwoven with the unconscious" intrudes into a space "interwoven with human consciousness," a similar psycho-spatial intrusion occurs between the telephone receivers and Benjamin's head in "The Telephone." Although Benjamin recalls how he took great efforts to stay in control of his senses just to reach the telephone, he loses all control once he puts his ear to the receiver, becoming "all ears," so to speak. The accompanying mood that Benjamin emphasizes is a complete giving-oneself-over to the mysterious Other. Instead of being able to ask himself, "what do I hear," like when he picks up the conch shell, all he

---

49 Rickels, *Aberrations*, 395. The telephonic suspension of "no" is so crucial that Avital Ronell begins her *Telephone Book* with the same reactive stance: "And yet, you're saying yes, almost automatically, suddenly, sometimes irreversibly. Your picking it up means the call has come through. It means more: you're its beneficiary, rising to meet its demand, to pay a debt. You don't know who's calling or what you are going to be called upon to do, and still, you are lending your ear, giving something up, receiving an order. It is a question of answerability" (Ronell, *Telephone Book*, 2).
50 Ronell, *Telephone Book*, 85.

can do with the telephone is say, "yes?"[51] This total lack of control, of giving-oneself-over to that the uncanny violence of the telephonic voice, will have resonances throughout many of the interpretations that follow: it is the same kind of *Verfassung* that, in the next chapter, forces both Nerval and Bertha to obsess over what they (think they have) heard and try to make sense of; it is also the same obsessive mood exemplified by one of Günter Eich's characters whom I discuss in Chapter Three. Like Benjamin at the telephone, the mood in which these listeners find themselves rattle them to their core, or in German, they are *außer Fassung geraten*. While the optical and acoustical unconscious, via various technological apparatuses like the camera or telephone, allow for greater analyzability of an encounter between, say, hand and metal, what I'm suggesting must be equally considered is the accompanying mode/mood of a certain *uncontrollability*, a condition that disrupts any previous sense (of self) or meaning (of words), of any attempt at a *Fassung*, be it a certain "version" of the past, a "wording," or keeping one's "composure." Perhaps more so than the optical unconscious, the acoustical unconscious does not "make" sense per se, but deprives one of it.

Beyond the parallels between Benjamin's description of the madeleine and the *Wiederhören* of early conversations on the telephone, references to time and the future also abound throughout "The Telephone," which point to the third characteristic of the acoustical unconscious explored in the previous section. "Each day and every hour (*Auf Tag und Stunde*), the telephone was my twin brother," Benjamin writes.[52] Many have commented on the telephone as his twin,[53] but none to my knowledge have discussed Benjamin's emphasis on its relation to time, and specifically its impact on previous modes of temporality: "The sound with which it rang between two and four in the afternoon, when a schoolfriend wished to speak to me, was an alarm signal that threatened (*gefährdete*) not only my parents' midday nap but the historical era (*die weltgeschichtliche Epoche* [1934]; *das Zeitalter* [1938]) in whose heart they surrendered to" (translation modified).[54] Like an alarm, the ringing of the telephone forewarns

---

51 Ronell explicitly asks the question that Benjamin's telephone encounter presupposes: "What does it mean to answer the telephone, to make oneself answerable to it in a situation whose gestural syntax already means yes, even if the affirmation should find itself followed by a question mark: Yes?" (Ronell, *Telephone Book*, 5).
52 Benjamin, *GS* 4:242 [*WuN* 11.1:507]; *SW* 3:349.
53 See Richter's reading of "two-ling" in chapter three of *Inheriting Walter Benjamin*.
54 Benjamin, *GS* 7:391 [*WuN* 11.1:508]; *SW* 3:350. Benjamin replaced a number of words in this sentence for the 1938 version. Benjamin writes in 1934 that the ringing telephone "disturbed [*störte*] not only my parents' midday rest, but the world-historical epoch, in the midst of which they surrendered to." In the revised 1938 version, it "not only threatened [*gefährdete*] the noonday rest of my parents, but the age in whose heart [*in dessen Herzen*] they surrendered

the end of his parents' era. With the coming of the telephone, to which the young Benjamin was now forever temporally bound, a particular mode of resting was forever lost.

But the noise (*Lärm*) of the telephone does not just sonically mark the end of an era. In its eventual graduation from the back of the dark corridor to the bright front room of the house, the telephone also holds out the possibility of hope for a younger, future generation:

> For once the chandelier, fire screen, potted palm, console table, gueridon, and alcove balustrade – all formerly on display in the front rooms – had finally faded and died a natural death, the apparatus, like a legendary hero once exposed to die in a mountain gorge, left the dark hallway in the back of the house to make its regal entry into the cleaner and brighter rooms that now were inhabited by a younger generation. For the latter, it became a consolation for their loneliness. To the hopeless who wanted to leave this wicked world, it shone with the light of a last hope. With the abandoned (*Verlaßnen*), it shared their bed.[55]

The telephone's "light of a last hope" and, as Ronell puts it, "sonic rescue missions" are directed toward the future. When Benjamin calls the ringing of the telephone "Nachtgeräusche," Eli Friedlander interprets them as similar to the flickering of the stars: "They are sounds whose meaning belongs to the future."[56] But whose future? If the telephone for Benjamin holds out hope for those who are otherwise hopeless or left behind, it is because its potential call – at any time on any day – helps to alleviate the anxiety of forever being alone and without hope. With its relation to hope and the future, even the silent telephone has an effect on the present mood of the receiver: the telephone's presence, now with its "regal entry into the cleaner and brighter rooms" inhabited by a younger

---

to." While the changes appear minor, the 1938 verb, "gefährdete," is more forceful and threatening than the 1934 verb, "störte." Benjamin's other minor revision, from the "Mitte" (the middle or midst) to the "Herz" (heart) of the era, could be due to a reference to the beating of his own heart at the end of the paragraph: "His [father's] hand, on these occasions, was a dervish overcome by frenzy. My heart would pound; I was certain that the employee on the other end was in danger of a stroke." By referring earlier to the heart of the epoch, Benjamin emphasizes the physical impact the telephone had upon the epoch's very corpus, in a way sounding its death knell.

55 Benjamin, *GS* 7:391 [*WuN* 11.1:508]; *SW* 3:350.
56 Friedlander, "Farben und Laute," 63. On the acoustic correlation to both the past and future in *Berlin Childhood around 1900*, Asmus Trautsch also writes succinctly in the same volume: what "can be heard [*vernehmen*] above all in Benjamin's *Berlin Childhood around 1900* is that the expected as well as the remembered lie in the ear" (Trautsch, "Die abgelauschte Stadt," 27).

generation, allows a potential future – the next phone call – to determine both their present and their past.

At the very end of "The Little Hunchback" ("Das bucklichte Männlein"), one of the last sections of *Berlin Childhood*, Benjamin describes how he never sees the hunchback, it only sees him. One of those places where the hunchback observes Benjamin is in front of the telephone:

> The little man preceded me everywhere. Coming before (*Zuvorkommend*), he barred the way. But otherwise he did nothing more to me, this gray reeve (*der graue Vogt*), than to collect a half portion of forgetting from each thing I came across. "When I go into my little room / To have my little sweet, / I find a little hunchback there / Has eaten half the treat." The little man was often found thus. Only, I never saw him. It was he who always saw me. He saw me in my hiding places and before the cage of the otter, on a winter morning and *before the telephone in the kitchen hall* (*vor dem Telefon im Küchenflur*) [emphasis mine], on the Brauhausberg with its butterflies and on my skating rink with the music of the brass band. He has long since retired [translation modified].[57]

Benjamin redacted a significant portion for the above 1938 version of *Berlin Childhood*. In the longer, 1934 version Benjamin further proposes that the hunchback saw even more the less Benjamin saw of himself: "And [he saw me] all the sharper, the less I saw of myself." (translation mine).[58] The hunchback's role here can be interpreted as a fantastical variation of how Benjamin explained the first experience of eating the madeleine: the more the taste becomes familiar, the more the first tasting becomes unconscious. It is no coincidence in the passage above that Benjamin cites the precise line in the poem when the hunchback has eaten a half-portion of his cereal (*Müßlein*). The less Benjamin is conscious of himself, which is to say, the less he is in control of his own senses, bearing or *Fassung*, the sharper is the hunchback's image of him, which nevertheless remains unconscious. I use "image" because in the redacted segment from 1934 Benjamin goes on to discuss how the hunchback has collected a series of images when the young Benjamin was in such a condition, so many that the hunchback can make a flip-book out of them. The hunchback becomes not only witness to Benjamin's half-conscious self – confirmed in the passage above when he sees Benjamin "before the telephone in the kitchen hall" – but is the author or *Verfasser* of a flip-book of images that both remain unconscious to Benjamin and together make up Benjamin's "whole life":

---

[57] Benjamin, *GS* 7:430 [*WuN* 11.1:490]; *SW* 3:385.
[58] "Und [es sah mich] desto schärfer, je weniger ich von mir selber sah" (Benjamin, *GS* 4:304). The Harvard translation does not include this crucial, redacted segment from the 1934 version of "The Little Hunchback," which is clearly crossed out in the *Werke und Nachlass* (Benjamin, *WuN* 11.1:376).

I think that that "whole life" which, according to some, pass before one's eyes when dying, consists of those images that the little hunchback has of us all. They whisk by quickly (*flitzen rasch vorbei*) like those pages of taut booklets that were once forerunners of our cinematographs. With a slight pressure, the thumb moved along its cut edge. Then images became visible in seconds, almost distinguishable from one another. In their fleeting cycle (*Ablauf*) they made recognizable the boxer while training and the swimmer struggling against the waves. The little hunchback also has the images of me. [translation mine].[59]

Despite this flip-book being a collection of unconscious "images" that only the hunchback is privy to, we nevertheless gain access to them in one of two ways: at the end of our life and via the Proustian *mémoire involontaire*, when they come upon us suddenly, unexpectedly, and "whisk by quickly" if we are not careful. The flip-book is thus comprised not of the highlights of our life, but of those fleeting moments, singular and otherwise irretrievable, which nevertheless have a lasting impact on our whole life, however unconscious those images have become. It is nothing other than the picture book of our distorted or displaced life, our *entstelltes Leben*.[60] In what follows, Benjamin will put his ear to a conch shell and ask, "what do I hear?" What he is listening for are not the sounds of the city or of music, that is, not the everyday sounds of conscious life, but rather, for those singular sound figures that, one could say, comprise the soundtrack to that flip-book of his life.

1.3 The Acoustical Un-conch-ious

The "Mummerehlen" is one of the more celebrated and discussed of all sections in *Berlin Childhood around 1900*. This is easy to understand: its varied material is so rich that much of Benjamin's theories concerning language, perception, mimesis and concentration are refracted through it like white light through a prism. What emerges from it are all the seven colors of the rainbow, which, for those who have read the Muhme Rehlen tales, will recall that this mythical aunt who lives in the forest wears seven cloaks, each one a different color of the rainbow.[61]

---

59 Benjamin, *GS* 4:304 [*WuN* 11.1:376].
60 That the *Männlein* takes "a half portion of forgetting" from each thing the young Benjamin came across is also consistent with his reference to the hunchback in his Kafka essay. There, Benjamin refers to the hunchback as the prototype of distortion (*Urbild der Entstellung*): he is "the occupant [*Insasse*] of distorted life" (Benjamin, *GS* 2:431–432). Like the figure of Odradek in Kafka's *Cares of a Family Man*, the hunchback can never be fully contained or controlled, and has neither a single origin nor place of residence (*Wohnsitz*).
61 The rainbow is a crucial image for Benjamin's concept of mimesis. See Peter Fenves, *The Messianic Reduction: Walter Benjamin and the Shape of Time* (Stanford, CA: Stanford University Press, 2010), esp. chap. 3.

As has already been mentioned, there are at least two versions of *Berlin Childhood* that Benjamin started roughly in the same year as the *Berlin Chronicle* (1932). Unlike the various versions of "The Telephone," which remain relatively unaltered, Benjamin revised and significantly diminished the "Mummerehlen" section in 1938. Not so well known, perhaps, is that the earlier 1934 version of the "Mummerehlen" is by far the one most often referred to, since it includes the recollections of a childhood photograph, links the "cloudy" existence of the Mummerehlen and Benjamin's own painting with watercolors, and ends with the famous story of the Chinese painter who jumps into his own painting. Little of this remains in the 1938 version of "Mummerehlen," except for Benjamin's reference to the conch shell; it is in fact the only element that survives fully intact from the earlier 1934 version. Furthermore, this "shell scene" stands at the very center of both versions: in the earlier version, Benjamin places the shell scene between the reflections on the photograph and the watercolors, as if he were housing or protecting it, placing the shell scene in its own textual shell. In the later version, the shell scene, being practically all that remains from the earlier version, is almost fully exposed. However, despite its central location and its survival through to the final version of 1938, Benjamin's shell scene is rarely discussed.[62] The following remarks attempt to remedy this silence by considering how applicable it is to both the *déjà entendu* and the acoustical unconscious.

Benjamin introduces the empty shell in both "Mummerehlen" versions with a reference to its status as a former dwelling place: "Thus I dwelt [*ich hauste*] in the nineteenth century like a mollusk dwells [*haust*] in its shell, which now lies hollow [*hohl*] before me like an empty shell. I hold [*ich halte*] it to my ear. What do I hear [*höre*]?"[63] Born in 1892, Benjamin's abode in the nineteenth century is none other than his childhood. Eduardo Cadava rightly compares this

---

62 Gerhard Richter comments on the shell scene in his chapter entitled, "Benjamin's Ear: *Berlin Chronicle*," employing it as more proof for Benjamin's inability to coincide with his own image (Richter, *Corpus of Autobiography*, 2000). Werner Hamacher makes numerous fascinating connections in his essay "The Word 'Wolke' – If It Is One," in *Benjamin's Ground: New Readings of Walter Benjamin*, trans. P. Fenves (Detroit: Wayne State University Press, 1988) but, surprisingly, never brings up the conch shell. One of the more careful readings I have come across of the shell – and I am indebted to Michael Levine for this reference – is by Eduardo Cadava in his book *Words of Light: Theses on the Photography of History* (Princeton, NJ: Princeton University Press, 1997). Unfortunately, Cadava makes no reference to the particular sounds heard when Benjamin picks up the shell. In the more recent collection of essays *Klang und Musik bei Walter Benjamin*, numerous scholars read the shell scene with an ear for the sounds that are heard, though none of them focus so particularly on the sounds and the words Benjamin uses to describe them as I do here.
63 Benjamin, *GS* 4:261 [*WuN* 11.1:215]; *SW* 3:392.

abode with a fragment in which Benjamin describes how the walls of children's rooms are closer together in memory than they are in reality:

> All the walls of a room that we occupy are *nearer* to us than to a visitor. That is the homely in the home [*das Heimliche am Heim*]. In the remembrance of our children's rooms, the walls are pressed closer together for us than in truth, more than if we would see them today. Their sight rips us apart [*Ihr Anblick zerreißt uns*] because we have appended ourselves to the walls [*uns an die Wände geheftet haben*] [italics original; translation mine].[64]

Like a mollusk who "expands until its formless figure inhabits its frame,"[65] our childhood memories fill every nook and cranny of the room in which we dwelt as a child, as if it was the space best proportioned and adapted to us despite our smaller frame.[66] Such a mode of dwelling is reminiscent of Benjamin's description of that long-forgotten moment in which the future "nests so eloquently." Nesting for Benjamin is the "homely in the home." If there is any doctrine of the uncanny for Benjamin, it is here: what becomes *unheimlich* (uncanny) is the act of severance from the walls to which we were earlier appended – like a mollusk from its shell – and of our seeing them now as a sight (*Anblick*). The walls from which we are torn become uncanny precisely because of their prior status as "the homely in the home"; in other words, there would be nothing uncanny that was also not previously homely, or in which we also once "nested so eloquently." No longer beholden to these walls, we see them now as a sight to behold.

The conch shell certainly is, or at least was, a nesting place. Just as interesting, however, is its bourgeois status as a trinket in the home or living room; it is often a collected artifact, perhaps from a past walk along a beach now distant in both space and time. As sexually charged a symbol as the forgotten glove or reticule, the shell is also *etui* and kitsch: it "lies hollow" before Benjamin in the longer version of the "Mummerehlen" section, apparently as one of the many props in the photographer's studio (although one might ask, what is a shell doing in the Alps?). As an empty, vertiginous nesting place, the shell is also the perfect "prop" for kitsch since, according to Benjamin, kitsch's seduction is like the feeling of "wrapping oneself in an old familiar coat."[67] In "Some Remarks

---

64 Benjamin, *GS* 6:203.
65 Cadava, *Words of Light*, 122.
66 I echo here Cadava's reference to Francis Ponge, in particular the relevance of dwellings in best proportion to one's size. See especially "Notes on a shell [*Notes pour un coquillage*]," in *Francis Ponge: Selected Poems*, ed. Margaret Guiton (Winston-Salem, NC: Wake Forest University Press, 1994), 62.
67 Benjamin, *GS* 6:186; *SW* 2:278.

1.3 The Acoustical Un-conch-ious — 53

on Folk Art," Benjamin fittingly aligns the wrapping-effect of kitsch with the experience of déjà vu: "for the situation [of déjà vu] is not experienced as by an outsider [*Außenstehende*]: it has come over us, we have enveloped ourselves in it."[68] We have already seen that, similar to the walls of a child's room or the life of a mollusk in its shell, the temporal experience of déjà vu similarly wraps the future into the past, implementing the beholder. But Benjamin makes the further point on "Some Remarks on Folk Art" that the déjà vu envelops the one experiencing it both spatially and temporally. While in *Berlin Chronicle* he describes the déjà vu experience in terms of a foreign entity (*eine Fremde*) who forgot words or gestures behind like a "forgotten glove or reticule," such foreignness in no way derives wholly from without. One should point out how the very act of listening already suggests the notion of envelopment and surroundability, which already plays a prominent role in "The Telephone" segment. Don Ihde notes in his *Listening and Voice* that "the auditory field surrounds the listener, and [that] surroundability is an essential feature of the field-shape of sound."[69] Surroundability is a feature shared by both listening to sound and, according to Benjamin above, the experience of déjà vu. Beyond Benjamin's suggestion at the end of *Berlin Chronicle* that the déjà vu should be thought more in terms of the audible rather than visual realm due to its affiliation with the echo, his reference in "Some Remarks on Folk Art" to the déjà vu as enveloping the person lends further credence to thinking of the phenomenon in terms of the "field-shape of sound." The way in which Benjamin describes putting the two telephone receivers to his ears, inserting himself into the circuit, and how he is subsequently at the mercy of whichever voice that spoke to him, exemplifies surroundability of acoustic phenomena as well as the envelopment of a mood (*Verfassung*) that, like the déjà vu, comes over us. And if such can be called "the architecture of the déjà vu,"[70] the empty shell also perfectly reflects this architecture, since its construction at every moment involves the folding of its exterior into its interior.

Let us return to the longer, 1934 version of the "Mummerehlen" section and pay particular attention to the architecture of the passage where the empty shell is introduced for the first time. As mentioned earlier, it is introduced through the back door of the studio, so to speak, as both a possible

---

[68] Benjamin, *GS* 6:187; *SW* 2:279.
[69] Don Ihde, *Listening and Voice: A Phenomenology of Sound* (Athens, OH: Ohio University Press, 1976), 75.
[70] Peter Krapp, *Déjà Vu: Aberrations of Cultural Memory* (Minneapolis: University of Minnesota Press, 2004), 36.

prop in a photographic studio and a metaphor for Benjamin's childhood life in the nineteenth century:

> I am standing there bareheaded, my left hand holding a giant sombrero which I dangle with studied grace. My right hand is occupied by a walking stick, whose curved handle can be seen in the foreground while its tip remains hidden in a cluster of ostrich feathers spilling in from a garden table. Over to the side, near the curtained doorway, my mother stands motionless in her tight bodice. As though attending to a tailor's dummy, she scrutinizes my velvet suit, which for its part is laden with braid and other trimming and looks like something out of a fashion magazine. I, however, am distorted by similarity [*Ich aber bin entstellt vor Ähnlichkeit*] to all that surrounds me here [*was hier um mich ist*].[71]

In *Words of Light*, Cadava suggests that the empty shell is the figure "toward which this entire photographic scene is oriented. We could even say that this empty shell forms the nucleus of the passage."[72] What is not explained, however, is how the empty shell, "which now lies before" Benjamin, got there in the first place. In the 1938 version of the "Mummerehlen," Benjamin deletes the photographic scene entirely; the empty shell, however, is still introduced as his abode, and is still preceded by the sentence, "But I am distorted by similarity to all that surrounds me here." While it is most certainly the nucleus of the passage, the shell scene nevertheless seems able to separate itself, like a mollusk from its shell, quite easily from the photographic scene described above. What is more difficult to separate from is its connection to Benjamin's abode in the nineteenth century.[73]

This is confirmed in what turns out to be the original setting of the shell scene, "The Lamp" (1933), from which later versions of the "Mummerehlen" and important sections of Benjamin's theses, "On the Mimetic Faculty" and

---

71 Benjamin, *GS* 4:261 [*WuN* 11.1:215]; *SW* 3:392.
72 Cadava, *Words of Light*, 124.
73 Another crucial element in this passage is how Benjamin describes his mother as she, from afar (*ganz abseits*), looks upon him in his velvet suit as if he were a tailor dummy. While this transformation into an inanimate object subsequently motivates Benjamin to describe his own distortion, what is left behind is that he was transformed initially through the eyes of his mother, via his mother's gaze. In an important article, "Walter Benjamin's Love Affair with Death" (in *New German Critique* 48 [Autumn 1989], 63–86), Rey Chow poses a question that is directly related the description of Benjamin's mother in the passage above: "Why does woman, against this background of allegorical dis-figuration, remain a figure?" (85). Chow's discussion of Benjamin's fascination with the inanimate and his reading of Baudelaire's "À une Passante" is equally relevant to the lost glove described in the first section of this chapter, which allowed Benjamin to "infer a stranger [*eine Fremde*,] had been there" (Benjamin, *GS* 6:518 [*WuN* 11.1:78]; *SW* 2:635). These important references to gender, language, the foreign and the mother require a much more elaborate investigation than can be addressed here.

"Doctrine of the Similar," derive.[74] In "The Lamp," the empty shell is itself disfigured; it is so fused with the lamp that Benjamin raises *both* to his ear:

> Here the lamp is fixed in position. Yet it was portable. And unlike our lighting systems, with their cables, cords, and electrical contacts, you could carry it through the entire apartment, accompanied always by the clatter of the tube in its casing and the glass globe on its metal ring – a clinking that belongs to the dark song of the surf which slumbers in the toil [*in der Mühsal*] of the century. When I bring it close to my ear [*Wenn ich sie meinen Ohren näh[e]re*], I do not hear the noise of field artillery, or the sounds of Offenbach's gala music, or the factory sirens.
>
> Now the nineteenth century is empty. It lies there like a large, dead, cold seashell. I pick it up and hold it up to my ear. What do I hear? I do not hear the noise of field artillery or of Offenbach's gala music; nor do I hear the factory sirens or the cry that goes up at midday on the stock exchange – not even the din of soldiers on parade or the long-drawn-out whistle on the train. I can of course imagine all these things. But what I hear when I put the shell up to my ear is something other [*ist ein anderes*]: it is the rattling noise of the anthracite that is emptied from the coal scuttle into the furnace; it is the dull pop with which the flame lights up the gas mantle; it is the jangling of my mother's keys in her basket, the clatter of the tube in its casing, the clink of the glass globe on its metal ring when the lamp is carried from one room to another [translation modified].[75]

This passage begins with being transported from the present day – and perhaps even the present moment, while Benjamin was writing this passage and presumably looked over at the lamp "fixed in position" next to him – to his childhood past in the nineteenth century, when lamps were oil-based and portable. This particular version of the shell scene diverges radically from its two variations in *Berlin Childhood* in that an oil lamp, usually hot and emanating light, suddenly takes on qualities of a cold, empty shell when lifted to one's ear: in carrying the lamp from room to room, one is always accompanied by "the dark song of the surf." Near the end of the passage and after the list of sounds Benjamin describes, the empty shell even echoes the two very specific sounds of the lamp: the clatter of the tube in its casing and the clink of the glass globe on its metal ring. What is therefore lost in the shell scenes found in both versions of *Berlin Childhood* is the transformation of lamp-as-shell. What can we make of this merging of lamp and shell, of light and sound? First, it recalls Johann Wilhelm

---

[74] The *Werke und Nachlass* conveniently bundles "The Lamp" under the heading, "Die Mummerehlen – drei Entwürfe," in the volume dedicated to *Berlin Chronicle* and *Berlin Childhood around 1900* (Benjamin, *WuN* 11.1:406–409). Despite this, I will refer to "The Lamp" strictly from the *Gesammelte Schriften*, since the multiple variations in the *Werke und Nachlass* requires an even more in-depth reading than the one presented here.
[75] Benjamin, *GS* 7:793; *SW* 2:692.

Ritter's multiple references to light and tone being one and the same. As is well known, Benjamin held Ritter in extraordinarily high esteem, and the latter's influence can be traced in such important works as the language essay and explicitly in Benjamin's habilitation.[76] Although Ritter is rarely attributed to influencing Benjamin's exploration of the mimetic faculty, Ritter's references to oscillation, energy transference and galvanism should be read as early, Romantic reflections on innervation, which for Benjamin informs his notion of the mimetic reception of the external world.[77]

Secondly, while the lamp and shell are both containers, one of light and the other of sound, their fusion should not be thought synasthetically (against which Benjamin also defends Ritter's work): the lamp's light does not "become" the shell's sound or vice versa.[78] Rather, the sounds retain their singular characteristics, while it is the container or *medium* that changes, as if the sounds were repeatable or reproducible through different media, even those that would not otherwise be able to transmit them. Not only was the lamp, like the shell, portable in the nineteenth century, but the lamp's singular sounds become themselves *tragbar* with the help of the mimetic faculty Benjamin is exploring in "The Lamp."

To return to the citation above: not only is the merging of lamp and shell left out of the two later shell scenes in *Berlin Childhood*, but an important

---

[76] See Thomas Strässle's "'Das Hören ist ein Sehen von und durch innen': Johann Wilhelm Ritter and the Aesthetics of Music," in *Music and Literature in German Romanticism*, ed. Siobhán Donovan and Robin Elliott (Rochester, NY: Camden House, 2004), 27–41. Strässle estimates that Benjamin first became acquainted with Ritter's work in the course of writing his dissertation around 1918/1919. In a 1924 letter to Scholem, Benjamin discusses and quotes in length Ritter's appendix to his *Fragmente aus dem Nachlasse eines jungen Physikers* (cited by Strässle, "'Das Hören,'" 35–36).
[77] See Buck-Morss quoted in Hansen, *Cinema and Experience*, 137. See also Ryder, "Innervation."
[78] Rather than maintaining the unique experience of a singular, unique sensation and its corresponding link to memory, synaesthesia merges two or more sensations to the point of indistinction. The oft-cited passage that illustrates Benjamin's own dissatisfaction with synaesthesia is found in the *Passagenwerk*, section J: "It would be an error to think of the experience [*Erfahrung*] contained in the *correspondences* as a simple counterpart to certain experiments with synesthesia (with hearing colors or seeing sounds) that have been conducted in psychologists' laboratories. In Baudelaire's case, it is a matter less of the well-known reactions, about which effete or snobbish art criticism has made such a fuss, than of the medium in which such reactions occur. This medium is the memory [*die Erinnerung*], and with Baudelaire it was possessed of unusual density" (Benjamin, *GS* 5:464; Walter Benjamin, *The Arcades Project*, trans. Howard Eiland and Kevin McLaughlin [Cambridge: Harvard University Press, 2002] [hereafter, *AP*], 367). For an in-depth reading of Baudelaire and synaesthesia, see Susan Bernstein, "The Other Synaesthesia," in *Points of Departure: Samuel Weber between Spectrality and Writing*, ed. Peter Fenves, Kevin McLaughlin, and Marc Redfield (Evanston, IL: Northwestern University Press, 2016), 131–147.

sentence is also left out that leads us back to the notion of the "other" nature of the camera in the artwork essay. In differentiating between the music of Offenbach and the noise of field artillery with the more idiomatic sounds that emanate from the shell, Benjamin writes: "I can of course represent all this to myself [*Vorstellen kann ich mir das alles wohl*]. But what I hear when I put the shell up to my ear is something other [*ist ein anderes*]" (translation modified).[79] The singular sounds that are heard in the shell are not readily representable (*vorstellbar*), but rather constitute "a something other" than representation, an other that is accessible only by putting one's ear to the shell. This is nothing other than that "other nature" that speaks to the camera in the artwork essay. Just as an other nature speaks to the camera, other sounds are being transmitted via the shell, sounds otherwise not representable to the naked ear. Like the importance of the camera for the optical unconscious, the shell constitutes that prosthetic or apparatus required to think the acoustical unconscious.

Sounds that emit from empty conch shells typically have more symbolic, religious, or even cosmic overtones. It is often characterized as a constant murmuring, perhaps of the waves, perhaps of the world or even the cosmos. From a different perspective, this is how William Wordsworth describes listening to a conch in a celebrated passage from his longest poem, "The Excursion" (1814):

> I have seen
> A curious child, who dwelt upon a tract
> Of inland ground, applying to his ear
> The convolutions of a smooth-lipped shell;
> To which, in silence hushed, his very soul
> Listened intensely; and his countenance soon
> Brightened with joy; for from within were heard
> Murmurings, whereby the monitor expressed
> Mysterious union with its native sea.
> Even such a shell the universe itself
> Is to the ear of Faith; and there are times,
> I doubt not, when to you it doth impart
> Authentic tidings of invisible things;
> Of ebb and flow, and ever-during power;
> And central peace, subsisting at the heart
> Of endless agitation.[80]

---

[79] Benjamin, *GS* 7:793 [*WuN* 11.1:407]; *SW* 2:692.
[80] William Wordsworth, *The Excursion* (London: Macmillan, 1935), 130.

Wordsworth's description of mysterious murmurings and the imparting of "authentic tidings of invisible things" echoes not only the experiences of putting an ear to a shell, but also Tibetan Buddhism and Hinduism, to name just two of the more prominent spiritual systems that involve conch symbolism. In these religions, the sounding of a conch evokes the primal sound of the void or cosmos, and as such symbolizes the source of all existence, like a cosmic womb.[81] In the two "Mummerehlen" versions of Benjamin's *Berlin Childhood*, no reference to such a cosmic sound exists. However, in the earlier fragment on "The Lamp," Benjamin describes how the two singular sounds of the lamp also belong "to the dark song of the surf [*dem dunklen Lied der Brandung*] which slumbers in the hardship of the century" (translation modified).[82] Considering the symbolic significance of the conch shell, Benjamin's singular sound events begin to take on cosmic proportions. What Benjamin hears in the empty shell might very well be the primordial murmurings of the universe, but if so, they are in the form of its smallest acoustical singularities. As such, they are auditory thresholds that sound out simultaneously the singular and the cosmic.

Such murmurings begin with Benjamin's use of specific words. We can begin with "Muschel," which is affiliated with the German verb, "mauscheln," and often associated with other words and phrases that indicate quiet or mumbled speech, like "whispering (*tuscheln*)," "speaking under one's breath" or "speaking inarticulately like small children."[83] Related to this sense of murmuring, Werner Hamacher refers to mummed speech as defiguration:

> Like so many other words that are closely related in Benjamin's texts – like *Marmarameer* and *Marmelade*, like *Murmelspiel* and *Marmorbelag* – *Mummerehlen* is a figure of murmuring, of inarticulate and mummed speech, a figure of defiguration, and so it can never be grasped in an entirely determined place and never in a completely determined sense.[84]

While Hamacher refers specifically to neither the word "Muschel" nor the sounds that emit from it, the word "Muschel" equally connotes an act of murmuring and

---

[81] In Tibetan Buddhism, for instance, the white conch is the symbol for Buddha's throat, an allusion to his voice that broadcasts the Dharma, considered as a call to arms or as an alert. In Indian Buddhism, Vishnu's conch is called *panchjanya*, and is said to emulate the primoridal sound of Aum (Om) from which all else is produced.
[82] Benjamin, *GS* 7:793; *SW* 2:692.
[83] Furthermore, the word "'Muschelei' has been used since the eighteenth century for all things secretive (*Geheimnistuerei*), dishonest schemes and deceitful games" (Klaus Schäfer, "Sprachliche Analyse zu 'Muschel,'" accessed 11 August 2021, www.schaefer-sac.de/klaus/sdc/z-pdf/MUSCHEL.PDF, 32; for more linguistic history of the word, "Muschel," see this extensive article by Schäfer).
[84] Hamacher, "Word 'Wolke,'" 163.

inarticulation, and even *means* a murmuring thing: the resounding shell. While the *Muschel* as an object can be physically grasped and held up to one's ear, neither its name nor its sound can be completely grasped "in an entirely determined place." Just as the photography session in the 1934 version falls away as the shell is picked up from an indeterminate location, it is equally unclear where the empty shell comes from in both "The Lamp" and the last, 1938 version of the "Mummerehlen" section.

Indeed, all that is left is the conch shell, Benjamin's ear, and what he hears and does not hear. Textually, one can imagine that the *Muschel* becomes a kind of object in which the word "Muschel" enters, but as dissembled from its own object. In this way, the word "Muschel" is paradoxically not a *Muschel*. Put another way, the *word* "Muschel" is the very exteriority of the shell, a kind of shell of the shell, which is itself nothing but an empty house or mere exterior. This aligns well with Hamacher's description of mummery: "dissemblance, disguise of words, things and persons: these are not exterior to them but rather, *as the exteriority of their exterior* [emphasis mine], constitute their very interior."[85] With Hamacher's vertiginous claims to interiority and exteriority and the exteriority of the exterior, it is strange that he makes no reference to the conch shell, which folds its exterior into its interior with divine proportion.

Even before the word "Muschel" is evoked for the first time in "The Lamp" fragment, another word is used that I would argue is what gives birth to the shell image in the first place. Let us return to the sentence when Benjamin describes how the sounds of the lamp belong to that dark song of the surf: "unlike our lighting systems, with their cables, cords, and electrical contacts, you could carry [the lamp] through the entire apartment, accompanied always by the clatter of the tube in its casing and the glass globe on its metal ring – a clinking that belongs to the dark song of the surf which slumbers in the hardship of the century [*das in der Mühsal des Jahrhunderts schläft*]" (translation modified).[86] Although he refers to the "dark song of the surf," Benjamin does not explicitly use the empty shell imagery until the next paragraph. Nevertheless, his description in the sentence about the song of the surf "sleeping" in the nineteenth century is rather awkward, especially since the song does not simply sleep in the nineteenth century but sleeps "in der Mühsal" of that century. Without the German original, it would be impossible to recognize that "Mühsal" sounds a lot like "Muschel," a disfiguration from toil to mussel. Benjamin's shell scene could very well derive from his play in "The Lamp" on the dark song of the

---

85 Hamacher, "Word 'Wolke,'" 162.
86 Benjamin, *GS* 7:793; *SW* 2:692.

surf that sleeps "in the hardship" or toil of the nineteenth century, which in *Berlin Childhood* becomes the mussel or seashell in which the nineteenth century is housed. Read this way, a whole new way of interpreting the shell scene becomes possible. Following how he "learned to disguise [himself] in words," one could say that the transformation of "Mühsal" to "Muschel" is one way in which Benjamin, as a child, similarly avoided hardship and difficult situations: by disguising it into a familiar, even kitschy abode.

The correspondence of the words "Mühsal" and "Muschel," while made explicit in this reading, is not particularly surprising, given the numerous similar examples that Benjamin himself offers in *Berlin Childhood*, like "Mark-Thalle" and "Näh-Frau."[87] As Werner Hamacher has shown, the phonetic transmogrification of "Worte" into "Wolke" is particularly emblematic of this phenomenon, since the meaning of cloud already means a blurring of boundaries and an unstable form in space and time. But one could take this a step further when studying more closely the singular sounds heard in the empty shell. From "The Lamp" fragment of 1933 to the final version of *Berlin Childhood* in 1938, the singular sounds heard in the shell are not altered in any significant way. Although the photograph sequence replaces the lamp in the 1934 version of the "Mummerehlen," the specific sound of the lamp is still heard in both shell scenes of *Berlin Childhood*.[88] Another significant feature that all of Benjamin's singular sounds share is that they are auditory thresholds signaling a change from one condition or place to another. "The brief clatter of the anthracite as it falls from the coal scuttle into a cast-iron stove, [and] the dull pop of the flame as it ignites in the gas mantle":[89] both of these sounds indicate a change of condition, an ignition. The two other sounds that Benjamin describes, "the clinking of the lampshade when a vehicle passes by on the street [and] the jingling of the basket of keys"[90] signal both an arrival and a passing from one place to another, respectively. Even the last "sound" that concludes the paragraph in both versions of *Berlin Childhood*, which is really a phrase, "Listen to my tale of the Mummerehlen," is like a portal from reality to fantasy, a narrative door opening to the fairy world. This characteristic is not only reminiscent of the tone that signals a change of

---

87 See n. 3 in this chapter.
88 In both versions of the "Mummerehlen" what remains of the lamp's echo in the shell is "the clinking of the lampshade on its brass ring when a vehicle passes by on the street" (Benjamin, *GS* 4:262; 7:417 [*WuN* 11.1:216, 539]; *SW* 4:375, 392).
89 Benjamin, *GS* 4:262; 7:417 [*WuN* 11.1:216, 539]; *SW* 4:375, 392.
90 Benjamin, *GS* 4:262; 7:417 [*WuN* 11.1:216, 539]; *SW* 4:375, 392.

picture in the "Kaiser Panorama" section,[91] but it also echoes "The Lamp" fragment when Benjamin reminisces about how lamps used to be portable, and how the sounds of the lamp accompanies him whenever it is "carried from one room to another." As sonic variants of disparate transits and transitions, these sounds are both defined by and echo a certain "transmitability." Such transmitability defines them, on the one hand, as not bound to any one medium: the sounds of the lamp are, for instance, equally transmittable in the empty shell. But they are also "carried over," in the literal translation of the German word for transmitting, "übertragen," from one room to another, and are themselves generated by a transition or change of condition. In this sense, they are both transmittable sounds and sounds *in* transport, transition and transference. As such, they are figurative signals – sonic signs – of the mimetic faculty which, like the phonetic blurring of the words "Mühsal" and "Muschel," names a becoming similar by way of the slightest alteration.

Another way to describe the function of these sounds is with the concept of the acoustical unconscious. Like the telephone receivers, the conch shell is certainly an acoustic apparatus, albeit more natural and divine than technological in origin.[92] Secondly, like the camera, an "other" nature speaks to the shell rather than to the naked ear, a nature that fully lends itself to hallucinatory and otherworldly effects. Lastly, the sounds temporally-bound to the nineteenth century are not just any sounds; they are not "the sounds of Offenbach's gala music" or "the din of soldiers on parade," all of which Benjamin can consciously represent to himself. Rather, what he hears when he "puts the shell up to [his] ear is something other [*ist ein anderes*]" (translation modified).[93] To return to Benjamin's vocabulary in the artwork essay, these other sounds recalibrate conscious and unconscious spaces, such that "a space interwoven with the unconscious steps into a space interwoven with human consciousness"

---

91 Eli Friedlander writes that "the ringtone of the panorama [is] associated with waking up, interrupting [*Unterbrechen*] and shaking awake – immediately before the machine the machine begins to move" (Friedlander, "Farben und Laute," 62). This signal tone as awakening will become crucial in Chapter Two, where I explore Benjamin's theory of forgetting in light of Ludwig Tieck's "Eckbert the Fair."
92 Significant parallels can also be made between the conch and the telephone, both of which are simultaneously receivers and transmitters. The distant whisperings of a conch shell is perhaps most readily comparable to the static of a disconnected telephone line. For instance, in Philip K. Dick's *Ubik*, the main character picks up the telephone, but he hears only "far-off static. From thousands of miles away [. . .] Eerie" (Philip K. Dick, *Ubik* [New York: First Vintage Books, 1991], 98).
93 Benjamin, *GS* 7:793; *SW* 2:692. See Introduction.

(translation modified).[94] The vertiginous echo chamber of the conch shell is itself not an unconscious space, whatever that may be, but its circular pathway is a zone or threshold in which these two spaces intermingle.

Let us listen even closer to these other sounds emerging from the empty shell in order to help us think the acoustical unconscious. The first thing to notice is that Benjamin uses a different, strange word for every sound. The specifically German words that designate the various sounds he hears, words like *Rasseln*, *Klirren* and *Scheppern*, all intermingle phonetically with the words that signify the objects affiliated with that sound. For instance, "Das kurze **Ra**sseln des Anth**raz**its": the "z" of *kurz* and the "ra-" of *Rasseln* are echoed in the German pronunciation for the word, *Anthrazits*. If this seems excessive or overly scrupulous, listen to the other examples: the syllables that reverberate between "der d**umpf**e Kn**all**" and "die **F**l**a**mme des Gasst**rumpf**s" (the "a" of *Knall* and *Flamme*, the "umpf" of *dumpf* and *Gasstrumpf*); the phrase "d**as Kl**irren der Lampen**glock**e" (the hard "k" of *Klirren* is found at the end of *-glocke*); the alliteration of "das **Schepp**ern des **Sch**lüsselkor**bs**;" and last but not least, the phrase "listen to my tale of the Mummerehlen [*Ich will dir was erzählen von der Mummerehlen*]" involves the rhyme of the last two syllables of the words, "er-zählen" and "Mummer-ehlen."[95] The German words that mean the sound of a "rattling," "dull pop," or "clang" are thus chosen by Benjamin not simply for the sounds they mean but for *the very sounds those words are comprised of*. Trautsch describes something similar when he writes that "the word comes loose from its defined meaning through this phonetic blurring of the word's threshold, which is produced by a quasi-musical hearing of the spoken word as pure sound" (translation mine).[96] This is certainly true of all those words that Benjamin blurs and disfigures, like "Mark-Thalle" or "Mummerehlen." What is different here is that these words mean a sound while also simultaneously being comprised of sounds that resonate with those of adjoining words. There are thus two ways of thinking "sound" here: as semantic or putative, on the one hand, and as "compositional" or paronymic, on the other. Both are held in suspension within and alongside each other, and each word's sounds begin to separate from the sound that that word means, like a mollusk from its shell. In this sense, every word that Benjamin uses to describe these sounds is like an empty shell that

---

94 Benjamin, *GS* 1:500 [*WuN* 16:241]; *SW* 4:266.
95 Distorted due to the verb "to narrate" (*erzählen*), the neologism *mummerehlen* sounds in German like a verb as much as it does a noun. As a verb, it might designate a kind of narrative *in silentio*, or a kind of mummed storytelling.
96 See Trautsch's excellent contribution, "Die abgelauschte Stadt und der Rhythmus des Glücks," in *Klang und Musik bei Walter Benjamin*.

might have at one point had its sound living within it, but which now lies empty before him.

In each version of *Berlin Childhood* in which Benjamin takes up the shell and puts it to his ear, he asks the rhetorical question, "What do I hear?" After reading carefully the words he uses in this passage to describe the sounds he hears, we should read this question as asking not what particular sounds he hears, but *whether* he is listening to the word's meanings that describe certain sounds, or to the sounds that comprise those words. Does Benjamin hear the sounds he describes, sounds that, like his acoustical *déjà vu*, awaken the present to a future echoing in a long-forgotten moment? Or does he hear the sounds of carefully chosen words that reverberate and phonetically bounce off each other like so many billiard balls, an acoustical vertigo spinning out the "whole distorted [*entstellte*] world of childhood" in divine proportion?[97] Whatever Benjamin is listening to, I propose that he is "hearing" these two possibilities simultaneously. For Benjamin, a sound is a word and vice versa; words are comprised of sounds as much as they are signs that impart meaning. "Rasseln" does not just mean "rattling" for Benjamin, but is also a sound that rattles and rustles within and alongside the word "anth**rac**ite." As we have seen in *Berlin Chronicle*, Benjamin confirms this emphasis on the word's sound when he considers an acoustical correlate to the *déjà vu*: "It is a word, a tapping, or a rustling," as if a word can also be nothing more than its sound. It is well known that "spoken words are oft-noted triggers to déjà vu illusions,"[98] so a word like anthracite as a sound leads Benjamin's ear back to an auditory *déjà vu*, not only to the sound of a "short rattling" but equally to the sounds of those two German words, "kurze Rasseln," that blend like acoustical watercolors into the sounds of "anth-ra-cite."[99]

In conclusion, it is important to return to the hunchback witnessing Benjamin's childhood experience in front of the telephone, since Benjamin significantly links the hunchback also to the sounds that are heard in the empty shell in the "Mummerehlen" fragment. After Benjamin lists all the places where the hunchback watched him, including at the telephone, he goes on to write how the hunchback, that grey reeve, "has long since abdicated. But his voice, which is like the hum of the gas burner [*das Summe des Gasstrumpfs*], whispers to me

---

[97] Benjamin, *GS* 7:417 [*WuN* 11.1:216]; *SW* 3:392.
[98] Anne M. Cleary and Alan S. Brown, *The Déjà Vu Experience: Essays in Cognitive Psychology* (New York: Routledge, 2021), 232.
[99] Another fascinating connection to Francis Ponge in this context would be his poem dedicated to anthracite, called "Anthracite, or Coal Par Excellence [*L'anthracite, ou le charbon par excellence*]," in *Francis Ponge: Selected Poems*, ed. Margaret Guiton (Winston-Salem, NC: Wake Forest University Press, 1994), 134–137.

over the threshold of the century [*die Jahrhundertschwelle*]: 'Dear little child, oh I beg you / Pray for the little hunchback too'" (translation modified).¹⁰⁰ If the hunchback is for Benjamin the prototype of distortion, the sounding out of those words, and of those words as sounds – "das Summe des Gasstrumpfs" – is the primal voice of disfiguration. Although the hunchback is never seen, his voice can still be heard whispering over the threshold of the century, like those earliest conversations on the telephone. It is a whispering that is perhaps transmittable across media but not representable in any putative sense. Defying representability, such singular sounds echo via an acoustic echo chamber that lies discarded and forgotten at the threshold of the nineteenth century, a conduit through which the whispering voice of disfiguration can be still heard.

In light of the shell scene, what constitutes the acoustical unconscious for Benjamin are not necessarily sounds per se, but the combination of sounding syllables that simultaneously assemble and dissemble words and their meanings. This process should be defined as neither homophonic nor onomatopoetic. Rather, Benjamin is primarily interested in the resonance chamber of language – its nondiscursive sonority, as if each word was an empty shell – that allows for the playful blurring of semantic fixity with paronymic possibility. The shell helps Benjamin play with the semantic and paronymic elements of words and phrases; but as an acoustical apparatus, the shell is also required for Benjamin to hear those longforgotten moments that the future has left so eloquently nestled in a distant past, like finding the lost glove of a stranger left curiously forgotten. The search for such lost sounds is sometimes as enchanting as the beholder who feels an irresistible urge to search a photograph for that tiny spark of contingency. Or to use a fitting German expression in this context: there isn't a pearl in every shell, but you have to open every one to find out.¹⁰¹ One could say that the conch shell helps bring to *conch*-iousness these very sound-pearls, these sound figures of distortion. The acoustical unconscious does not lie hidden under the folds of fixed meanings and contexts of words, but constitutes the very exteriority of words, their sounding out.

It has been said that neither Freud nor Benjamin was particularly interested in the unconscious "itself" as much as they were interested in the pathways *between* conscious and unconscious knowledge. For both, language is critical for laying the groundwork of those pathways. And yet, not only do they employ language in different ways, their intentions for seeking out those paths between conscious and unconscious knowledge directly impact the contours of their divergent paths. As we shall see in the next chapter, Freud wishes to make intelligible –

---

100 Benjamin, *GS* 7:430 [*WuN* 11.1:236]; *SW* 3:385.
101 "Es sind nicht in allen Muscheln Perlen, aber man muss sie alle durchsuchen."

his word is "anschaulich," i.e., intelligible and visual or vivid – those unconscious pathways, which are always mental pathways, so as to find a meaning that was always already there, attempting to reveal and establish a closed circuit. Benjamin exceeds Freud, first by recognizing those pathways are not just mental but inextricably linked to the body and to sense experience. They are always possible but accidental, sudden, when we least expect it, and above all *von fremder Seite*, that is, they require an other for us to recognize them in the first place. As Benjamin writes in his essay on Franz Kafka in 1934, "the forgotten [. . .] is never something only individual [*ist niemals ein nur individuelles*]." As the next chapter will elucidate, Benjamin's particular version of the unconscious is closely aligned with his theory of forgetting: just as that which is forgotten is not just individual, Benjamin's version of the unconscious is never strictly limited to the psyche of a single individual but is "shared," so to speak. Whether it is a shell emitting sounds not otherwise representable, a forgotten glove or reticule left in the home that suddenly "lets us infer that a stranger had been there" (translation modified)[102] or, as we shall see in the next chapter, a stranger reminding someone of a dog's name – words, objects and sounds *von fremder Seite* are necessary foreign entities that allow the unconscious to merge, however fleeting, with human consciousness. They "speak" to us in a way that we could not otherwise imagine or represent, that catches us off-guard, but that nevertheless tell us something fundamental about ourselves. In other words, they speak like that "other nature" speaks to the camera, or the way those first telephone conversations are "other" than today, or the singular sounds that emit from the shell are other than what is representable. While in this first chapter the other may have seemed scattered throughout, always accompanying but incidental or *beiläufig* – which like the hunchback, is its nature – the other and its relation to the acoustical unconscious takes center stage in Chapter Two.

---

[102] Benjamin, *GS* 6:518–519 [*WuN* 11.1:77]; *SW* 2:634–635.

2 Of Birds and Barks: Listening in on the Forgotten in Freud, Benjamin, and Tieck

> Dear friend, who knows? The pupils of the dying are said to retain the last image they received . . . what if this ear-shaped snail stored the sounds it heard at some critical moment – the agony of mollusks, maybe?[1]

In *Gramophone, Film, Typewriter* (1986), Friedrich Kittler cites in its entirety a fantastical tale by Maurice Renard, originally entitled "Death and the Shell" ("La mort et le coquillage," 1907),[2] in which an accomplished composer attempts one night to transcribe the sounds he hears from a conch shell. Despite being "among the most famous" of composers, Nerval is unable to transcribe the mysterious sounds "dictated" to him, and later that night – after recognizing the impossibility of his task – he dies. The entire story of Nerval's death is narrated by one of Nerval's friends, left unnamed, who is speaking to Nerval's doctor. The friend wants to prove to the doctor that the latter's diagnosis for Nerval's death, a stroke,[3] was incorrect. What killed Nerval, according to his friend, was listening to the conch shell, a fate that the friend thinks he will soon share himself:

> Do you believe that there are poisons for the ear [*poisons de l'öuie*] modeled on deadly perfumes and lethal potions? Ever since last Wednesday's acoustic presentations [*l'audition*] I have not been feeling well. It is my turn to go . . . Poor Nerval! . . . Doctor, you

---

[1] "Qui sait, mon cher? On dit que les prunelles des mourants conservent l'image des visions suprêmes . . . . Si ce colimaçon, de forme auriculaire, avait enregistré les sons qu'il a perçus lors d'un instant critique – l'agonie du mollusque, par exemple?" Maurice Renard, "La mort et le coquillage," in *Le voyage immobile, suivi d'autres histoires singulières* (Paris: Georges Crès, 1922), 101–109. The English translation, the title of which is "Death and the Shell," is taken from Friedrich Kittler's *Gramophone, Film, Typewriter*, translated by Geoffrey Winthrop-Young and Michael Wutz (Stanford, CA: Stanford University Press, 1999), 54. In both the German original (Friedrich Kittler, *Grammophon. Film. Typewriter* [Berlin: Brinkman & Bose, 1986]) and English translation of Kittler's text, the source of "La Mort et le Coquillage" is falsely cited as being in Renard's collection, *Invitation à la peur*.
[2] The title is altered by Kittler. Instead of "Death and the Shell," Kittler replaces "Death" with "Mann." It is unclear why this subsitution is made, other than for its alliterative appeal in German: "Der Mann und die Muschel."
[3] In the original French, which is found in the following footnote, the doctor's diagnosis for Nerval's death is "une congestion," which is then translated into English as congestion. It seems more likely, however, that Nerval died not from a very bad cold, but rather "une congestion cérebrale," or a stroke.

claim he died of a stroke . . . and what if he died *because he heard the sirens singing? Why do you laugh [emphasis original]?*[4]

Laughter is the only indication of the doctor's response throughout the story. We are left to wonder whether the doctor is laughing at the narrator's own madness, finding the whole story scientifically untenable, or perhaps whether the doctor actually knows the story to be true, and is laughing at the poor narrator for finding out only too late. Indeed, interpreting the doctor's laughter is about as impossible as transcribing the sounds supposedly emitting from the conch shell: both may lead to madness.

Renard's tale succinctly refers back to Benjamin's two auditory examples in Chapter One. As we have seen, the conch shell is something quite different in *Berlin Childhood around 1900*: "like a mollusk in its shell, I had my abode in the nineteenth century, which now lies hollow before me like an empty shell."[5] In the hands of Benjamin, the shell houses the singular sounds of his childhood experience, a linguistic supplement that transmits both the word and the word's sounds carried along with it. But the shell in Renard's tale is equally reminiscent of the two telephone receivers through which the young Benjamin was ruthlessly delivered over to the uncanny violence of the telephonic voice. Kittler himself makes the correlation between Nerval's shell and the telephone explicit: the shell "takes the place of the mouthpieces [*die Muschel*] of a telephone or loudspeaker capable of bridging temporal distances [*Zeitenfernen*] in order to connect [Nerval] to an antiquity preceding all discourse [*vor jedem Diskurs*]."[6] Whereas Benjamin's shell involves long-forgotten sonic, but nevertheless singular experiences that reveal themselves through the very materiality of specific words, Kittler interprets Nerval's shell like a telephone that transmits a mysterious "antiquity preceding all discourse." As such, they elicit two very different bridges crossing distant temporal shores: one apparently pre-linguistic, the other making legible the intensive temporality of singular sense phenomena.

The present chapter takes up another fantastical tale, Johann Ludwig Tieck's "Eckbert the Fair" ("Der blonde Eckbert" [hereafter, "Eckbert"], 1797), which also

---

[4] Maurice Renard, "La mort et le coquillage," in *Le voyage immobile* (Paris: Georges Crès, 1922), 109. Cited by Kittler, *Gramophone, Film, Typewriter*, 55. Original emphasis.

[5] Walter Benjamin, *Gesammelte Schriften* (Frankfurt a.M.: Suhrkamp, 1972) (hereafter, *GS*), 4:261; Walter Benjamin, *Selected Writings*, ed. Michael W. Jennings, Marcus Bullock, Howard Eiland, and Gary Smith, trans. Rodney Livingstone and Edmund Jephcott (Cambridge: Harvard University Press, 1996–2003) (hereafter, *SW*), 3:392.

[6] Kittler, *Gramophone, Film, Typewriter*, 55; *Grammophon. Film. Typewriter*, 88.

blurs the distinction between the two bridges above.⁷ Sounds reverberate throughout Tieck's story, from a dog's bark to a magical bird's song. And like Renard's tale above, Tieck's story concludes with an acoustical aporia that appears to lead to madness. Although "Eckbert" involves no characters putting their ear to a conch shell, the story nevertheless reflects the two different ways of listening as exemplified by both Benjamin in the "Mummerehlen" fragment and Nerval in Renard's story cited above. Just as Benjamin's empty conch shell reverberates with sounds and words from his own past, Bertha's memory in Tieck's "Eckbert" is triggered by hearing the name of a dog that sends her back in time to a cottage wherein she once dwelled. And yet, the madness of the composer Nerval is just as evident in "Eckbert", in that repeated sounds and words in "Eckbert" act like *poisons de l'öuie* in Bertha and Eckbert's ears.

Apart from the story's emphasis on repeated sounds, one of the main reasons for examining Tieck's "Eckbert" is Benjamin's fascination with it throughout his life. Although he never directly interprets it, he makes a number of important references to the story. In a letter to Scholem in 1925, for instance, Benjamin mentions that he plans to write an essay on it. Nearly ten years later, in his essay, "Franz Kafka: On the Tenth Recurrence of His Death-day" ("Franz Kafka. Zur zehnten Wiederkehr seines Todestages," 1934), Benjamin refers to the story as "profound" (*tiefsinnig*), reminding the reader that Kafka was not the only writer for whom animals were "receptacles [*Behältnisse*] of the forgotten."⁸ Then in a letter to Adorno in 1940, Benjamin makes the bold claim that the story is the "locus classicus of his theory of forgetting."⁹ Finally, in the *Arcades Project*, Benjamin refers to notes on the story that are now lost: "The theory of not-yet conscious knowing may be linked with the theory of forgetting (notes on *Blonde Eckbert*) and applied to the collective in its various epochs."¹⁰ All of these references prove that Tieck's story played a central role in Benjamin's notion of forgetting.

While none of these references are significant enough to grasp Benjamin's interpretation of the story, the point of this chapter is not to reconstruct Benjamin's analysis of "Eckbert" as the locus classicus of his theory of forgetting.¹¹

---

7 My reading of Tieck's "Eckbert" in this chapter derives partly from an earlier article, "Of Barks and Birdsong: Listening in on the Forgotten in Tieck's *Der blonde Eckbert*," *Goethe Yearbook* 25 (Spring 2018), 55–76.
8 Benjamin, *GS* 2:430; *SW* 2:810.
9 Benjamin, *GS* 1:1134; *SW* 4:413.
10 Benjamin, *GS* 5:1031; *AP* 861 <O°,50>.
11 Interestingly enough, an extended interpretation of Tieck's story has been written in which it is at least *claimed* that Benjamin played a significant role. In a three-page postscript to a

Rather, Tieck's story will be examined first as exemplary of two notions that are closely related to the Benjaminian unconscious that we have been pursuing thus far: 1) a notion of forgetting that is neither simply individual nor relegated to the past, but is related to that "forgotten glove or reticule" in Chapter One that makes us infer a stranger, the future, was in our house of memory; and 2) a certain logic of repetition, one that disrupts rather than establishes identities and narratives.[12] What is particularly advantageous about Tieck's "Eckbert," and why it is crucial to discuss in a book oriented around the notion of the acoustical unconscious from a Benjaminian perspective, is that these two notions – a forgetting that is tied to the stranger and the future, and a repeatability that works to disrupt sameness and the self – can be discussed in terms of the sounds that reverberate throughout the story. The repeated sounds – the barking of the dog and the bird's song – fall under the rubric of repeatability above: instead of establishing fixed positions and character identities, they tend to disrupt and make impossible any fixed place from which to hear them, the extreme case of which is exemplified in the final sentence of the story. It will also be argued that the sound of the dog's bark is what drowns out Bertha's ability to remember the dog's name. How she comes to remember the name through a stranger, moreover, will also be described as an alarm clock that awakens her to her fate.

The unique conditions and consequences for the forgetting and sudden remembrance of the dog's name are perhaps why "Eckbert" has been one of the most frequently analyzed of Tieck's stories – the history of its subjection to psychoanalytical critique alone is vast – but they are also likely why Benjamin referred to the story as "tiefsinnig" and the locus classicus of his theory of forgetting. Since the forgetting and sudden remembrance of the dog's name are so central to the story, I wish to begin by first looking at another famous example of forgetting a name in the history of psychoanalysis: Sigmund Freud's explanation of his Signorelli parapraxis that opens the *Psychopathology of Everyday*

---

fragment entitled "Bilder des Déjà vu," Ernst Bloch recalls discussing Tieck's story with Benjamin one night in 1924 on the island of Capri. Since Benjamin himself never recorded this discussion in any of his notes, and since Bloch published this fragment in his *Verfremdungen* nearly forty years later in 1962, it will never be known to what extent Benjamin actually influenced Bloch's reading of Tieck. While this postscript of Bloch's will be referenced throughout the current chapter, I will not attempt to discern what Benjamin may or may not have contributed to it.

12 I am gesturing here toward Derrida's reformulation of the unconscious as a certain iterability whereby every single event or moment is in itself split and "multiplied in advance by its structure of repeatability" (Derrida, cited by Samuel Weber, *Benjamin's -abilities* [Cambridge: Harvard University Press, 2008], 6). See also the end of the Introduction.

Life. An examination of the way Freud justifies his forgetting of the name "Signorelli" is helpful as a counterexample to the way Bertha forgets the dog's name "Strohmian" in Tieck's "Eckbert." The comparison reveals, first, differences between Freud's theory of the unconscious, which is based on the individual and a repression of the past, and a certain process of forgetting that both implies an other's participation and impacts the future. Second, the comparison exposes the distinction between seeing and hearing, respectively: whereas Freud relies on a rebus (*Bilderrätsel*) that pictorially maps out parallel syllables that make "anschaulich" (both visible and intelligible) the functioning of his unconscious processes, Bertha and Eckbert are caught in a web of repeated sounds that only further disorient time and space to the point where nothing becomes identifiable, including any distinction between the two of them.[13] In stark opposition to Freud's *Bilderrätsel*, Tieck's story leaves itself open to dissonances that, as we will see at the end of the chapter, echo the "imagistic dissonance" (*Bilddissonanz*) – to use one of Benjamin's terms from another context – that is characteristic of the amorphous marks and vagabond memories affiliated with the acoustical unconscious.

Despite these differences, two common threads connect Freud and Bertha's forgetting. First, both are reminded of what was forgotten by someone else: Bertha is reminded of the dog's name by Walther, and Freud is reminded of the name Signorelli, as he mentions in a footnote, "von fremder Seite," which can be translated as either "from the other side" or from someone else, a stranger or foreigner. Second, both Freud and Bertha repress the forgotten name due to a certain anxiety: Freud concludes that he forgot the name because he had just learned that one of his patients committed suicide; Bertha represses the name because she knew that what she had done in the past was wrong and yet she chose to ignore it. Although the previous chapter already involved sounds heard from a forgotten childhood soundscape, this chapter focuses even more so on the role of memory and forgetting, not only because the unconscious in general cannot be thought without it, but also to illustrate that the memories associated with the acoustical unconscious cannot be purely individual, but rather always involve a word or sound *von fremder Seite*.

---

13 This comparison might at first appear to rely on a traditional distinction between sight and sound: that seeing something makes things intelligible while only hearing something increases the potential for doubt, disorientation and delusion. While this is a common trope in German Romantic literature, I am interested here less in the connection between music and madness than I am in the role these sounds have in the process of forgetting, and how they inscribe the other into that process. For an excellent reading of music and its correlation to madness via language, see John Hamilton's *Music, Madness, and the Unworking of Language* (New York: Columbia University Press, 2008).

2.1 Freud's trompe l'oreille

> It is consistent to define psychoanalytic case studies, in spite of their written format, as media technologies.[14]

In some of his first demonstrations of the existence of the unconscious around 1900, as well as his earliest work on the theory of neuroses, Freud uses examples of forgetting.[15] In "The Psychical Mechanism of Forgetfulness" ("Zum Psychischen Mechanismus der Vergeßlichkeit," 1898) and *The Psychopathology of Everyday Life*, Freud considered forgetting, like slips of the tongue, to be a parapraxis symptomatic of ongoing repression. We have already seen that Benjamin refers to the latter text when formulating his theory of the optical unconscious in the artwork essay. Freud begins the *Psychopathology of Everyday Life* with his own story about having forgotten the name of an Italian Renaissance painter, Luca Signorelli. Freud's classic analysis includes substitute names (*Ersatznamen*), such as "Botticelli" and "Boltraffio," that tend to replace the forgotten name: these "are cases in which a name is in fact [*nämlich*] not only *forgotten*, but *falsely remembered*."[16] The name is not accidentally forgotten, but forgotten for a reason: "I wanted therefore to forget something; I had *repressed* something [*ich hatte etwas* verdrängt]" (emphasis original).[17] As is well known, the unconscious for Freud involves an active mode of forgetting called repression (*Verdrängung*).[18]

---

14 Kittler, *Gramophone, Film, Typewriter*, 89; *Grammophon. Film. Typewriter*, 139.
15 See in particular Freud's "Neuro-psychoses of Defense" ("Die Abwehr-Neuropsychosen," 1984) in Sigmund Freud, *Gesammelte Werke* (London: Imago, 1940–1952) (hereafter, *GW*), 1: 57–75; Sigmund Freud, *The Standard Edition of the Complete Psychological Works of Sigmund Freud*, trans. James Strachey (London: Hogarth Press, 1953–1974) (hereafter, *SE*), 3:41–61.
16 Freud, *GW* 4:6; *SE* 6:1. The translators are right *not* to translate the adverb "nämlich" as "namely," since it functions here as a conjunctive adverb, reinforcing the previous statement. Unfortunately, the English phrase "in fact" covers up the tongue-in-cheek irony of "nämlich" that Freud uses. The irony resides, namely, in "nämlich" taking the place of the subject, "der Name." Freud thus performs a kind of *Ersatznomina* while simultaneously describing his theory of *Ersatznamen*.
17 Freud, *GW* 4:8; *SE* 6:4.
18 On the relationship between the unconscious and repression, Freud remains fairly constant throughout his theoretical work, as he makes clear nearly thirty years later in *The Ego and the Id* (*Das Ich und das Es*, 1927): "We obtain our concept of the unconscious [. . .] from the doctrine of repression [*Lehre von der Verdrängung*]" (Freud, *GW* 13:241). But the relationship between the two is precise: in the opening paragraph of *The Unconscious* (*Das Unbewußte*, 1915), Freud writes "[e]verything that is repressed must remain unconscious; but let us state at the very outset that the repressed does not cover everything that is unconscious" (Freud, *GW* 10:264). This pattern, as Samuel Weber notes, is one "that Freud repeatedly evokes: B is a

Freud explains why he forgets the name Signorelli: it is not because he was repressing the Italian painter's frescoes of the "Four Last Things" in the Orvieto cathedral, but rather because he was unconsciously adding something to the name, "Signorelli": namely, the topic of death and sexuality, and in particular the story of one of his patients who had recently committed suicide on account of an incurable sexual disorder. Despite Freud's insistence that the unconscious addition of his patient's story and the names associated with it helped him to repress the painter's name, I will argue that a certain external force equally provoked Freud's repression of the name: the one figure in the Orvieto frescos who stares back at Freud.

The names associated with his patient's story, like where the patient was from (Trafoi), suggest to Freud possible avenues into the unconscious that help to reconstruct why he "forgot" the name in the first place, that is to say, what he unconsciously associated with the name but repressed. The result of his analysis is a rebus or *Bilderrätsel* of substitute names, which looks like an almost poetological schema of linked phonemes (Fig. 2.1).

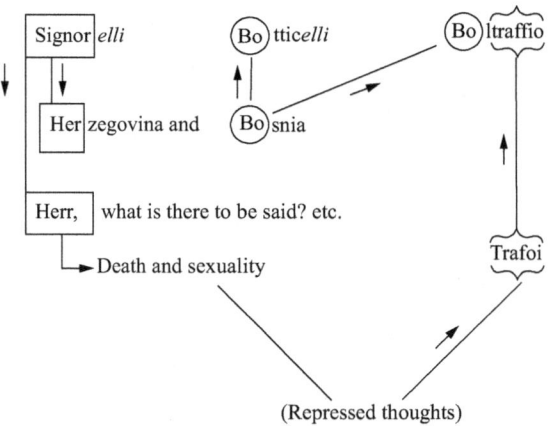

Fig. 2.1: Sigmund Freud, "Zum psychischen Mechanismus der Vergesslichkeit [The Psychical Mechanism of Forgetfulness]," *GW* 1:519–527; *SE* 3:287–297.

Freud's Signorelli parapraxis is important for two reasons: it is, according to Michael Molnar, the "first detailed examination of unconscious processes ever

---

characteristic of A, but not all B is A, hence B does not suffice to explain A." See Samuel Weber, "Anxiety: The Uncanny Borderline of Psychoanalysis?" *Konturen* 3 (2010): 51.

to be published;"¹⁹ and second, unlike Freud's other studies on Leonardo and Michelangelo,²⁰ the original images of Signorelli's frescoes take no part in Freud's examination of the name. It is as if Freud dissolved Signorelli's fresco "into words and fragments of words,"²¹ drawing up his own fresco of phonemes. Freud's insistence on the artist's name over the artist's work derives, in this case at least, from his interest not in the visual images depicted in the frescoes, but in the sonic *Verschiebungen* of syllables. The passage in which Freud describes the rebus also clarifies in which "images" he is most interested:

> The name *Signorelli* has undergone a division [*zerlegt worden*] into two pieces. One of the pairs of syllables (*elli*) recurs without alteration in one of the substitute names, while the other, by means of the translation of *Signor* into *Herr*, has acquired a numerous and miscellaneous set of relations to the names contained in the repressed topic, but for this reason it is not available for [conscious] reproduction. The substitute for it [for *Signor*] has been arrived at in a way that suggests that a displacement [*Verschiebung*] along connected names of "*Her*zegovina and *Bos*nia" had taken place, without consideration for [*ohne Rücksicht auf*] the sense or for the acoustic demarcation of the syllables.²²

Freud takes into consideration – in German, *Rücksichtnehmen*, to take a look back – the shared phonemes between words, creating an image out of sonic associations that his conscious mind did not "see" at the time. Only by linking the shared phonemes together is Freud able to derive any sense of the names that substitute Signorelli; we literally "see" in the diagram that Freud derives meaning from syllabic association. This "first detailed examination of the unconscious" thus functions at the level of largely acoustic association, in that the shared phonemes allow Freud to mine his own unconscious choices in order to make sense of them.²³ Another way to say this is that, instead of the trompe-l'oeil that Signorelli frequently employs to frame his frescoes in the

---

19 See Michael Molnar's essay "Reading the Look," in *Reading Freud's Reading*, ed. Sander L. Gilman (New York: New York University Press, 1994), 77.
20 For Freud's analyses of Leonardo da Vinci's *Virgin as Child* and Michelangelo's *Moses*, see "Eine Kindheitserinnerung des Leonardo da Vinci" and "Der Moses der Michelangelo" in Freud, *GW* 8 and 10, respectively.
21 Molnar, "Reading the Look," 77.
22 Freud, *GW* 4:10; *SE* 6:4–5.
23 In *The Fact of Resonance: Modernist Acoustics and Narrative Form* (New York: Fordham University Press, 2020), Julie Beth Napolin suggestively calls Freud's schema a *sound bleed*: "In Freud's image, we can see an edifice or, rather, a receptacle, one that might 'contain' the dispersed and multitudinous phonemes of human languages" (Napolin, *Fact of Resonance*, 107). But as receptacle of the forgotten, it contains only what Freud wants it to contain, which is very different from the scattered and strewn receptacles of the forgotten that Benjamin is most interested in.

Orvieto cathedral, Freud is actually most interested in the *trompe l'oreille* that is produced by his own unconscious, "revealed" sonically in the *Ersatznamen*.²⁴ The names Boticelli and Boltraffio are composed of acoustical phonemes that "frame" the repressed name: while they both stand in for Signorelli, they also both stand between its acoustical components and Freud's unconscious associations. Freud's *Ersatznamen* thus act as thresholds between acoustically conscious and unconscious data.

When confronted with Freud's schematic *Bilderrätsel* of words and word fragments, a reader might not be entirely convinced that these and *only* these cross-lingual and cross-phonetic associations actually happened for the reasons Freud describes. In his first written account of the Signorelli parapraxis, which he described in a letter written to Wilhelm Fliess on 22 September 1898, Freud is most excited about his discovery of the apparently unconscious phonetic correlations. But he too was troubled that it might not be entirely convincing: "How can I make this credible [*glaubwürdig*] to anyone?"²⁵ One is indeed tempted to ask whether Freud's correlations are not in fact concealing other links he either did not hear at the time or, to echo his own theory of repression, he did not want to hear. Why, for instance, does Freud associate the place in which he first heard of his patient's death, Trafoi, and not the patient's name, with the *Ersatzname* "Boltraffio"? Did the patient's name, which Freud never reveals, not fit into the overall schema of shared syllables? Why not add his

---

24 Freud's own interest in trompe-l'oeil is perhaps best recognized in the mechanism of secondary elaboration, the fourth mechanism of dream symbolization in the *Interpretation of Dreams*. Samuel Weber describes it thus: the "desire to make sense out of what we see [. . .] provides the condition of possibility for the trompe-l'oeil of secondary elaboration: our waking mind is so eager to find meaning that it will readily ignore absurdities to get at what seems to be sensible" (Samuel Weber, *Legend of Freud* [Stanford, CA: Stanford University Press, 2000], 11).

25 Freud to Fliess, 22 September 1898, in Sigmund Freud, *The Complete Letters of Sigmund Freud to Wilhelm Fliess 1887–1904*, trans. Jeffrey Moussaieff Masson (Cambridge, MA: Belknap Press, 1985), 327. In a subsequent letter to Fliess written five days later, Freud makes a passing reference to the Signorelli parapraxis again, saying that he has written "a short essay" about it and sent it to the publishers of the *Monatsschrift für Psychiatrie und Neurologie*. The essay was inevitably published under the title, "Zum Psychischen Mechanismus der Vergesslichkeit" a year later (1898), but at the time Freud was still uncertain whether it would be published. In the event that it would be refused, Freud writes, he would use "an old idea of [Fliess's] [. . .] and offer the thing to the Deutsche Rundschau, for example." Freud's consideration to send the article to the highly influential literary and political periodical is further evidence that he had serious doubts about making the Signorelli parapraxis credible to a scientific community. See Sigmund Freud, *Aus den Anfängen der Psychoanalyse; Briefe an Wilhelm Fliess, Abhandlungen und Notizen aus den Jahren 1887–1902* (London: Imago, 1950), 282–283; in English, *Complete Letters of Freud to Fliess*, 326–328.

own? It has been suggested, for instance, that the first syllable of Signorelli corresponds to Freud's given name, *Si*-gmund (see top left of diagram below). And if places were so important, would not the name of the place in which Signorelli's frescoes are found, Orvieto, also figure somehow into his Signorelli schema of displacement? The last -o at the end of "Orvieto" might further solidify the ending of the *Ersatzname*, Boltraffi-o, which seems about as valid as Freud's dependency on the first two letters that connect *Bo*tticelli, *Bo*snia, and *Bo*ltrafio. With these suggestions, Freud's diagram could be extended thus (Fig. 2.2):

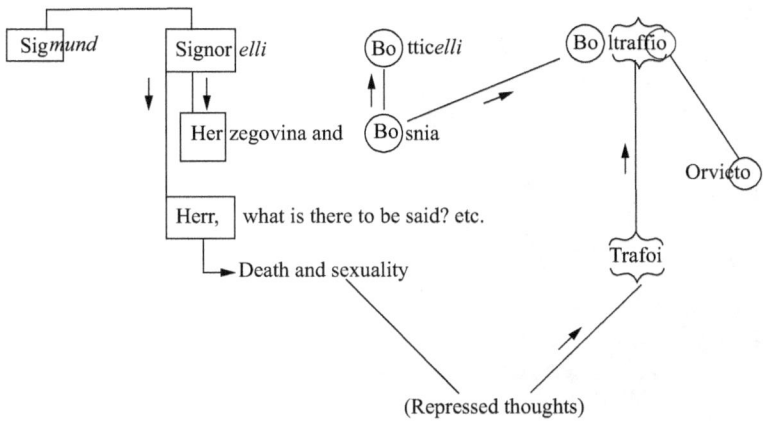

Fig. 2.2: Variation on Sigmund Freud's diagram [see Fig. 2.1].

While Freud writes that his rebus attempts to approximate the dynamic activity of his own unconscious mind, it can be easily shown how Freud consciously limits them to only specific associations. The expanded rebus above proves visually how phonemes cannot simply be contained in any closed system but echo beyond borders, creating new associations – like a constellation – that in turn put into question previous attempts at establishing meaning. Comparing Freud's attempt at a self-contained "sound map" to Benjamin's playful use of words and their sounds in the "Mummerehlen" fragment clearly illustrates the limitations of the Freudian schema for the acoustical unconscious.

Focusing on one other element of the Orvietto paintings will further help explain why Freud was so adamant to reestablish visually his authority over the name, Signorelli. Perhaps the most intriguing of the associations that we know Freud consciously leaves out in the first chapter of *Psychopathology of Everyday Life* is the fact that Signorelli painted himself into one of the frescoes at the Orvieto cathedral. Freud was well aware that Signorelli signed his *Deeds of the Antichrist* fresco by painting his entire body into the bottom left-hand corner of the frame. Of all the figures in the fresco, Signorelli is the only one that looks directly out at the fresco's viewers (Fig. 2.3).

Fig. 2.3: Self-portrait of Signorelli looking back in the Fresco Cycle of the San Brizio Cathedral in Orvieto, Spain.

However, Freud relegates this detail to a footnote in the chapter following the Signorelli parapraxis in *Psychopathology of Everyday Life*, as if he could not fit Signorelli's signature into his overall schema of the first chapter, relegating it instead to a footnote in the second. Freud admits in the footnote that, while Signorelli's name still remained inaccessible (*unzugänglich*) to him, "the visual memory that I had of the series of frescoes and of the self-portrait which is introduced into the corner of one of the pictures was *ultra-clear* [*überdeutlich*], at any rate much more intense than visual memory-traces normally appear to me" (emphasis original).[26] In the absence of the name "Signorelli," Signorelli's image haunts Freud by staring back but refusing to speak. Only after Freud remembers the name is he able to replace the image of Signorelli staring back

---

26 Freud, *GW* 4:18; *SE* 6:13.

with the painter's name, and by extension, Signorelli's frescoes with Freud's own rebus.[27] Considering this replacement of Signorelli's image with the remembrance of his name, Molnar claims that it is "as if clarity of vision and of verbal consciousness were incompatible" for Freud.[28] Indeed, Freud unconsciously works to relieve the anxiety he feels about the painter who keeps staring back, demanding with his return gaze to solve the riddle of his name and destabilizing Freud's own analytical gaze in the process. Freud's situation here recalls the Karl Kraus quotation Benjamin cited frequently, "the closer you look at a word, the more distantly it looks back," except in this case, it is the fresco's creator looking back at Freud. Only by reacquiring the painter's name and finding its echoes in various *Ersatznamen* is Freud finally able to affix "Signorelli" for all time on the page, into a rebus and thereby reestablish his own analytical gaze. In drawing out his rebus and making sure he understands all the reasons why he forgot the name in the first place, Freud reduces Signorelli from a *Signor* to a sign.

In the *New Introductory Lectures* (*Neue Folge der Vorlesung zur Einführung in die Psychoanalyse*, 1933), written more than thirty years after *Psychopathology of Everyday Life*, Freud uses the metaphor of a modern painting to explain how to make the psychic intelligible:

> If we wish to do justice to the specificity of the psychic, we must not seek to render it through linear contours, as in a drawing or in a primitive painting, but rather through blurred fields of color, as in a modern painting. After we have separated, we must permit what we have separated to coalesce once again. Do not be too hard on this initial attempt to make the difficult and elusive domain of the psychic intelligible [*anschaulich*].[29]

This plea could easily be applied to Freud's initial hopes between 1898–1901 to make his Signorelli parapraxis not only *glaubwürdig* (credible) but also *anschaulich*, that is to say, both visible and intelligible, intelligible *because* visible.[30] Near the end of chapter one in *Psychopathology of Everyday Life*, Freud states that the mechanism of paramnesia (*Fehlererinnerns*) reflected in his Signorelli example is not applicable to every case of forgetting a name.[31] All that he has done is added a motive (*ein Motiv hinzugefügt*) to those moments that

---

27 Precisely how Freud remembers the name "von fremder Seite" will become important in the following section.
28 Molnar, "Reading the Look," 80.
29 Freud, *GW* 15:85–86; translation in Weber, *Legends of Freud*, 33.
30 Another way to translate "anschaulich," especially in terms of psychology, is "eidetic." And yet, while Freud is discussing an image that reappears or "coalesces" over time, it is not an eidetic image per se. Eidetic memory and so forth is not popularized in psychology until the latter half of the twentieth century.
31 Freud, *GW* 4:10.

have been long recognized as having the capacity to cause the forgetting of a name.³² What he does not readily admit to in 1901 is that his diagram of the *Ersatznamen* is potentially refutable, or that the painter whose name he "forgot" but who incessantly stares back at him from the painting is really the one who motivates Freud to reestablish his dominance over both his memory and its unconscious processes. Freud thus draws the lines that produce meaning from syllabic echoes, giving the impression of reestablishing vision's dominance, seniority or *Herrschaft* over the names that once sonically reverberated the forgotten name. And yet, in giving an explanation, in making them *anschaulich*, he explains *away* the threat of not knowing. Freud's visual rebus replaces the sonic environment in which the words and names might have continued to reverberate beyond his fixed schema, cancelling or tuning out the sonic differences and dissonances in order to "get at what seems to be sensible."³³ In Tieck's "Eckbert," however, such dissonance is amplified rather than diminished, which only further destabilizes any fixed place from which one can look and listen.

2.2 The Signorelli-Strohmian Strain

> What has been forgotten [. . .] is never something only individual. [translation modified].³⁴

A number of common threads connect Freud's Signorelli parapraxis to Tieck's "Eckbert," not the least of which is the remembrance of a name. On the other hand, a comparison between the circumstances of remembrance illustrates two very different ways of thinking about the forgotten: whereas in Freud, the forgotten lies repressed in other names and words that can be and eventually are revealed through psychoanalysis, the forgotten in Tieck's story throws the individual into question by leaving open the influence of an enigmatic other to help with one's own memory, thereby destabilizing the notion of any "one." In order to parse out these similarities and differences, it is worth reminding ourselves at least of Bertha's childhood story, the circumstances under which it is told, and how she is reminded of the dog's name and by whom.

Although Tieck's "Eckbert" does not immediately begin with Bertha recounting her childhood narrative, the section devoted to her story comprises just over half of the whole tale. At the request of her husband, the knight Eckbert, Bertha

---

32 Freud, *GW* 4:10.
33 Weber, *Legends of Freud*, 11.
34 Benjamin, *GS* 2:430; *SW* 2:809.

agrees to tell her story to an invited guest, Pierre Walther, who is Eckbert's closest friend. After sitting down around a warm fire, she begins to explain to her intimate audience of two that, when she was young, she was accused by her poor parents of being "a stupid, foolish child [. . .], [who] could not be trusted to carry out even the simplest of tasks."[35] Her father, a shepherd by the name of Martin, one day threatens her with daily punishment if she does not learn the most basic household skills. In fear of such punishment, Bertha runs away. She wanders through strange lands, including what seems like an unending field of boulders, and finally comes upon a forest. There she finds an old woman, who feeds the young and starving Bertha and brings her back to the small cabin in the forest. Bertha lives with the old woman for many years, learning how to sew, read, and care for the old woman's pet bird and a small dog, whose name, Bertha explains to Eckbert and Walther, she has long since forgotten. The old woman, whom Bertha refers to as *die Alte*, often goes on excursions into the forest, leaving Bertha in charge of the cabin and her pets. After four years, the old woman trusts Bertha enough to tell her that the bird is actually a magical bird that lays eggs containing pearls and jewels. The old woman also warns her:

> "You're a good child," [the old woman] once said to [Bertha] in a rasping tone. "If you go on in this way, you will do well. But if you stray from the path of righteousness [*der rechten Bahn*], punishment will surely follow, however long it will be."[36]

Although Bertha does not fully understand the old woman's warning, she understands from all the fairytales she has been reading at the cabin that such pearls and jewels could be exchanged for riches and a beautiful life as a princess. Bertha never seems to have explicit intentions to steal, but one day, when the old woman announces that she would again be going on another excursion and "this time for longer than usual,"[37] Bertha becomes especially nervous. A few days after the old woman leaves the cabin, Bertha is still arguing with herself about whether to run away or not: "two warring spirits seemed to be fighting for possession of my soul."[38] Nevertheless, almost as if in a trance, Bertha

---

35 "Ein einfältiges, dummes Kind [. . .], das nicht das bedeutendste Geschäft auszurichten wisse." The original German is found in Ludwig Tieck, *Schriften in zwölf Bänden* (Frankfurt: Deutscher Klassiker Verlag, 1985), 6:126–148. Unless otherwise noted, the English translation is taken from Ludwig Tieck, "Eckbert the Fair," in *Six German Romantic Tales*, trans. Ronald Taylor (London: Angel Books, 1985). In citing page references, the German pagination will come first, followed by the English – in this case, Tieck, *Schriften*, 128; "Eckbert," 18.
36 Tieck, *Schriften*, 135–136; "Eckbert," 24. Jack Zipes translates *rechter Bahn* as "straight path." See Jack Zipes, *Spells of Enchantment* (New York: Penguin Group, 1991).
37 Tieck, *Schriften*, 136; "Eckbert," 25.
38 Tieck, *Schriften*, 137; "Eckbert," 25.

leashes the dog up to the cabin, takes the bird and a box of jewels, and runs away from the old woman forever. Upon returning to her parents' home, however, she discovers that they passed away long ago. Also, when the magical bird Bertha stole begins to sing a new song, reminding her of the old woman's cabin and Bertha's betrayal, she finds the song too painful to bear and strangles the bird. Bertha abruptly finishes her narrative to her husband and his friend once she recalls how she soon after gave her hand to a knight whom she had known for some time, the Ritter Eckbert.

While this marks the end of Bertha's narrative, this is far from the end of "Eckbert." As Bertha gets up to retire for bed, Pierre Walther "bade her goodnight with a kiss on the hand and said: 'Thank you, dear lady. I can well imagine [*recht vorstellen*] you with the strange bird, and how you gave little *Strohmian* his food'" (translation modified).[39] While there is much more to discuss in Tieck's tale – so much has already been left out – it is necessary to stop here at Walther's naming of the dog. It would likely be as difficult to discuss Freud's work and influence without alluding to the unconscious as it would be to discuss Tieck's literary influence on German Romanticism without mentioning the dog's name, Strohmian. Moreover, the story has historically been linked to psychology in yet another way: since at least Otto Rank's analysis of "Eckbert" in 1912, it has been subject to much psychoanalytical interpretation, and the apparently symbolic role of Strohmian is a case in point.[40] Of the two Jungian analyses that have been published, it is not surprising to read that Strohmian represents trust and is loosely affiliated with either Anubis, the jackal-headed god associated with mummification and the afterlife, or the child that Bertha will never have.[41] These

---

39 Tieck, *Schriften*, 140; "Eckbert," 28.
40 Otto Rank, *Das Inzest-Motiv in Dichtung und Sage*, 2nd ed. (Leipzig and Vienna: Franz Deuticke, [1912] 1926), 570–571. The following are five articles and references that have since Rank explicitly offered a psychological reading of Tieck's story, listed in chronological order: Robert Stanley, "Tieck's Der blonde Eckbert and Flaubert's Saint Julien: Blood and Guilt in Two Tales," *Journal of Evolutionary Psychology* 5, no. 3–4 (August 1984): 245–253; Timothy F. Sellner, "Jungian Psychology and the Romantic Fairy Tale: A New Look at Tieck's Der blonde Eckbert," *Germanic Review* 55 (1980): 89–97; Kurt Fickert, "The Relevance of the Incest Motif in 'Der blonde Eckbert,'" *Germanic Notes* 13, no. 3 (1982): 33–35; Victoria L. Rippere, "Ludwig Tieck's 'Der blonde Eckbert': A Psychological Reading," *PMLA: Publications of the Modern Language Association of America* 85, no. 3 (May 1970): 473–486; and Valentine C. Hubbs, "Tieck, Eckbert und das kollektive Unbewußte," *PMLA: Publications of the Modern Language Association of America* 71, no. 4 (September 1956): 686–693.
41 See Hubbs, "Tieck, Eckbert und das kollektive Unbewußte," 690. Also see Rippere, "Tieck's 'Der blonde Eckbert,'" in which Strohmian is interpreted as a baby-figure: "Abandoned to starve in the forest, [Strohmian] comes to represent the child [Bertha] will now never have" (Rippere, "Tieck's 'Der blonde Eckbert,'" 482).

interpretations have since been eclipsed by more rigorous and less conventionally psychoanalytical studies by Thomas Fries and Liliane Weissberg.[42]

But in the history of psychoanalytical readings of "Eckbert," no one has examined the particular way Bertha forgets the name and how it compares specifically to Freud's Signorelli parapraxis that begins the *Psychopathology of Everyday Life*. Perhaps this is because the two circumstances appear to be both very similar and at the same time irreducibly different. Similar because of Freud's theory of repression: one may easily – all-too-easily – determine that for Bertha the dog's name is what houses her repressed guilt of betraying the old woman, a repression that is so great that it overtakes Bertha's ability to remember the name itself. But the two examples are also very different, since Freud develops a whole theory of *Ersatznamen* that reveals the logic of his unconscious at work; no such analysis is offered in Tieck's "Eckbert." Even though Bertha and Freud are both recounting a personal story of the past, Bertha does not scrutinize her story to discover possible reasons as to why she has forgotten the name, as does Freud. Indeed, we would do well to remind ourselves, as Freud does, that his Signorelli parapraxis is not applicable to every case, Bertha's included.

And yet, names and their affiliation to other names in "Eckbert" appear to echo Freud's rebus of *Ersatznamen* the closer we look at them. Although Bertha does not produce any of her own substitute names, many names in Tieck's story appear to be substitutions for one another. Perhaps the most obvious are the names Eck-*bert* and *Berth*-a. Their relation does not become obvious until the end of the story, when it is revealed that Bertha unknowingly married her own half-brother. A less obvious example is the name "Walther," who is Eckbert's friend and who utters the dog's name. Again, only at the end of the story is it revealed that the old woman is a kind of magical shape-shifter, and that she disguised herself as Walther in order to punish Bertha and Eckbert. This explains why Walther knew the dog's name without Bertha having uttered it: because Walther was in fact the old woman. But had Bertha perhaps been more like Freud, she might have noticed that "Walther" hides the word "Alte" within it, which is the word that Bertha used to refer to the old woman throughout her narrative.[43] In

---

[42] See Thomas Fries, "'Ein romantisches Märchen: Der Blonde Eckbert' von Ludwig Tieck," *MLN* 88, no. 6 (December 1973): 1180–1211, and Liliane Weissberg, "Wiederholungen," in *Erinnern und Vergessen in der Europäischen Romantik*, ed. Günter Oesterle (Würzburg: Königshausen & Neumann, 2001), 177–191. Weissberg dedicates a middle section to Freud's theory of repetition compulsion and trauma that informs her reading of Tieck's "Eckbert." We will return to Weissberg's article at the end of this chapter.
[43] I attribute Walter as *Ersatzname* for "die Alte" to Maria Tartar's reading in "Unholy Alliances: Narrative Ambiguity in Tieck's 'Der blonde Eckbert,'" *MLN* 102, no. 3 (April 1987): 623.

this sense, the name "Walther" is as much of an *Ersatzname* for "die Alte" as "Botticelli" is for Freud's "Signorelli." And with Benjamin's own fascination with names and how they tend to keep secret the persons they name, including his own, it is little wonder why *Walter* Benjamin wanted to write an essay on Tieck's story.

There are of course obvious differences that distinguish the *Ersatznamen* in Tieck's story from those in Freud's parapraxis: they neither offer a closed visual schema nor do they relate in any way to the single name that is forgotten, "Strohmian."[44] And yet, how Freud and Bertha are confronted with the name is eerily consistent. Although Freud dominates the discussion of his parapraxis by establishing connections between *Ersatznamen* in order to find unconscious motivations for his "forgetting," his description about how he was finally reacquainted with the name is cursory, almost parenthetical: "[w]hen I learnt the correct name from someone else [*von fremder Seite*], I recognized it at once and without falter [*ohne Schwanken*]."[45] Encapsulated in this tangential sentence is the central event in Tieck's "Eckbert": both Freud and Bertha recognize the correct name instantly and from a foreign entity. The difference is that, whereas Freud seems to pride himself on recognizing the name without any feeling of doubt or without being shaken (*ohne Schwanken*), Bertha is forever shaken by this encounter *von fremder Seite*:

> Was it coincidence [*Zufall*]? Did [Walther] just guess the dog's name? And if he knows it, did he mention it on purpose? What connection is there between this man and my destiny? Sometimes I try to convince myself that I am merely imagining this strangeness [*Seltsamkeit*], but it is certain, only too certain. A terrible fear took over me when this total stranger [*ein fremder Mensch*] helped me with remembering the past [translation modified].[46]

Freud similarly claims that the coincidences that make up his Signorelli rebus are anything but accidental: "It is no longer possible for me to take the forgetting of the name *Signorelli* as a chance event [*zufälliges Ereignis*]."[47] The difference between Freud and Bertha's "coincidences" is control over the *Fremde*: for Bertha, Walther is wholly other, so much so that she is no longer in control of either her childhood memories or her fate; for Freud, on the other hand, everything derives from an unconscious that, although he may not be fully aware of at the time, has its own motivations that, eventually, he is able to deduce

---

44 A more extended analysis of this vagabond name follows in the next section.
45 Freud, *GW* 4:7; *SE* 6:2.
46 Tieck, *Schriften*, 141–142; "Eckbert," 29.
47 Freud, *GW* 4:8; *SE* 6:4.

and thereby control. By relegating the moment of remembrance to a footnote, Freud establishes a concept of the forgotten that is significantly other from the one reflected in Tieck's story. From his cursory note on how he remembered Signorelli "von fremder Seite" to the full-fledged schema of his *Bilderrätsel*, Freud's own motivation as a scientist is, if not to eradicate the influence of the enigmatic other that throws the individual into question, then at least to call it by another name: the unconscious.

At stake in this distinction between Bertha and Freud's forgetting of their respective names is precisely how one establishes a definition of the unconscious. In Freud's example, the forgotten is motivated by unconscious processes that are limited to the individual. This means that, while the unconscious may be inaccessible to self-consciousness, it is for Freud only ever a mental, and therefore internal, process.[48] By contrast, Tieck's story illustrates a forgetting and a remembrance that emphasizes the role of the other, an idea perhaps best expressed by Benjamin in his essay on Kafka: "What has been forgotten [. . .] is never something purely individual."[49] In adding to Bertha's personal memory, Walther calls into question the limits of Bertha as an individual and with it the notion of strictly internal mental processes. If the unconscious is no longer limited to the internal psyche, what other systems and natures might it be comprised of? In Chapter One we explored how Benjamin thought of an other nature speaking to the camera than to the naked eye, and from this other nature Benjamin developed the notion of the optical unconscious. In "On Some Motifs in Baudelaire" ("Über einige Motive bei Baudelaire," 1939), Benjamin admits that he is as interested as Freud is in discovering "other systems" that explain how memory traces (*Erinnerungsreste*) are most powerful "when the incident which left them behind was one that never entered consciousness."[50] But whereas Freud develops the theory of a psychic shield serving to protect against external stimuli that can then be

---

48 In the same letter in which he first communicates his Signorelli parapraxis (September 22, 1898), Freud expresses to Fliess their shared interest not to leave psychology "without any organic foundation [*organische Grundlage*]," but he also sees no way of bringing psychology and physiology together, neither theoretically nor therapeutically (see Freud, *Anfängen der Psychoanalyse*, esp. 282; *Complete Letters of Freud to Fliess*, 326). Fifteen years later, around the same time that Freud writes his important essays on repression and the unconscious, Freud continues to deal only with the psychological at the expense of the physiological, and the unconscious is exemplary of this distinction: "To come closer to it [the unconscious] from the angle of *physical* processes [emphasis original] [. . .] still seems completely impossible. It [the unconscious] must therefore remain an object of psychology" (Freud, *GW* 8:406).
49 Benjamin, *GS* 2:430; *SW* 2.2:809.
50 Benjamin, *GS* 1:612–613; *SW* 4:317. See also chapter four of Freud's *Jenseits des Lustprinzips* (Leipzig/Wien/Zürich: Internationaler Psychoanalytischer Verlag, 1921).

bypassed, Benjamin turns to Proust for one such "other system," the *mémoire involontaire des membres*.[51] The "other system" exemplified here in Tieck's "Eckbert" involves awakening to the "other" of familiarity, to that which we thought was closest-at-hand – such as our childhood memories – but which is suddenly most foreign, shockingly most *fremd*. In the case of "Eckbert," the figure who best illustrates the other is Eckbert's "closest friend," Walther.

For the purposes of defining the unconscious according to Benjamin, the consequences of this foreignness is that one is left open precisely to the status of "one." In other words, whereas unconscious motivations are ultimately discernible in Freud's Signorelli example, awakening to the other involves a distinctive experience that does not subsume the other into any internal process. One experience that makes such foreignness explicit, and which was already relevant in Chapter One, is the experience of déjà vu. As we have seen in *Berlin Chronicle*, Benjamin conceives of déjà vu in terms of both an echo and a lost glove or reticule left behind by a stranger (*eine Fremde*). In the postscript to his fragment, "Images of the déjà vu" ("Bilder des Déjà vu"), Ernst Bloch further accentuates this foreignness of the déjà vu, and explicitly in reference to Tieck's "Eckbert":

> So it is not only the case, as Bertha says, that a stranger [*ein fremder Mensch*] helped to provide her with her memories and she was therefore afflicted with extreme horror; rather, as if illuminated from above, the *déjà vu of the other* casts her in not even the slightest shadow wherein she could flee [emphasis mine].[52]

The structure of the déjà vu is indeed relevant to the Strohmian moment, since one of déjà vu's most salient features is that it appears to repeat that which

---

51 This is an important footnote in Benjamin's "Some Motifs in Baudelaire," which is entirely left out of the Harvard English translation: "Proust deals with these 'other systems' in many ways. He prefers to represent them through the limbs, and he never tires of speaking about the memory images [*Gedächtnissbildern*] deposited in them: how they, independent of any hint of consciousness, nevertheless abruptly [*unvermittelt*] break into consciousness when a thigh, arm, or shoulder blade in bed is involuntarily put into a position that it had once been in a long time ago. The *memoire involontaire des membres* is one of Proust's favorite subjects" (translation mine; Benjamin, *GS* 1:613).
52 Ernst Bloch, *Verfremdungen* (Frankfurt a.M.: Suhrkamp, 1965), 35. All translations from Bloch's "Déjà vu of the Other" are my own. One should add here that, even if Benjamin and Bloch discussed Tieck's "Eckbert" once on the island of Capri in 1924, which is what Bloch claims in his postscript, it is unclear whether they would have agreed on the phrase, "déjà vu of the other." Bloch has come under critique for this phrase. Thomas Fries, for instance, rejects this idea as absurd, and instead posits that déjà vu typically do not happen beyond the one experiencing it: no one can experience another person's déjà vu (Fries, "'Ein romantisches Märchen,'" 1198). And yet this is precisely the problem in terms of a kind of collective unconscious.

never was, opening up the dangerous possibility of anything being repeatable at any moment. What intrigues both Benjamin and Bloch about forgetting generally – and which is experienced in the structure of the déjà vu and in Tieck's story in particular – is not a psychological reading whereby discovering an individual's repressed memories explains what is forgotten and why. This only relieves the anxiety of the alternative: that one's forgotten past may blindside you at any moment and *von fremder Seite*.

In this situation, there is no way of knowing when it will happen or what will trigger it. It is also often the closest things that suddenly become most foreign, like Eckbert's supposedly best friend, Pierre Walther. Often they come in the form of a sound, which is the way Benjamin writes about déjà vu at the end of the *Berlin Chronicle*.[53] While Benjamin never fully explains why these moments tend to strike us in the form of a sound, one sound that typically shocks us in this way is an alarm clock. If Benjamin's description of the *déjà entendu*, as explored in the previous chapter, can be read as one of the clearest examples in his work that supports the concept of an acoustical unconscious, then another central motif of the acoustical unconscious, apart from the conch shell, is the sound of an alarm clock. Alarms resound throughout Tieck's "Eckbert," perhaps the most alarming being Walther's utterance of the dog's name. In this sense, Walther is as much *die Alte* as he is Bertha and Eckbert's *Wecker*: even his name appears to be a combination of the two words superimposed upon each other. One could visualize it in a rebus, echoing Freud's Signorelli diagram:

die ⟦Alte⟧
|
⟦W⟧ – ⟦althe⟧ – ⟦r⟧
\   /
der ⟦W⟧ecke⟦r⟧

In what follows, both the dog's bark and the bird's song will also sound out as if they are alarms, awakening both Bertha and Eckbert to the darkness of a past life. Instead of being "set" for a particular moment to ring, all of these alarms are unexpected and disarming, upsetting any sense of time and unsettling whoever hear their repeated ringing.

---

53 Benjamin, *GS* 6:518 [Walter Benjamin, *Werke und Nachlass: Kritische Gesamtausgabe* (Frankfurt a.M.: Suhrkamp, 2008–) (hereafter, *WuN*), 11.1:77]; *SW* 2:634.

2.3 The Bark of the Forgotten

Much has been written about the name "Strohmian." Although it is as central to Tieck's story as Signorelli is to Freud's parapraxis, it promises no new syllabic correspondences to any other names in the story. Even the meaning of the word, "stromian," foregrounds its own inability to "fit in." The *Grimms Dictionary* defines "stromian" (without the h) as "probably a derivation of *strom* 'vagabond, vagrant' [. . .] with meaning restricted to its external appearance: 'wild, unkempt beggar.' apparently limited to low German. probably used only half-jokingly."[54] Although the name is resistant to any systemized rebus, a stromian's tendency to wander nevertheless permeates nearly every character in the story. We have already seen how the old woman, for instance, often took multiple excursions away from the cabin. Bertha's flights both from her parents' home and later from the old woman's cabin are other examples of a wandering vagrant who "passed through a number of villages and began to beg."[55] Finally, in the second half of the story, Eckbert increasingly wanders without any goal in sight. He first leaves Bertha's deathbed with the intention of going hunting,[56] but after killing Walther in the forest, discovers that he "had been wandering in the forest for hours."[57] Near the end of the story, after Eckbert thinks he had seen his newest friend, Hugo, speaking to Walther, whom Eckbert thought dead, he leaves his castle "with no particular direction in mind and paying scant heed to the countryside around him."[58] Even the memory of the name, "Strohmian," seems to wander away from Bertha and into the memories of others like Walther. In this sense, although Strohmian the dog remains leashed to the cabin and left to die, the word "stromian" is both a rogue memory and a theme that roams throughout the story and its characters.

In the postscript to his déjà vu fragment, Ernst Bloch writes that stromian is also "the word for a crime."[59] As such, the name is typically understood in terms

---

54 See "stromian" in *Das deutsche Wörterbuch von Jacob und Wilhelm Grimm auf CD-Rom und im Internet* (digitized version in Wörterbuchnetz des Trier Center for Digital Humanities, version 01/21, https://www.woerterbuchnetz.de/DWB): "'verwilderter, struppiger kerl'. anscheinend aufs nd. beschränkt. wohl nur halb scherzhaft gebraucht."
55 Tieck, *Schriften*, 129; "Eckbert," 19.
56 Tieck, *Schriften*, 142; "Eckbert," 30.
57 Tieck, *Schriften*, 142; "Eckbert," 30.
58 Tieck, *Schriften*, 144; "Eckbert," 32.
59 Although no *Bilderrätsel* like Freud's can be drawn between names and their syllables in Tieck's "Eckbert," the name "Strohmian" is nevertheless itself a *Buchstabenrätsel*: with the "h" it is an anagram for "romantish," without the "c." This anagram was identified by Albrecht Koschorke who, in his article "Imaginationen der Kulturgrenze. Zu Ludwig Tiecks Erzählung

of Bertha's crime of betraying the old woman's trust. But when the name Strohmian also wanders into Benjamin's essay on Kafka, the crime is more of a mysterious guilt:

> Kafka is not the only writer for whom animals are the receptacles [*Behältnisse*] of the forgotten. In Tieck's profound story, *Blonde Eckbert*, the forgotten name of a little dog, Strohmi, is the chiffre for a mysterious guilt [*einer rätselhaften Schuld*]. One can understand, then, why Kafka never tired of learning about the forgotten by listening to animals [*abzulauschen*]. They are surely not the goal; but it does not work without them [translation modified].[60]

To introduce the role of animals in Kafka by way of the "little dog, Strohmi," illustrates first and foremost the centrality of "Eckbert" for Benjamin: Strohmian is nothing less than the precursor to Kafka's animals. Defined as a vagabond or *Landstreicher*, that is to say, someone "who is not sedentary, often without a fixed residency, [and who] migrates aimlessly from place to place,"[61] the term "stromian" does not stray far from Kafka's vagabond, Odradek.[62]

‚Der blonde Eckbert,'" admits that he did not himself discover the anagram, but that Michel Chaouli, Professor of German and Comparative Literature at Bloomington-Indiana, was present during an earlier version of his paper and had noticed it right away. Koschorke, who "for weeks had puzzled over this name," was surprised that for Chaouli the anagram "was apparently all-too evident!" The important point here, although it is one that Koschorke does not dwell on, is that such a discovery parallels both Freud and Bertha's remembrance of their respective forgotten names: it can only ever come *von fremder Seite*. Similar to Freud's remembrance of the name, with which he was able to develop his "first detailed examination of unconscious processes," Koschorke's identification of the anagram has major consequences for all future readings of "Eckbert": now that it has been pointed out, "Strohmian" will be recognized by Koschorke, and indeed for the entire German literary community, as an anagram "immediately and without falter." See Albrecht Koschorke, "Imaginationen der Kulturgrenze. Zu Ludwig Tiecks Erzählung ‚Der blonde Eckbert,'" in *Kultur-Schreiben als romantisches Projekt: romantische Ethnographie im Spannungsfeld zwischen Imagination und Wissenschaft*, ed. David Wellbery (Würzburg: Königshausen & Neumann, 2012), 135–153.
60 Benjamin, *GS* 2:430; *SW* 2:810. Although it is not the point of the present discussion to link Strohmian to an enigmatic guilt, Benjamin nevertheless gestures here toward the understanding of guilt in his essay on *Destiny and Character* (*Schicksal und Charakter*, 1921): "insofar as something is fate, it is misfortune and guilt [soweit etwas Schicksal ist, ist es Unglück und Schuld]" (Benjamin, *GS* 2:174; *SW* 2:203). In his article on "Eckbert," Thomas Fries continues this reading of Strohmian and Benjamin's notion of destiny by characterizing the old woman's revelations at the end of the story as follows: "The old woman's answers speak not only for themselves [. . .]. On the question of a failed human destiny, they declare the 'natural' wisdom of all those who are able to sleep calmly with the saying, 'from injustice follows punishment'" (Fries, "'Ein romantisches Märchen,'" 1203).
61 "Landstricher," in Duden's *Das große Wörterbuch der deutschen Sprache*.
62 The similarities between Odradek and Strohmian are striking: both are small creatures affiliated with a place or dwelling but who also move in and out of both space and time with

But an equally important feature in the passage above is the way Benjamin describes Kafka's relationship to animals: Kafka does not tire of learning about the forgotten by *listening in on* them. *Ablauschen* means both to ascertain something by thorough investigation and to experience something by way of overhearing or without being noticed (the root verb, *lauschen*, means to overhear or eavesdrop).[63] For Benjamin, Kafka does not simply learn about the forgotten from animals, but learns by listening to them. Kafka also listened to the strangeness of his own body, and in this way "one can understand why Kafka called the cough that broke out from his insides, 'the animal.'"[64] Like Kafka listening to his cough, we should not turn a deaf ear to Strohmian's bark, through which one may learn about what is forgotten in "Eckbert."

Or perhaps one should say: through which one is *awakened* to the forgotten, however distant in the past it may lie. This forgotten, as we have recognized in both Benjamin's shell scene and Bertha's experience when Walther mentions the dog's name, is something forgotten in the distant past of childhood. As Benjamin writes above with respect to Kafka's animals, they are not themselves the goal, but "without them it does not work." Like the shell, animals act as passageways that allow access to that most distant past, which is otherwise neither repeatable nor representable. In the case of a barking dog, the appropriate metaphor is less a passageway than a signal or alarm that suddenly awakens one to the forgotten. Tieck's "Eckbert" is not the only text in which a dog's bark acts as an alarm, reminding the listener of a distant, mysterious past. In Friedrich Nietzsche's "The Vision and the Riddle" ("Vom Gesicht und Rätsel"), Zarathustra recounts to the ship's crew a strange story concerning his ascent up a mountain path, an argument he has with the dwarf who accompanies him, and eventually the sound of a dog howling. Near the end of his tirade against the dwarf, Zarathustra recalls how he began to speak softer and softer, "for I was afraid of my own thoughts and the thoughts behind those thoughts":

> Then, suddenly, I heard a dog *howl* nearby.
> Had I ever heard a dog howl like this? My thoughts raced back. Yes! When I was a child, in my most distant childhood:

---

relative ease. Despite having strange and foreign names, both are familiar creatures whom we address in the "du" form. Whereas one laughs, the other barks.

63 In Duden's *Das große Wörterbuch der deutschen Sprache*, "ablauschen" is defined as *"von jmdm. durch aufmerksames Hin-, Zuhören erfahren:* jmdm. ein Geheimnis a." In the German dictionary, *Wahrig*, the word is defined as *"(unbemerkt) von jmdm. etwas erfahren; (fig) durch gründliche Beobachtung herausfinden, gestalten;* er hat seinen Roman dem Leben abgelauscht."

64 Benjamin, *GS* 2:431; *SW* 2:810.

> – then I heard a dog howl like this. And I saw him too, bristling, his head up, trembling, in the stillest midnight, when even dogs believe in ghosts:
> – so that I felt pity. For just then the full moon, silent as death, passed over the house; just then it stood still, a round ember – still on the flat roof, as if on a stranger's property,
> that was why the dog was terrified: for dogs believe in thieves and ghosts. And when I heard such howling again I took pity once more.
> Where did the dwarf go? And the gate? The spider? The whispering? Was I dreaming? Did I wake up? Between wild cliffs I stood all at once, alone, deserted, in the most deserted moonlight [translation modified].⁶⁵

Without delving too deep into the numerous analyses of this important section and its relation to Nietzsche's eternal return in particular, including Heidegger's influential reading of it, it suffices here to emphasize how the dog's howl "nearby" signals Zarathustra's sudden return to his "most distant childhood." Just as Benjamin writes about Kafka's animals, the dog heard here by Zarathustra is not "the goal," but without it, Zarathustra would never have regained access to the vision subsequently recalled and recounted. Equally significant is the way in which the dog's howl is heard: not just "nearby" and "suddenly," but also in the process of his own speech becoming "ever quieter" (*immer leiser*) due to growing fears about the path his own thoughts were taking. Unable to explain this anxiety, in a sense becoming choked up over it – a choking that foreshadows the shepherd choking on the snake – the dog's howl is what allows for a continuation of thought, but of thought that *raced* back (*lief zurück*), suddenly and out of Zarathustra's control. His subsequent conflicting questions about what had happened as he heard the dog's repeated howl – "Was I dreaming? Did I wake up?" – eerily echoes Bertha's own series of questions when reflecting on how Walther could have possibly known the dog's name: "Was it coincidence? Did [Walther] just guess the dog's name? [. . .] Sometimes I try to convince myself that I am merely imagining this strangeness [*Seltsamkeit*], but it is certain, only too certain. A terrible fear took over me" (translation modified).⁶⁶

It would therefore not be an exaggeration to say that, when Bloch writes about the dog's bark in Tieck's "Eckbert," his comments are equally applicable to Nietzsche's howling dog in "The Vision and the Riddle":

---

65 Friedrich Nietzsche, *Sämtliche Werke* (Berlin/New York: De Gruyter, 1999), 4:201; Friedrich Nietzsche, *Thus Spoke Zarathustra*, trans. Adrian del Caro (Cambridge: Cambridge University Press, 2006), 125.
66 Tieck, *Schriften*, 141–142; "Eckbert," 29.

> We can in any case not see our current lived moment, neither the "I" that lives it, nor the immediate content that is respectively lived. But this darkness is also the place of an invariable "forgetting" of I-know-not-what; animals that disgust or terrify us conspicuously live there, a single barking dog can likewise bring us back there [*dahin zurückholen*].[67]

Bloch is relying here on a phrase that was already prominent in the first version of his *Spirit of Utopia* (*Geist der Utopie*, 1918): the darkness of the lived moment (*das Dunkel des gelebten Augenblicks*). Benjamin was well aware of this phrase, comparing it to Proust's experimental relocation of furniture in the Arcades Project.[68] Bloch argues that, far from being comparable merely to forgotten or past events, this darkness of the lived moment introduces punctual breaks in the flow of consciousness,[69] and in this sense is comparable to what Benjamin calls a *Bruchstelle*.[70] With these incisive breaking points or places, which for neither Bloch nor Benjamin are "primarily negative or privative in character," Bloch emphasizes its peculiar *darkness*. At first glance, this darkness seems to contradict the other word in Bloch's phrase that relies on the metaphor of sight: *Augenblick*. This later term, which is as essential to Benjamin as it is to Nietzsche, is difficult to translate, since it is not merely an "instant" or "moment," but a literal translation might be an instantaneous "eye-glance." Samuel Weber defines the *Augenblick* as "the glance of an eye whose sight is always split between what it is and what it sees."[71] To read this definition of *Augenblick* into Bloch's use of the term helps to elucidate the essential unseeability of the *Augenblick* that Bloch is attempting to attribute to it with the notion of the darkness of a lived moment: as a glance that is already split, one does not merely see darkness, but sees without any secure notion of a self seeing. The unseeable in the *Augenblick*, its "darkness," is therefore not necessarily the opposite of sight, but a kind of seeing darkly without an I.

Despite Bloch's emphasis on the *darkness* of the lived moment, our sense of hearing apparently remains intact, since "a single barking dog can bring us

---

67 Bloch, *Verfremdungen*, 36.
68 "Awakening is the exemplary case of remembering [*des Erinnerns*] – that case in which we succeed in remembering the nearest, the most obvious [*das Nächsten, Naheliegendsten*] (to the I). What Proust means with the experimental rearrangement of furniture, what Bloch recognizes as the darkness of the lived moment, is nothing other than what here is verified at the level of the historical and collectively. There is a 'not-yet-conscious knowledge' of *what has been*: its extraction [*Förderung*] has the structure of awakening [h° 2]" (Benjamin, *GS* 5:1057–1058; *AP* 883).
69 See Ernst Bloch, *Das Prinzip Hoffnung* (Frankfurt a.M.: Suhrkamp, 1959), 338; Ernst Bloch, *The Principle of Hope*, vol. 1, trans. Neville Plaice, Stephen Plaice, and Paul Knight (Cambridge: MIT Press, 1986), 1:290–291.
70 See Weber's discussion of "Bruchstellen" in *Benjamin's -abilities*, 167.
71 Weber, *Benjamin's -abilities*, 168.

back there."⁷² What reverberates is not only a return to the logic of repetition and the eternal return, but more precisely the return to a memory that is unexpectedly triggered by an other: in this case, an animal whose sonic call makes possible a certain unexpected and sudden recall. The hearing of a single dog's bark (Tieck) or howl (Nietzsche) sends the listener back to a place that by definition can never be seen, that is to say, a breaking-place (*Bruchstelle*) that cannot, in Freud's sense, be made visible and therefore intelligible (*anschaulich*). Not only is sight split apart, disorienting place – Zarathustra asks "Where did the dwarf go? And the gate? The spider? The whispering? Was I dreaming? Did I wake up?" – but hearing the howl or bark throws off the listener's sense of time: both Zarathustra and Bertha are "sent back" (*zurückholt*) to another place and another time with the acoustic signal. In this sense, Bloch's darkness refers to a knowing of neither where nor *when* you are. The latter, moreover, is related to the unexpected: like the nature of the déjà vu examined in the last chapter, one cannot "see" it coming. While Zarathustra first hears the dog's howl and only then sees "him too, bristling, his head up, trembling," Zarathustra's vision is nevertheless seen "in the stillest midnight [*in stillster Mitternacht*], when even dogs believe in ghosts." The reference to midnight is not accidental: while the rest of Zarathustra's vision is described in an eerie moonlight, the "stillest midnight" refers to the witching hour, when time itself stands still.⁷³ As we shall see in Tieck's "Eckbert," the sounds of the dog's bark also sends the listener back to a darkness that destabilizes the listener's sense of both place and time.⁷⁴

Strohmian's bark is heard three times in Tieck's "Eckbert." The first time occurs during Bertha's narrative, when she follows the old woman to the cabin for the first time. The dog's bark simultaneously announces Bertha's arrival to the cabin and the dog's entrance into the narrative:

> We climbed over a hill covered with birches [*Birken*] and looked down from the top on to a green valley also full of birches, and in the middle of the trees [*Bäumen*] stood a tiny cottage [*Hütte*]. A cheerful bark [*ein munteres Bellen*] reached our ears, and soon a nimble

---

72 Bloch, *Verfremdungen*, 36.
73 In the *Trauerspiel* book, Benjamin examines the "hatchway of time [*Luke der Zeit*]" of baroque mourning plays, discussing the importance of midnight or the witching hour, and the widespread notion, "that at this hour time comes to a standstill, like the arm of a balance" (Benjamin, *GS* 1:313; Walter Benjamin, *Origin of the German Trauerspiel*, trans. Howard Eiland [Cambridge: Harvard University Press, 2019] [hereafter, *OGT*], 135).
74 For an important discussion of animal sounds in relation to language opening up to non-language in the form of exclamation and *Ausruf*, see Daniel Heller-Roazen, *Echolalias: On the Forgetting of Language* (New York: Zone Books, 2005).

little dog [*ein kleiner behender Hund*] was jumping up at the old woman, wagging his tail. He came towards me, looked at me from all sides, then went back cheerfully to his mistress.[75]

The affiliation of dog with the hut, of *Hund* with *Hütte*, not to mention the alliteration of *Birken*, *Bäumen* and *Bellen*, illustrates the interconnection of the domestic animal and the domicile, or in a word: the *Haus-tier*. This interconnectedness of house and animal is precise: it is a relation based neither on protection nor servitude, but rather on a sense of belonging.[76] The words similarly belong to and contextualize each other: in surrounding the dog and the domicile, the *Bellen* and the *Birken* belong to each other in the sense of interweaving semantically and syllabically both landscape and soundscape.

We should not forget that this is Bertha's recollection of her first encounter with the dog, and that at this moment in Tieck's story she still has no access to the dog's name. The second time she tells us of the dog's bark is still during her childhood narrative, therefore still before Walther mentions its name. After having just leashed up the dog and stolen the jewels and bird, she recalls: "The farther I went, the less I heard [*hörte*] the barking, until finally it stopped altogether [*hörte es ganz auf*]. I wept and was on the point of turning back, but the urge to see something new [*etwas neues zu sehn*] drove me on" (emphasis mine).[77] The hearing (*hören*) that finally stops (*hört auf*) not only repeats the same verb stem, but also stops because of Bertha's need to *see* something else beyond the old woman's cottage in the forest. This need to move forward, furthermore, directly opposes what she is able to hear. Belonging as much to the dog as to the hut, the bark becomes a sonic signifier for that to which she turns her back. Bertha's relation to the dog's bark can now also be related to the way Freud reacted to the painter who stared back at him from the fresco at the Orvieto cathedral: like Signorelli staring back at Freud without relinquishing his

---

75 Tieck, *Schriften*, 132; "Eckbert," 21.
76 In his *Fundamental Concepts of Metaphysics* (*Grundbegriffe der Metaphysik*, 1929–1930), Martin Heidegger is most specific on this point: "Let us consider the case of domestic animals [*die Haustiere*] as a striking example. We do not describe them as such simply because they turn up in the house [*weil sie im Haus vorkommen*] but because they belong to the house [*weil sie zum Haus gehören*], i.e., they serve the house in a certain sense. Yet they do not belong to the house in the way in which the roof belongs to the house as protection against storms. We keep domestic pets in the house with us, they 'live' with us" (Heidegger, cited by Jacques Derrida, *The Animal that Therefore I Am*, trans. David Wills [New York: Fordham University Press, 2008], 158). The dog that Bertha encounters for the first time *belongs* to the cabin in precisely the way Heidegger describes in this passage: it does not protect the cabin as much as it is an extension of it.
77 Tieck, *Schriften*, 137–138; "Eckbert," 26.

name to the psychoanalyst, the dog's bark is sonically *überdeutlich* to Bertha: it is as if the bark replaces the dog's name with a kind of "substitute sound," blocking sonically the name from memory. Like Signorelli's stare that disrupts Freud's fixed position as observer and analyst, Strohmian's bark rings out in Bertha's memory, disrupting her ability to recollect the name. But unlike Freud, who builds a rebus to explain why he forgot the name and thereby regain control, Bertha is forever haunted by what the sudden remembrance of the name portends and, unable to escape what she has done, dies.

The third and last time the dog's bark is heard comes at the very end of Tieck's "Eckbert." After Bertha dies and Eckbert apparently murders Walther only to run away from his only other friend, Hugo, Eckbert wanders aimlessly into a forest: "As if in a dream he found himself climbing a hill. Suddenly he seemed to hear the cheerful bark of a dog close at hand [*ein nahes munteres Bellen*] and birch trees [*Birken*] rustled."[78] Although there is no mention of Eckbert ever having been to the old woman's cabin, the combination of the words *Bellen* and *Birken* once again announce the cabin's sonic surroundings. The adjective "munter" also accompanied the dog's bark the first time Bertha described it during her childhood narrative: "A *cheerful* bark [*munteres* Bellen] came towards us" (emphasis and translation mine).[79] Similar to the leitmotif technique of the Homeric epithet, the *munteres Bellen* that resounds at the end of the story repeats the first time it was heard, but this time with neither the dog nor the same person who had originally heard it. Through the repetition of the bark, the identities of Bertha and Eckbert begin to blur and become indistinguishable. If the bark is an *Ersatzlaut* for a forgotten name, it carries with it a sense of guilt that is now shared by more than one.

We will be able to return to the end of the story a second time after examining the iterations of the bird's song. For now, it suffices to add one final note on the vagabond memory of the dog, Strohmian, which is also the case with the bird. Since Bertha seemed to have left the dog to die, and since she strangled the bird with her own bare hands, this should mean that the bark and song should have died along with her. And yet, the animals live on well after Bertha dies. One could argue that the animals appear to be mere projections of the old woman's malignant power. But the two animals are – like the old woman – immortal, which returns us once again to the question of time: the forgotten that resounds in the animal trumps not only the human and the subject, but also temporal continuity. While the animals belong to the cabin, they also belong to

---

78 Tieck, *Schriften*, 145; "Eckbert," 32.
79 Tieck, *Schriften*, 132.

a time both before and after the time of human history. Another way to say this is that, like Zarathustra's howling dog in "stillest midnight," these animals live in the absence of history, when time is at a standstill. In the case of Tieck's "Eckbert," they awaken Bertha and Eckbert not simply to a past event, but also to their shared fate, as did Walther with the utterance of the name, Strohmian.

2.4 Waldeinsamkeit – Wiederhörbarkeit

> Aloft, in secret veins of air,
> Blows the sweet breath of song,
> O, few to scale those uplands dare,
> Though they to all belong![80]

The old woman in "Eckbert" owns both a dog by the name of Strohmian and a magical bird that daily lays an egg containing either a pearl or jewel. As Bertha explains in her narrative, the old woman waited for four years before she entrusted the young Bertha with this secret.[81] Bertha's subsequent betrayal of the old woman's trust is what ultimately leads to both Bertha and Eckbert's downfall. But rather than focus on Bertha's *Unrecht* towards the bird and its trajectory through to the end of the story, this final section is devoted to the bird and its song. Unlike the dog, the old woman's bird has no name.[82] It is nevertheless affiliated with a single word, "Waldeinsamkeit." If the name "Strohmian" is defined as a vagabond or vagrant without a home, the bird's repeated references to "Waldeinsamkeit" certainly gives the impression that the term is not simply a feeling of "forest solitude," but that solitude is also its home. The first time Bertha hears the song, she has just encountered the dog and seen the hut:

---

80 Ralph Waldo Emerson, "Waldeinsamkeit," in *The Complete Works of Ralph Waldo Emerson: Poems*, by Ralph Waldo Emerson (Cambridge, MA: Riverside Press, 1904), 9:249.
81 Tieck, *Schriften*, 134; "Eckbert," 22.
82 It is also not the only bird in the story. As Bertha recalls, before she found the old woman, she experienced many sleepless nights alone and scared in the forest, trying to figure out what she was hearing in the night: "I heard the strangest sounds in the night, and took them for wild beasts in one moment, the next for the wind that wailed through rocks, then for strange birds" (translation mine; Tieck, *Schriften*, 130). During her first night in the old woman's cabin, however, the sounds are less unknown and more comforting and dreamier: "Such a wonderful medley [*Gemisch*] was heard with the birch rustling in front of the widow and the song of a distant nightingale, that I kept feeling as if I was not awake, but rather as if I had fallen into an even more strange dream than before" (translation mine; Tieck, *Schriften*, 133).

As we descended the hill, I heard an extraordinary song coming from the direction of the cottage, like a bird singing:

›Waldeinsamkeit,
Die mich erfreut,
So morgen wie heut
In ewger Zeit,
O wie mich freut
Waldeinsamkeit.‹

These few words were repeated over and over. If I were asked to describe it, I would say that the sound made me think of pipes and horns playing in the distance.[83]

Nowhere in the story does the bird actually speak back; no matter whether the old woman or Bertha speaks to the bird, its "only response was to go on repeating its song."[84] In this sense, although the bird is adorned with feathers of all possible colors, it is no parrot.[85] The simple verse appears to be a translation of the natural song of the bird into human language. It remains unclear, however, whose translation it is: it certainly is not Bertha's, who seems to have heard the song as words. Also unique to this "translation" is the neologism, *Waldeinsamkeit*, as if the German language was insufficient to express what the bird was singing about. Nearly every line, furthermore, has the same number of syllables as the single word, *Waldeinsamkeit*, giving the impression that each line is but a variation on the word, echoing not the word itself but all that is affiliated with it. Indeed, just as each line is a kind of *Ersatzphrase* for the otherwise untranslatable word, we can imagine that the word itself stands in for a four-note bird motif.

With the second reiteration of the bird's song, however, what is "heard" by Bertha takes on a different meaning altogether. By this point in Bertha's narrative, she has already stolen the bird and left the cabin. Just as Bertha was beginning to forget the old woman and become satisfied with her new life, the bird suddenly changes its tune. Bertha explains:

The world was by no means as wonderful as I had imagined, but my memory of the old woman and my years with her faded even further into the background, and on the whole, I was quite content with my lot [*im Ganzen recht zufrieden*].

---

[83] Tieck, *Schriften*, 132; "Eckbert," 21.
[84] Tieck, *Schriften*, 133; "Eckbert," 22. There is no reference in the story to the bird speaking back, but only singing its song. In this sense, the bird in Tieck's "Eckbert" is quite different to the talking raven in Günter Eich's *Sabeth*. See below, Chapter Three, section five.
[85] Tieck, *Schriften*, 134; "Eckbert," 22. The rainbow colors of the bird are reminiscent of the *Muhme Rehlen*, who owned seven coats, each one a different color of the rainbow.

The bird had stopped singing some time ago. Then one night, to my horror, it suddenly started again, but this time it was a different song:

›Waldeinsamkeit
Wie liegst du weit!
O dich gereut
Einst mit der Zeit. –
Ach einzge Freud
Waldeinsamkeit‹[86]

More than any other version of the song, this one appears to be a reminder of the *Unrecht* that Bertha has committed. The question naturally arises: what is the relationship between this new song and Bertha's unconscious anxiety? Whose unconscious is it anyway? In reading Lacan's "Position of the Unconscious," Derrida concludes that, at least for Lacan, there

> is no desire, and thus no unconscious, except for the human; it in no way exists for the animal, unless that be as an effect [*l'effet*] of the human unconscious, as if the domestic or tamed animal translated within itself [*en lui*] the unconscious of man by some contagious transference or mute interiorization. [. . .] Its thesis is clear: the animal has neither unconscious nor language, nor the other, except as an effect of the human order, that is by contagion, appropriation, domestication.[87]

But are we limited to this *effect* of the human unconscious? It does not seem sufficient to conclude that this second version of the bird's song is simply the echo of Bertha's unconscious, brought about via some "contagious transference."

And yet, the bird seems particularly prescient of Bertha beginning to *forget* what she has done. In this second hearing, the bird's altered song thus functions, like Walther's utterance of "Strohmian," like an alarm clock: upon hearing the new song, Bertha explains how she "was unable to sleep the whole night, all [her] thoughts of the past came back."[88] Like the dog's bark and Walther's utterance of the dog's name, the song carries Bertha back to her singular transgression, not allowing her to forget. A single line in the new song also points forward, beyond even the end of Bertha's childhood narrative: "O dich gereut." This phrase, meaning something like "Oh repent," is enigmatic, since the previous phrase, "How far away you are [*Wie liegst du weit*]," appears to address "Waldeinsamkeit" in the informal "du" form. Although it makes sense that the feeling of forest solitude might now be distant for the bird, how

---

86 Tieck, *Schriften*, 139; "Eckbert," 27.
87 Derrida, *L'animal*, 165; *Animal*, 120.
88 Tieck, *Schriften*, 139; "Eckbert," 27.

2.4 Waldeinsamkeit – Wiederhörbarkeit — 97

can *Waldeinsamkeit* be repentant or rueful?[89] Does the "du" pronoun now refer to Bertha when the bird sings, "O dich gereut"? Whatever the phrase means in the song, the word "reuen" returns almost immediately, but only *after* Bertha finishes narrating her childhood story. As if to pacify his friend Walther, who sat patiently throughout Bertha's narrative, Eckbert hastily adds after she is done, "[Bertha] seemed to me like a miracle, and my love for her was beyond measure. I had no possessions of my own, but I came to this fortune through her love, and we made our home here. Not for a single moment have we had cause to *rue* our union [*hat uns bis jetzt noch keinen Augenblick* gereut]" (emphasis mine).[90] Within the next three sentences, they all get up, wish each other a good night, and Walther mentions the name, Strohmian. But "reuen" returns: "Also Walther went to bed, leaving Eckbert pacing uneasily up and down the room. 'How foolish one can be!' he said to himself. 'It was I who suggested that my wife should tell her story and now I *regret* having trusted Walther so completely! [*und jetzt* gereut *mich diese Vertraulichkeit!*]" (emphasis mine).[91] The word "gereut," making its first appearance only when the bird sings a second time during Bertha's narrative, functions in a similar way to Walther's utterance of the name "Strohmian": it echoes far beyond the limits of its own context, sounding out in its own ambiguity but also foreshadowing and even framing Eckbert's first moment of regret since he married Bertha. If ever there is a "contagious transference," it occurs not between the bird and Bertha's unconscious, nor even necessarily between the bird and its owner, Walther *die Alte*. Rather, the echoing word functions contagiously at the linguistic level, disrupting both the narrative and temporal boundaries between Bertha's supposedly self-contained childhood story and the tale that Tieck continues beyond it. The "contagious transfer" of *reuen* that breaks down narrative boundaries between the bird, Bertha and Eckbert thus functions the way character names echo each other and, in the process, destabilize any apparently individual identities.

This breakdown of both narrative structure and character identity is accomplished through repetitions that, as we have seen, work at the level of words and names. Liliane Weissberg comes to a similar conclusion in her article, which is fittingly entitled, "Repetitions":

> Repetition becomes a substantial linguistic problem, in that the name [Strohmian] is no arbitrary word. It is not so much a carrier of identity than a trigger; its articulation constitutes identities anew, while they once appeared seemingly established. Its articulation

---

[89] The German verb, "reuen," now antiquated, is etymologically related to the English "rue."
[90] Tieck, *Schriften*, 140; "Eckbert," 28.
[91] Tieck, *Schriften*, 140; "Eckbert," 28.

puts the plot into action. The repeated name accomplishes a process similar to Freud's notion of becoming conscious [translation mine].[92]

Typically, that which is repeated and articulated tends to constitute and stabilize meanings, memories, and identities. The problem in Tieck's "Eckbert" is that the comparison between a "mark" and its repetition – words like *gereut*, the name *Strohmian*, and the dog's bark – becomes no longer tenable; that is to say, the comparison to its "earlier occurrence" disrupts rather than reinforces identity and continuity. Repetition in Tieck's "Eckbert" is repetition without equality, blurring boundaries rather than establishing them by making things identifiable.

More than either of the two earlier variations, the third and final version of the bird's song thematizes such repetition and return. Just as the *munteres Bellen* recalls the first time the dog was heard by the young Bertha, the final version of the song describes the bird's return to happiness, to a place apparently free of sorrow and envy:

Waldeinsamkeit
Mich wieder freut,
Mir geschieht kein Leid,
Hier wohnt kein Neid,
Von neuem mich freut
Waldeinsamkeit.[93]

This happiness is of course congruent with the mental state of neither Eckbert nor Bertha, unconscious or otherwise. There are many ways to interpret this final variation of the bird song, but it is clear that the bird is imparting joy at the return to a place from which it was once forcibly taken. Much like the function of a coda in music, it repeats the beginning in order to bind the piece into a single whole; in returning to the place where it once was at the beginning of the story (i.e., within Bertha's narrative), it seems to close the circle. But in closing the circle, it also closes the net around Eckbert: just as the bird was once bound to the cage, it now binds Eckbert to his own "horrifying loneliness," a cage from which he can never escape.

While the final song thematizes a return to that which has been, the last sentence of the story once again involves a repetition without closure: "Eckbert lay on the ground, crazed and dying [*wahnsinnig und verscheidend*]; stupefied and bewildered, he heard the old woman talking, the dog barking, and the bird's

---

[92] Weissberg, "Wiederholungen," 185.
[93] Tieck, *Schriften*, 145.

song repeating [*den Vogel sein Lied wiederholen*]." (translation mine).[94] What is interesting about the scholarship that comments on this last sentence is that, while everyone addresses the final sonic environment that Eckbert seems to drown in, few offer a convincing reason for Tieck's emphasis on sound in the first place. John Ellis points out, for instance, that the sounds produce "confusion in [Eckbert's] mind; the physical world has no clear orientation points for him anymore. [. . .] these sounds in the final words of the story [. . .] suggest the final slipping away of all contact with the outside world."[95] But how is it possible to deduce the "physical world" from anything else, especially in a story like "Eckbert"? Liliane Weissberg also comments on the final sentence as follows: "Any silence, the stillness of the *Waldeinsamkeit*, is broken here, not only through the word, but through the word heard repeatedly."[96] Although Weissberg emphasizes the repeated word as *heard*, she does not say why it is important to hear it as opposed to reading it. Finally, Thomas Fries seems to avoid the problem altogether: "Whether [Eckbert] 'really' heard the dog and the bird, and really saw the old woman, peu importe!"[97] Fries is right: it is not important at all whether Eckbert "really" hears the old woman speak, the dog bark, and the bird repeat its song because there is, in a sense, nothing "real" about Eckbert's hearing *as* a sense. Whether heard in reality or not, what is important is neither the actuality of the sounds nor the "slipping away" of the outside world, but rather the *possibility* of the sounds' continued repetition beyond the existence of Bertha and Eckbert, beyond Bertha's narrative, and indeed reverberating beyond the end of Tieck's story. What is important, in terms of iterability, is not the sounds' actuality but their *Wiederhörbarkeit*, their possibility of being forever heard over and over.

In order to further clarify this relation between repetition and sound at the end of Tieck's "Eckbert," let us return to the notion of *déjà entendu*, especially the way Benjamin describes it in *Berlin Chronicle*: as "a sound that seems to have been heard somewhere in the darkness of a past life."[98] Notice first the use of a Bloch's "darkness" here. But second, this is a past life that is at once foreign to Eckbert – Bertha's childhood experience – and yet absolutely familiar, since he is not only Bertha's husband and brother, but carries her name within his own, Eck-*bert*. Like the structure of the *déjà entendu*, the acoustical

---

[94] Tieck, *Schriften*, 146. Unlike the Taylor translation, I prefer to translate the verbs into their gerund form in order to suggest the continuation of these sounds echoing through eternity.
[95] John M. Ellis, "Tieck: 'Der blonde Eckbert,'" in *Narration in the German Novelle: Theory and Interpretation*, by John M. Ellis (London: Cambridge University Press, 1974), 92.
[96] Weissberg, "Wiederholungen," 191.
[97] Fries, "'Ein romantisches Märchen,'" 1202.
[98] Benjamin, *GS* 6:518 [*WuN* 11.1:77]; *SW* 2:634.

unconscious always functions within a certain logic of repetition, of repeating sounds. But instead of a repetition that establishes a unified self-consciousness, the repetition of the acoustical unconscious disperses rather than fixes meaning, amplifies the foreign elements of what is heard with only half an ear, and makes strangely familiar what at first might sound completely foreign, as is the case with Eckbert.

In differentiating between Freud's looking and Bertha's listening, let me conclude this chapter by comparing Freud's rebus (*Bilderrätsel*) with the notion of "imagistic dissonance" (*Bilddissonanz*). This latter term, coined by Benjamin in another context altogether,[99] poses an alternative to Freud's rebus in that it offers a description of what goes on in the dissolution of identity and at the breaking of place.[100] The fact that "dissonance" involves "an inharmonious or harsh sound or combination of sounds"[101] only makes the term more relevant to the "sound images" that echo throughout "Eckbert." This is not to say that the sounds themselves are dissonant, but rather that they have the effect of generating structural dissonance upon the narrative, distorting meaning, time and any previously established distinction between characters. While Freud seeks out syllabic consonance between words and word parts, the words, names and sounds in Tieck's "Eckbert" all resound dissonantly, and we are left, like both Eckbert and the poor composer Nerval that began this chapter, riddled with sound and with no way out.

The next chapter takes up the acoustical unconscious in terms of radio by turning to both Benjamin's and Rudolf Arnheim's reflections on the medium. With the introduction of regional radio broadcasting in Germany in October 1923, radio was becoming increasingly ubiquitous throughout Germany during the Weimar Republic and became even more so with the National Socialist takeover of the radio industry only ten years later. While at first glance there may appear to be little in common between this chapter and the next, a number of threads link the unconscious as it has been examined in this chapter to the way the acoustical unconscious will be approached in the following two chapters on radio. For one, Benjamin's particular version of the unconscious is, as we have seen, closely aligned with his theory of forgetting: just as that which is forgotten

---

99 For Benjamin's reference to *Bilddissonanz*, see "Two Poems by Friedrich Hölderlin [*Zwei Gedichte von Friedrich Hölderlin*]" (Benjamin, *GS* 2:117; *SW* 1:29). Samuel Weber (*Benjamin's -abilities*, 279) refers to this term.

100 Weber notes that, like "rhythm, which it echoes, ['the dissonance of the image'] involves sameness without self, repetition without equality" (Weber, *Benjamin's -abilities*, 279).

101 "Dissonance," *Oxford English Dictionary*, 2nd ed. (Oxford: Oxford University Press, 1989) (hereafter, *OED*), s.v.

is not just individual, Benjamin's version of the unconscious is never strictly limited to the psyche of a single individual, but is "shared," so to speak. Whether it is a receptacle of the forgotten that Kafka learns about by listening, a conch that emits sounds that cannot otherwise be representable, or a forgotten glove or reticule left in the home that suddenly "let us infer that a stranger had been there" (translation modified)[102] – words, objects and sounds *von fremder Seite* are necessary foreign elements that allow the unconscious to bleed through into human consciousness. As we shall see, a number of Benjamin's fictional persona in the two radio plays for children, *The Cold Heart* and *Bustle about Kasperl*, need also be reminded by strangers of what was forgotten. These strangers "speak" to us in a way that we could not otherwise imagine, that catches us off-guard, but that nevertheless tells us something fundamental about ourselves. This is what Kasperl experiences at the end of *Bustle about Kasperl*: the recording and play-back of his voice not only catches him off-guard, revealing a fragment of his own existence, but it even forces him to conclude that he now has heard "what radio is." The estranged voice that speaks back at the end of *Bustle about Kasperl* echoes how that "other nature" of the camera speaks to the eye differently than our own. And like that "other nature" of the camera, or the unique sounds in the conch shell, the radio also allows for the *possibility* of not only hearing words and things, but even ourselves, otherwise.

---

[102] The phrase comes from Benjamin's *Berlin Chronicle,* cited in Chapter One (Benjamin, *GS* 6:518–519; *SW* 2:634–635).

3 Voices Carry: Benjamin and Arnheim on Radio

Between 1927 and 1933, Walter Benjamin worked for Radio Berlin and Radio Frankfurt, writing for and sometimes delivering via radio roughly eighty or ninety broadcasts.[1] He wrote a myriad of texts, from literary radio talks to a series of "radio stories for children," a few radio plays, and even some short radio dialogues he referred to as "Hörmodelle." He also reflected on the medium in a few short texts, most of which were published during his lifetime. But in his unpublished, two-page exegesis, "Reflections on Radio" ("Reflexionen zum Rundfunk," 1931), Benjamin is, among other things, concerned with how radio has not been properly heard because of the continued practice of distancing the practitioners from the listeners. He argues that the most important element of any cultural institution is that it gives its public the opportunity to become experts by virtue of its forms and techniques (*kraft seiner Formen, seiner Technik*). Instead of being given the chance to react critically, the radio public has been converted into "dull, inarticulate masses – the 'public' in the narrower sense of the word that has neither yardsticks for its judgment nor a language for its sentiments."[2] During this short diatribe against the present state of the medium, he compares it to other cultural institutions like theater and film: "There has never been another genuine cultural institute that has failed to authenticate itself by taking advantage of its forms or technology – using them to *awaken* [erweckt] in the public a new expertise" (emphasis mine; translation modified).[3] In Harvard's

---

[1] See Lecia Rosenthal's excellent overview of Benjamin's relatively short engagement with radio in her introduction to Walter Benjamin, *Radio Benjamin*, ed. Lecia Rosenthal, trans. Jonathan Lutes (London/New York: Verso, 2014). Rosenthal not only references the small pool of scholarship on Benjamin's radio work, including Sabine Schiller-Lerg's seminal *Walter Benjamin und der Rundfunk* (Munich: K. G. Saur, 1984), but also gives reasons why Benjamin's radio texts have historically been overlooked by both media theorists and Benjamin scholars alike. See also the massive two-volume set, 9.1 and 9.2, of Walter Benjamin's *Werke und Nachlass: Kritische Gesamtausgabe* (Frankfurt a.M.: Suhrkamp, 2008–) (hereafter, *WuN*), which for the first time collects all of Benjamin's radio work into a single volume. At just under 950 pages, volume 9.2 includes all drafts, edits and both typewritten and handwritten corrections for every text, allowing scholars to see what the editors of *Werke und Nachlass* refer to as Benjamin's "processuality" (*Prozeßhaftigkeit*) of the texts he wrote and revised for and about radio.

[2] Walter Benjamin, *Gesammelte Schriften* (Frankfurt a.M.: Suhrkamp, 1972) (hereafter, *GS*), 2:1506 [*WuN* 9.1:531]; Walter Benjamin, *Selected Writings*, ed. Michael W. Jennings, Marcus Bullock, Howard Eiland, and Gary Smith, trans. Rodney Livingstone and Edmund Jephcott (Cambridge: Harvard University Press, 1996–2003) (hereafter, *SW*), 2:544.

[3] Benjamin, *GS* 2:1506 [*WuN* 9.1:531]; *SW* 2:544.

English translation of this sentence, "erweckt" is mistranslated as "created."[4] In light of the previous chapter and Benjamin's fascination with *awakening* – its relation to the body and consciousness in writers like Proust, Tieck and Bloch, among others – it is difficult to take his use of the word lightly. Radio, for Benjamin at least, has the same potential as film and theater to verify or authenticate itself (*sich beglaubigen*) by allowing the public to *awaken* to its forms and techniques (*Technik*). Every cultural institution involves a process whereby the public, awakened in such a manner, learns to judge it. Critique derives from such awakening.

In order to awaken the public to radio's forms and techniques, Benjamin is specific: "it would not be at all easy to circumscribe (*zu umschreiben*) the behavior of the voice (*das Benehmen der Stimme*) in relation to language – for this is what is involved" (translation mine).[5] The Harvard translation of the phrase, "to describe the way the voice relates to the language used," erases the care with which Benjamin wrote this sentence.[6] Two important elements stand out: the first is the nominalization that Benjamin attaches to the voice, "das *Benehmen der Stimme*," the "behavior" or "comportment" of the voice.[7] By altering Benjamin's reference to the voice from a subjective genitive – from *das Benehmen* der *Stimme* – to a direct object, "the voice," the English translation misleads us into thinking that "the voice" can be directly approached or "described." A few sentences earlier, Benjamin explains why it is so easy for listeners to turn off the radio:

> It is the voice, the diction, the language (*die Diktion, die Sprache*) – in a word, the technical and formal side of the matter, which so frequently make the most desirable programs unbearable for the listener. Conversely, for the same reason but very rarely, programs that might seem totally irrelevant can hold the listener spellbound. (There are speakers who one listens to even for the weather report.) [translation modified].[8]

Benjamin is already not speaking about just the voice, but also diction and language. It was of course already a common trope at the time to describe how radio, and then sound film, brought with it a renewed interest in and attention to the "materiality" of the voice, which for many offered an alternative mode of

---

4 In *Radio Benjamin*, Jonathan Lutes translates "erweckt" as "inculcated" (Benjamin, *Radio Benjamin*, 363).
5 Benjamin, *GS* 2:1507 [*WuN* 9.1:532–533].
6 Benjamin, *GS* 2:1507 [*WuN* 9.1:532–533]; *SW* 2, 544.
7 In the *Werke und Nachlass* volume, it appears that Benjamin first wrote "das Verhalten der Stimme" but then crossed the first word out and wrote "Benehmen" instead (Benjamin, *WuN* 9.1:532).
8 Benjamin, *GS* 2:1507 [*WuN* 9.1:532]; *SW* 2:544.

meaning that was categorially different to what words themselves supposedly mean. Benjamin gestures in this direction with the phrase, "das Benehmen der Stimme," but with it also distances himself both from any reference to materiality in the phenomenological sense and from the Romantic impulse, found in writers such as Rousseau, Novalis and Herder, to return to that *Urzeit* when language was more musical.

We know little about Benjamin's thoughts concerning the voice in general, but in the opening pages of the *Trauerspiel* book he aligns voice with gesture when distinguishing between speech and prose: a speaker uses voice and gesture to construct an "often vacillating and vague train of thought [*Gedankengange*], as if projecting a signifying sketch [*andeutende Zeichnung*] in a single stroke" (translation modified).[9] A speaker's voice carries the listener away – we travel with the voice (*mitreisen*), are enthralled by it (*begeistert*) – from the contemplative mode of presentation, which is more dominant in the written word and, for Benjamin at least, the only style suitable for philosophical reflection. Voice and gesture in speech are like the expansive and constant waves of the sea, in distinction to the broken, rocky shoreline of the written word. We should thus think of Benjamin's *Benehmen* of the voice not simply as its "comportment," but also in terms of its root verb, *nehmen*, to take: the verb, *benehmen*, is not simply what one "takes away" from the voice as expressive, but also names a process through which the listener is taken away from being able to fully contemplate what is being said. Voice, much like the constant flow of images in cinema, can make the listener dazed or stupefied; in a word, *benommen*. Duden's *Etymological Dictionary* defines "benommen" as "actually 'the revoking of consciousness.'"[10] Unable to remain conscious of all that passes, the listener is taken up and carried away by a voice's "com-portment," its taking-with, much like how the young Benjamin, in putting his head between the two telephone receivers, was ruthlessly put at the mercy of the telephonic voice. "Comportment" then refers not to a collection of properties that identify, characterize or essentialize the voice. Rather, Benjamin's reference to the voice's "comportment" involves, on the one hand, this "taking" up of the listener's consciousness. But just as importantly, "comportment" must also be read alongside his reflections on gesture, for such taking or carrying-with is consistent with gesture's etymological

---

9 Benjamin, *GS* 1:209; Walter Benjamin, *Origin of the German Trauerspiel*, trans. Howard Eiland (Cambridge: Harvard University Press, 2019) (hereafter, *OGT*), 3–4.
10 "Schwindlig, betäubt (eigentlich 'dem Bewußtsein entzogen')." See "nehmen," in *Das Herkunftswörterbuch, Etymologie der deutschen Sprache*, 2nd ed., ed. Günther Drowsdowski (Mannheim: Dudenverlag, 1989), 7:483.

roots, *gerere* or *gestum*, designating the action of bearing or carrying. Benjamin's *Benehmen der Stimme* thus suggests the com-porting or demeanor – from *se demener:* to carry or conduct oneself – of the voice, that is, the gestural conduct of the voice, or vocalic gestures (*Stimmgebärden*). We will return to Benjamin's link between voice and gesture later in this chapter.

But is it possible to describe or explain this comportment of the voice? Let us return to the sentence in *Reflections on Radio*: "It would not be at all easy to circumscribe (*zu umschreiben*) the comportment of the voice (*das Benehmen der Stimme*) in relation to language – for this is what is involved" (translation mine).[11] The Harvard translation renders the verb as "to describe,"[12] but *umschreiben* is anything but an explicit description: one cannot describe the voice's comportment precisely because it does not refer to a series of properties that characterize or identify it. Rather, the comportment of the voice must be "circumscribed," encircled. How is that possible? Benjamin gives no further clues in "Reflections on Radio" about how to begin such a task. But let us return once more to the "Epistemo-Critical Preface," where Benjamin discusses the idea: "As the shaping of a complex in which the singular-extreme stands with its like, the idea is circumscribed."[13] Interestingly, Benjamin uses the same verb, *umschreiben*, when discussing both the idea and the comportment of the voice. Despite both being related to a kind of complex or arrangement that "affirms the uniqueness of a certain singularity,"[14] it would be a mistake to subsume the voice under Benjamin's specific notion of idea, because the idea is much more closely aligned with the word, specifically the word-as-symbol, as Weber concisely puts it:

> This is why the "idea" can only be "circumscribed" – *umschrieben* – but never simply *beschrieben*, described. For the idea is not simply visible or describable, except perhaps in the literal sense of writing and language: "The Idea belongs to language, namely, in

---

11 Benjamin, *GS* 2:1507 [*WuN* 9.1:532–533].
12 In *Radio Benjamin*, Jonathan Lutes retains the "behavior of the voice." But I would hesitate to translate *umschreiben* as "to adapt" (Benjamin, *Radio Benjamin*, 364) as Lutes does, since it implies that the voice's comportment would in some way have to adapt to the language. This raises the question: what is the nature of the relationship between language and the voice's behavior? Benjamin's answer, as we shall see in section three, involves gesture.
13 "Als Gestaltung des Zusammenhanges, in dem das Einmalig-Extreme mit seinesgleichen steht, ist die Idee umschrieben" (Benjamin, *GS* 1:215). I follow Samuel Weber's translation in *Benjamin's -abilities* (Cambridge: Harvard University Press, 2008), 8, since both official English translations render *umschreiben* as either "explained" (Walter Benjamin, *The Origin of German Tragic Drama*, trans. John Osborne [London: New Left Books, 1977], 35) or "described" (Benjamin, *OGT* 11).
14 Weber, *Benjamin's -abilities* 8.

the essence of the word it is in each case that moment in which the word is symbol [*Die Idee ist ein Sprachliches, und zwar im Wesen des Wortes jeweils dasjenige Moment, in welchem es Symbol ist*]."[15]

The idea is "something linguistic (*ist ein Sprachliches*)," it "belongs to language."[16] As such, the idea is constitutive of that second half of the task that Benjamin prescribes in *Reflections on Radio*: what is involved is circumscribing the comportment of the voice *in relation to language* (*im Verhältnis zur Sprache*). This last phrase does not simply refer to the language used, such as German, French or any other, but rather to the essence of the word whereby at any given moment it is a symbol. This word-as-symbol, moreover, is something that can be "heard" or perceived, albeit not empirically, for in the very next sentence after defining the idea, Benjamin writes:

> In empirical listening (*empirischem Vernehmen*), in which words have been disintegrated (*sich zersetzt*), there attaches to them, along with their more or less hidden symbolic side, an overt, profane meaning. It is the concern of the philosopher, through staging (*Darstellung*), to reestablish in its primacy the symbolic character of the word [. . .]. Since philosophy may not presume to speak in tones of revelation, this can happen only though a remembering that goes back first of all to original listening (*Urvernehmen*) [translation modified].[17]

We should not confuse the task of the philosopher here with the task of awakening the listening public to radio's forms and techniques. But already in what Benjamin calls here empirical listening, the "more or less hidden symbolic side" of words still remain attached, despite the words' disintegration and their adherence to overt meaning. The question becomes whether words can potentially echo that "more or less hidden symbolic side" beyond the realm of philosophy, that is to say, whether a certain staging of them can elicit an originary listening/perceiving linked to remembering. One such staging are the words as sounds in the "Mummerehlen" fragment of *Berlin Childhood*. One could also argue that Benjamin plays around with the staging of words in his radio work, especially in his two *Hörspiele für Kinder*, that is, "hearing plays" or even "listening games" for children, experimental playgrounds for such a staging of words to be heard.

The present chapter is divided into two parts. The first half focuses on the radio theory of the contemporaneous media theorist, Rudolph Arnheim. As we have already seen in Chapter One, Benjamin cites a passage about slow motion

---

15 Weber, *Benjamin's -abilities* 8.
16 Benjamin, *GS* 1:216; *OGT* 13.
17 Benjamin, *GS* 1:216–217; *OGT* 14. See also the opening pages of the Introduction.

from Arnheim's *Film as Art* (1932) in the last version of the artwork essay. However, it is unlikely that Benjamin ever read Arnheim's short reflections on radio, which the latter began publishing sporadically between 1927 and 1933, the same years Benjamin worked in radio. The latter would also certainly have never had the opportunity to read Arnheim's next book-length project, *Radio as Aural Art (Rundfunk als Hörkunst)*, which he completed while exiled in Italy after 1933, but which was only published for the first time in its original German in 1979. In *Radio as Aural Art*, Arnheim is as interested as Benjamin in the comportment of the voice, even if he does not quite "describe" it in like manner. Arnheim is also concerned with the receptive conditions of the radio listener in his penultimate chapter, "The Psychology of the Radio Listener." While Arnheim's extra-formalist considerations will become an exception to his later approach to both media and art in general, it nevertheless coincides with Benjamin's similar emphasis on the radio listener's receptivity, including the hopes for "awakening" the listeners' expertise.[18] By analyzing both Arnheim's formalist discussion of voice and sound in radio as well as his reflections on the psychology of the radio listener, it will be possible to see the extent to which Benjamin and Arnheim's reflections on radio complement each other, where they part ways, and what elements of their radio theory might inspire thinking toward an acoustical unconscious specific to an acoustic medium like radio.

In the second half of this chapter, I will focus on some of Benjamin's own work for radio. Having given his first broadcast on 23 March 1927, Benjamin already noted in a letter to Gershom Scholem in February 1925 that he had a friend in broadcasting, Ernst Schoen, who was "able to put in a good word" for

---

18 Arnheim has been typified as the German formalist of classical film theory, and often in stark contrast to his contemporary, the "social critic," realist and author of *Theory of Film* (1960), Siegfried Kracauer (see in particular Eric Rentschler's "Rudolf Arnheim's Early Passage between Social and Aesthetic Film Criticism," in *Arnheim for Film and Media Studies*, ed. Scott Higgins [New York: Routledge 2011], 51–68). Foregrounding some of the major differences between Arnheim's *Film als Kunst* in 1932 and its English adaptation in 1957, Rentschler suggests that "it might be more accurate to say that Arnheim *repressed* (rather than *resolved*) the tensions posed by the social and historical incentives of his early writings" (Rentschler, *Film and Media Studies*, 65). Much recent scholarship attempts to reconstruct Arnheim's (somewhat self-imposed) image of the rigid formalist of film and media criticism in an attempt to understand why he might have "repressed" the social and political aspects of his early work, including his reflections on radio. See Shawn Vancour's essay, "Arnheim on Radio: *Materialtheorie* and Beyond," in the same volume (*Arnheim for Film and Media Studies*, ed. Scott Higgins [New York: Routledge, 2011], 178–194), which is primarily concerned with these extra-formalist tendencies in Arnheim's radio work.

him.[19] Despite his radio work giving him a much-needed and often consistent source of income, Benjamin regularly dismissed it as having no value, which is perhaps one reason why Benjamin scholars have routinely ignored it.[20] But in his letter to Gershom Scholem dated 28 February 1933, while disparaging his radio work once again as being "of no interest except in economic terms," Benjamin singles out his radio play, *Bustle about Kasperl* (*Radau um Kasperl*, 1932), stating that it is notable "from a technical point of view perhaps."[21] The final section of this chapter will focus on how Benjamin was explicitly playing with voices and experimenting with the aural in/of language in two of his many but often overlooked radio plays from 1932, *The Cold Heart* (*Das kalte Herz*) and *Bustle about Kasperl*.

3.1 Materiality and Expression in Arnheim's (Radio) Art

In the opening pages of *Radio as Aural Art*, Arnheim is clear about his overall project: to make conscious a new aural education through wireless. In this he appears in alignment with Benjamin's hope for the awakening of the public to radio's forms and techniques. For Arnheim, however, this new education of the ear

> does not consist only of training our ear to recognize sounds, so that it can distinguish the hissing of a snake from that of steam [..]. But it is more important that we should get a feeling [*Gefühl*] for the musical in natural sounds; that we should feel ourselves back in that primeval age [*Urzeit*] where the word was still sound, the sound still word.[22]

---

19 Rosenthal, citing Scholem, in Benjamin, *Radio Benjamin*, xviii. For a much more thorough biographical overview of Benjamin's radio years, see Rosenthal's introduction in Benjamin, *Radio Benjamin*, esp. xviii–xix.
20 Rosenthal in Benjamin, *Radio Benjamin*, xvii–xx.
21 Walter Benjamin and Theodor Adorno, *Adorno & Benjamin: The Complete Correspondence, 1928–1940*, trans. N. Walker (Cambridge: Harvard University Press, 1999), 403–404. See also Rosenthal in Benjamin, *Radio Benjamin*, xx. Jonathan Lutes creatively translates Benjamin's title as "Much Ado about Kasperl," but I have chosen to retain the reference to noise that "Radau" implies: a racket, banging, crashing, hubbub or bustle. I have also chosen "bustle" for a number of reasons: it often comes with the preposition, "about" (as in, "what's all this bustle about?") and the German *um* can mean both "around" and "about." The word also connotes not simply "noisy activity and movement," but also "a pretense of haste intended to confuse the victim when borrowing or begging for money; *on the bustle*: by means of this or a similar fraud. Cf. 'hustle'" (*Oxford English Dictionary*, 2nd ed. [Oxford: Oxford University Press, 1989] [hereafter, *OED*], s.v.). Both noise and confusion abound in *The Bustle about Kasperl*.
22 Rudolph Arnheim, *Rundfunk als Hörkunst und weitere Aufsätze zum Hörfunk* (Frankfurt a.M.: Suhrkamp, 2001), 26–27; Rudolph Arnheim, *Radio*, trans. Margaret Ludwig and Herbert Read (London: Faber & Faber, 1933), 35.

Arnheim unapologetically adopts a clearly phonocentric approach to language as derived from German Romantic theories of art, sharing Novalis's goal of rediscovering the musical "in sound and speech," which Arnheim writes is "one of the greatest artistic tasks of radio."[23] His reference to Novalis illustrates just how important the Romantic tradition for Arnheim was to the artistic potential of this budding medium called radio. Arnheim was certainly not the first to claim that radio would help revive the Romantic project of returning the voice to its previous musical magnificence, but he was certainly among those who hailed it as such.[24]

Adopting Novalis's claim for rediscovering the music of language via radio is just one example that illustrates Arnheim tendency to evaluate the new media of reproducibility primarily in terms of traditional forms of art, a tendency that Benjamin criticizes and works against throughout his reflections on both film and radio. But what makes Arnheim useful for the present study is that he does not simply fall back on Romantic theories of music and language, adopting their vocabulary whole-cloth and with it the phonocentric hopes of reviving a supposedly more musically or sonically-attuned primeval age. Arnheim's initial title for his radio book was *Radio in Search of its Form* (*Rundfunk sucht seine Form*), a title he had used earlier for one of his many short texts on radio. What this title reveals is that Arnheim, much like Benjamin, was searching for form, a form that only radio could offer. Although we should turn a deaf ear neither to his traditionalist impulses nor to his Gestaltist premises, Arnheim's search for radio's form led him to both an idiosyncratic definition of "materiality" in terms of the radiophonic voice, on the one hand, and to educating the distracted radio listener on the other. The latter will be reserved for the next section.

As was already mentioned, the rise of radio – and then sound film – brought with it a renewed interest in and attention to the "materiality" of the voice. For his part, Arnheim already called his own theory of film a *Materialtheorie*, but we should pause for a moment at his unique definition of "material," which Arnheim defines in the opening pages of *Film as Art*. His film theory is designed to "show that artistic and scientific descriptions of reality are cast in molds that derive not so much from the subject matter itself as from properties of the medium –

---

23 Arnheim, *Rundfunk*, 26–27; *Radio*, 35.
24 For an excellent overview of Arnheim's accord with his contemporaries, like Alfred Döblin und Arnold Zweig, who believed that radio would return to the literary genre that lost tonal language developed in the oral tradition, see Harro Zimmermann, "Kult der Anschauung – Blinder Funk. Nachbemerkungen zur Radiotheorie von Rudolf Arnheim," *Jahrbuch zur Kultur und Literatur der Weimarer Republik* 9 (2004): 225.

or *Material* – employed."[25] "Material" for Arnheim refers not to the things themselves but to the inherent properties of the medium being used. Put another way, it is the medium's specific properties that hypostatize its subject (into) matter. Arnheim's *Materialtheorie* is therefore always already a theory of medium and/as perception: what he means by "material" is less any phenomenological theory of things than the characteristics or properties made perceptible through the medium in question. And for Arnheim, radio was no exception. One may in fact adapt for radio a comment that Gertrud Koch originally formulated when referring to Arnheim's theory of film: his arguments "refer to the intrinsic structural laws of [radio]'s material aspect, not to the relationship between [radio] and reality."[26]

One way to think radio's "materiality" as Arnheim employs the term, comes close to the way Benjamin calls for writing around the comportment of the voice. Although Arnheim dedicates no single chapter to the voice, he nevertheless makes scattered references to it throughout the chapter, "In Praise of Blindness." The bulk of the chapter deals specifically with examples that illustrate the artistic advantage gained "from the 'defect' [*Manko*] of blindness."[27] His first group of examples, which includes aural surprise and the uncanny to sound-motifs and the careful foregrounding of "sound-scenery," all involve concrete, acoustical scenes that differ from visually constructed scenes, but which nevertheless can, according to Arnheim, be imagined visually. But he goes on to name and privilege a second group of examples, "in which the optical part [*optische Part*] not only weakens the effect but is also generally speaking impossible" (translation modified).[28] This second group, which might best be referred to as "pure radio images"[29] – acoustical images that allow no recourse to visual suggestion

---

25 Arnheim, cited by Noël Carroll, *Philosophical Problems of Classical Film Theory* (Princeton, NJ: Princeton University Press, 1988), 35.
26 See Gertrud Koch's article, "Rudolf Arnheim: The Materialist of Aesthetic Illusion – Gestalt Theory and Reviewer's Practice," *New German Critique* 51 (Autumn 1990): 170.
27 Arnheim, *Rundfunk*, 109; *Radio*, 171.
28 Arnheim, *Rundfunk*, 109; *Radio*, 172. It is much clearer in the German original that Arnheim's use of the word, "Part," is in reference to an instrumental or musical score, as in a partiture.
29 In an article entitled "The Visible, Invisible and Divisible: Thoughts on the Acoustic and Literary Image" (*Belgrade Journal of Media and Communications* 1 [2009]: 31–50), Samuel Weber writes about the radio image that "involves both the 'visibility of the invisible' and, inseparably linked to it, that of the 'invisibility of the visible'" (Weber, "Visible, Invisible and Divisible," 34). Arnheim's categorization presupposes there are certain radio images that cannot be visualized, that do not fall under the category of the "visibility of the invisible." Nevertheless, both Arnheim and Weber are interested in how the indeterminacy of the radio image (Arnheim calls it a "deficiency" in scare quotes) entails its greatest potential for effect.

or optical counterpoint – involve, for Arnheim at least, all symbolic figures and personifications, including the possibility of giving voice to inanimate objects. One of his main examples is Brecht's radio play, *Lindbergh Ballad*:

> All forces and characters are translated into voices – so that even inanimate objects play a part, and it makes a fine effect when, for instance, in Brecht's *Lindbergh Ballad* the airman contends with the Mist, the Snow-storm and Sleep, which try to frighten or lull him by their words. The physical struggle of the airman with the elements is transported to the sphere of words.[30]

The vocal representation of inanimate objects and natural forces, including animals and all other imaginary creatures who typically cannot speak, is a cross-cultural hallmark of radio drama that often gives it its fairy-tale like quality, hence the popularity of radio plays for children.

Another one of Arnheim's more interesting examples is when he describes various voice-types and their tonal interaction by suggesting that all human voices be categorized according to the musical instrument that sounds most similar to them. One may speak, for instance, "of flute- and cello- or of the trombone- or harp-voices. Then it would be clear what instrumental part would fall to the vocal character of the human voices in a sound-drama."[31] As preposterous as this may sound, it clearly illustrates the direction in which Arnheim wished to redefine the human voice in terms of radio: the radiophonic voice becomes less *human* and more *instrumental*, in the sense of an orchestra of "vocalic" instruments. As musical instrument, the voice becomes separated from its usual tendency to express a unifying self and becomes part of a larger orchestration of multiple tonalities and timbres.

On the one hand, Arnheim's treatment of the voice as instrument recalls Deleuze and Guattari's deterritorialization of the voice in *Thousand Plateaus*.[32]

---

30 Arnheim, *Rundfunk*, 115; *Radio*, 182. In his preface to the English reprint of 1971, Arnheim continues to refer to Brecht's *Lindbergh Ballad* as a formative example of "terse, poetical language that has become typical of many radio plays since" (Arnheim, *Radio*, 10–11).
31 Arnheim, *Rundfunk*, 28; *Radio*, 38.
32 "Music is a deterritorialization of the voice, which becomes less and less tied to language [. . .]. Voice and instrument are carried on the same plane in a relation that is sometimes one of confrontation, sometimes one of compensation, sometimes one of exchange and complementarity [. . .] a becoming-molecular in which the voice itself is instrumentalized – where the instruments speak no less than the voice, and the voice plays no less than the instrument" (Gilles Deleuze and Félix Guattari, *A Thousand Plateaus: Capitalism and Schizophrenia*, trans. Brian Massumi [Minneapolis: University of Minnesota Press, 1987], 96; see also 302–307). For a stimulating reading between the voice, becoming-insect, and music in Kafka's *Metamorphosis*, see Marcel Cobussen, "Music and Network: The Becoming Insect of Music," in *Music and Networking*, ed. T. Markovic and V. Mikic (Belgrade: University of the Arts, 2005), 19–27.

It is also helpful to think of timbre as one possible way of thinking radio's "material aspect," especially the way Jean-Luc Nancy examines it in *Listening* (*À l'écoute*, 2002). On defining timbre, Nancy first adopts Antoine Bonnet's two claims that timbre is both "the modern name for sound" and "the *real* of music."[33] Then Nancy adds a third definition: timbre is "sonorous matter, and sonorous matter is precisely what, while still remaining matter (voluminous and impenetrable: in the present case, rather strongly penetrating), spreads itself out in itself and resounds in (or from) its own spacing [*son propre espacement*]."[34] Leaving aside terms like resounding (*retenir*) and proper placement – terms that would require their own place in a more extended analysis of Nancy's philosophical concern with materiality – it is nevertheless helpful to pause at timbre as sonorous material, for Arnheim is equally concerned in both film and radio with "a new material world, just as material as the 'real' one."[35] Especially in the passage mentioned above concerning the radiophonic voice as orchestral instrument, Arnheim seems to be gesturing towards the sonorous "material" of timbre when he describes how the characterization of various instruments' timbres are equally attributable to human characteristics.[36] For Nancy, timbre opens "immediately onto the metaphor of other perceptual registers."[37] Because timbre cannot be fixed or contained by any one perceptual register, it resists closure and unity, and on this point Nancy is clear: "Timbre is above all the unity of a diversity that its unity does not reabsorb."[38] Timbre should therefore also be distinguished from consciousness because, as "the unity of a diversity," timbre works against any consciousness that posits and requires a unified self. If anything, timbre as "the unity of a diversity" is more in line with the unconscious, which challenges the unity of both consciousness and perception.

---

33 Jean-Luc Nancy, *À l'écoute* (Paris: Éditions Galilée, 2002), 76; Jean-Luc Nancy, *Listening*, trans. Charlotte Mandell (New York: Fordham University Press, 2007), 40. Unless otherwise noted, all English translations are taken from Nancy's *Listening*.
34 Nancy, *À l'écoute*, 77; *Listening*, 40.
35 Arnheim, *Rundfunk*, 122; *Radio*, 194.
36 Arnheim's passage continues as follows: "The 'character' of a sound conveys qualities which can be traced back to the structure of its source. In music one speaks of the 'vocal character' of instruments. The part each instrument plays in the piece of music is determined very essentially by its vocal character. There is the pomp, breadth and might of deep brass and the double bass; the bright, sharp force of the trumpet; the thin nasal woodwind; the versatility of the violin: soft vibrant singing, graceful agility. As we can see, these characteristics are most naturally described by the same terms that are used to denote human characteristics, and this is no mere chance" (Arnheim, *Rundfunk*, 28; *Radio*, 38).
37 Nancy, *À l'écoute*, 80; *Listening*, 42.
38 Nancy, *À l'écoute*, 79; *Listening*, 41.

This is supported by a fascinating footnote by Nancy, who cites Jules Lagneau in his *Course on Perception* (*Cours sur la perception*) as early as 1898 on timbre:

> Since it is not by a distinct act of mind that we compose the idea of timbre, it is perhaps not true to call it perception; perceiving timbre, we measure nothing [..] Intensity and timbre are immediate sensations, in which we can note complexity only by using external analysis. There is something ultimate there for consciousness.[39]

Because becoming conscious of timbre is not simply "perceiving" it, it is hard to say whether one is ever fully "conscious" of timbre in the first place. As an "immediate sensation" it passes through consciousness and, as Herder already revealed, is the human experience of sound: "it is the concept to which we must turn to describe the immediacies of how sounds strike our ears, how they affect us."[40] Parroting Lagneau, there is perhaps something ultimate here for the acoustical unconscious: timbre is akin to both the non-discursive sonority of language with which we began and, as we shall see later in this chapter, the gestural quality of the voice as Benjamin examines it. Resisting closure, timbre equally rebuffs signification – it is as uniquely expressive as it is capable of mimesis.[41] Put another way, timbre is, like Benjamin's comportment of the voice, neither simply hearable nor describable, but can only be circumscribed – *umschrieben*: it surrounds us while being semantically impenetrable; or as Lagneau writes, in perceiving it, "we measure nothing." Arnheim's insistence on orchestrating human voices into instruments in his *Radio* book is one way to think how attention to timbre is amplified via radio and hypostatized into sonorous matter, so long as we maintain Arnheim's *Materialtheorie* that defines matter not as phenomenologically grounded but as properties made perceptible, perhaps for the first time, by the intrinsic structural laws of the medium in question.

Another theoretical tool that appears both related to and expands upon his *Materialtheorie* is what Arnheim explicitly calls the "expressive quality" of objects. In *Film as Art*, Arnheim employed an explicit theory of expression, which he revealed in a late essay called, "On the Nature of Photography" (1974): "The

---

39 Lagneau, cited by Nancy, *À l'écoute*, 78; *Listening*, 83.
40 Emily I. Dolan, *The Orchestral Revolution: Haydn and the Technologies of Timbre* (Cambridge: Cambridge University Press, 2013), 88. For an excellent analysis about how the burgeoning discourse around timbre in the eighteenth century not only coincided with the birth of the aesthetic but "*was* the birth of the aesthetic" (Dolan, *Orchestral Revolution*, 88), see her chapter two, "The Idea of Timbre."
41 See Dolan's discussion about the sonority of the glass harmonica as not only an approximation but the ideal version of the human voice (Dolan, *Orchestral Revolution*, 61–65): "Underlying such comparisons is the idea of mimesis" (Dolan, *Orchestral Revolution*, 64).

strategy [in *Film as Art*] was therefore to describe the differences between the images we obtain when we look at the physical world and the images perceived on the motion picture screen. *The differences could then be shown to be a source of artistic expression*" (emphasis original).[42] As Noël Carroll has convincingly argued, the expressive qualities of film singled out by Arnheim are specifically those that develop out of the creative use of the *limitations* of the medium in question.[43] But like his notion of materiality, Arnheim conceives of expression as something quite different from its phenomenological definition:

> To see the expression of an object means to see the general dynamic characteristics inherent in its particular appearance. In a functional-looking object, we may see the dynamics of pouring, soaring, containing, receiving, etc. We also see such "character traits" as flexibility, sturdiness, gracefulness, strength, etc., which, just as in a representational work of fine art, are intimately and totally related to the theme: the gracefulness of the spout consists in the graceful pouring it displays visually; the sturdiness of the Doric column consists in its supporting the roof sturdily. Expressive properties are adverbial, not adjectival. They apply to *the behavior of things*, not the things themselves [emphasis mine].[44]

Arnheim's theory of expression should be thought in terms of his *Materialtheorie*, that is, as referring less to any static, "material" aspect of a thing than to the dynamic process of adverbial expression, to its expressive properties or "behavior," given to it by the particular medium in question.

Arnheim's divergence from any strict phenomenological reading of *Material* is, moreover, consistent with Benjamin's own use of the term on at least one point: for both critics, the "materiality" of objects is never separable from its signifying structure. The crucial difference between Arnheim and Benjamin lies in the very mode of signifying. Signification for Arnheim arises *directly* from expressive qualities that are universally transferable from and immediately present in an object's (or artwork's) "material" and functional traits. This

---

42 Rudolph Arnheim, "On the Nature of Photography," in *New Essays on the Psychology of Art*, by Rudolph Arnheim (Berkeley: University of California Press, 1986), 108.
43 See Carroll, *Philosophical Problems*, esp. chap. 1, "Cinematic Expression: Rudolf Arnheim and the Aesthetics of Silent Film," 17–91. Arnheim begins with his deficiency principle which then leads him to artistic expression: by stating that nothing is "deficient" and everything is there, the subsequent task is to exploit these apparent "limitations" and make them "a source of artistic expression" unique to the medium in question. A number of scholars have explored the inherent limitations of and offered possible solutions to Arnheim's own paradigm of expression. See Koch, "Materialist of Aesthetic Illusion," 177–178. Koch cites Noël Carroll, as well as Nelson Goodman and Catherine Elgin, when discussing the paradigm of expression in Arnheim's theory of art.
44 Rudolph Arnheim, "Function to Expression," in *Toward a Psychology of Art: Collected Essays* (Berkeley: University of California Press, 1994), 208.

becomes a central tenant in his later book, *Toward a Psychology of Art*: for Arnheim, "in a successful painting the essential meaning is *directly* expressed in the properties of the visual form" (emphasis mine).[45] At best, Arnheim refers to this procedure of directly expressing meaning as a "translation" of physical functions into expressive qualities. A revealing example of such translation is his description of the lost "spiritual overtones" of a doorway:

> A door is, in many of our modern buildings, nothing better than the hole that will let you in or out. [. . .] A true door, however, may embody the architectural gesture of inviting entrance. It *translates* its physical function into the perceptual expression of openness for reception, and, in a medieval church, is fashioned in such a way that the gesture conveys the experience of spiritual initiation [emphasis original].[46]

Arnheim's use of "gesture" seems reminiscent of Benjamin's emphasis on gesture and its relation to the "comportment of the voice" with which this chapter began. But despite similar words and phrases, Arnheim means something quite different. For Arnheim, the "architectural gesture" of invitation is expressive, it "conveys the experience of spiritual initiation." This experience appears to be the door's "essential meaning" – what makes it a "true door" – which for Arnheim is directly conveyed and expressed by such an "architectural gesture." This is undoubtedly a traditional understanding of gesture: something done or expressed in order to convey a specific intention or attitude. But as Weber points out, such a conventional definition of the term is precisely what Benjamin challenges: "For 'gesture' as [Benjamin] employs it with respect to Epic Theater, and in general, involves not the fulfillment or realization of an intention or of an expectation but rather its disruption and suspension. It entails not so much expression as interruption."[47] Like Freud's deliberate intention with his rebus discussed in the previous chapter, where he connects phonemes of disparate words in order to explain why he forgot the name, Signorelli, Arnheim is similarly so consumed with discovering the true meaning of expressive properties to be aware of any possible disruptions or interruptions. Put another way, Arnheim is so concentrated on the direct experience and spiritual meaning of passing through a true door that he overlooks the possibility of tripping at its threshold.

---

45 Arnheim, *Toward a Psychology of Art*, 258. Like Nancy after him, Arnheim adopts the language of what is "proper" and with it the language of property. The phrase "essential meaning" reveals the essentialism that runs throughout much of this passage specifically and Arnheim's later work in general.
46 Arnheim, *Toward a Psychology of Art*, 209.
47 Weber, *Benjamin's -abilities*, 98.

A parallel example in Arnheim's *Radio* book to the doorway image mentioned above, which conflates expressive meaning with the existence and even essence of the image in question, is the sound of coins jingling in a radio play:

> How radically the existence of a person is reduced to a partial utterance, and what a powerful effect can be achieved in this way, is shown in a very successful scene from a radio play [Arnheim gives no reference – RGR], where a desperate unemployed man hears his neighbor counting her money through the wall. One does not hear the woman speak or move, she exists only as the jingling of coins; her essence [*ihr Wesentliches*] is concentrated with wonderful consistency. Only a characteristic sound, very emphatic by its rhythm and monotony and so very suggestive, remains of a person![48]

What the spiritual door and jingling of coins have in common is how their "physical function" is translated into an expressive quality that for Arnheim immediately conveys a specific meaning. Arnheim's structure of signification, illustrated by his notion of gesture above, is a one-way path to a particular meaning understood by all. This is one reason why Arnheim's paradigm of expression has been interpreted as having a "symbolic" signifying structure.[49] It is a closed process, one that closes the door, so to speak, on alternative modes of signification. As is well known, Benjamin's preferred mode of signification is allegorical, not symbolic: he is dedicated less to any one meaning with respect to its mode of articulation than to a plurality of meanings that determine themselves in part through the differential relations of the (non)discursive language in which they play a part.[50] Because they determine themselves differentially, meanings themselves are never complete nor immediately expressed, but are instead always interrupted, suspended or delayed. This is one way to think of timbre as Benjamin might have conceived it in relation to the comportment of the voice: not merely as "sonorous material" as Nancy describes it nor simply as one of Arnheim's adverbial "expressive properties," but as always maintaining a degree of open determination that allows it to distinguish one instrument or voice or sound from another. The problem of timbre ultimately requires thinking a non-appropriative process of relative determination, not unlike the amorphous marks and signs of the *Merkwelt* referred to in Chapter One. This

---

48 Arnheim, *Rundfunk*, 101; *Radio*, 159.
49 See in particular Koch, "Materialist of Aesthetic Illusion," 177.
50 The word-as-symbol, to which I referred earlier when highlighting how the idea for Benjamin can only be circumscribed, is quite different from Arnheim's symbolic signifying structure. For Benjamin, the symbol is always fundamentally linked to theological, not aesthetic, concerns. While this tendency runs throughout Benjamin's writings, it can perhaps best be grasped in his distinction between tragedy and the German *Trauerspiel*. See especially Benjamin's "*Trauerspiel* and Tragedy" (Benjamin, *GS* 2:133–137; *SW* 1:55–58).

process is not descriptive in the sense of producing a single, "essential" meaning, but modular, relational, differential; in a word, circumscriptive. Perhaps only the distracted listener, who listens with half an ear, can take part in this non-appropriative procedure.

3.2 Arnheim's Art of Not Listening

"Listening with half an ear" is a common English and German idiom typically defined as listening to something without giving it one's fullest attention. It is often derogatory, and often begins with the word "only," which is the way the famous film music composer, Bernard Herrmann, once used the phrase when referring to music in film: we listen to film music with only half an ear.[51] Anatomists commonly distinguish between the external, middle, and internal ear, referring to the multiple parts that make up the organ of hearing in both humans and animals. But to listen with half an ear implies, at least figuratively speaking, that the ear is also a measurable unit like an hour of time, which can be halved, quartered and so on. This figurative division of the ear is of course nothing new. Multiple instances of an eye or ear too many or too few can be found in religious, mythical, literary, and philosophical traditions, and often imply significant advantages or deficiencies. While the cyclops Polyphemus is perhaps the most famous example of a one-eyed mythological creature, one is also reminded of Friedrich Hölderlin's remark of King Oedipus having "perhaps one too many eyes,"[52] where having an additional eye is a source of sorrow and pain. At the other extreme, Nietzsche's discussion of "listening with the third ear" – and Theodor Reik's adoption of it in his book of the same name (*Listening with the Third Ear*, 1948) – is an example of how having more than two ears or eyes implies an additional, even supra-sensual capacity beyond the limits of human capacity.

With their emphasis on an eye or ear too few or too many, these examples imply a norm that is either not being reached or is being surpassed. The same can be said of listening with only half an ear. When we are "all ears," we are

---

51 "'I think a short phrase has certain advantages,' [Bernard Herrmann] said in 1975. 'The short phrase is easier for audiences, who listen with only half an ear.'" See Steven C. Smith, *A Heart at Fire's Center: The Life and Music of Bernard Herrmann* (Berkeley/Los Angeles/London: University of California Press, 2002), 78.
52 "Ein Auge zu viel vielleicht." See Friedrich Hölderlin, "In lieblicher Bläue. . ." (1823)/"In lovely blueness. . .," in *Poems and Fragments*, by Friedrich Hölderlin, bilingual ed., trans. Michael Hamburger (London: Anvil Press Poetry, 2004), 792–793. We will return to this discussion in Chapter Four.

supposedly giving something our fullest attention.[53] But when we are listening with only half an ear, we are paradoxically both listening and not listening at the same time. Arnheim struggles with this paradox in his *Radio* book, specifically in his penultimate chapter on the "Psychology of the Radio Listener," explaining as follows: "The art of *not* listening to radio, which, as we have seen, is such an important element of the art of listening to radio, can hardly be taught by wireless itself."[54] This apparently mutually inclusive relationship between the art of listening and the art of not listening to radio – as if one could not be thought without the other – is the central paradox of Arnheim's chapter, one that he continued to grapple with in the foreword to his 1970s reprints of *Radio* in both German and English. Additionally, Arnheim grafts a pedagogical element onto this curious art of "not listening," in that it "can hardly be taught by radio itself." Arnheim was as dedicated as Benjamin was to training the public on how to listen to radio, wrote a number of articles promoting a more informed and disciplined mode of listening, and described the "ideal" radio listener, who was "independent in thought, feeling and action."[55] But if the passive or distracted listener "plays an important part" in the art of listening to radio, the question thus remains: is passive listening a preliminary stage for Arnheim that would inevitably be surpassed with improved radio programming concomitant with "appropriate ideas" (i.e., his ideas) about the meaning and function of radio as art? Or is there something about the psychology of passive listening itself that will *always* remain essential – and perhaps even beneficial – to the art of radio listening more generally?[56]

Throughout Arnheim's chapter, a tension remains unresolved between radio's modern characteristic to elicit passivity in the listener and a "corresponding counter-development which will again encourage the activity and independence of the individual within society."[57] To a large extent, Arnheim calls for the same interactive role of the radio listener that Brecht and Benjamin promote in their

---

53 This is also one of the primary discussion points in Reik's *Listening with the Third Ear* (New York: Farrar, Straus & Giroux, [1948] 1983), to which we will have a chance to return. See in particular Reik's chapter, "Free-floating Attention" (Reik, *Listening*, 157–172). See also John Mowitt's chapter "Whistle," in *Sounds: The Ambient Humanities*, by John Mowitt (Berkeley: University of California Press, 2014), 40–57.
54 Arnheim, *Rundfunk*, 234; *Radio*, 274.
55 Arnheim, *Rundfunk*, 169; *Radio*, 272.
56 This section derives partly from an earlier article, "Rudolph Arnheims *Rundfunk als Hörkunst* und die Kunst, nicht Rundfunk zu hören," in *Phono-Graphien. Akustische Wahrnehmung in der deutschsprachigen Literatur von 1800 bis zur Gegenwart*, ed. Marcel Krings (Vienna: Universität Wien Verlag, October 2011), 367–378.
57 Arnheim, *Rundfunk*, 123; *Radio*, 273.

respective radio reflections, just as he adopts the same thesis as Döblin, Zweig, and others who recognized radio's potential to bring back that lost tonal language from the literary culture before the written word. Arnheim is therefore not describing anything new when he begins his chapter by emphasizing the real dangers of succumbing to a mode of listening that is imposed upon, rather than initiated by the listener. A hallmark of Arnheim's radio theory, and media theory more generally, is the extent to which he professes the "innocence" of the medium itself. The divesting of the listener's mental labors, for instance, is not due to the intrinsic nature of the radiophonic medium, but is due rather to the lack of discipline on the part of the listener. Arnheim's argument in the "Psychology of the Radio Listener" and throughout much of the book is to show that radio is a tool, and precisely *how* this tool is used determines whether it has a more detrimental or educational effect. This thesis is most poignantly stated in the last sentences of the chapter, which are also his last words about radio as a medium: "radio has a detrimental effect only if – with the one-sidedness of its character, which is not to be condemned as negative in itself – it promotes a harmful tendency already existing. The instrument is never to blame, but always the one who takes it up [*sondern wer es handhabt*]" (translation modified).[58]

Given this argument, Arnheim cannot condemn outright the tendency to listen passively to radio, which leads to the following question: in what ways does Arnheim recognize the potential usefulness of passive listening, that is to say, how can a certain degree of "inattentive listening" be productive? The unresolved tension in Arnheim's last chapter on radio revolves precisely around this issue. On the one hand, Arnheim criticizes how the wireless is a "new, dangerous tempter" that can be detrimental to independent thought. On this point he echoes Benjamin's claims about how a speaker's voice and gestures make contemplation and philosophical reflection impossible: "the wireless listener bobs like a cork on the waves, hears one after another an endless succession of totally unconnected things, and so entirely without a breathing space that he does not manage subsequently to ponder and consider what he has heard."[59] Arnheim is adamant that this inability to reflect on what's being heard is "naturally [. . .] not the fault of radio but is due to a lack of discipline in the listener."[60]

This dependency on the self-disciplined listener, however, appears inconsistent with how he describes passive listening as an *art* of not listening to radio. Can this art of not listening be learned? Two passages are relevant here.

---

58 Arnheim, *Rundfunk*, 171; *Radio*, 275.
59 Arnheim, *Rundfunk*, 165; *Radio*, 265.
60 Arnheim, *Rundfunk*, 165; *Radio*, 265.

The first is Arnheim's short description of the "passive listener." He starts by inviting the reader to imagine an extraordinary case:

> It would be extraordinary if a man, whose whole life from the time he was born was so enveloped in musical sounds that he did not notice them any more than the light or the air around him, should still be able to succumb to the magic of a violin or the power of an orchestra. Should we not expect the rising generation to be the most unmusical that has ever lived [translation modified]?[61]

At the time of writing this radio manuscript, Arnheim had not only just moved to Italy, but he had also not yet turned thirty years old. It is likely that Arnheim included himself in this rising generation who are able listen to music more ubiquitously than ever before, and so the rhetorical question above should be read ironically. While he duly recognizes the dangers of increased passivity in the listening radio public, he also shows that inattentive listening should not be labeled outright as degenerative or "condemned as negative in itself." Without explicitly describing its potentially positive or useful effects, Arnheim is doubtful that an increased practice of inattentive listening in and of itself necessarily leads to an overall degradation of the way we listen.

A second passage describes more directly the unavoidable tendency to listen inattentively to radio. It is not true, Arnheim writes, that radio commandeers the listener at all times. While there are certain events broadcast, like boxing matches or the polling of votes, to which full attention must be paid, the radio listener is often distracted. Indeed, the coming of radio inaugurates the modern-day concept of "multitasking," as the following passage illustrates. Because the power of a broadcast to attract aural attention must often work

> *against* the listener's surrounding, it usually manages to gain only half the listener's ear. Above all, the special psychological need, commensurate with wireless, of needing to be busy, is satisfied by a superficial listening-in [*ein oberflächliches Hinhören*]. The daily life in the home makes all sorts of demands, so the listener never sits "idly" in front of the loudspeaker, but does all sorts of useful and useless things at the same time. [..] The concentration which is enhanced in church or concert-hall by the entire situation must be fought for by the listener *against* his surroundings, and he rarely succeeds in doing this. Wireless is a permanent guest [*Dauergast*], and such a person is notoriously "made no fuss of": life goes on as if he were not there [emphasis original; translation modified].[62]

Arnheim is more explicit here about the psychological need that is both satisfied by a "superficial listening-in" and made more recently possible by the ubiquity

---

61 Arnheim, *Rundfunk*, 168; *Radio*, 271.
62 Arnheim, *Rundfunk*, 166–167; *Radio*, 268.

of radio: the need to feel busy or "fill up time," *das Beanspruchtseinwollen*.⁶³ But again, Arnheim is careful to attach neither overtly positive nor negative connotations to the fulfillment of this psychological need. In an article on Arnheim's radio theory, Harro Zimmermann appropriately suggests that Arnheim's

> theory of "listening with half an ear" is precisely not a sign of the self-relinquishment of radio as a cultural medium, but is rather an acknowledgment of the social gravitas, the sensory deadweight and the mediatedness of (subjective) receptivity in the face of this new word (and image) medium [translation mine].⁶⁴

Similar to the previous passage about the most unmusical of generations, Arnheim does not condemn the tendency of radio listeners to listen with only half an ear as inherently negative. He recognizes that, with the ubiquity of radio, a new way of listening has begun, one that is at least partly constitutive of not listening, of listening with half an ear.

Writing nearly thirty years later in the *Introduction to the Sociology of Music* (*Einleitung in die Musiksoziologie*, 1962), Adorno denounces outright this mode of listening, which he calls entertainment listening (*Unterhaltungshören*). Comparing the role of the entertainment listener in society to the social approbation of alcohol and smoking, Adorno describes how such a conduct of listening "attaches itself to technology, which is already affectively engaged. There can be no more drastic demonstration of this compromising character than the conduct of a man who has the radio playing while he works [*der gleichzeitig das Radio tönen läßt und arbeitet*]" (translation modified).⁶⁵ Like a descent into Dante's *Inferno*, Adorno's chapter on the "Types of Musical Conduct" ("Typen musikalischen Verhaltens") describes six types in all, each one progressively worse. He begins with the expert listener – "the fully conscious listener who tends to miss nothing and at the same time, at each moment, accounts to himself for what he has heard"⁶⁶ – and ends with the *Unterhaltungshörer*, who are "resolutely passive and fiercely opposed to the effort which a work of art demands."⁶⁷ Passive listening for Adorno is in direct opposition to critical activity, and can be adequately described "only in the context of the mass media, of radio, film, and television."⁶⁸ While Adorno

---

63 In the 1936 English version, the German word is translated into the phrase, to "fill up time."
64 Zimmermann, "Kult der Anschauung," 236.
65 Theodor Adorno, *Gesammelte Schriften* (Berlin: Directmedia, 2003), 14:193. See Theodor Adorno, *Introduction to the Sociology of Music*, trans. E. B. Ashton (New York: Continuum, [1976] 1988), 15–16.
66 Adorno, *Gesammelte Schriften*, 14:182; *Introduction to the Sociology of Music*, 4.
67 Adorno, *Gesammelte Schriften*, 14:194; *Introduction to the Sociology of Music*, 16.
68 Adorno, *Gesammelte Schriften*, 14:196; *Introduction to the Sociology of Music*, 17.

states that it is not his intention "to disparage representatives of the described listening types negatively,"[69] it is clear that technology has certainly not increased the number of expert listeners, but quite the contrary. One might even question whether there can ever be such a thing as an "expert radio listener" according to Adorno and his taxonomy of listeners.

Back in his 1933 manuscript, Arnheim already assumed there were "ideal" radio listeners: "even today there exist here and there 'ideal' radio listeners, inasmuch as there is today a considerable number of people independent in thought, feeling, and action."[70] What Arnheim does not explore, to the detriment of his overall argument, is whether these "ideal" – that is to say, intellectual and independent – listeners nevertheless rely also on "the art of *not* listening" while listening to radio. Is it possible for men capable of independent thought to maintain critical engagement while listening "thoughtlessly"? Or more to the point: do listeners "of action" benefit from a potentially productive mode of passive listening? Because Arnheim does not adequately explain *how* not-listening is a part of or even benefits his "ideal" radio listener, he nowhere justifies why these two modes of listening might be interconnected. Arnheim must have recognized this in his 1979 German publication, which is why he strikes out the phrase referring to the "art of *not* listening to radio" as being an explicitly "important element to the art of listening to radio."

If, according to Arnheim, future masters of radio will have to consider what is not heard in order to master radio *as* listening art, the question remains how this art of not listening can be learned. Taking a cue from Arnheim's chapter title, "Psychology of the Radio Listener," one answer might come from psychology itself. In "Recommendations to Physicians Practicing Psychoanalysis" ("Ratschläge für den Arzt bei der psychoanalytischen Behandlung," 1912), Freud endorses a listening attitude that he calls free-floating attention (*gleichschwebende Aufmerksamkeit*). Employing the metaphor of the telephone, Freud explains how the physician should bend his own unconscious in order to receive the patient's emerging unconscious:

> Just as the patient must relate all that self-observation can detect and must restrain all the logical and affective objections which would urge him to select, so the physician must put himself in a position to use all that is told him for the purposes of interpretation and what is hidden in the unconscious, without substituting a censorship of his own for the selection which the patient forgoes. Expressed in a formula, he must bend his own unconscious like a receptive organ toward the emerging unconscious of the patient, be as the receiver of the

---

69 Adorno, *Gesammelte Schriften*, 14:196; *Introduction to the Sociology of Music*, 17.
70 Arnheim, *Rundfunk* 169; *Radio*, 272.

telephone to the disc. As the receiver transmits the electric vibrations induced by the sound-waves back again into sound-waves, so is the physician's unconscious, which has directed his associations, from the communications derived from it.[71]

The art of "bending one's own unconscious like a receptive organ" requires analysts to let go of conscious listening and to "listen to themselves – that is, to be aware of their own stream of consciousness" – in the act of listening to their patients.[72] This patient-physician relation has been called the classical view of countertransference, "conceptualized as the therapist's largely unconscious, conflict-based reactions to the patient's transference."[73] While there emerges in Freud's work an ambivalent attitude toward countertransference, what is important in the context of Arnheim's radio theory is that Freud advocates for analysts a mode of listening with only half an ear: while one half is turned toward what the patient is saying, the other half is turned inward, listening to the analyst's own unconscious censors so as to "hear better" their patients' own emerging unconscious. Moreover, just as Arnheim writes that radio itself cannot teach the art of not listening, Freud also describes how free-floating attentiveness also cannot be taught by psychoanalysis per se, since it requires the analyst's *conscious* recognition of his own unconscious censorship, of "resistances in himself," and "of those complexes of his own which would be apt to interfere with his grasp of what the patient tells him."[74] Such listening requires a mode of self-analysis: in order to use it productively, analysts must be aware of their own unconscious inhibitions and censors. Both Arnheim's ideal radio listeners and what can be called Freud's "ideal analysts" thus share the characteristics of self-discipline and self-awareness, which equally coincides with Arnheim's overarching thesis that the instrument itself is not to blame, but rather the one who uses it.[75]

---

71 Sigmund Freud, *Gesammelte Werke* (London: Imago, 1940–1952) (hereafter, *GW*), 8:381–382; Sigmund Freud, *The Standard Edition of the Complete Psychological Works of Sigmund Freud*, trans. James Strachey (London: Hogarth Press, 1953–1974) (hereafter, *SE*), 12:328.
72 David Livingston Smith, *Approaching Psychoanalysis: An Introductory Course* (London: Karnac Books, [1999] 2005), 77.
73 Charles Gelso and Jeffrey Hayes, *Countertransference and the Therapist's Inner Experience: Perils and Possibilities* (Mahwah, NJ: Lawrence Erlbaum Associates, 2007), 5.
74 Freud, *GW* 8:382; *SE* 12:329.
75 Directly after his formulation of the analyst as telephone receiver, Freud also refers to the analyst's use of his unconscious in terms of an instrument: "But if the doctor is to be in a position to use his unconscious in this way as an instrument [*als Instrument*] in the analysis, he must himself fulfil one psychological condition to a high degree. He may not tolerate any resistances in himself which would hold back from his consciousness what has been perceived by his unconscious; otherwise he would introduce into the analysis a new species of selection and distortion which would be far more detrimental than that resulting from concentration of

Such a comparison, of course, overlooks some of the more obvious distinctions that need to be kept in mind. Perhaps the most important one, which again echoes the theoretical disparities between Arnheim and Benjamin, is Arnheim's propensity for the dialectics of negation. Simply put, nowhere in his advice for physicians does Freud suggest that free-floating attention involves *not* being attentive. Rather, the analyst bends or turns (*zuwenden*) his unconscious "like a receptive [*empfangendes*] organ toward the emerging unconscious," allowing his own consciousness to turn inward, or at least elsewhere. What Freud is describing is movement and directionality, not negation or cancellation. Free-floating attention "schwebt," in the sense of moving back and forth,[76] hovering between, or even "revolving or circling" as a searchlight might over land and sea.[77] Freud's is therefore more in line with the non-binary "logic" of listening with half an ear, with which this section began, than with the binary logic that dictates Arnheim's art of not listening. This is why Freud typically speaks not of deficiency or indetermination but of overdetermination, with Nietzschean resonances. And it is towards this non-binary logic of ambivalence, as expressed by both free-floating attention and listening with half an ear, that I wish to turn or "bend" the concept of the acoustical unconscious.

In *Listening with the Third Ear*, Theodor Reik explicitly states that Freud's notion of free-floating attentiveness must be distinguished from any binary logic of attention: "The withdrawal of attention does not give rise to inattention, but to a shifting of attention, to a readiness to receive a variety of stimuli emerging from the unconscious or the unknown."[78] This is a crucial insight with respect also to the acoustical unconscious: comparable less to Arnheim's "art of not listening" than to Freud's free-floating attention, the acoustical unconscious would name a receptive organ that involuntarily turns its free-floating attention to the amorphous marks and signs of the acoustical *Merkwelt*. A useful analogy that Reik uses when discussing this peculiar mode of attentiveness is that of the searchlight:

---

conscious attention" (Freud, *GW* 8:382; *SE* 12:329). Just as Arnheim thinks of radio as an instrument that can be used for good or ill, so does Freud recognize that the analyst's use of his own unconscious *as an instrument*, when used improperly, would only add another level of distortion to the one already unavoidably communicated by the analysand, one potentially far worse than being fully attentive.

76 Duden's *Herkunftswörterbuch* refers to old high German's *sweben* as "sich hin und her bewegen" (*Das Herkunftswörterbuch*, s.v.).

77 This is how Theodor Reik describes Freud's notion of "free-floating attentiveness," to which we will turn momentarily. See Reik, *Listening*, 157–163.

78 Reik, *Listening*, 171.

> If we drive at night along a road near New York, we may notice that a searchlight in the middle of the road is scouring the surrounding country uninterruptedly. It illumines the road, is then directed to the fields, turns toward the town, and swings in a wide curve back to the road, and so repeats its circuit. This kind of activity, which is not confined to one point but is constantly scouring a wide radius, provides the best comparison with the function of free-floating attention.[79]

This is a useful analogy indeed, but one dominated by visibility, a centrally fixed tower that scans its surroundings. The model of a free-floating attentiveness related to the acoustical unconscious would involve no searchlight on a flat surface, but rather the distant echoes of sounds in the ocean, with the receiver floating in whichever direction in three-dimensional space it is attracted to at any given moment. In other words, the listener is carried along by the sonic waves – which travel far greater distances in water than in air – similar to how consciousness is carried away by the comportment of the voice. Following Freud and Reik, such a carried-away consciousness describes acoustical attentiveness that is both a giving up of control to and a readiness to receive acoustical stimuli "emerging from the unconscious or the unknown," an openness to hear that which is unheard (of). This is not to say that Arnheim's "art of not listening to radio" is irrelevant to any notion of the acoustical unconscious. But it reveals, precisely in what it is not, how it should be distinguished from the acoustical unconscious, which follows a mode of receptivity that resists any binary opposition between passive or active, attentive or inattentive.

One other important distinction that differentiates Freud's free-floating attentiveness from Arnheim's art of not listening to radio is that, while both tend to describe modes of not-fully-conscious receptivities, their end goals are quite different. Whereas both Freud and Reik emphasize the free-floating attentiveness as flitting between the internal self and the internal other,[80] this is certainly not the case with Arnheim. Although he is never explicit, Arnheim's art of not listening refers more to a mode of receptivity related to a kind of distracted listening. This is not to say that Freud's free-floating attentiveness has

---

79 Reik, *Listening*, 163.
80 Reik borrows Nietzsche's reference to a third ear for this very reason: The third ear "can catch what other people do not say, but only feel and think; and it can also be turned inward. It can hear voices from within the self that are otherwise not audible because they are drowned out by the noise of our conscious thought-processes" (Reik, *Listening*, 146–147). One can even go so far as to say that the third ear is that which is turned toward the acoustical unconscious, whether one's own internal unconscious or those of others.

nothing to do with distraction – both, one could say, are singular countermodels of attentiveness[81] – but the way distraction figures into it is unique: Freud suggests that the analyst be fully conscious of his own otherwise unconscious "inhibitions and censors" so as *not* to be distracted by them, which in turn allows him to give "equal notice to everything" in the hope of extracting some interpretive clarity. Arnheim, on the other hand, is simply wishing to develop an artistic ear for the aesthetic forms that emerge from radio, which for him is at least partly dependent on "not listening," which I read as being both receptive and distracted. This coincides with the way he describes the "superficial listening-in" of the radio listener at home, who "does all sorts of useful and useless things at the same time."

Distraction also requires us to return to Benjamin. Like Freud's free-floating attentiveness, Benjamin's notion of distraction, influenced both by his reading of Alois Riegl's *The Group Portraiture of Holland* (*Das holländische Gruppenporträt*, 1902) and Louis Aragon's *Paris Peasant* (*Paysan de Paris*, 1926), is also neither a lapse of attention nor inattention: in this "strange zone," as Aragon puts it, *all* is distraction (tout *est lapsus*); we are carried along by the relentless "current of objects" in this modern-archaic "underwater world."[82] Benjamin's theory of distraction is grounded not in psychology but in a theory of perception. In all three versions of the artwork essay, Benjamin writes that *"reception in distraction [. . .] is a symptom of profound changes in apperception"* (italics original).[83] As such, distraction for Benjamin should not be thought in the negative or deficient sense, as in "the bored student, dissolute citizen or the absentminded professor," but rather how Paul North describes it in his book, *The Problem of Distraction*: "Benjamin's *Zerstreuung* gestures toward an untold abundance and fertility [. . .] *Zerstreuung* names a complete deformation of the perceptual-mental order."[84] Benjamin's notion of distraction, which for North is "the stage in which the 'Sinneswahrnehmung' is no longer organized and not yet organized," does not inaugurate a "new perceptual order but the condition for its possibility."[85] A mode of distracted listening, then, extracted from Benjamin's theory of distraction and read alongside Arnheim's art of (not) listening to radio, comes perhaps

---

81 On Freud's "evenly suspended attention," see Jonathan Crary, *Suspensions of Perception: Attention, Spectacle, and Modern Culture* (Cambridge: MIT Press, 2001), 368.
82 Cited by Howard Eiland in his essay, "Reception in Distraction," *boundary 2* 30, no. 1 (Spring 2003): 51–66.
83 Benjamin, *GS* 7:381; *SW* 3:120. Howard Eiland writes that distraction for Benjamin "is a covert measure of the ability to perform new tasks of apperception, for *successful* reception in distraction presupposes that a mastery of certain tasks has become habitual" (Eiland, "Reception in Distraction," 57).
84 Paul North, *The Problem of Distraction* (Stanford, CA: Stanford University Press, 2012), 155.
85 North, *Problem of Distraction*, 145.

even closer to the notion of an acoustical unconscious for radio than, say, Reik's third ear or Freud's free-floating attentiveness: while both Benjamin and Arnheim borrow from psychology in their own way, their reflections on distraction are related less to psychology than to the possibility of a new perceptual order.

Benjamin's notion of the optical unconscious is certainly one way he is exploring the possibility of profound changes in optic apperception. Despite the ambiguity and underdeveloped theories in Arnheim's chapter on the "Psychology of the Radio Listener," their implications nevertheless point toward an early instance in German radio theory that calls for a productive mode of distracted listening, which makes it relevant to the acoustical unconscious explored here. Why? Because Arnheim's binary logic is explicitly codependent: the art of not listening is interwoven with the art of listening. Benjamin's introduction of the optical unconscious in the artwork essay – as "a space [*Raum*] interwoven with human consciousness giving way to a space interwoven with the unconscious" – is another way, albeit more nuanced, of describing Arnheim's codependency between listening and not listening to radio: the art of listening gives way to, and in so doing is modified by, an as-yet-determined art of *listening in distraction*. The task of the oft-distracted radiophonic ear, which is not quite the same as the third ear, is thus to train itself in recognizing the blurring of these spaces and the merging of these modes of acoustic perception. Arnheim's attempt to articulate a mode of distracted listening that is not a detriment or deficiency but an "art" amounts to a recognition, however underdeveloped, that profound changes in apperceptive listening are becoming possible with the growing ubiquity of radio. It also marks the beginning of thinking the acoustical unconscious in radio, which points less to what is heard or left "unheard" than to *how* one listens in distraction, bearing in mind that reception in distraction already problematizes the very limits of hearing/seeing/thinking, of any preconceived perceptual-mental order. The acoustical unconscious names one such condition of possibility, and as such offers a way of thinking the modern radio listener's own condition or bearing, their *Benehmen*, not simply in front of the radio, but in the age of technology.

3.3 The Gesticulating Voice in Benjamin

Much has been written on Benjamin's repeated emphasis on gesture, especially when he writes about Bertolt Brecht, Franz Kafka, and Karl Kraus, the latter of which was an Austrian journalist, critic, playwright, poet and editor of *The Torch* (*Die Fackel*). Less well-known perhaps is Benjamin's consistent alignment of gesture with voice. As mentioned earlier, the etymological roots of gesture, *gerere* or *gestum,* suggest the action of bearing or carrying that underscores Benjamin's careful use of the phrase, "the comportment *(das Benehmen)* of the voice." Gesture was also examined in Arnheim's example of the true door above: whereas gesture for Arnheim involves the fulfillment of a true intention or expectation, gesture for Benjamin entails interruption, disruption and a halting of direct meaning. Two published essays by Benjamin, "Karl Kraus" (1931) and "The Problems in the Sociology of Language" ("Probleme der Sprachsoziologie," written in 1934 and published 1935), bring Benjamin's reflections on voice and gesture surprisingly to the fore.

Benjamin had already gone to Kraus's reading of Offenbach's *La vie parisienne* at the end of March 1928, and in the years following attended other readings by Kraus on Shakespeare and Johann Nestroy. By the time Benjamin published his major essay, "Karl Kraus," in the *Frankfurter Zeitung und Handelsblatt* in March 1931, he had more than enough first-hand experience to write the following about Kraus's use of his own voice in these performances:

> It is as if the demon in the man [*der Dämon des Mannes*] sought the tumultuous atmosphere of these dramas, shot through with all the lightning flashes of improvisation, because it alone offered him the thousand opportunities to break out, teasing, tormenting, threatening. In them his own voice tries out the demonic abundance of personae [*den dämonischen Personenreichtum*] inhabiting the performer – per-sona: that through which it resounds [*das, wohin durch es hallt*] – and about his fingertips dart the gestures of the figures that live in his voice [*die Gebärden der Gestalten, welche in seiner Stimme wohnen*] [translation modified].[86]

For Benjamin, "eine Person" is anything but a single person, personality or individual (*Einzelperson*). Between hyphens, Benjamin refers instead to the Latin "per sona," that through which sound passes. In early Greek theater, "per sona" referred to the mouthpiece of the mask through which the voice sounded out.[87] Here Kraus – more specifically, his voice – tries out not just one but a multiplicity of mouthpieces. Such plurality continues with its connection to the gestures that live within it. Kraus's voice becomes both that which tries out different "per sona" and is a part of the body wherein gestures live. Given that gestures for Benjamin are "indissolubly bound up with, although not reducible to, the body," it is no wonder that the voice is equally populated by gestures.[88] But while they may have a home in the voice, the voice should not be seen as a vessel wherein they are housed or contained, just as Weber reminds us that the body for Benjamin is to

---

86 Benjamin, *GS* 2:327; *SW* 2:442.
87 See Donald R. Mathis, *Melodic Sculpturing: The Art and Science of Singing* (Bloomington, IN: Arthur House, 2009), 139.
88 Samuel Weber, *Theatricality as Medium* (New York: Fordham University Press, 2005), 47.

be understood "not in the Aristotelian sense, as a vessel or container, but rather in terms of its *articulations*" (emphasis mine).[89] Gestures are always on the move, always articulating, as in the passage above: they dart through Kraus's fingertips. They are articulated not only in the bodily joints that make movement possible but also through the articulations of the voice, via various "per sona." This is reminiscent of Benjamin's bearing or comportment of the voice, so long as "voice" is conceived not as a vessel but like any other bodily joint that articulates, however disjointedly. For Benjamin, the voice gesticulates no less than the hand.

This relation between voice and gesture become even more apparent in Benjamin's 1934 report, *Problems in the Sociology of Language*. Benjamin admits he was out of his depth with this overview, telling Scholem in a letter dated December 1934 that he wrote it not as an expert but as a learner.[90] Despite it being relatively overlooked in Benjamin scholarship, *Problems in the Sociology of Language* nevertheless reveals a host of topics that pepper Benjamin's writings, including gesture, language and mathematics, the magic of words, and above all mimesis.[91] But throughout the overview, Benjamin also focuses on one issue that he rarely gives any sustained attention to elsewhere: the mimetic-gestural capacity of the voice. Benjamin examines how recent sociological theories of language have overcome the onomatopoeic principle of language, a principle that began, as he reminds us in the opening paragraphs, with Herder: "Man himself invented language! – from the sounds [*Tönen*] of living nature" (translation modified).[92] Benjamin then cites Lévy-Bruhl, who adds a variant of the onomatopoetic theory that echoes some of Benjamin's own comments about Kraus's voice above:

> the language of the Ewe tribe is richly endowed with the means of reproducing an impression directly through sounds [*unmittelbar durch Töne*]. This abundance [*Reichtum*] bespeaks their almost irresistible tendency to imitate all they hear [*alles Hörbare nachzumachen*]. Likewise, everything that is seen, and in general what is perceived [..] first and foremost the movements [*die Bewegungen*]. But these vocal imitations or reproductions, these sound images

---

[89] Weber, *Theatricality as Medium*, 47.
[90] Benjamin, *GS* 3:674.
[91] In their annotations to the report, the editors of the *Gesammelte Schriften* reference Benjamin's letter to Werner Kraft from January 1936, where he admits that he deliberately, if not explicitly, set up the report to lead "exactly to the place where my own theory of language, which I laid down in Ibiza several years ago in a very short programmatic note begins" (translation mine; Benjamin, *GS* 3:674). This programmatic note, the editors add, is Benjamin's "On the Mimetic Faculty" ("Über das mimetische Vermögen").
[92] Herder, cited by Benjamin, *GS* 3:453; *SW* 3:69. I modified the translation to reflect Benjamin's punctuation.

> [*Lautbilder*], also cover sounds, odors, tastes, and tactile impressions [. . .]. Properly speaking, they are not onomatopoetic inventions; rather, they are descriptive vocal gestures [*beschreibende Stimmgebärden*] [translation modified].[93]

Benjamin's extended citation of Lévy-Bruhl emphasizes not only the latter's preference for vocalic gestures over onomatopoesis, which Benjamin no doubt shared, but also how these *Lautbilder* imitate movements above all else, reminiscent of gestures always being on the move. But the language of gesture, which can be seen as the central motivating factor guiding Benjamin's entire overview, always bumps up against language's phonetic element.

For instance, Benjamin reserves his inclusion of Richard Paget's "surprising definition of language" for near the end of his overview: Paget "understands [language] as the gesticulation of the speech organs [*eine Gestikulation der Sprachwerkzeuge*]. Here the gesture, not the sound [*Laut*], is primary [. . .]. According to Paget the phonetic element is founded on a mimetic-gestural one."[94] With the work of Paget and others, Benjamin concludes, not only has the obsolete onomatopoetic theory of language been "supplanted by a mimetic theory in a far wider sense," but a new task for language theory has opened up, one that involves the exploration of a "physiognomic phonetics," that is to say, the inherently expressive means of language.[95] And here Benjamin cites Paget on the voice's gestural components:

> It is remarkable, and a sign for how extraordinarily slowly human development proceeds, that the civilized human being has not yet learned to do without head or hand movements as expressive elements [*Ausdruckselemente*] of his opinions. [. . .] When will we learn to play so skillfully and rationally on the wonderful instrument of the voice as to attain a range of sounds of the same scope and perfection? What is certain is that we have not yet completed this course of learning. [. . .] All the existing works of literature and eloquence [*Beredsamkeit*] are as yet merely elegant, inventive compositions [*Gestaltungen*] of formal or phonetic elements of language which, in themselves, are wholly wild and uncultivated, since they have been formed naturally without any conscious intervention by humans [translation modified].[96]

On the one hand, Paget's hope for learning to play on the "wonderful instrument of the voice" is reminiscent of Arnheim's suggestion to orchestrate voices in a radio sound-drama according to the musical instruments they best tonally imitate. On the other hand, Paget's description of how far off we still are from "completing this course of learning" echoes the difficulty that Benjamin acknowledges when

---

93 Lévy-Bruhl, cited by Benjamin, *GS* 3:455–456; *SW* 3:70.
94 Benjamin, *GS* 3:476; *SW* 3:82.
95 Benjamin, *GS* 3:478; *SW* 3:84.
96 Paget, cited by Benjamin, *GS* 3:479; *SW* 2:85.

attempting to circumscribe the behavior of the voice in relation to language. For what is involved is bringing to consciousness these "wholly wild and uncultivated" phonetic gestures "formed naturally without conscious intervention." Paget's phraseology, translated into German by Benjamin himself, articulates the latter's interest in what could be called the "acous-mimetic" articulation of the voice, which would be one way to approach or circumscribe Benjamin's "comportment" of the voice in its relation to gesture.

Since these acous-mimetic articulations "have been formed naturally without any conscious intervention by humans," in what way are they linked to the acoustical unconscious proposed in this study? Before introducing the optical unconscious in the final version of the artwork essay, Benjamin lists a number of situations that we do every day – the act of walking, picking up a cigarette or spoon – but then emphasizes how we know nothing of what is really going on "during the split second when a person actually takes a step," or what goes on "between hand and metal, and still less how this varies with different moods [*Verfassungen*] in which we find ourselves."[97] These unconscious actions are similar to the auto-acoustic mimesis of the voice described above. Similar to slips of the tongue, which passed more or less unnoticed until Freud isolated and made them analyzable in *On the Psychopathology of Everyday Life*, human voices' acous-mimetic articulations were only first becoming theorized about and isolated by such sociologists of language during Benjamin's lifetime. For Benjamin, the very act of taking a step or picking up a spoon is isolated and made analyzable for the first time through film. When it comes to any acoustic medium, be it radio, the gramophone or telephone, Benjamin's notion of the optical unconscious should orient our definition of the acoustical unconscious: just as we discover the optical unconscious for the first time through the camera, so do we discover the acoustical unconscious through the microphone. Only through audio recording and play-back is it possible for the first time to isolate and make analyzable the comportment of the voice, which includes both the auto-acoustic-mimesis described above, that is, its articulative, gestural component, which cannot be separated from the mood of the speaker, as well as its effect upon the listener, specifically, how the voice picks up and takes away, via its com-portment, the listener's capacity to fully contemplate, leaving the listener numb, *benommen*. The gesticulatory voice is itself not the acoustical unconscious, but only via acoustic media like radio, the gramophone and telephone can its sonic articulations be analyzed and augmented, captured near or far, and thus offer the possibility of new acoustic experiences never before heard. This

---

97 Benjamin, *GS* 1:500 [*WuN* 16:240]; *SW* 4:266.

augmented realm (*Raum*) of acoustic apperception, as it enters into the space of human consciousness, is that of the acoustical unconscious.[98]

Before turning to Benjamin's radio plays for children, one other topic covered in *Problems in the Sociology of Language* that will help inform the following readings: how children listen to and use language. In the previous section, we examined how the distracted listener of radio – Arnheim's "art of not listening" – should be thought not in any negative sense but as a condition for the possibility of a new perceptual order, in which the senses are "no longer organized and not yet organized."[99] Children's relation to and reception of language already presupposes this not-yet organized perceptual mode, though it is labeled developmental rather than distraction. Benjamin highlights the then-contemporary work of Jean Piaget, known today for being one of the greatest influences on modern child psychology. Benjamin succinctly summarizes Piaget's theory of the language of children, which moves along two different tracks: "It exists as a socialized language on the one hand, and as egocentric language on the other."[100] Benjamin focuses on the latter, which exists solely for the speaking subject itself and remains otherwise unintelligible "unless accompanied by the context of the situation in which it arose."[101] In modern child psychology, one example of Piaget's egocentric language is called echolalia, a subset of various echophenomena, whereby sounds are automatically imitated "without explicit awareness."[102] While such echophenomena and Piaget's egocentric language are present both during normal childhood development and in various neuropsychiatric disorders, Benjamin underscores its prevalence in behavioral disorders and the performing of difficult tasks because, as he gleans from the Russian child psychologist, Lev Vygotsky, it is generated in interruption: "Whenever they encountered a difficulty, our children exhibited an increase in egocentric language [. . .] Thinking is brought into action when an

---

98 It may be tempting to compare these reflections on the acoustical unconscious and the gesticulatory voice with the "theoretical failure" that Lacoue-Labarthe finds in Theodor Reik's emphasis on voice, the unconscious and the language of gesture in *Surprise and the Psychoanalyst*. But we should keep in mind how devoted Reik was to Freud's concept of the unconscious, which is not the same as Benjamin's, as I examined in Chapter Two. See in particular Philippe Lacoue-Labarthe, *Typography: Mimesis, Philosophy, Politics* (Cambridge: Harvard University Press, 1989), 162–164.
99 North, *Problem of Distraction*, 155.
100 Benjamin, *GS* 3:475; *SW* 2:82.
101 Benjamin, *GS* 3:475; *SW* 2:82.
102 See Christos Ganos, Timo Ogrzal, Alfons Schnitzler, and Alexander Münchau, "The pathophysiology of echopraxia/echolalia: Relevance to Gilles de la Tourette syndrome," *Movement Disorders* 27, no. 10 (September 2012): 1222.

activity which has run unhindered up to then is interrupted."[103] This last sentence from Vygotsky could apply just as easily to Brecht's epic theater, a link that Benjamin must have also recognized immediately. But conscious of his reading public, he instead adds this revealing statement: "In other words, in early childhood egocentric language takes exactly the place reserved at a later stage for the thinking process [*Denkvorgang*] itself. It is the precursor, indeed the teacher, of thinking [*die Lehrerin des Denkens*]" (translation modified).[104] Then again, perhaps his sociologist readers might not have fully comprehended Benjamin's own *Denkvorgang* here, since he is also referring to the kind of thinking that define the heroes of Brecht's plays: according to Benjamin, "Brecht undertook to make the thinker, or even the wise man, the hero of the drama. It is from this perspective that one can define his theater as epic theater."[105] Indeed, just as Piaget's egocentric language is distinct from socialized language, Brecht's heroes share an attitude (*Haltung*) that for Benjamin is "essentially dubious, unsympathetic, or self-interested [*eigennützig*]."[106] And just as egocentric language is unintelligible without recourse to the specific situation in which it arises, epic theater "is less concerned with developing plots as with representing situations [*Zustände*]," discovering them for the first time, which can only "take place [*sich vollziehen*] through interruption of the action."[107] It is little wonder that Benjamin highlights Piaget's notion of egocentric language, as it is the ontogenetic counterpart to Brecht's modern theatricality.

The connection to Brecht is not frivolous. Benjamin's comment that egocentric language is the teacher of thought aligns with Brecht's pedagogical views on theater and his *Lehrstücke* in particular, the explicit goal of which was getting his audience to think. For both Brecht and Benjamin, radio was also a richly potential site for pedagogical effect, which Benjamin perhaps best emphasizes in *Theater and Radio*, a short, published text from 1932 that we will turn to at the end of the chapter. But in the process of researching for and writing *Problems in the Sociology of Language*, Benjamin learned that egocentric language, in contrast to socialized language, is comprised of mimetic-gestural elements. If children acquire "the syntax of language before the syntax of thought," then appealing to their attentiveness to egocentric language in stories, theater and radio plays may help lead them to develop their own capacity for critical thinking.[108] Benjamin imbues the various "per sona" that populate

---

103 Vygotsky, cited by Benjamin, *GS* 3:475; *SW* 2:82.
104 Benjamin, *GS* 3:475; *SW* 2:82.
105 Benjamin, *GS* 2:534; *SW* 4:303.
106 Benjamin, *GS* 2:633 [*WuN* 9.2:479]; *SW* 2:367.
107 Benjamin, *GS* 2:535; *SW* 4:304.
108 Vygotsky, cited by Benjamin, *GS* 3:475; *SW* 2:83.

his radio plays, especially those in *The Cold Heart* and *Bustle about Kasperl*, with the mimetic, gestural elements of egocentric language through sonic interruptions, mishearings and even a dialogue based entirely on echoes.

3.4 Per Sona and Rustling Papers in *The Cold Heart*

In the opening scene of *The Cold Heart* (*Das kalte Herz*, 1932), a children's radio play Benjamin cowrote with childhood friend and director of Radio Frankfurt, Ernst Schoen, the fictional characters show up to the radio studio only to be told by the radio director that they must leave everything else behind if they want to enter "Stimmland" (Voice Land). From the outset, Benjamin and Schoen stage a metatheatrical moment by turning their listeners' attention, who are likely almost entirely children, to the very medium through which they have "tuned in." The fictional radio director – in German, *der Sprecher* or speaker/announcer – addresses the characters, telling them that, if they wish to enter Voice Land, they must shed all belongings but their voice: "Whoever wishes to enter Voice Land must be very frugal [*ganz bescheiden*]. He must surrender all finery and relinquish all external beauty, so that nothing is left but his voice [*so dass von ihm nur die Stimme bleibt*]. However, his voice will then be heard by thousands of children simultaneously."[109] This was ostensibly the main reason for the fairytale characters to seek out the radio station in the first place. But more is happening in this prologue than meets the eye: a few characters express dismay because they think they will not be able to see the ground in Voice Land and are afraid of stumbling over roots, at which point the main character, the coaler Peter Munk, exclaims without waiting for the announcer to confirm, "[o]ne certainly can see in Voice Land, but one cannot be seen." The announcer then placates the characters: "if anything goes wrong – that's why I'm here: the Announcer [*der Sprecher*]. We in radio know our way around Voice Land like the back of our hands [*wie in unserer Tasche*]."[110] Much can be teased out of this short exchange between seeing and "stumbling" around blind in Voice Land – the fear of not finding one's way through to the end of a radio script is Benjamin's main problem in his short text, *On the Minute* (*Auf die Minute*, 1934)[111] – but this early emphasis on sight also marks the beginning of a tension between the visible and invisible that runs throughout the radio play. With the inclusion of dense fog, pipe smoke and the night in other scenes – not to

---

[109] Benjamin, *GS* 7:320 [*WuN* 9.1:91]; *Radio Benjamin*, 225.
[110] Benjamin, *GS* 7:319 [*WuN* 9.1:91]; *Radio Benjamin*, 224.
[111] See Robert Ryder, "On the Minute – Out of Time: Reading the Misreading of Time in Walter Benjamin's 'Auf die Minute' (1934)," *Germanic Review* 91, no. 3 (2016): 217–235.

mention the deliberate hiding of the Little Glass Man, a magical dwarf and apparent shape-shifter who grants wishes – Benjamin and Schoen make explicit the indeterminacy, not the absence, of sight and seeing while listening to radio.

There is so much going on in Benjamin's radio adaptation of *The Cold Heart* that it is difficult to know where to begin. Let me start with some connections back to Brecht, pedagogy and gesture. Benjamin must have chosen to adapt this well-known fairytale, written in 1827 by Wilhelm Hauff, in part because of its central moral: money cannot buy you happiness, but can turn your heart to stone. This ethical value echoes one of Brecht's main subject areas, which Benjamin had already pinpointed in his 1930 radio lecture titled, "Bert Brecht." Benjamin concludes by stating that, whosoever wants to limit oneself to one sentence about Brecht, the most crucial thing to say would be: "His subject is poverty." In *The Cold Heart*, the main protagonist, Peter Munk, is dissatisfied with his job as charcoal burner, which has a meager salary. Envious of the other men whose careers, abilities or sheer luck have made them "super rich" (*steinreich*), he seeks out the Little Glass Man, who Peter has heard can grant three wishes and who also goes by the name of *Schatzhauser*, "Keeper of Wealth." The radio adaptation skips over a long section in the original where Peter loses all the money and assets he gained from his first two wishes, but the Little Glass Man would not grant him a third wish as foolish as his first two. Desperate, Peter visits Dutch Michael, whom he had learned could also grant him all the riches he could ever wish for, except that Dutch Michael would take his heart in exchange. Suffice it to say, after giving Dutch Michael his heart and receiving a stone heart in exchange, Peter no longer feels any emotions and becomes a greedy, bad tempered rich man. While the fairytale ends on a happy note, with Peter Munk learning the folly of his ways and eventually getting his heart back from Dutch Michael through cunning, this is enough of the story to realize its pedagogical impetus and its connection back to Brecht. For Benjamin, Brecht's version of poverty is not any mystical or poetic view of poverty, but "more like a uniform and is calculated to confer a high rank on anyone who wears it. It is, in short, the physiological and economic poverty of man in the machine age."[112] When the fairytale characters were instructed in the opening of *The Cold Heart* to take off their clothing and keep behind their money in order to enter Voice Land, Benjamin was clearly playing with the idea of radio as another variation of man's poverty in the technological age: being stripped of everything but one's voice.

Benjamin writes only a few stage directions for the accompanying music and voice acting in *The Cold Heart*. Early on, however, a scene in the original fairytale,

---

[112] Benjamin, *GS* 2:667 [*WuN* 9.1:483]; *SW* 2:370.

which must also have been a major impetus for its radio adaptation, involves Peter Munk falling asleep while trying to remember the verse he needs to recite in order for the Little Glass Man to appear and grant him three wishes. The stage directions in the scene instruct that "a little music is heard, to which coal Peter sings along in a drowsy voice" the three lines he remembers, but not the last one.[113] It is not clear where the music is coming from, and one assumes it must be nondiegetic music (which was also composed by Schoen). Then six chimes are heard, after which we hear Peter snoring, and finally "music approaches softly. One hears 1–2 verses sung."[114] This music, however, is no longer nondiegetic but is coming from the window beyond Peter's bedroom, which he confirms for his listeners only after waking: drowsily (*schlaftrunken*), he says, "huh, a music box (*Spieluhr*) for an alarm clock. I would like to wake up to lovely music every morning, like a prince. But no, it's coming from outside: apprentice craftsmen!"[115] As in the original fairytale, the singing apprentices are what jog Peter's memory in the radio play, allowing him to remember the last line of verse. This scene thus rivals the scene in Tieck's "Eckbert," when Bertha also remembers the dog's name: both are helped by strangers, *von fremder Seite*, to remember what was forgotten. In Hauff's original text, one sentence stands out that appears to be a sonic variant of Benjamin's notion of shock: the apprentice's song "drove through Peter's ear like a brilliant flash of lightning."[116] What Benjamin further adds in the radio play to Hauff's original is the state in which Peter hears it: Peter is in a half-sleeping state, just waking up. Benjamin thus injects into this scene a Proustian acoustic involuntariness in which Peter is listening with only half-an-ear. And while it remains unclear in the original tale why Peter forgot the line in the first place – perhaps as unclear as Bertha's mysterious guilt – a hint is offered in Benjamin's radio adaptation that points to the medium itself: the line Peter forgot ends in the verb "sehen," to see. The entire verse is as follows:

Schatzhauser in green fir forest,	Schatzhauser im grünen Tannenwald,
You are already many hundred years old	Bist schon viel hundert Jahre alt
Yours is all the lands where firs stand	Dein ist all das Land, wo Tannen stehn,
You let only Sunday children see you.	Läßt dich nur Sonntagskindern *sehn* [emphasis and translation mine].[117]

---

113 Benjamin, *GS* 7:327 [*WuN* 9.1:100]; *Radio Benjamin*, 231.
114 Benjamin, *GS* 7:327 [*WuN* 9.1:100]; *Radio Benjamin*, 231.
115 Benjamin, *GS* 7:327 [*WuN* 9.1:100]; *Radio Benjamin*, 231.
116 "Das Lied fuhr wie ein leuchtender Blitz durch Peters Ohr" (Wilhelm Hauff, *Das kalte Herz: Ein Märchen* [Berlin: Holzinger, 2016], 15).
117 Benjamin, *GS* 7:328 [*WuN* 9.1:102].

In radio, nothing is "seen" per se, which suggests that Peter forgot the last line at least in part because of the very indeterminacy of any line of sight, of any way of seeing in Voice Land. Put another way, he only remembers the forgotten line of verse about seeing when he overhears a song from strangers. But even more revealing is the line itself: Schatzhauser only lets Sunday children see him. It is made clear in both the original and Benjamin's radio adaptation that a Sunday child is anyone born on a Sunday at noon, and in German, a "Sonntagskind" is an idiomatic term referring to anyone born under a lucky star. As Peter reveals earlier in the story, he is one such lucky person, meaning that the verse he forgot refers to *himself*. But it could also very well refer back to any *Sonntagskind* being read the story or, in the case of the radio play, listening in. This single line of verse, forgotten until recalled indirectly and apparently accidentally via a stranger's song, thus interrupts the narrative by referring beyond it, to both the protagonist's self-forgetting and that of the listening public. It also breaks narrative by calling attention to the medium itself: rather than refer to any absence of seeing, it instead invites those lucky children to see Schatzhauser through their ears. Via radio, the children are allowed to see not just without being seen, but also without seeing in any empirical sense. It goes without saying that the Little Glass Man can also be read as a variant of Benjamin's hunchback, which further problematizes any way of "seeing" him: not only could Benjamin never see him, "[he saw me] all the sharper, the less I saw of myself."[118] Peter needed to be reminded of the rhyme with seeing in order to recognize that it also referred to himself as a Sonntagskind, no doubt all the while being observed by the all-knowing but invisible Little Glass Man.

Another element through which Benjamin interrupts the narrative of the radio play and calls direct attention to the medium is when the radio announcer returns. Recall the announcer's original admission that he and his colleagues know their way around Voice Land like the back of their hands. The fairytale characters then asked if he could be their guide in Voice Land, to which he agreed, saying, "[w]ell then, I will guide you, only don't be upset if my papers occasionally rustle. (*Rustling paper*) Without my map [*Plan*], even I can't find my way around in Voice Land."[119] What rustles here is a "map" of Voice Land insomuch as a radio script maps out the successive scenes, mapping out what comes next. The danger here is not following the script to the letter and losing one's way. The sounds of rustling paper are a clear indication of the current radio script, and in this way is no different from Arnheim's example of the jingling of coins above

---

118 Benjamin, *GS* 4:304.
119 Benjamin, *GS* 7:321 [*WuN* 9.1:92]; *Radio Benjamin*, 225.

that immediately conveys a specific meaning. But it is also ostensibly the source, so to speak, of the words being spoken, and so already reflects back to the medium, adding another level of indeterminacy to what is the "original" or authentic text. This indeterminacy is compounded when the radio announcer reappears in the narrative. After Peter speaks to Schatzhauser for the first time, who disappears in a cloud of "smoke so thick, [Peter] can hardly see him," the announcer speaks:

> ANNOUNCER: Yes, well then, where were we? You children have just listened in on the conversation between our good Peter Munk and our little Keeper of Wealth. You heard the foolish wishes Peter made, and how the Little Glass Man disappeared in a cloud of good Dutch tobacco. Now let's see what comes next [*müssen wir also weitersehen*]. (*He rustles some papers*). Hm, hm! (*Louder rustling*).
>
> LITTLE GLASS MAN (*whispering*): What's going on? Why aren't we continuing the play?
>
> ANNOUNCER (*whispering*): I have no idea what to do next, Mr. Keeper of the Wealth. Fancy that! The forest wind must have blown away some of the pages and now we're in a jam. I have no idea how we will ever find our place again [*wie wir uns weiterfinden soll*].[120]

Beyond the repeated leitmotif of the rustling papers, which immediately reminds us of the announcer's "map" of Voice Land, what becomes clear is that parts of the script were inadvertently "blown away" with the wind, and their guide – both radio announcer and ersatz narrator – is no longer able to find the narrative path. What the rustling papers now elicits is a frantic search for that which has been lost or misplaced, a kind of acoustic gesture that both foregrounds the medium and highlights the interruption of narrative flow. And like a lost glove or reticule, what has been misplaced, however temporarily, is the future. As Weber writes, "[c]ited as citable, gesture is never simply present, but split between past and future, invoking the past to portend an unpredictable future."[121] Far from Arnheim's jingling of coins, whose expressive quality leads only to a closed system of signification, the rustling of papers hearkens back to the announcer's "map" only to open up to incompleteness and imminent unpredictability. As part of the machine that makes the radio play work – along with the microphone, broadcast equipment, voice actors, etc. – the script's rustling reveals the growing possibility of a disjointed piece of the mechanical body, of its imperfections. If the essence of gesture, as movements of the body, are to be found in its series of articulations, that is, in "the joints that make such movement possible,"[122] the rustle of papers exemplifies such an acoustic articulation of the radiophonic machine.

---

[120] Benjamin, *GS* 7:330 [*WuN* 9.1:105]; *Radio Benjamin*, 234.
[121] Weber, *Theatricality as Medium*, 46–47.
[122] Weber, *Theatricality as Medium*, 47.

Eventually the radio announcer, with the help of the fairytale characters themselves, is reminded of the plot, specifically that Peter Munk had gambled away not only all the wealth he acquired from the first wish that was granted to him, but also became so indebted that he also had to sell the glass factory, which he acquired from his second wish. The announcer remembers the line: "Hold on: had to sell – had to sell – ? There it is on page sixteen! Thank God, I've found the thread again! Let's go, people, we can continue!"[123] Benjamin did not need to have the announcer lose his place in the script, which simultaneously derails the plot and allows it to be surreptitiously moved forward. But just as Peter was reminded of the verse from the apprentice's song, so here the announcer is reminded by fictional "per sona" from the narrative, only after which they are able to continue. In both instances, forgetting or losing one's way interrupts the narrative flow; both Peter and the announcer are aided *von fremder Seite*. Such remembering is, moreover, related to listening in both cases: for Peter, it is a distracted listening that he originally mistook for an alarm clock, and for the announcer it constitutes a listening in on the fictional characters bickering about what happens next in the fairytale, as if the announcer was now part of the radio play's attentive listening audience rather than its guide. Of course, neither instance stages language in any particularly egocentric way, nor does either "per sona" participate in a kind of originary listening that reveals the word-as-symbol. But both instances represent the two poles of listening to radio: either wholly attentive, as in the case of the announcer, or distractedly so, like Peter. Taken together, they offer insight into how Benjamin and Schoen were looking to draw attention not only to the medium within the medium, that is, to its potentialities and indeterminancies, but also to the receptivity of the listener. In a way, these two Brechtian "situations" are perhaps meant to jolt the listening audience into thinking about their own com-portment, that is, whether they are being carried off by the narrative as much as they are by the voices being perceived. In both cases the listening children are invited to reflect on not just what they hear but *how* they are listening in, and whether their listening is not at least in part also a kind of seeing (Schatzhauser letting himself "be seen" by lucky children) or a reading (of the rustling script). Whatever intentions Benjamin and Schoen had with these metatheatrical stagings, they certainly emphasize the pedagogical impetus that shapes much of Benjamin's radio texts.

---

[123] Benjamin, *GS* 7:331 [*WuN* 9.1:106]; *Radio Benjamin*, 235.

3.5 Mickey and Kasperl

Benjamin's experimentation with radio's pedagogical potential is even more multifaceted in his other radio play for children, *Bustle about Kasperl*, which was broadcast twice in 1932. One explicitly pedagogical goal Benjamin had for the radio play was to ask the children to guess the sounds they heard in every scene, and to send their opinions back to the radio station for a potential prize (Fig. 3.1).

> 19.45 (7.45) **SWF (M)**
> **Radau um Kasperl**
> Ein Hörspiel für Kinder
> von **Walter Benjamin**
> Hauptpersonen:
>   Kasperl
>   Herr Maulschmidt
>   Rundfunkansager
> Nebenpersonen:
>   Fischweib
>   Empfangschef
>   Bahnhofsvorsteher
>   Löwenwärter
>   Taxichauffeur
>   Eiliger Herr
>   Kasperls Frau Puschi
>   viele Tiere
> Leitung: Der Verfasser
> (Uebrigens sind Kasperls Erlebnisse in diesem Hörspiel, wie schon der Titel sagt, mit Radau verbunden. Die Kinder werden gebeten, zu erraten, was die hierbei auftretenden Geräusche bedeuten und ihre Meinung darüber dem Südwestfunk mitzuteilen.)

Fig. 3.1: "(Incidentally, Kasperl's experiences in this radio play are, as the title already suggests, connected to hubbub. The children are asked to guess what the noises mean and to send their opinion about them to the Südwestfunk.)" (translation mine).[124]

This extradiegetic task, whereby the young listeners need to think about what sounds they are hearing, indicates the extent to which Benjamin wished to convert radio, as Brecht writes elsewhere, from a *Distributionsapparat* into a *Kommunikationsapparat*.[125] In an as-yet untranslated outline of the radio play, "Kasperl

---

[124] Benjamin, *GS* 7:832.
[125] See Bertolt Brecht, "Der Rundfunk als Kommunikationsapparat" (in *Bertolt Brecht: Gesammelte Werke* [Frankfurt a. M.: Suhrkamp, 1967], 8.2:127–134), which was originally written in 1932. A translation can be found in Bertolt Brecht, *Brecht on Film and Radio*, ed. Marc Silberman (London: Methuen, 2000), 41–48.

and the Radio: A Story with Noise" ("Kasperl und der Rundfunk: Eine Geschichte mit Lärm"), Benjamin is even more specific: the basis of each episodic scene "consists of various characteristic types of sounds [*Geräuscharten*], which are interrupted now and then by hints and words."[126] The children are meant to guess, based on a combination of sounds, words and hints in the dialogue, where Kasperl "is." Similar to the last line of forgotten verse in *The Cold Heart*, where the Little Glass Man allows himself to be seen only by lucky children, here Kasperl is hiding in the midst of indeterminate sounds interspersed with words and hints, and the listening children are invited to rummage through these sounds to find him. But the sounds are not *of* something specific; that is to say, Benjamin is not asking his young listeners to identify the sounds heard. Rather, the announcer should present listeners with the task of "envisioning [*sich ausmalen*] the episodes left indeterminate [*im Ungewissen gelassen*] according to their imagination and liking [*nach ihrer Fantasie und ihrem Gefallen*], using the respective sounds as a basis, and sending the solutions back to the broadcaster."[127] Clearly Benjamin is less interested in whether the children can correctly identify the sounds than what they imagine or would like those sounds to be, which in turn will help them envision – or paint a picture, *ausmalen* – the episodes that are otherwise left indeterminate. Put another way, Benjamin is wishing his listeners to utilize less any conventional, socialized mode of hearing than to tap into their egocentric abilities, asking them what they hear according to their fantasy or likes. Requesting that they paint a mental picture amounts to becoming authors of the scene, painting themselves into it, and in this way exercising their mimetic faculty, much like how the Chinese painter steps into his own painting in Benjamin's "Mummerehlen" fragment of *Berlin Childhood*.

This task is not the only element of *Bustle about Kasperl* that concerns egocentric language and a kind of mimetic faculty linked specifically to what is heard via radio. Throughout the radio play, Kasperl continuously exercises his capacity for egocentric language to the dismay of every adult he encounters. In the opening scene, where Kasperl finds himself in a dense fog at the market while buying a fish to bring home to his wife, he inadvertently bumps into another man.[128] They both ask each other's name, and the discussion gets increasingly heated:

---

[126] Benjamin, *GS* 7:832 [*WuN* 9.1:51]. Only the first paragraph has been translated by Jonathan Lutes in Benjamin, *Radio Benjamin*, 220, n. 3.
[127] Benjamin, *GS* 7:832 [*WuN* 9.1:51]; *Radio Benjamin*, 220, n. 3.
[128] That Krespel is out at the market buying a flounder is yet another nod to Brecht, whose protagonist, Gala Gay, is also out buying a flounder in the opening scene of *Man Is Man*.

HERR MAULSCHMIDT: Who are you anyway? You impertinent fellow!

KASPERL: Pardon me, but to whom do I have the honor of introducing myself?

HERR MAULSCHMIDT: Maulschmidt.

KASPERL: Who are you?

HERR MAULSCHMIDT: Maulschmidt.

KASPERL: I have to ask, good man, since when are mouths smithied? I thought at best they were stuffed.

HERR MAULSCHMIDT: You ruffian, you! I'm not a mouth-smith, I'm called that [*Ich bin nicht Maulschmidt, ich heisse so*].

KASPERL: Sure, good man, but I just asked you who you are [*wer Sie sind*].

HERR MAULSCHMIDT: Don't you mean, what you are?

KASPERL: Whoever you are, whatever you are, you can kiss my behind goodbye.

HERR MAULSCHMIDT: How dare you! [*Unterstehen Sie sich nicht!*] I am a respected person [*eine Respecktsperson*].

KASPERL: For someone who eats a lot of bacon [*eine Specksperson*], you seem pretty gaunt [*mager*] to me [translation modified].[129]

Although such jokes are themselves rather thin at times, this short, introductory dialogue exemplifies Kasperl's egocentric approach to language throughout the radio play; that is, he hears what he wants to hear rather than what is socialized, conventional or acceptable. Often names are converted to words with literal or ludicrous meaning, like *Maulschmidt* as "mouth-smith" above, or a word like *Respektsperson* is reworked and takes on a different meaning altogether.

Herr Maulschmidt turns out to be a radio announcer by trade. Just like in *The Cold Heart*, Benjamin explicitly references in *Bustle about Kasperl* the medium within the medium itself, never allowing his young listeners to forget the medium through which the story is being told. The word that is also a name, "Maulschmidt" or mouth-forger, further "satirizes radio as 'giving voice,'" as if the radio announcer helps forge mouths for the battle of voices that erupts on radio.[130] Upon realizing to whom he is speaking, Maulschmidt invites Kasperl to speak on the radio. At first Kasperl is unwilling, commenting that, were he to speak on the radio, "with all those sparks [*Funken*] flying around [*rund*], I might try to catch one and then I'd catch fire myself."[131] He is finally convinced and, once in front of the radio, immediately begins cursing and swearing at an enemy of his in Putzingen, hoping that his enemy is listening to him at that very moment.

---

129 Benjamin, *GS* 4:675 [*WuN* 9.1:60]; *Radio Benjamin*, 202–203.
130 Rosenthal in Benjamin, *Radio Benjamin*, xxvi.
131 Benjamin, *Radio Benjamin*, 204.

Much of the remainder of the radio play involves Maulschmidt and two of his colleagues chasing Kasperl from one place to another, from the train station and the market, to a carnival, zoo and eventually back to Kasperl's home.

One may wonder whether Kasperl is inadvertently mishearing such words or whether he is deliberately being a ruffian or lout (*Rüpel*), as Maulschmidt admonishes above. The answer, at least when first speaking to Maulschmidt, is clearly the latter: Kasperl is taking deliberate joy in redirecting words and phrases back at his interlocutors, not just upsetting them but upsetting any logical sequence or socialized convention. With Kasperl, a perceived lack of understanding – *Verstehen Sie mich?* – can quickly turn into a rebuke: "Unterstehen Sie sich!" His relation to language as one of distortion and disjointedness, moreover, is reminiscent of how gesture for Benjamin involves the articulation of bodily joints not as perfect or continuous, but as a "loosening of joints to the limits of the possible."[132] We should be mindful of the fact that, long before Benjamin's transfer of Kasperl to the radiophonic stage, Kasperl was and continues to be a famous puppet found throughout German-speaking countries since at least the eighteenth century. Without getting into the various styles and forms that Kasperl and his puppet theater has taken since, it is enough to emphasize how a puppet's joints not only stretch the limits of the possible, but are altogether otherworldly, as Heinrich von Kleist's essay, "On the Marionette Theater," famously elucidates. In the same passage in "What is Epic Theater?" Benjamin further writes: "'It can happen that way, but it can also happen entirely differently [*ganz anders*]' – this is the basic attitude of anyone who writes for epic theater. He relates to the story the way that a ballet teacher relates to his pupil."[133] For Benjamin writing the radio play, *Bustle about Kasperl*, the phrase could be slightly altered but amounts to the same thing: "It can be heard that way or it can be heard entirely otherwise."

Kasperl's cunning way of distorting echoes turns back on himself later in the radio play, resulting in an idiosyncratic logic based entirely on syllabic repetition. At one point while at the carnival, Kasperl enters the tent of the spirit Lipsuslapsus, who is billed by the booth owner outside as an "invisible, all-knowing and great magician" who can "discover lost objects, teach you foreign languages while you sleep, interpret your dreams [*deutet Ihnen Träume*], and do your school-

---

132 Benjamin, *GS* 2:536. Taken from the first version of "What is Epic Theater?" – which is not translated in the Harvard edition. Both this translation and the next are from Weber, *Theatricality as Medium*, 47.
133 Benjamin, *GS* 2:536; Weber, *Theatricality as Medium*, 47.

work."[134] Beyond the direct reference to Freud's *Interpretation of Dreams* (*Traumdeutung*), the wizard's name is also a play on what Freud called in his early psychoanalytic theory a "lapsus," a slip of the tongue.[135] The whole scene can thus be read as a comical refutation of Freud and the limits of psychology, especially Kasperl's criticism after he exits the tent: "[y]ou won't get any wisdom from this spirit. That wasn't right. Besides, I have a hunch it was the booth owner, whose spirit I'm now gonna turn black and blue."[136] But let us remain in the tent with Kasperl a little longer, since the "conversation" that occurs therein, which Benjamin in the stage directions calls an *Echospiel*, stages theatrically how an audible echo separates from the person uttering it to take on an entirely different meaning.

Let me first differentiate between this *Echospiel* and some other instances of echoes in the present study. Kasperl's "dialogue" between himself and the spirit who echoes the last few syllables back to him is far from Benjamin's night noises of the earliest telephone conversations that echo otherwise (*anders*) in his ears from those of today. Nor are Kasperl's echoes those of a long-forgotten moment. And in the next chapter, where a similar *Echospiel* occurs in Eich's radio play, *Sabeth*, word-parts are put forward (*proférer*) from which a name is echoed back, making one scholar conclude that the scene stages nothing less than the "birth of language from itself!"[137] Far from aspiring to such lofty intentions, the Lipsuslapsus scene in *Bustle about Kasperl* stages, if anything, the practice of psychoanalysis as a comedic series of echoes between analysand and analyst. The content, moreover, is reminiscent of *The Cold Heart*, since Kasperl is also searching, like Peter, for a way to find both wealth and happiness. Because of the incommensurable singularity of these syllabic echoes that resist any translation to another language, like the words "Maulschmidt" and "Specksperson" above, a select few will suffice:

> KASPERL: So, I need to find a lucrative line of work?
> LIPSUSLAPSUS: Work!
> [. . .]
> KASPERL: Well, maybe I'll become a doctor.
> LIPSUSLAPSUS: Idiot! (*Thor!*)

---

134 Benjamin, *GS* 4:684 [*WuN* 9.1:71–72]; *Radio Benjamin*, 210.
135 As mentioned earlier, Benjamin directly references Freud's slips of the tongue in section thirteen of Harvard's third version of the artwork essay, just before introducing the optical unconscious (Benjamin, *GS* 1:498 [*WuN* 16:239]; *SW* 4:265).
136 Benjamin, *GS* 4:686 [*WuN* 9.1:73]; *Radio Benjamin*, 211.
137 Peter Märki, *Günter Eichs Hörspielkunst* (Frankfurt a.M.: Akademische Verlagsgesellschaft, 1974), 46. See also the section on Eich's *Sabeth* in Chapter Three.

KASPERL: You don't think medicine would be gratifying (*erfreulich*)?

LIPSUSLAPSUS: Of course! (*Freilich!*)

KASPERL: And important for living (*Leben*)?

LIPSUSLAPSUS: Sure! (*Eben!*)

KASPERL: What then is missing from a doctor's luck (*Glück*)?

LIPSUSLAPSUS: Happiness! (*Glück!*)

KASPERL: Well, then I'll be a statesman.[138]

Whether or not this short exchange should be read as yet another snub against Freud's profession, what is certain is that the whole scene satirizes the role of the analyst both in general and, one could even say, the technique of free-floating attentiveness: instead of being like Freud's ideal analysts, who are conscious of their own unconscious inhibitions so as to better "interpret" what their patients tell them, the spirit of Lipsuslapsus is simply an echo machine with no consciousness of its own. As such, the scene both criticizes psychoanalysis and exemplifies how Kasperl's voice is already being mediated through the radiophonic apparatus: his voice is taken from him and echoed back in such a way that it is no longer recognizable to him. When speaking to Maulschmidt earlier, Kasperl appeared in full control of the disjointedness of words and their signifying misdirection. But here, Kasperl seems to be at the mercy of a vocalic repetition that returns the same, albeit without the self. Two points should be made here. First, Kasperl's final syllables and their return not only part with his self, becoming other than his own words, but it stages how language also parts with itself. That language takes leave of itself to become something other than it was, but without any additional intervention from without, is at the heart of Benjamin's theory of language. As Weber notes, language for Benjamin "is (immediately) the ability or the capacity to impart without recourse to anything else. Impart here entails what the word in English, as in German, implies: a process of *partitioning*, of *parceling out* 'oneself,' thereby becoming something else."[139] Language's "capacity to impart," its impart*ability*, consists for Weber "in its transformation, its becoming-other."[140] This does not mean that in becoming-other, language becomes completely other than language. It does however suggest that language has the capacity within itself, without any further mediation (in this case "un-mittelbar," im-mediate), to no longer remain the same.

---

138 Benjamin, *GS* 4:686–686 [*WuN* 9.1:72–73]; *Radio Benjamin*, 211.
139 Weber, *Benjamin's -abilities*, 44.
140 Weber, *Benjamin's -abilities*, 44.

The echo play illustrates this point well: Kasperl's question above, whether medicine would be gratifying, ends with "erfreulich" ("gratifying"), the response to which by Lipsuslapsus is, "Freilich! ("of course!"). The word in its transformation retains a syllabic and sonic semblance or trace of the word from which it has departed, but also becomes something else with a completely different meaning. This is why Weber emphasizes the double nature of "im-parting" above, the German equivalent of which is "mit-teilen": in the very act of communicating or imparting, a process of partitioning occurs such that language splinters and transforms into something else.

But is language the only element that parts with itself? What about Kasperl's voice? In the stage directions for this scene, Benjamin is adamant: the "following play of echoes must emerge solemnly and sustained [*getragen*, which could also refer to the musical term, *sostenuto* – RGR] throughout. The answers especially must be characterized as if echoes from afar" (translation modified).[141] Radio for both Schaeffer and Chion is acousmatic in nature because anyone who "speaks on the radio are acousmêtres in that there is no possibility of seeing them."[142] During Benjamin's echo play, Kasperl's voice becomes even more acousmatic, one could even say doubly-acousmatic: already separated from a visible body due to radio, Kasperl's voice also separates from its radiophonic source, from Kasperl's vocalic identity. And yet this is also not quite the whole story, since every listener realizes that Lipsuslapsus's answers are nothing but Kasperl's echoes; everyone, that is, but Kasperl himself. For Kasperl, the voice he hears is the voice of Lipsuslapsus, whereas for every young listener, it is merely an echo of Kasperl's voice, a phenomenon that might be called acousmatic irony.

Rather than rely on Chion's somewhat narrow definition of the radio acousmêtre, I would first turn to Jean-Luc Nancy's notion of *partage des voix*, which is both the French title of his 1982 book and a variation of the German "im-parting" so central to Benjamin's theory of language described above. For like the German word, "mit-teilen," which implies the double move of imparting and parting with, the French verb, "partager," can mean to both share and split, a sharing that is also a splitting. For instance, one shares money by splitting or dividing it between interested parties. Nancy's title, *partager des voix*, often translated as "sharing voices," equally refers to their splitting and distribution into a plurality of voices, to which Nancy pays equal heed. Without delving into Nancy's focus on *logos* and

---

141 Benjamin, *GS* 4:684 [*WuN* 9.1:72]; *Radio Benjamin*, 210.
142 Michel Chion, *The Voice in Cinema*, trans. Claudia Gorbman (New York: Columbia University Press, 1999), 21. It should be pointed out that even here, in his two radio plays for children from 1932, Benjamin is playing with the very possibility of seeing through one's ears, a notion that Chion does not seem to consider.

the hermeneutic voice, let me simply emphasize that, as with any play of echoes, any single voice, in the very act of sharing it with the external world, becomes both split and plural in order for it to be shared. Kasperl's voice is simultaneously his own and shared with Lipsuslapsus, and therefore split between both. One cannot therefore speak of any single voice or "the" voice, but always of its singular plurality. Radio seems to be the medium par excellence of the *partage des voix*.

If in the echo play Kasperl seems oblivious to how his voice splits from himself, he learns in the final scene of the radio play how his voice can be stolen from him. After returning home and speaking briefly with his wife, Maulschmidt knocks at the door. Upon entering, Maulschmidt gives him a thousand marks, telling Kasperl that, unbeknownst to him, Kasperl has been on the radio the whole time, and that the money being given was payment for his services.

> KASPERL: What's that supposed to mean?
>
> HERR MAULSCHMIDT: It means that you spoke on the radio, even if you didn't know it.
>
> KASPERL: Well, that must have been in my sleep.
>
> HERR MAULSCHMIDT: Not in your sleep, but in your bed.
>
> KASPERL: In bed?
>
> HERR MAULSCHMIDT: He who laughs last, laughs loudest. We in radio are even cleverer than you. While you were out in the city perpetrating your scandalous deeds, we secretly installed a microphone in your room, under your bed, and now we have everything you said, on record, and I just happened to bring one along for you.[143]

At this point, both Kasperl and the listening audience hear a crackly recording of his brief discussion with his wife from just moments ago. In the Introduction to *Radio Benjamin*, Rosenthal rightly posits this scene as highlighting "the structural significance of sound recording and surveillance to radio," whereby "the voice is subject to new and unseen forms of expropriation."[144] This is no doubt true, but let us also consider the correlation of this scene with the echo play above. Both scenes involve Kasperl's voice returning back to him, but whereas with Lipsuslapsus he was unable to recognize his own voice echoing back, here Kasperl hears and understands that voice to be his own. In both cases his voice is split and shared – in the case of Maulschmidt's recording, Kasperl's voice is even shared with the fictional listening audience *within* the radio play, effectively doubling the audience – but only in this final scene is Kasperl able to *hear* this voice as his own, as if for the first time. Kasperl thus finds himself as split as Bertha was when hearing the name, Strohmian: while

---

143 Benjamin, *GS* 4:694–695 [*WuN* 9.1:84–85]; *Radio Benjamin*, 219.
144 Rosenthal in Benjamin, *Radio Benjamin*, xxvii–xxviii.

certainly not as inexorably linked to his fate as the dog's name is to Bertha's, the recording does capture Kasperl's plans to break every bone in Maulschmidt's body. He has thus learned perhaps to be more cautious about what he says. It is also no coincidence that Maulschmidt hid the microphone under the bed, and that Kasperl suggests that he must have been recorded in his sleep: beyond the blurring of private and public spheres is the potential to record the sounds of sleep and even, as we shall see in the next chapter, dreams.

But there are other, more important reasons why this is a culminating moment in *Bustle about Kasperl*. One reason involves Benjamin's written stage directions for the moment when the recording of Kasperl's voice is heard: "the above text comes over the record, but somewhat distorted [*etwas entstellt*] in tonal coloring [*Tonfärbung*]" (translation modified).[145] Kasperl, like Benjamin's image of the hunchback, is not only diminutive in size, but also cannot be seen in the radio play, just as the hunchback could never be seen. They also both share distorted voices: at the end of *Berlin Childhood*, the hunchback whispers back to Benjamin "like the hum of the gas burner [. . .] over the threshold of the century,"[146] whereas the recording of Kasperl's voice is equally distorted, albeit via technology rather than memory. Indeed, Benjamin's opening phrase in "The Telephone" – whether "it lies with the construction of the apparatus or with that of memory"[147] – reflects the two ways in which the voices of Kasperl and the hunchback – both of which are always more than one – have become distorted, as if memory and technology are inexorably linked in disfiguration.

Another, equally diminutive figure that must be added to this lineage and who is even better aligned with the radiophonic Kasperl is Mickey Mouse. Given Benjamin's reflections on Mickey Mouse, one can go one step further and posit that Benjamin's Kasperl on radio functions as Mickey's acoustical variant. For one, both are almost universally recognizable: Benjamin calls him "the globe-encircling Mickey Mouse."[148] But let us begin with Benjamin's opening comment in his unpublished 1931 fragment on Mickey Mouse: "here we see for the first time that it is possible to have one's own arm, even one's own body, stolen."[149] Or in Kasperl's case at the end of the radio play, one's own voice. Whether such scenes are interpreted as more comical or horrifying, any comprehensive analysis of Disney films for Benjamin "should start from the ambiguity of situations which have both a comic and horrifying effect. As the reactions of children show, comedy and horror

---

145 Benjamin, *GS* 4:695 [*WuN* 9.1:85]; *Radio Benjamin*, 219.
146 Benjamin, *GS* 7:430 [*WuN* 11.1:236]; *SW* 3:385.
147 Benjamin, *GS* 7:390 [*WuN* 11.1:507]; *SW* 3:349.
148 Benjamin, *GS* 7:377 [*WuN* 16:132]; *SW* 3:118.
149 Benjamin, *GS* 6:144; *SW* 2:545.

are closely related."¹⁵⁰ Kasperl is certainly left stunned, perhaps even horrified, when listening to his distorted voice speak back to him. But the next line of Benjamin's "Mickey Mouse" fragment is equally relevant: the "route taken by Mickey Mouse is more like that of a file in an office than it is like that of a marathon runner."¹⁵¹ While Kasperl is clearly running away from his pursuers throughout the radio play, he tends to flit from one telltale scenario to another, with their sequence not nearly as important as simply getting from one to another. We should also not forget that Kasperl is originally a puppet. In this way, both Mickey and Kasperl are more like flying papers blowing in the wind than human runners laser focused on the finish line; they are more prop than person or, in the case of Kasperl, a prop "per sona." Miriam Hansen succinctly describes the relation of Mickey Mouse to a prop in light of Benjamin's comments:

> As a prototype of innervation, Benjamin's Mickey Mouse competes with the figure of the screen actor [. . .]. In contrast with the stage actor, the performer on screen forgoes the aura of "his presence in the here and now"; his performance or accomplishment (*Leistung*) is to a much greater degree determined by heteronomous agents, from the director and cinematographer to the sound engineer and editor. Thus fragmented and remote-controlled, he or she no longer dominates the scene by psychologically identifying with a role but, in tendency at least, functions like a prop – "a thing among things," as Kracauer was wont to put it – a moving object that interacts with and is acted upon by other objects, animate or inanimate, in a scenic space constituted by the apparatus.¹⁵²

Much of Hansen's incisive reading of Mickey Mouse can be applied to Benjamin's radiophonic Kasperl, including the citation that follows Hansen's passage above, which she gleans from Benjamin's artwork essay: "'Film is thus the first artistic medium which is able to show how matter plays havoc with human beings [*wie die Materie dem Menschen mitspielt*].' This makes film 'an excellent means of materialist exposition.'"¹⁵³ The same can be said of radio, and especially *Bustle about Kasperl*, from the stolen voice at the end to the initial pedagogical task of submitting my mail what its young listener's think they hear to the radio station, which is its own kind of *mitspielen*, of cooperating or playing along.

With the word "material," we have also returned, in a roundabout way, to Arnheim's reflections on materiality in the opening section of this chapter. While it would be a mistake to conflate Arnheim's material theory with Benjamin's use of the word, recall that materiality for Arnheim refers less to any phenomenological

---

150 Benjamin, *GS* 7:377 [*WuN* 16:132]; *SW* 3:130.
151 Benjamin, *GS* 6:144; *SW* 2:545.
152 Miriam Hansen, *Cinema and Experience* (Berkeley: University of California Press, 2012), 177.
153 Hansen, citing Benjamin in *Cinema and Experience*, 177.

materiality of things than to characteristics or properties made perceptible through the medium in question.[154] One such characteristic in film is slow motion, which Benjamin adopts directly from Arnheim to illustrate how film offers wholly new, otherworldly movements not otherwise seen before, leading Benjamin to his theory of the optical unconscious. Kasperl's recorded voice at the end, "somewhat distorted in its tonal coloring," is another, albeit acoustic, example of distortion that leads Kasperl – and his young listeners – to a completely different way of hearing his voice, which Kasperl was previously unable to perceive with Lipsuslapsus. This is one reason why Kasperl, after hearing his recorded voice in this new, otherworldly way, responds by saying, "I've just heard for the first time, what radio is [*wie der Rundfunk ist*]."[155] This revelation, brought about by the recording of Kasperl's voice and his realization of its technical reproducibility – which allows for the possibility of perceiving by means of radio one's own most intimate voice in an otherworldly way never before heard – is not just a conscious realization of radio's horrifying capacity to expropriate voices, though it is certainly that as well. But it is also a revelation about what and especially how we are now able to hear, and in Kasperl's case, of hearing one's own voice otherwise. The scene thus stages a becoming conscious of radio's acoustical unconscious, where Kasperl's consciousness becomes interwoven with the acoustical unconscious to which radio grants access.

The way Benjamin reads Mickey Mouse in earlier versions of the artwork essay is yet another way in which Kasperl, as Mickey's acoustical equivalent, becomes affiliated with the unconscious. In the second version of the artwork essay, Benjamin introduces the optical unconscious in section sixteen. Curiously, all references to Mickey Mouse in this section were stricken from the third version of the essay, a redaction that Miriam Hansen has reflected on most effectively and which I cannot hope to better here.[156] Benjamin aligns Mickey Mouse to the unconscious in earlier versions of the artwork essay because film has invalidated the "ancient truth expressed by Heraclitus, that those who are awake have a world in common, while each sleeper has a world of his own." Film achieves this not via "depictions of the dream world," but rather with the "creation [*mit der Schöpfung*] of figures of the collective dream, such as the globe-encircling Mickey Mouse" (translation modified).[157] This sense of creating anew as opposed to depicting or representing the dream world once again aligns with how Benjamin, just a paragraph earlier, reads

---

154 For a reading of Benjamin's use of "material" in distinction to Kracauer's use of the same, see the first section of Chapter Five.
155 Benjamin, *GS* 4:695 [*WuN* 9.1:85]; *Radio Benjamin*, 219.
156 See Hansen's chapter "Micky Maus" in *Cinema and Experience*.
157 Benjamin, *GS* 7:377 [*WuN* 16:132]; *SW* 3:118.

Arnheim's comments on how slow motion in film reveals not just familiar aspects of movement, but "discovers in these known aspects wholly unknown [*entdeckt in diesen bekannten ganz unbekannte*] aspects of movement" (translation modified).[158] As a new figure of the collective unconscious imparted by film, Mickey Mouse had the capacity for Benjamin to preemptively diffuse, through collective laughter, those "dangerous tensions which mechanization [*Technisierung*] and its consequences have engendered in the masses at large – tensions which at critical stages take on a psychotic character" (translation modified).[159] Hansen is therefore right to situate Benjamin's reception of Mickey Mouse "at the crossroads between fascism and the possibility of its prevention."[160]

While it would be a stretch to position Benjamin's radiophonic Kasperl at those same crossroads, he is nevertheless intended to elicit not only collective laughter throughout but also a deliberate learning moment at the end. This moment, when Maulschmidt unexpectedly knocks on Kasperl's door and enters the scene, is modelled on what Benjamin elsewhere described as fundamental to Epic Theater: "The most basic example would be a family scene that is suddenly interrupted by the entrance of a stranger."[161] But Maulschmidt is not the only stranger that interrupts the family scene between Kasperl and his wife, Puschi. Maulschmidt's play-back of Kasperl's "somewhat distorted" voice is also a sonic interruption, made even more apparent by the way Benjamin describes, in his notes on "Kasperl and Radio," how this final noise should be heard: "One hears for a while just static and then fragments [*Bruchstücke*] of what Kasperl has just said" (translation mine).[162] Benjamin's reference to fragments or "break-pieces," a term that is not found in the radio play proper, further emphasizes the interruptability and therefore pedagogical function of this sonic experience. The implications of interruption have proliferated throughout this chapter, from Vygotsky's claim, cited by Benjamin, that "[t]hinking is brought into action when an activity which has run unhindered up to then is interrupted," to how the rustling papers in *The Cold Heart* signaled simultaneously the interruption of narrative flow and the foregrounding of the radio as medium. And in Benjamin's other major text on radio, "Theater and Radio: On the Mutual Control of Their Educational Program" ("Theater und Rundfunk: Zur gegenseitigen Kontrolle ihrer Erziehungsarbeit," 1932), written in the same year these two radio plays were broadcast, he is even more explicit:

---

158 Benjamin, *GS* 7:376 [*WuN* 16:131]; *SW* 3:117.
159 Benjamin, *GS* 7:377 [*WuN* 16:132]; *SW* 3:118.
160 Hansen, *Cinema and Experience*, 168.
161 Benjamin, *GS* 2:535; *SW* 4:304.
162 Benjamin, *GS* 7:836 [*WuN* 9.1:57].

This is not the place to expound on the theory of Epic Theater, much less to demonstrate how the development and structure of *gestus* is nothing but a retro-transformation [*Zurückverwandlung*] of the methods of montage so critical to broadcasting and film – from a technological undertaking to a human one. Suffice it to say that the principle of Epic Theater, like that of montage, is based on interruption. Only here, interruption is not characterized as a stimulus, but has a pedagogical function. It brings the action to a halt, and thus forces the listener [*dem Hörer*] to take a position on [*zur Stellungnahme*] what is happening, and the actor [*den Akteur*] to take a position on his role [translation modified].[163]

With Benjamin's reference at the end to both listener and actor, the latter of which is not simply a stage or "seen" actor (*Schauspieler*), the blurring of radio and Epic Theater is heightened and with it, interruption as a mutual pedagogical function. Lutes translates "Stellungnahme" as "critical position," but Benjamin's point is clear: the interruption of action forces the listener to *think* about what is going on, and the actor to reflect on their role.[164] With the play-back of Kasperl's voice, Benjamin forces both his young listeners and his main protagonist to do just that. Only via this sonic interruption is Kasperl – and by extension, his listeners – able to reflect critically on what he hears for the first time: not just what but also how radio is (*wie der Rundfunk ist*).

In his essay, "Franz Kafka, On the Tenth Anniversary of His Death" ("Franz Kafka. Zur zehnten Wiederkehr seines Todestages," 1934), Benjamin compares Kafka's situation to experiments that "have proved that a man does not recognize his own gait on film or his own voice on the phonograph."[165] Hansen calls this a "salutary miscognition," one that, according to Benjamin, leads Kafka to study (*auf das Studium anweist*), where he "perhaps encounters fragments of his own existence."[166] Kasperl's situation here is the same: for a moment he is able to study the medium and recognize it for what it is, while simultaneously encountering a fragment of his own existence outside himself. But study is what keeps the students in Kafka's *Castle* awake, writes Benjamin: "While they study, the students are awake, and perhaps their being kept awake is the best thing about their studies."[167] While it is but a momentary sonic interruption for Kasperl, the technological estrangement and *Entstellung* of his own voice awakens him to what radio is. Benjamin thus stages at the end of *Bustle about Kasperl* how the main protagonist awakens to radio's forms and techniques, which brings us back not only to the opening pages of this chapter and Benjamin's *Reflections*

---

163 Benjamin, *GS* 2:775 [*WuN* 9.1:525]; *SW* 2:584–585.
164 Benjamin, *Radio Benjamin*, 367.
165 Benjamin, *GS* 2:436; *SW* 2:814.
166 Benjamin, *GS* 2:436; *SW* 2:814.
167 Benjamin, *GS* 2:434; *SW* 2:813.

on Radio, but also to the importance of bringing this expertise to radio's listeners. Given this final scene, what is involved in circumscribing the comportment of the voice in radio is not simply a kind of measuring of the immeasurable, nor just timbre that resists closure; it also cannot be limited to the acous-mimetic articulations of the voice, nor to its "com-portment," that is, its taking away of the listener's capacity to contemplate. It is all these elements and something more: the capacity of the speaker to be astonished by the sound of their own voice, and awaken to that most intimate part that has been forgotten. And this can only be heard *von fremder Seite*, which in Kasperl's case, is radio.

Benjamin's last broadcast was "From an unpublished collection of sketches, Berlin Childhood around 1900" ("Aus einer unveröffentlichten Skizzensammlung Berliner Kindheit um 1900") on 29 January 1933.[168] The very next day, Hitler was appointed chancellor and with that, the history of German radio's Weimar era came abruptly to an end. But Benjamin's last broadcast was arguably also the first publication of his *Berlin Childhood*, which he began working on in 1932, the same year his two children's radio plays were aired. Though he would have no other opportunity to broadcast this "collection of sketches" via radio, *Berlin Childhood* should perhaps be read through the lens of his radio work that began in 1927 and culminated in 1932. Instead of taking Benjamin at his word that none of his work for radio had any value "except in economic terms," his attention to voice and language, to the mishearings of words and their sounding out in his radio work should be recognized as laying the groundwork for the same in his autobiographical work, especially *Berlin Chronicle* and *Berlin Childhood around 1900*.

Like Benjamin, the young Günter Eich also recognized that radio could have an economic benefit to his chosen career as writer. But unlike Benjamin's radio career, which was curtailed in January of 1933, Eich's career became increasingly lucrative as he continued working in radio throughout the National Socialist regime. Eich's complicity during WWII will be discussed at some length in the next chapter, but it would already seem to put Benjamin and Eich at odds. And yet, Eich's acute sensitivity to the word – the fragile relationship between its meaning and its sonic elements, the word's distorted echoes in similarly sounding words and names – recalls themes in keeping with both Benjamin's radio and autobiographical work, and the acoustical unconscious in this and previous chapters. Eich's love of language bordered on the mystical, and his attendance at Martin Heidegger's early-1950 lectures will allow us to consider the extent to which Eich

---

168 See Rosenthal in Benjamin, *Radio Benjamin*, xx. Unfortunately, while there is a record that this final broadcast occurred, the typescript for it did not survive.

adapted some of Heidegger's reflections on technology, poetry and receptivity for radio. Perhaps most importantly, we shall see how Eich, after having once helped perpetuate the National Socialist regime, was paradoxically able to almost single-handedly awaken the listening public not just to the artistic and pedagogical potential of radio, but above all to its political impact.

4 Glimpsing the World through Our Ears: Günter Eich and the Acoustical Unconscious

Günter Eich wrote some of the most important work for German radio directly after WWII, which garnered him the title "grandfather" of the modern German *Hörspiel*, even if the next generation of *Hörspielmacher* vehemently rejected his radio work.[1] Unlike even Benjamin's relatively minor radio projects, all of which have been translated and collected in a single volume,[2] fewer than five of Eich's over one hundred radio plays have been translated into English.[3] Eich was also an influential post-war lyricist, but as one publisher of his selected poetry rightly attests, Eich is "unjustly neglected in English" because only small selections of his poetry are available. Whether remembered in Germany more for his radio plays or for his poetry, Eich continues to remain practically unknown in North America today.

Perhaps because of this, readers of Eich or Benjamin – and this may be one of the few similarities they share – almost inevitably overlook their radio work. Both authors not only garnered a fairly stable income from the texts they wrote for radio, but they also reflected on the medium in short, critical texts. As we have

---

1 In his book, *Das Hörspiel – Mittel und Möglichkeiten eines totalen Schallspiels* (1961), Friedrich Knilli inspired the next generation of *Hörspielmacher* with a new theoretical approach to the German radio play that emphasized sound over language, and which distanced itself from Eich's more traditional approach. For a brief overview of the history of the German radio play between the 1950s and 1960s, see Hans-Jürgen Krug, *Kleine Geschichte des Hörspiels* (Konstanz: UVK Verlagsgesellschaft mbH, 2008), esp. 69–77.
2 See both Walter Benjamin, *Radio Benjamin*, ed. Lecia Rosenthal, trans. Jonathan Lutes (London/New York: Verso, 2014), and Walter Benjamin, *Werke und Nachlass: Kritische Gesamtausgabe* (Frankfurt a.M.: Suhrkamp, 2008–) (hereafter, *WuN*), vol. 9 (2017).
3 Hofmann, cited by Axel Vieregg, "The Spanner in the Works," in *The Berlin Review of Books*, 30 March 2011, http://berlinbooks.org/brb/2011/03/the-spanner-in-the-works/. In *German Radio Plays*, (The German Library 86, ed. Everett Frost and Margaret Herzfeld-Sander [New York: Continuum, 1991]), two of Eich's radio plays are translated: "Dreams" and "Don't Go to Al-Kuwaid!" See also Günter Eich, *Journeys: Two Radio Plays* (London: Cape, 1968), in which two other radio plays by Eich are translated by Michael Hamburger: "The Rolling Sea at Setubal" and "The Year Lazertis." As far as I am aware, only one radio play has ever been produced in English: *The Other and I* (*Die Andere und Ich*), for which he won the prestigious Blind War Veterans' Radio Play Prize (Hörspielpreis der Kriegsblinden) in 1952, was produced in English in 1984 under the auspices of the Hörspiel/USA project, led by Klaus Schöning and cosponsored by the West Deutsche Rundfunk (WDR). The most recent collection of his poetry translated into English is from 2010: Günter Eich, *Angina Days: Selected Poems of Günter Eich*, trans. Michael Hofmann (Princeton, NJ: Princeton University Press, 2011).

seen, Benjamin recognized early on that radio still had an equal chance as film, theater or any other art form to authenticate itself once the public was given the opportunity to *awaken* to its form. At first glance, Eich uses the medium of radio in the 1950s, and the genre of the radio play in particular, to do just that. For instance, the main motivation behind Eich's most famous radio play, *Dreams* (*Träume*, 1951), is to wake up.[4] By emphasizing the all-too-human character of Nazi Germany's crimes and extending them into the moral malaise of Western capitalism as a whole, Eich uses *Dreams* to criticize the listening public both for their passive acceptance of the former's crimes and for their desire to integrate into the latter's culture. The most famous line of the radio play encapsulates this call to rise against submission: "Be obstreperous, be as sand, not oil in the machinery of the world!" ("Seid unbequem, seid Sand, nicht das Öl im Getriebe der Welt!"). In this way, Eich shared Benjamin's hopes to awaken the public ear to the artistic, pedagogical but above all political potential of radio. As paradoxical as it sounds, Eich's *Dreams* helped awaken the German public to their post-war condition: according to Heinz Schwitzke in his classic text of 1963, *The Radio Play: Dramaturgy and History* (*Das Hörspiel: Dramaturgie und Geschichte*), Eich's *Dreams* "was the birthing hour, via the radio play, of the inevitable challenge to the German public."[5]

While Eich arguably employed an emerging aesthetic awareness of radio in the 1950s to confront the German listening public with their passive acceptance, his own complicity with the propaganda machine of the Third Reich certainly muddles his post-war convictions.[6] Moreover, as Bernhard Siegert and others argue, Eich's radio plays of the 1950s are constitutive of a Romantic aesthetic that foregrounds a "highly problematic worship of the word," which ultimately contributes to the erasure of radio as a medium.[7] In other words, Eich's radio plays of the early 1950s emphasized not an exploration of the medium's unique form

---

4 Two lines from the poem that ends the radio play indicate the absolute wakefulness that Eich calls for: "Wake up, because your dreams are bad [*schlecht*]! / Stay awake, because that which is horrible is approaching [*näher kommt*]" (translation mine; Günter Eich, *Gesammelte Werke* [Frankfurt a.M.: Suhrkamp, 1973] [hereafter, *GesW*], 2:321).
5 Heinz Schwitzke, *Das Hörspiel: Dramaturgie und Geschichte* (Köln: Kiepenheuer und Witsch, 1963), 300–308. Similarly, Axel Vieregg writes that in *Dreams* "Eich describes our waking state as a sleep 'into which we have all been lulled' while to dream means in fact to awaken in the true reality" (Vieregg, "Spanner in the Works," http://berlinbooks.org/brb/2011/03/the-spanner-in-the-works/).
6 I will address Eich's radio career during the National Socialist regime in section 2 of this chapter.
7 Bernhard Siegert, "1953, March 26. The Bayrische Rundfunk broadcasts Max Frisch's radio play *Herr Biedermann und die Brandstifter*," in *A New History of German Literature*, ed. David Wellbery, 861–866 (Cambridge: Harvard University Press, 2004), 863.

and techniques, of sound over language, but rather a continuation of a Romantic, decidedly phonocentric aesthetic that Eich himself employed throughout his prolific radio career during the Third Reich.

Siegert's critique about Eich's conservative radio plays would suggest their unsuitability to the acoustical unconscious examined thus far: Eich's emphasis on language throughout his work in radio has been argued by German radio historians and media theorists as doing away with radio as a medium, such that there would be no difference between reading one of Eich's radio plays or listening to it performed, whether on the radio or live. I certainly concede this point: Eich's decidedly literary approach to the radio play genre no doubt limited the palette of sonic experiences and experimental soundscapes that radio producers were already exploring during the Weimar Republic; Eich inserts no radio announcer to interact with various persona into his radio plays, as Benjamin did in both *The Cold Heart* and *Bustle about Kasperl*. But while Eich's postwar radio work contributes to the 1950s' "radio play of inwardness" and the "disappearance" of radio as medium, I propose that Eich was nevertheless interested in the radiophonic medium precisely because it allowed for an *amplification* of the fissures of language in the absence of the written word. Much like how Benjamin carefully chose words that not only describe sounds but also echo the words' sounds, or the way Kafka wrote with an ear for how words in a sentence may sound during a public reading, Eich was similarly attuned to the way in which sounds of words would be heard if one's eyes were closed and only the ears were awake.[8] Eich's emphasis on the sonic dispersion of language, meaning and vocalic identity in his plays, despite his otherwise conventional use of the medium, correlate to some of the features of the acoustical unconscious examined in previous chapters. Language for Eich certainly stands at the very center of his thought, but it does not follow that language as a "medium" – whether read or only heard via radio – is therefore absent or disappears. The task here is to interrogate Eich's emphasis on language and consider the extent to which it aligns with or diverges from Benjamin's own reflections on language and radio, how much Eich relies on traditional notions of aestheticism, and whether any of this helps elucidate an acoustical unconscious relevant to German radio after WWII.

---

[8] See Kata Gellen, *Kafka and Noise: The Discovery of Cinematic Sound in Literary Modernism* (Evanston, IL: Northwestern University Press, 2019), especially her third chapter on Kafka's problematic relationship to recitation.

4.1 "Dichterisch wohnet der Eich": Eich and Heidegger

Already at a young age, Günter Eich was an active writer of radio adaptations and radio series from the National Socialists' seizure of the radio industry in March 1933 to the end of the war in 1945. He had even applied to join the Nazi Party as early as 1 May 1933, although the application was never confirmed, apparently due to the flood of applications at the time.[9] Eich's activity as a professional radio writer during the Nazi regime continues to be regarded by many critics as suspicious at best. The majority of his radio work from 1933 to 1945 amounts to radio adaptations of existing literary resources – over a hundred and fifty radio pieces in all – from popular German fairytales such as Baron von Münchhausen and the brothers Grimm to eighteenth and nineteenth-century authors such as Eichendorff, Storm, Hebel and Tieck.[10] But he also wrote a handful of radio plays and co-wrote with Martin Raschke seventy-five of the ninety total episodes for the radio series, *Monthly Scenes from the Country Postman* (*Die Monatsbilder des Königswusterhäuser Landboten*). The series, whose main protagonist involved a country mailman and his trusty dog Troll, was broadcast between October 1933 and May 1940 and was regarded at the time as not merely tolerated but "singled out as *the* model radio program of the Third Reich."[11] The debate about Eich's radio work for the Nazis was further exacerbated in 1993 when a recording of Eich's final Nazi-era radio play, *Rebellion in Gold City* (*Rebellion in der Goldstadt*) was discovered. The radio play is decidedly anti-capitalist, illustrating the fall of greedy British capitalists through an uprising in one of its African colonies. It was broadcast on 8 May 1940, a few months after Goebbels began his anti-British propaganda campaign and four

---

[9] Hans-Ulrich Wagner, *Günter Eich und der Rundfunk. Essay und Dokumentation* (Potsdam: Verlag für Berlin-Brandenburg, 1999), 55. But Martin Heidegger, who also applied to be a party member on the same day as Eich, had his application accepted, and maintained his membership until the end of the war. For an overview of the correspondence between Eich and Heidegger, see Walter Kühn, "Das alte Buch. Eichs Beitrag zur Festschrift von Martin Heidegger," *Berliner Hefte zur Geschichte des literarischen Lebens*, vol. 7 (Berlin: Institut für deutsche Literatur, 2005), 152–171.

[10] Matthew Philpotts, "Surrendering the Author-function: Günter Eich and the National Socialist System," in *Modes of Censorship: National Contexts and Diverse Media*, ed. Francesca Billiani (New York: Routledge, 2014), 265.

[11] Glenn R. Cuomo, *Career at the Cost of Compromise: Günter Eich's Life and Work in the Years 1933–1945* (Amsterdam: Rodopi, 1989), 80. In chapter four of his book, Cuomo gives an excellent overview of the NS reception of *Die Monatsbilder des Königswusterhäuser*, as well as situating the radio series within Eich's ouvre ("In terms of sheer quantity, it is also [Eich's] most voluminous work ever" [Cuomo, *Career*, 78]). See also Axel Vieregg, *Der eigenen Fehlbarkeit begegnet. Günter Eichs Realitäten 1933–1945* (Eggingen: Edition Isele, 1993), esp. 26–35.

months before Nazi bombers raided London on 7 September 1940.[12] With the discovery of *Rebellion in the Gold City*, it was no longer a question of whether Eich was complicit, but for what reasons he continued his radio career under the Nazi regime, whether for practical, opportunistic or political reasons.

No one can deny that Eich was one of the more prolific writers for the National Socialists' radio propaganda machine. And yet, his decision to work in radio was his own, and it was apparently more of an opportunistic than political choice. Critics cite a passage in one of his letters to a friend in 1932 as the turning point away from what he deemed was his ideal career as poet to entertainment writer: "Dear Erhard! [. . .] It's important (at least for me) to tell you that, due to lack of talent, I'm giving up my studies. I'm thinking to earn my daily bread as an author (Proof of which I will reserve until better times)."[13] Despite this turn away from a career as poet, a surviving radio play from 1932, *A Dream at Edsin-gol* (*Ein Traum am Edsin-gol*) is certainly worthy of being called "Eich's poetically most demanding text of this time," at least for radio.[14] It was to be broadcast in 1932 via an ambitious literary program led by Eugen Kurt Fischer and Arno Schirokauer before it was cancelled due to a drastic personnel shake-up at the Mitteldeutschen Rundfunk AG (MIRAG) in Leipzig. Pointing both to the passage in his 1932 letter above and to radio projects like *A Dream at Edsin-gol*, Matthew Philpotts and others suggest that the twenty-five year old Eich was already setting himself up to become a professional writer before the National Socialists officially seized the radio industry in March 1933.[15] Even his application to the NSDAP two months later was, as Hans-Ulrich Wagner writes, nothing more than "a consciously opportunistic move towards his media-literary career [. . .]. The young author believed to increase his chances with radio. This is why he applied, while privately he mocked it and distanced himself from it at the same time: 'Dear Addi! Everything's more or less fine here (. . .) Nothing else new to report, other than I've joined the NSDAP. Heil Hitler. Günter.'"[16]

Already by June 1933, less than six months after Benjamin's final broadcast, Eich had enough stability to buy a piece of land in Poberow and to buy a DKW

---

12 The book, *"Unsere Sünden sind Maulwürfe." Die Günter-Eich-Debatte* (Amsterdam: Rodopi, 1996), edited by Axel Vieregg, is a rich collection of critical essays and previously published newspaper articles that spans the critical reactions engendered by the sudden discovery of Eich's *Rebellion in der Goldstadt* in 1993.
13 Eich, cited by Hans-Ulrich Wagner, *Günter Eich und der Rundfunk. Essay und Dokumentation* (Potsdam: Verlag für Berlin-Brandenburg, 1999), 42. Unless otherwise noted, all references to Wagner's work are my own.
14 Wagner, *Günter Eich und der Rundfunk*, 39.
15 Philpotts, "Surrendering the Author-function," 268.
16 Wagner, *Günter Eich und der Rundfunk*, 55.

from the "not inconsiderable sum of 1200 Reichsmarks."[17] One reason why it is so difficult for scholars of Eich to accept his successful radio career during the National Socialist regime is because of he began his literary career before the war denouncing politics over aesthetics. In one of his more frequently cited texts from the immediate pre-war history, "Observations on Poetry" ("Bemerkungen über Lyrik," 1932), Eich emphasizes what he believes to be the poet's ultimate duty: to trace the inner movement of the unified *Ich* over any external influences like society and politics:

> The poet decides on nothing, he is interested only in himself [*sein Ich*]. He creates no second or third-person world like the epic poets or the dramatists, since for him only the isolated I that is devoid of society exists. And precisely because he decides on nothing, he collects time as intrinsically whole, and lets it be seen again in the unclouded mirror of his I. For the transformations of the I are the essence of a time.[18]

Eich published this in *The Column* (*Die Kolonne*), a short-lived journal whose overriding principle was arguably "the defense of the apolitical sphere of literature."[19] Throughout "Observations on Poetry" and much of his work for *The Column* prior to 1933, Eich defends poetry as "inner dialogue," a concept touted by Gottfried Benn before him. Benn constitutes, according to one critic, "the prime exponent of timeless lyric inwardness," and it is from Benn that Eich adopts a "Romantic aestheticism emphasizing the primacy of aesthetics over politics, the individual over society, intuition over ratio, nature over civilization."[20]

Eich's penchant for this brand of Romantic aestheticism should also be seen as one of the reasons why he was later able to distance himself after WWII from both political complicity with the Third Reich and, especially with *Rebellion in Gold City* and the *Country Postman* radio series, the ofttimes blatant propaganda that pervades his radio work between 1933 and 1945. Indeed, Eich's pre-war proclivity towards Romantic and apparently apolitical aestheticism helped him procure not just amnesty by the Americans after the war but the license to publish his work in the American occupation zone by 1946. On behalf

---

17 Wagner, *Günter Eich und der Rundfunk*, 56–57.
18 Eich, *Gesammelte Werke* [Frankfurt am Main: Suhrkamp] 4, 459). All subsequent references to Eich's *Gesammelte Werke* will be labeled *GW* followed by volume and page number.
19 Matthew Philpotts, *The Margins of Dictatorship: Assent and Dissent in the Work of Günter Eich and Bertolt Brecht* (Oxford: Peter Lang, 2003), 180. For slightly different views on the political viability of and Eich's poetological stance in *Die Kolonne*, compare Cuomo's references to the journal in chapter two of his *Career at the Cost of Compromise* with Philpotts's section entitled "Ideological conservativism?" (Philpotts, *Margins*, 175–184).
20 Dolan and Richardson, cited by Philpotts, *Margins*, 178.

of Eich, friend and author Hermann Kasak wrote the following evaluation of his work for the Americans:

> [Günter Eich] has always rejected Nazi ideology. In his essence, he is an individual who, because of his lyrical view of the world, approaches all political questions in a naïve and disinterested way. Instinctively, he rejected Hitlerism. In neither his poems, nor his dramas, nor his plays for the radio have I come across a single line which has been political or, in the slightest way, Nazi in nature. For him, it is a question of pure poetry [translation Philpotts's].[21]

In this plea for Eich's political neutrality, Kasak relies heavily on the notions of "purity" and poetry as inherently apolitical, thereby hoping to separate Eich's supposedly untainted work from Nazi politics. Scholars have of course since questioned such posturing, pointing to his prodigious radio output during the Third Reich as anything but "pure" from political influence. Nor can one say, especially in light of the mole-like subversiveness in both his poetry and radio plays after WWII, that Eich remained apolitical. And yet, his earlier Romantic aestheticism was nevertheless used like an umbrella to weather the political storms in which he found himself, allowing him to work for both the National Socialists during the war and the Americans in West Berlin almost immediately thereafter.

It is therefore with suspicion that one must turn to the Romantic aestheticism and lyricist elitism that Eich continued to promote even after WWII, especially in his reflections on language and radio. Eich's output as essayist is limited by both variety – his topics invariably revolve around either language, lyricism or radio – and volume: apart from a number of prize speeches after 1950, his reviews and essays are often compendious in style and scope. While much work has been done to tease out Eich's Romantic aestheticism via his literary influences and output prior to WWII, especially with his connection to *The Column* circle, much less scholarly attention has been given to its relation to his reflections on radio.[22] The radio play is praised by Eich as "a wonderful

---

21 Cited by Cuomo, *Career*, 137; translation in Philpotts, "Surrendering the Author-function," 274.
22 In *Career at the Cost of Compromise*, Cuomo briefly surveys two German radio theorists who wrote influential texts prior to the Third Reich's takeover: Hermann Pongs's *Das Hörspiel* (1930) and Richard Kolb's *Das Horoskop des Hörspiels* (1932). While Cuomo follows Gerhard Hay's suggestion that both works could be seen as developing "the theoretical foundation for the National Socialist radio plays," he does not take up either work in relation to Eich's own view of language or reflections on radio. However, the affinities between Kolb's concept of the word as described in *Horoskop des Hörspiels* and Eich's emphasis on language is striking. Bernard Siegert rightly links Eich's "problematic worship of the word" back to Kolb's influential book: "Kolb's theory of the radio play centered on the idea of the word as a creative force which, liberated from the exterior world, would trigger an 'image of the absolute' in the

artform" because it "is set only to language [*Sprache*]. Language is what I'm interested in. In any case I see the world through the ear, which means through language, much more than through the eye."[23] This frequently repeated sentence from an interview conducted as late as 1967 clearly indicates how much Eich continued to think of language as heard rather than seen or read on a page: "seeing the world through the ear" is synonymous for Eich with comprehending it "through language." Eich's emphasis on speech in radio recalls those early twentieth-century authors and media theorists like Arnheim, Döblin, Zweig and others, who called for radio to rediscover that lost tonal language that Rousseau and German Romanticists like Novalis and Herder first imagined to be at the heart of the origin of language. For Eich, then, radio was a conduit of spoken language through which both the world and, more importantly, the self and its "inner dialogue" could be perceived. Radio becomes less a medium of reproducibility than a technology that allows for listening in on what for Eich is the essence of an era: "the transformations of the I."[24]

Eich was fully aware that he would be considered by many as a traditionalist. But already in his 1953 prize speech for winning the *Radio Play Prize of Blind War Veterans* (*Hörspielpreis der Kriegsblinden*), Eich announced that labeling him a Romantic idealist would be a mistake: "Don't misunderstand me as an idealist who mourns the passing of time, when there was still no electronic microscopes, no Hollerith machines, no eight tracks or mechanical brains [*mechanischen Gehirne*]."[25] In this particular paragraph, Eich is concerned with the role of technology in the modern world, as well as with the limits of human sense perception:

> In some respects, humankind is quite simply blind, and I don't just mean the blind. Our sense organs always apprehend only a part of reality. Our ears do not hear the screech of bats, and we don't see infrared or ultraviolet. Humankind therefore creates substitute organs, radar equipment of every description, and measuring instruments that apparently work more precisely and faster than eye or ear. Our hubris appears convinced that there are no fundamental limits to such development. That may be; however, it appears that the more we see, the more blind we become. For we can actually only get closer to that which we love, and we are really only capable of recognizing that [object of love]. The blind hand

---

listener. [. . .] Between 1933 and 1940, Günter Eich, whose language-centered radio plays dominated the scene after 1945, wrote several plays for radio, and he no doubt absorbed many of Kolb's ideas about the creative force of the word. In particular, Eich's postwar texts for radio betray a continuation, in some sense, of Kolb's doctrine that the action and the characters of radio plays are not in front of the listeners, but inside their heads" (Seigert, "1953, March 26," 864).

23 Eich, *GesW* 4:504.
24 Eich, *GesW* 4:459.
25 Eich, *GesW* 4:610.

that, full of love, touches a flower, sees better than the eye that indifferently registers a whole garden. The world has been broadened by its measurability, but has become smaller in its intimacy [*Innigkeit*].[26]

Such are the reasons why, according to Eich, he should not be branded an idealist.[27] And in a sense he was right: much of what he describes in the above passage, particularly his reference to the increased number of measuring instruments that expand our perception of the world while reducing our intimacy with it, is an echo of contemporaneous discourse on technology at the time, especially in the philosophical work of Martin Heidegger, with whom Eich became acquainted only a few years earlier and whose lectures Eich regularly attended.

In *Mixed Conditions: Heidegger in the Literary and Philosophical Life of the 1950s* (*Vermischte Zustände. Heidegger im literarisch-philosophischen Leben der fünfziger Jahre des zwanzigsten Jahrhunderts*, 2015), Walter Kühn dedicates an entire chapter to examining the private, institutional, and intellectual encounters between Eich and Heidegger, including what they might have read or heard of each other's work throughout the 1950s. Eich's and Heidegger's successful careers during the Third Reich in the 1930s and 1940s make their acquaintance all the more understandable and problematic. While Kühn makes no mention of their previous careers during the war, he nevertheless reports with great detail the first extended encounter between Eich and Heidegger, which occurred in August 1951, when Eich was invited to attend a small gathering of poets and intellectuals for a few days in Austria, including Friedrich Georg Jünger and Clemens Podewils. They played boccia every day, but also visited churches and went on communal walks to nearby lakes. One evening, a short lecture and a subsequent poetry reading were planned: both Eich and Jünger recited a few of their poems, and Heidegger presented his work-in-progress, "Building–Dwelling–Thinking" ("Bauen–Wohnen–Denken"). As Eich later wrote in his diary about this evening: "Then a few days in the princely castle in Austria, Heidegger gave his lecture on 'building–dwelling–thinking' (a strong influence, I must read something of his)."[28] Only a half-year later, in January 1952, Eich was again invited to a small gathering in order to listen and respond to a

---

26 Eich, *GesW* 4:609–610.
27 The flower to which he refers is not the blue flower of the Romantics but the trophy awarded to Eich in the form of two hands holding a flower, which as Eich comments, "epitomizes [*versinnbildlicht*] the tactile world of the blind die" (translation mine; Eich, *GesW* 4:609–610).
28 Eich to Rainer Brambach on 29 August 1951. Cited by Walter Kühn, *Vermischte Zustände. Heidegger im literarisch-philosophischen Leben der fünfziger Jahre des zwanzigsten Jahrhunderts* (Würzburg: Königshausen und Neumann, 2015), 110. Kühn's next section is an intricate reading of Heidegger's "Building–Dwelling–Thinking" alongside Eich's *Sabeth*.

portion of Heidegger's new lecture, "What is Thinking?" ("Was heißt denken?"). Four months after that, in April 1952, Eich participated at a conference on "Art and Technology" at the Munich Academy, which was not only co-organized by Heidegger but in which Heidegger gave a lecture entitled, "Poetically Man Dwells" ("Dichterisch wohnet der Mensch"). Whether or not Eich followed up with his need to read something more from Heidegger, the number of lectures he attended between 1951 and 1952 suggests a keen interest in Heidegger's work. Thanks to this timeline of the early 1950s that Kühn so meticulously describes, much of Eich's reflections on poetry, language and technology should be read in light of Heidegger's own lectures and publications of the time. Eich's prize speech before the blind war veterans, which he presented on 3 March 1953 and which Heidegger apparently read later that year, is no exception.[29]

Eich must have been as moved by Heidegger's "Poetically Man Dwells" as he was with "Building–Dwelling–Thinking": as is well known, Heidegger takes up in the former Hölderlin's late poem "In lovely blueness" ("In lieblicher Bläue") to discover that "poetry is a measuring" completely other than the measurements taken by various mechanical instruments:

> Yet it strikes us as strange that Hölderlin thinks of poetry as a measuring. And rightly so, as long as we understand measuring only in the sense current *for us* [emphasis original]. In this sense, by the use of something known – measuring rods and their number – something unknown is measured out [*abgeschritten*] and thus made known, and so is confined within a quantity and order which can always be determined at a glance. Such measuring can vary with the type of apparatus employed. But who will guarantee that this customary kind of measuring, merely because it is common, touches the nature of measuring?[30]

The similarities here between Heidegger's reflections in "Poetically Man Dwells" and Eich's comments in his prize speech before the blind war veterans about modern instruments are striking. In his pursuit to examine poetry as a measuring, Heidegger continues with Hölderlin's poem to deduce that the measure for poetry is the godhead, or more precisely, God as the unknown which is imparted through images of the familiar. This too Eich suggests in his prize speech: while he does not follow Heidegger's specific trajectory via Hölderlin to the godhead, Eich nevertheless ends his speech by turning to theology:

---

29 Kühn, *Vermischte Zustände*, 143.
30 Martin Heidegger, *Gesamtausgabe* (Frankfurt a.M.: Klostermann, 2000) (hereafter, *GA*), 7:203. The English translation, slightly modified, is from ". . . Poetically Man Dwells . . ." in Martin Heidegger, *Poetry Language Thought*, trans. Albert Hofstadter (New York: Perennial Classics, 2001) (hereafter, *PLT*), 222. Subsequent page references to Heidegger will be indicated first as *GA*, followed by *PLT*, indicating Hofstadter's English translation, unless otherwise noted.

Basically, I mean that there is for everything written – which also comes down to something else for the radio play – something that I can't justify for you, neither short, long or in any way. It is something that I must ask you to accept as a personal opinion and confession: It comes down to everything written approaching theology.[31]

Once again, Eich is wary not to be labeled an idealist or evangelist by immediately listing what he does not mean by his reference to theology. "What then do I mean?" he writes, and his answer follows: "We avail ourselves of words, sentences, language. Every word preserves a reflection [*Abglanz*] of that magical state where the word is one with its intended object, where it is identical to creation."[32] In one of his notebooks from the 1950s, Eich went even further: "Poetry is an attempt to meditate on the thoughts of God."[33] For Eich, each word thus retains or preserves (*bewahrt*) the trace of some magical state or theological being that, as he must have already heard in Heidegger's lecture on Hölderlin the summer before, could not be measured by any instrument of measurement, but was subject only to a certain measuring of the immeasurable.[34]

Another noteworthy resemblance between Eich's prize speech in March 1953 and Heidegger's Hölderlin lecture attended by Eich in the summer of 1952 is a mutual reference to the blind. It is no surprise that Eich would mention the blind to a speech to and for blind war veterans of WWII. In the extended passage cited

---

31 Eich, *GesW* 4:611.
32 Eich, *GesW* 4:612.
33 Eich, *GesW* 4:365.
34 Eich had likely not read Benjamin's early essay, "On the Language of Man and on Language as Such," so he would not have been aware that, for Benjamin at least, "the fundamental problem [*das Urproblem*] of language is its magic" (Walter Benjamin, *Gesammelte Schriften* [Frankfurt a.M.: Suhrkamp, 1972] [hereafter, *GS*], 2:142–143; Walter Benjamin, *Selected Writings*, ed. Michael W. Jennings, Marcus Bullock, Howard Eiland, and Gary Smith, trans. Rodney Livingstone and Edmund Jephcott [Cambridge: Harvard University Press, 1996–2003] [hereafter, *SW*], 1:63–64). Benjamin's reading of language's magic is of course much more complex than Eich's brief turn to theology in this *Kriegsblinden* speech. But when Benjamin speaks about the magic of language, he also emphasizes not that which imparts *through* but what imparts *in* language: "What does language 'communicate' or impart? It imparts the spiritual being [*das geistige Wesen*] that speaks to it [. . .] Spiritual being imparts *in* a language and not *through* a language [. . .] For precisely because nothing imparts *through* language, that which imparts itself *in* language [i.e., the spritual being – RGR] cannot be limited or measured from without" (Benjamin, *GS* 2:142–143; *SW* 1:63–64). Benjamin's reflections on language not only appear to coincide with Eich's "personal creed" that every word carries along with it a reflection of some magical state, but also echoes Eich's comments – which echo those of Heidegger's above – on the nature of measuring: the spiritual being which imparts itself in language cannot be measured externally. To consider all that is written "as nearing theology" thus means, for Eich by way of Benjamin, to consider the immeasurability of the spiritual as it imparts itself *in* language.

above, Eich refers to man – and not just to the blind – as being incapable of perceiving certain sensations like infrared light or the sonic waves of bats. In "Poetically Man Dwells" Heidegger also refers to man's blindness, although in terms of man's dwelling unpoetically. "Do *we* dwell unpoetically?" he asks.

> Presumably we dwell altogether unpoetically. If that is so, does it give the lie to the poet's words; are they untrue? No. The truth of his utterance is confirmed in the most unearthly way. For dwelling can be unpoetic only because it is in essence poetic. For a man to be blind, he must remain a being by nature endowed with sight. A piece of wood can never go blind. But when man goes blind, there always remains the question whether his blindness derives from some defect and loss or lies in an abundance and excess [*Überfluß und Übermaß*]. In the same poem that meditates on the measure for all measuring, Hölderlin says (lines 75–76): "King Oedipus has perhaps one eye too many."[35]

Once again, the issue for Heidegger is that of measuring: one's blindness to poetry is not a question of simultaneously perceiving and not perceiving, of some paradoxical combination of presence and absence, but rather how such blindness derives from "a curious excess [*ein seltsames Übermaß*] of frantic measuring and calculating." It is this overmeasuring of measuring, moreover, that conceals the true nature of measuring.

To avoid this tendency and to learn to know the poetic, Heidegger does not stray far from an equally curious mode of listening. The measure of poetry, the unknown and immeasurable god against which man measures himself, is

> a strange measure for ordinary and in particular also for all merely scientific ideas, certainly not a palpable stick or rod but in truth simpler to handle than they, provided our hands do not grasp but are guided by gestures befitting the measure to be taken [*sondern durch Gebärden geleitet sind, die dem Maß entsprechen, das hier zu nehmen ist*]. This occurs with a taking which never clutches [*an sich reißt*] at the measure but rather takes in the collected perception that remains a listening [*sondern es nimmt im gesammelten Vernehmen, das ein Hören bleibt*].[36]

From here it is a short step to the way Eich thinks he perceives the world less with his eyes than with his ears. Both Heidegger and Eich's emphasis on listening amounts to a certain mode of receptivity that "takes in" rather than grasps for or clutches at. It is a receptivity that avoids the passive/active divide and remains open to an excess (*Übermaß*) that would otherwise threaten to overwhelm our senses and distort our understanding of and intimacy (*Innigkeit*) with the world around us. On the one hand, this *taking in* of collected perception that remains a listening is immediately reminiscent of Freud's technique of free-floating

---

35 Heidegger, *GA* 7:206–207; *PLT* 225.
36 Heidegger, *GA* 7:201–202; *PLT* 223.

awareness examined in the previous chapter. It also shares some affiliation with Benjamin's *Urvernehmen*, or primal listening, which he refers to in his "Epistemo-Critical Preface" and which has been referred to at several points in this study.[37] But beyond all these variants of a kind of ideal open receptivity that remains a listening, which Heidegger contrasts here with a futile attempt of grasping at, there is also Benjamin's com-portment or behavior of the voice, specifically its ability to sweep up and carry the listener away, leaving them stupefied, *benommen*. This constant oscillation between a receptive "taking in" by the open ear and a "taking away" of consciousness by the comportment of the voice offers another way to think the radio listener's own condition or "bearing" in modernity, which is never fixed or whole. The following analyses of three radio plays by Eich explore such oscillations.

4.2 Awakening in *Dreams* to Eich's Soundscapes

> Dream interpretation is Günter Eich's poem, and one can hardly say more about his fame than this: he poetizes all of our dreams.[38]   *Frankfurter Allgemeine Zeitung*, 13 March 1954

Imagine a world in which the dreams of others were not only accessible but newsworthy: a world in which journalists could gain access to the dreams of our political leaders or the dreams of everyday people around the globe in the course of a single day; where reporters could cite these dreams, and we could see and hear the dream images of others on television or radio; a world in which such "dream reports" would be as significant as the summary of world events or national news. By finding out what a group of people dream about from a given region or country, we would gain access to their collective unconscious. If we compared what people were dreaming about on a global scale, we might even catch a glimpse of what affects everyone, regardless of country or culture. Now imagine that we could only *hear* these dreams. Such would be the world that Günter Eich invites us to listen to with his most famous radio play, *Dreams* (*Träume*, 1951).[39]

---

37 While a more sustained comparison is called for between Heidegger's collected perception that remains a listening and Benjamin's primal listening in the "Epistemo-Critical Preface," what Heidegger's collected perception lacks is Benjamin's emphasis on a retrospective memory that is inseparable from his notion of *Urvernehmen*.
38 "Traumdeutung ist Günter Eichs Gedicht, und man kann zu seinem Ruhme wohl nicht mehr sagen, als daß er unser aller Träume dichtet" (translation mine).
39 This section is derived from an earlier article, "When Only the Ears are Awake: The Acoustical Unconscious and Günter Eich's Radio Plays," in *Germany in the Loud Twentieth-Century: An Introduction*, ed. Alexandra Merley Hill and Florence Feiereisen (Oxford: Oxford University Press, 2012), 35–50.

The initial reaction of the German public to Eich's *Dreams*, which was broadcast at 20:50 on 19 April 1951, was unanimously negative. During its premiere, the telephone operator at Hamburg Northwest German Radio (NWDR) was overwhelmed with callers complaining about its indecent content.[40] It is not difficult to understand why Eich's *Dreams* triggered so visceral a reaction by the German listening public: the five dreams unambiguously suggest scenes of deportation, execution, cannibalism, and the threat of being either hunted by an unknown enemy or consumed from within for attempting to be happy or content in a post-war consumerist society. Despite this inauspicious beginning of his post-war career, Eich went on to write many radio plays, and is now generally lauded as having initiated the "golden age" of German radio in the early 1950s. As Mark E. Cory writes, the public anger provoked by Eich's *Dreams* was "one measure of his achievement," while his other, "more telling measure of achievement [. . .] was the proliferation of dream plays, as studio after studio became a kind of 'acoustical dream laboratory.'"[41]

Many have discussed Eich's *Dreams* in psychological and socio-political terms, while others have read it in accordance with reception theory. All of these critics have limited themselves to an examination of either the written page or the play's effects on society. While it is necessary to understand the play's impact on its contemporary radio audience and the history of German radio drama in general, what has been lost in previous critical analyses is, simply put, its *acoustical* transmission, which includes listening to the comportment of voices in relation to the language used.[42] In 2007, the original broadcast was made available

---

40 Karl Karst's extensive notes in the dust jacket of the 2007 compact disc release transcribes a selection of callers' vehement reactions to the radio play. Also included on disc three is a "Musikalischer Epilog" arranged by Hans Schüttler, who mixes concrete sounds and rhythmic beats with fragments of callers' reactions originally recorded in 1951.
41 Mark E. Cory, "Soundplay: The Polyphonous Tradition of German Radio Art," in *Wireless Imagination: Sound, Radio, and the avant-garde*, ed. Douglas Kahn and Gregory Whitehead (Cambridge: MIT Press, 1992), 351.
42 In 1974, two years after Eich's death, Peter Märki describes in *Günter Eichs Hörspielkunst* that his radio art, while appreciated mainly in terms of content and stylistic characteristic, has been subject to no close readings by literary scholars (Peter Märki, *Günter Eichs Hörspielkunst* [Frankfurt a.M.: Akademische Verlagsgesellschaft, 1974], 11–12). Märki was the first to do so in earnest by including three close readings of Eich's *Dreams*, *Sabeth*, and *The Other and I* (*Die Andere und Ich*). Unfortunately, Märki fails in his interpretations to *listen* closely to the plays' voices and sounds, despite writing a little further on that, whenever we interpret radio plays, "we must remember that the text is initially nothing more than a score [*der Text zunächst nicht mehr als eine Partitur ist*]" (translation mine; Märki, *Günter Eichs*, 13).

to the public for the first time in over fifty-five years and has since been made available online via YouTube.[43]

Eich shared Benjamin's hopes in the early 1930s to awaken the public ear to the artistic possibilities of radio. But why would Eich employ dreams in particular to awaken his listeners to their bad conscience and moral proclivities? There are multiple reasons for this, some of which are related to the history of Weimar radio itself. But I will limit myself to three general dimensions: a peculiar characteristic of the auditory sense, radio's apparent affinity with dreams, and the significance of dreams in psychology. These three parameters can more generally be categorized under phenomenological, radiophonic, and psychological headings, but all of them affect each other and combine to make dreams the most useful vehicle for Eich's call to wakefulness.

The first parameter involves what it means to listen. More than any sight that we behold, sounds penetrate us. Don Ihde writes in his *Phenomenology of Sound* that our auditory field and auditory focus is "not isomorphic with visual field and focus, it is *omnidirectional*":

> In the shape of the auditory field, as a surrounding thing, the field-shape "exceeds" that of the field-shape of sight. Were it to be modeled spatially, the auditory field would have to be conceived of as a "sphere" within which I am positioned [. . .] If I hear Beethoven's Ninth Symphony in an acoustically excellent auditorium, I suddenly find myself *immersed* in sound which *surrounds* me. The music is even so *penetrating* that my whole body reverberates, and I may find myself absorbed to such a degree that the usual distinction between the senses of inner and outer is virtually obliterated. The auditory field surrounds the listener, and surroundability is an essential feature of the field-shape of sound [italics original].[44]

While these are not unique claims, they clarify just how permeable the threshold is between the hearer and the heard. Unlike vision, where the perceiver and the perceived can be clearly demarcated, the acoustical realm more easily allows for the fluid *interpenetration* of perceiver and perceived. The breakdown of the boundary between inner and outer, subject and object, that defines the acoustical sphere, is one of the most intriguing characteristics that distinguish the auditory realm from the visual one, and by extension sound studies from visual studies. As we will see in the examples that follow, the localizing of the

---

43 As of this publication, all five dreams can be found on YouTube, the first one being here: https://www.youtube.com/watch?v=5gQcvu1YgCE. The compact disc release also includes a new dramatization of the radio drama performed and recorded in 2007, allowing for the rare opportunity to compare vocal and theatrical techniques in the original broadcast with those used today.
44 Don Ihde, *Listening and Voice: A Phenomenology of Sound* (Athens, OH: Ohio University Press, 1976), 75.

listener in relation to what is being heard in Eich's *Dreams* becomes especially problematic when there is an added ambiguity between reality and fantasy.

This leads to the second reason why Eich employs dreamscapes: because of their affinity to the medium of radio, and to the radio play in particular. As Justus Fetscher writes, "the radio play's presentation of sound material is unable to distinguish the fictitious from the factual, dream from reality, the paranormal from the normal."[45] How much this affinity of the genre is due to its reliance on the omnidirectional auditory field described above is debatable. It is indeed one thing to be immersed in Beethoven's Ninth Symphony in a concert hall and quite another to listen to Eich's *Dreams* on the radio or headphones. While it is true that the lines between both subject/object and reality/fantasy tend to blur in the radio play, it does not follow that the lack of a subject/object dichotomy necessarily leads to a blurring of reality and fantasy. And yet, this is often what occurs in Eich's radio plays. Radio plays tend to "epitomize illusion and auditivity by playfully exploiting and challenging them, and thus making them conscious for the listeners."[46] The challenge is to think of these illusions as the playful and conscious exploitation of otherwise unconscious auditory marks that, instead of imposing the unity demanded by self-consciousness, are allowed to echo in their ambiguities.

Last but not least, Eich's use of dreams cannot be thought without reference to the field of psychology. The most significant contribution to dream psychology, Freud's *Interpretation of Dreams* (*Traumdeutung*, 1901), was published exactly fifty years prior to the first broadcast of Eich's *Dreams*. Unlike Freud, Eich does not ask his listeners to interpret the dreams they hear, nor does Eich appear to offer any direct interpretation of the dreams himself. However, much of what has already been discussed in the first two paradigms above, from its "envelopment" (Ihde) to the radio play's affiliation to dreams, can be further elucidated via Freud's distinction, in *The Interpretation of Dreams*, between day and night dreams. In the daydream, the position of the dreamer is at least in part structurally fixed and unified, over and against the objects of his fantasies, which are also fixed. In the night dream, however, the position of the subject is no longer unitary because the "objects" of the dream are themselves no longer unified: they are "signifiers," "marks," and must be re-marked in the interpretation, which in turn also resituates the marker, or in this case, the dream-interpreter. While I examined this line of argument in the introduction with

---

45 Justus Fetscher, "Blindness and 'Showside': Non-Visual Aspects of German Radio and Radio Plays in the 1950s," *Monatshefte* 98, no. 2 (Summer 2006): 246.
46 Fetscher, "Blindness," 246.

regard specifically to the acoustical unconscious, its relation to the experience of night dreams should also be emphasized here. As we will see in the interpretation of *Dreams* that follows, Eich causes an acoustic crisis of localization on the part of the radio listener, such that the position of the listening "dream-interpreter" becomes split and dispersed. Eich uses this instability of the hearing-I not only to break down the distinction between the hearer and the heard, but also to implicate the listener, as both prisoner and prosecutor, into the acoustic experience. What links Freud's psychology with Eich's sonic dream laboratories, and with *Dreams* specifically, is the need to awaken to unconscious mental processes. But what Eich adds to Freudian psychology via radio is twofold: a prototheory of dreams premised on sound, which runs counter to Freud's insistence that there are no voices in dreams, and the possibility of sharing collective dream experiences.[47] Whereas Freud in *Interpretation of Dreams* wished to improve the overall mental health of the individual patient, Eich wants to awaken each citizen's moral responsibility concerning the recent atrocities of the Holocaust.

It will be difficult to avoid returning to these three paradigms. German radio theory has always dealt with the medium's affinity with the fantastic and the dream, if not the psychotic.[48] Specifically for Eich, however, these three key elements – the interpenetration of the hearer and the heard, the play between reality and fantasy, and the night-dream in which the subject becomes dispersed and resituated – help us understand why Eich uses dreams to pursue his agenda of social and political awakening in his radio play, *Dreams*. In what follows, I focus on some of the ways in which the use of voices and sounds in *Dreams* accentuate acoustic indeterminacy, and, instead of requiring or imposing a unified listening subject, challenge the listener's mode of hearing in the *dispersion* of a "listening subject." In this way, Siegert's claim that Eich always puts the listener into the heads of his radio plays' characters is helpful only up to a point. The following reading suggests a slight variation, namely, that Eich is playing with the notion of a "unified" listener and their placement in his plays; in some instances, the listener's position can no longer be fixed. One could further extrapolate this reading into the realm of social critique and say

---

47 See Mikko Keskinen, "Hearing Voices in Dreams: Freud's Tossing and Turning with Speech and Writing," *PSYART: A Hyperlink Journal for the Psychological Study of the Arts*, accessed 28 January 2021, http://psyartjournal.com/article/show/keskinen-hearing_voices_in_dreams_freuds_tossing_.
48 For an excellent overview of especially German radio history and its affiliation to psychosis, see Wolfgang Hagen's *Das Radio: Zur Geschichte und Theorie des Hörfunks – Deutschland, USA* (Munich: Wilhelm Fink, 2005).

that Eich uses the radiophonic medium to propose that the grounds for a unified society are just as illusory and untenable as a unified subject, and that a functional society requires not just unification but subversive, destabilizing elements that warn a society's members of becoming oil in the machinery of the world. But to use a fitting albeit pre-industrial idiom, this would be putting the cart before the horse.

4.3 Eich's *poisons de l'öuie*

Heinz Schwitzke once wrote that the first dream of Eich's *Dreams*, "the railroad dream, is one of Eich's most impressive sketches in terms of both subject matter and execution."[49] The following analysis of Eich's railroad dream (*Eisenbahntraum*) is meant as a model of reading – and listening to – particular elements like voice and sounds that signal a becoming conscious of acoustically unconscious signs and marks heard in the dislocation of a listening subject. We will listen closely to three exemplary moments in the first dream: the first two involve the manner of speech and the spacing out of the voice(s), while the third example analyzes the ambiguous role of the sounds heard.

Each of the five dreams begins with a short description of the dreamer, narrated as if it were a news broadcast. The first dream is introduced by a female voice:

> In the night from the first to the second of August 1948, the locksmith Wilhelm Schulz from Rügenwalde in Hinterpommern, which is now Gütersloh in Westfalen, had a dream that was not particularly pleasant. [. . . It was a dream] that should not be taken seriously, since Schulz, who has since passed away, was evidently suffering from a stomach disorder. Bad dreams come from a stomach that is either too full or too empty.[50]

The dream that we subsequently hear is not only one that must have been previously "recorded," since the fictional locksmith who dreamt it has since died, but it should apparently also not be taken seriously, since Schulz was suffering from stomach cramps. We will return to the relationship between body and dream content later. For now, I wish only to point out how listening to a dead man's dream is reminiscent of Maurice Renard's fantastical tale, "La mort et le coquillage," which I took up at the beginning of Chapter Two. Just as it remains unclear whether the composer Nerval died of congestion (as the doctor said he did) or from listening too closely to the sounds emitting from the conch shell, it also remains ambiguous here whether the locksmith Schulz died because of a

---

49 Schwitzke, *Das Hörspiel*, 110.
50 Eich, *GesW* 2:289.

stomach illness or from a bad dream. The suggestion, of course, is that both Schulz and Nerval's death were caused by something more than a mere physical ailment; perhaps by those "poisons de l'öuie," rumored to exist by the narrator of Renard's tale, a phrase that admirably characterizes all five dreams heard in Eich's radio play.

The first dream invites the listener to imagine a group of people in a freight car devoid of lights. The incessant noise of a slow-moving train and other, distant voices in the wagon are all that are heard at first, but grow ever louder. A dialogue begins between an old couple who can just barely remember when they used to live in a world beyond the four walls of the freight car. Two other generations of their family, their grown-up grandchildren and their great-grandchild, Frieda – the only character with a name in the entire dream sequence – are also in the freight car. It becomes clear that, while the old couple might have once led a happy existence at some time before they found themselves in the freight car, everyone else has no recollection of the outside world, nor do they believe there is one.

As in many of his other plays, like the fragment *An Hour with the Dictionary* (*Eine Stunde Lexikon*, 1931) or *The Year Lazertis* (*Das Jahr Lazertis*, 1953), Eich introduces characters that are fascinated with a particular word or phrase. The old man and woman keep remembering strange words from a temporally (and ever more spatially) distant world. One word in particular, "Löwenzahn" (dandelion) is repeated multiple times because, like the distant memory of the outside world, the word itself becomes increasingly difficult to remember with each passing minute. The old woman earlier tells her husband, "dandelion, – you use the strangest of words," only to ask him not long thereafter:

> OLD LADY: "What was the name of the flower that you spoke of earlier, the yellow one?"
> OLD MAN: "Dandelion [*Löwenzahn*]."
> OLD LADY: "Dandelion, ah yes, I remember."[51]

The focus on words and names that either are constantly being forgotten or mutate into *Ersatznamen* is a hallmark of Eich's radio work, revealing how attuned he was to the acoustic fragility of a word and how it is remembered. Particularly significant is the way Eduard Marks, who plays the old man in this original 1951 broadcast, articulates the word "Löwenzahn": he hesitates on and then repeats the first syllable, "Löw-" when answering his wife, as if he is himself having trouble remembering the word in its entirety. The breakdown of the word's

---

[51] Eich, *GesW* 2:291.

articulation by Marks, which is impossible to read on the page without listening to the original broadcast, further makes conscious the word's combination of "Löwe" (lion) and "Zahn" (tooth). What breaks apart is the relationship between signifier and signified: words and names peel away from their putative meaning and become almost meaningless sounds.[52] This exemplifies the unique play between diction and language made possible by radio. Its unique, other nature allows a word, through its very mode of articulation, to more easily split from its given meaning because of how the word's sounds are enunciated. In radio at least, the conscious meaning of a word more easily gives way to the word's sonic parts: its individual syllables and how it is pronounced. Eich was very aware of this potential, which is one way that radio sounds out the indeterminacy related to the acoustical unconscious.

Another example of the specific use of the voice in radio involves less a play between diction and language than between vocal direction and displacement. A significant moment in the dream occurs when the characters recognize a hole in the wall, through which they can glimpse the outside world:

OLD MAN: "If there's a hole in the wall, we should be able to look out."
GRANDSON: "Good, I'll look out."
OLD MAN: "What do you see?"
GRANDSON: "I see things I don't understand."
WIFE: "Describe them."
GRANDSON: "I don't know the words that belong to them."
WIFE: "Why aren't you looking out anymore?"
GRANDSON: "No, I'm scared."[53]

After the grandson retreats from the hole, the old man and old woman look through and recognize things they have not seen for forty years, including a field of dandelions. Instead of relying on the text to analyze this passage, it is important to listen carefully to the voices heard in the original 1951 broadcast. When the middle-aged grandson looks out of the hole, the direction of his voice

---

[52] This reaches its thematic height and ethical significance in the dream when the grandchild, a grown man, complains to the old man that he should not speak of such meaningless words: "Regardless of whether it is true or not, do you think we will be happier if you tell us that [. . .] there is something you call a yellow flower, and some kind of beings you call animals, and that you have slept on something you call a bed, and that you have drunk something you call wine? All words, words – what are we to do with them? [*was sollen wir damit?*]" (translation mine; Eich, *GesW* 2:292).
[53] Eich, *GesW* 2:294.

changes considerably: instead of speaking to one or another family relative, he seems to speak directly into the microphone, which gives the acoustical illusion that he is speaking directly into the ears of the radio audience. Clearly audible is how director Fritz Schröder-Jahn decided in 1951 to record the voice significantly closer to the microphone whenever any of the characters "look out" from the hole, giving the impression that they are not just "looking out" but actually "speaking out" through the crack of the freight car in which they are encaged.[54] Two inferences can be made from this change of vocal direction at this crucial juncture. First, we might conclude that the characters are speaking directly to us: our ears are on the other side of the hole, perhaps even the hole itself. The idea that they glimpse the outside world through our ears describes a unique version of synesthesia, whereby one looks through an ear to see out into the world. According to this reading, however surreal it may sound, the radio audience would thus have to be positioned *outside* of the freight train and therefore part of the outside world. But a second inference may also be pursued: if we imagine the characters' voices as not external from us but internal – as speaking from within our mind – then their view of the outside world merges with our own. In this second reading, in which our mind doubles as the freight car, the grandson looks through our eyes and speaks with our voice. At this point in the dream, the listener may even be induced to open his or her eyes and "look out" into the outside world along with the grandson, the old man and old woman, and confront the history of the world that they all share with the listener. Günter Eich and director Schröder-Jahn thereby split the position of the radio audience between these two scenarios: on the one hand, the radio audience is outside of the freight car listening in – their ear is the hole through which the characters in the dream perceive the outside world – but on the other hand, with the freight car doubling as the mind's stage, the radio listeners may simultaneously be located inside the freight car with them looking out. This fundamental displacement of the listener, involving at once implication and observation, generates a crisis of localization whereby the listener is unable to fix herself to a single acoustical place, and as such is always on the alert, always listening for a way to find a foothold. This displacement and subsequent alertness are generated not through the diction of the voice, but through its direction and projection.[55]

---

54 In 2007, radio director Alexander Schuhmacher did not use this vocal technique when theatricalizing this particular dream. He did, however, significantly modify the soundscape of this dream from the earlier version. One unique example is his use of a high-pitched tone to sonically imitate the *Sonnenstrahl* (sunbeam) that streams through the hole when it is first discovered.
55 The listener's ear of Eich's *Dreams* is split in a similar way that Bertha's eye (and therefore also place) is split in Tieck's "Eckbert the Fair." See Chapter Two.

My final example further complicates the issue of displacement, this time not through the voice but through another acoustical feature of the 1951 recording: the accompanying sounds of the freight train heard throughout the dream. All five dreams feature a particular sound that not only lends structural unity to the dream as a whole, but is also integral to the narrative of the dream. In the fifth and final dream, for instance, the sound of termites devouring the insides of buildings and humans alike is heard both by the characters within the dream and by the listening audience, a technique often referred to as point of audition. In *Audio-Vision* (1994), Michel Chion argues that one should rather speak "of a place of audition, or even zone of audition," since it is the image of audiovisual counterpoint that "always creates the point of audition, which in this case is worthy of the term *point*" (emphasis original).[56] Chion's zone of audition is more appropriate for radio, since it has no filmic image. Radio also blurs the two meanings that Chion attributes to point of audition: its spatial sense (from where am I listening?), and its subjective sense (which character is hearing what I hear?). In the radiophonic zone of audition, space and subject comingle, allowing for the radio listener to enter that zone as if they were a character in that space, an ambiguity that will become important in what follows. It should also be noted that the incessant sounds that comprise the "zones of audition" in Eich's *Dreams* – whether they be drums in the distance (fourth dream), the heavy approach of footsteps (third dream), or even the sounds of the train speeding up (first dream) – slowly increase in volume as each dream nears its end. This technique, admittedly hackneyed, nevertheless also implies the nearing threat to the listener's safety, a threat that Eich explicitly describes in the line from the closing poem already cited.

Returning to the first dream, the acoustical mise-en-scène involves, as I have already mentioned, the unmistakable sounds of a train rolling over tracks and the rhythmic sounds of a steam engine. The train itself could be anywhere, but it is clear that the voices heard are inside the train and that it is on the move. As the dream unfolds, however, the incessant sounds of the slow-moving freight train begin to suggest other sounds, in particular, the sounds of someone sleeping. The low, rhythmic booms of the train moving over the tracks imply the beating of a heart, while the higher sighs of the distant steam engine conform almost uncannily to the *deep breathing of a sleeper*. That the sounds of the slow-moving train parallel the sounds of a body sleeping – which, again, can only be experienced by listening to the play – returns us to the issue of unconscious bodily perception. As we observed with the threshold experience of awakening in Chapter

---

56 Michel Chion, *Audio-Vision* (New York: Columbia University Press, 1994), 91.

Two, consciousness of the self is possible only after the body distinguishes its "self" as separate from the objects or marks surrounding it. The same can be said of dream-consciousness: the body's own physical or internal sounds are also what determine, at least in part, dream content. Recall that the dreamer, Wilhelm Schulz, is suffering from stomach illness. The radio audience adopts not simply the point (or place) of audition of the characters on the train, but simultaneously hears the very sounds of the dreamer's body as it translates unconsciously the sounds of its internal organs into the acoustical sound-image of a train. This is the only instance in Eich's *Dreams* where the fictional dreamer's presence is implied, albeit obliquely, but it is also an indication of how radio can make heard the translation of unconscious bodily stimuli into an acoustical dream image. Just as the sounds of a word begin to separate from its meaning, and just as the listener is split between participation and impartiality, the point-of-audition sounds oscillates disjunctively between signifying a train's movement in dream-consciousness and the body's unconscious interpretation of itself sleeping.

Benjamin describes a similar process in fragment K1, 4 of *The Arcades Project*. The way a sleeper's internal bodily noises and feelings are translated into dream images acts as a model for how Benjamin conceives of the Parisian arcades: as generated by the dreaming collective communing with its own insides.

> [J]ust as the sleeper [. . .] sets out on the macrocosmic journey through his own body, and the noises and feelings of his insides, such as blood pressure, intestinal churn, heartbeat, and muscle sensation [. . .] generate, in the extravagantly heightened inner awareness of the sleeper, illusion or dream image which translates and accounts for them, so likewise for the dreaming collective, which, through its arcades, communes with its own insides.[57]

In Eich's *Dreams*, the sounds of a freight train that are generated by the dreamer's heartbeat and slow breathing echoes these remarks if we consider the dreamer as the German dreaming collective. In this reading, we hear neither a train nor the internal organs of the locksmith Wilhelm Schulz, but the deep breathing of the sleeping, German collective body. Eich's method is to awaken that dreaming collective precisely by turning its unconscious "ear" upon itself, by forcing it to listen consciously to its own breathing in sleep and how it unconsciously translates the sounds of its own body into the dream-image of freight trains. The German dreaming collective thus awakens to its own internal processes, to what it hears unconsciously prior to any conscious hearing of itself. In learning to hear consciously what the collective body – with what Benjamin calls above its "exceptionally

---

[57] Benjamin, *GS* 5:491; Walter Benjamin, *The Arcades Project*, trans. Howard Eiland and Kevin McLaughlin (Cambridge: Harvard University Press, 2002) (hereafter, *AP*), 389.

heightened inner awareness" – unconsciously translates into dream, the dreaming collective awakens and is forced to contend with its own body as collective history.

Much more can be said about how the listeners of Eich's *Dreams* awaken to previously unconscious acoustical knowledge of voices and sounds, both in this dream and the four remaining ones. Eich perfects in *Dreams* a radiophonic language that tends to decenter rather than unify the listener by calling attention to the disjunction between word and sound and by disclosing the unconscious translation of sounds into acoustical dream-images. While Siegert and others are generally correct when they criticize Eich for imprisoning the radio listener in the minds of his characters, this should not deter us from considering Eich's keen interest in systematically dismantling the security of the ear: through the sound of words, Eich banishes the private realms that would otherwise allow an individual refuge from what Frederic Jameson has called the omnipresence of history and the implacable influence of the social.[58] Explicitly calling for a future community that must no longer seek refuge in either its history or its dreams, Eich recruits a radiophonic – as opposed to a phonocentric – approach to language whose other nature speaks a different constellation of acoustically conscious and unconscious data. Subsequent readings of Eich's work should account for awakening to this new configuration, a mode of hearing when only the ears are awake.

4.4 Eich's Echoes: *Sabeth*

Written in the same year as *Dreams*, the story of *Sabeth* (original broadcast in 1951),[59] which Märki describes as having "the simplicity of a folk tale,"[60] recalls less the nightmarish vignettes of *Dreams* than the fantastical settings of Tieck's "Eckbert the Fair." The hour-long radio play, divided into "chapters," is about a family of farmers, the Fortners, whose daughter teaches a giant raven how to speak. In the process of learning the language of man and becoming a close friend of the Fortner family, the giant raven gradually loses the ability to communicate with other ravens, forgets how to fly and realizes near the end that he

---

[58] Frederic Jameson, *The Political Unconscious: Narrative as a Socially Symbolic Act* (Ithaca, NY: Cornell University Press, 1981), 20.
[59] As of this publication, the 1954 broadcasting of *Sabeth or the Guests in Black Robes* (*Sabeth oder die Gäste im schwarzem Rock*) can be accessed via this YouTube link: https://www.youtube.com/watch?v=Khp-nv4n5YA.
[60] Märki, *Günter Eichs Hörspielkunst*, 34.

is no longer even a raven: "I have learned your language. I am no longer a raven but have not become a human either."[61] On the one hand, Sabeth's identity complex may be interpreted as the result of Sabeth's marked distanciation from the *Urtext* as he learns the language of man. Learning how to use words, in this interpretation, is the equivalent of forgetting the *Urtext* common to all ravens.[62] But this metalinguistic interpretation cannot be thought without the way it makes use of radio's ability to personify – that is to say, to "give a voice" to or make a "per sona" of – both animate and inanimate objects.[63]

The play is divided into eight sections, the first three of which are "Tales" (*Erzählungen*) narrated by three different characters. The first tale is narrated by Therese Weisinger, who is the teacher of the Fortners' young daughter, Elisabeth. Weisinger is suspicious of the young girl, who has been admitting in class that she has spoken with a giant raven. Weisinger decides to visit the Fortner family, who lives on the settlement furthest from the village of Reiskirchen. During Weisinger's visit, Sabeth enters the Fortner home unexpectedly, and Weisinger faints from "seeing" a giant raven in the doorway. Frau Fortner, who narrates the second tale, explains to a slowly recovering Weisinger the story of how the family first met Sabeth. Much can be examined in this second chapter of the play, from its largely narrative exposition to the way in which Frau Fortner, when speaking about her first encounter with Sabeth, describes a feeling of déjà vu, as if she had long known the giant talking raven. Her vague sense of already having known the raven is comparable, for instance, to Bertha's experience of encountering the name, Strohmian. Such a comparison, however, should not overlook the narrative and structural differences, perhaps the most important being Frau Fortner's explanation of her déjà vu experience *within* the narrative, while Bertha's "déjà vu des Anderen" (according to Bloch) is "external" to it, that is, "external" to the narrative in the sense that the name's utterance wholly restructures, reopens, and displaces Bertha's apparently closed, childhood narrative.

By the end of the first two tales, we have only heard *about* the "black coat incarnate" – Sabeth's epithet, *der Leibhaftige im schwarzen Rock* may also be translated as "the devil in the black coat" – while all the characters have already

---

61 Eich, *GesW* 2:373.
62 This is largely Döhl's interpretation: Sabeth "appears [. . .] as a being from that world in which *word and thing* are one. By learning the language (of man) and using it, he removes himself ever further away from the primal text [*Urtext*], and finally dissolves completely" (translation mine). See Richard Döhl, "Zum Hörspielwerk Günter Eichs," WDR 3, 13 December 1976, accessed 22 August 2021, http://www.reinhard-doehl.de/eich1.htm.
63 Compare also with Rudolf Arnheim's discussion of how symbolic figures and inanimate objects can be given a voice in radio, which is referred to in the first section of the last chapter.

"seen" him. Only in the third chapter do we hear Sabeth's voice for the first time. In these first two chapters, Eich uses a technique reminiscent of the way Fritz Lang initially conceals his main protagonists from the film screen in both *M* and *The Testament of Dr. Mabuse*: characters in *Sabeth* have seen, spoken with, and even befriended the giant raven long before the radio listener hears his voice for the first time. To set the scene for our first vocal encounter with Sabeth, Eich changes the narrator once again in the third chapter. This time, the child Elisabeth narrates how she used to go into the forest in search of the ravens that she and her family had seen in the forest. Only once she has given up her search does she suddenly see a giant raven hiding in the bushes. She runs up to it, and here Elisabeth's narrative turns into dialogue form:

> ELISABETH: Good day, raven! I've been looking for you for a while. Where did you all go? My parents are also wondering why none of you come by anymore. Have I seen you before? I don't know, you all look the same.
> *Pause.*
> My name's Elisabeth.
>
> SABETH *(slowly and struggling):* Sa – beth.
>
> ELISABETH: You can speak!
>
> SABETH: Sabeth.
>
> ELISABETH: No, not Sabeth! Elisabeth!
>
> SABETH: Sabeth.
>
> ELISABETH: Sabeth! I'll name you Sabeth then. Is that what you want?
>
> SABETH: Sabeth.
>
> ELISABETH: When you've learned it correctly, you must call me Elisabeth. But your name is Sabeth.[64]

In his dated but otherwise insightful reading, Peter Märki writes enthusiastically of this moment how "Elisabeth's speech simultaneously awakens Sabeth's linguistic character [*Gestalt*]. A birth of language from itself!"[65] The parallels between the Echo myth and Eich's *Sabeth* are also not lost on Märki, to which we will return to momentarily.[66] But what remains after Märki's reading of this passage is, once again, the comportment of the voice. Kurt Lieck's voice for Sabeth in the original recording that premiered on 26 October 1953, is dark, low and monotone, almost guttural, as if it was rising out of the depths of the ocean. Lieck's low voice is interspersed with the high chirps of Elisabeth's voice, performed in the premier by Ute

---

64 Eich, *GesW* 2:369.
65 Märki, *Günter Eichs Hörspielkunst*, 46.
66 Märki, *Günter Eichs Hörspielkunst*, 46.

Zschaler and which can now, like *Dreams*, be accessed via YouTube. If we follow Derrida's reading of the Echo myth, as a "dissymmetrical, unequal correspondence, unequal, as always, to the equality of the one to the other,"[67] we can actually hear this relational dissymmetry in the two very disparate voices. The unequal correspondence between these two voices mirrors acoustically – one might say, echoes – the unequal relationship of Echo and Narcissus.

It may at first seem counterintuitive to raise Derrida's treatment of the Echo myth, which can be found in his introduction to *Rogues: Two Essays on Reason* (*Voyous: Deux essais sur la raison*, 2005), since it appears to take us further away from the voices heard in *Sabeth* and deeper into metalinguistic concerns. Derrida's reading, however, is relevant because of his equal concern for what slips away – and slips in – when echoes are heard otherwise: while Echo "repeats, without simulacrum, what she has just heard, another simulacrum slips in [*s'insinue*] to make her response something more than a mere reiteration."[68] In this context, Derrida is not referring, as I am here, to the voice as that which makes Echo's responses more than mere echoes. Rather, he suggests that Echo is feigning her repetition of Narcissus's last syllables "in order to proffer something else [*pour proférer autre chose*]."[69] Derrida is questioning Echo's intentions,[70] which also means questioning the way we listen to Echo: for Derrida, she might be uttering something other than what we hear and understand, that is to say, other than what we *want* to hear.[71] This is inferred in the Sabeth scene precisely when Elisabeth interprets the raven's parroting of her name as his own. Elisabeth, we can say, hears what she wants to hear in the echoes: his name.

---

67 Jacques Derrida, *Voyous* (Paris: Éditions Galilée, 2003), 10; Jacques Derrida, *Rogues: Two Essays on Reason*, trans. Pascale-Anne Brault and Michael Naas (Stanford, CA: Stanford University Press, 2005), xii.
68 Derrida, *Voyous*, 10; *Rogues*, xii.
69 Derrida, *Voyous*, 10; *Rogues*, xii.
70 When questioning Echo's intentions, at least in the context of *Rogues*, Derrida might not be referring to (listening to) a voice. But Jean-Luc Nancy *is* referring to the audible realm when he discusses intension in his extended essay, *Listening*: "Sound (and/or sense) is not at first intended. It is not first 'intentioned': on the contrary, sound is what places its subject, which has not preceded it with an aim, in tension, or under tension" (Jean-Luc Nancy, *À l'écoute* [Paris: Éditions Galilée, 2002], 42; Jean-Luc Nancy, *Listening*, trans. Charlotte Mandell [New York: Fordham University Press, 2007], 20).
71 "Echo thus lets be heard by whoever wants to hear it, by whoever might love hearing it, something other than what she seems to be proffering" (Derrida, *Voyous* 10; *Rogues* xii). In the original translation, "proférer" has been translated as "saying," but this misses the sense of putting something forward, uttering, or even "saying loudly" (*Oxford English Dictionary*, 2nd ed. [Oxford: Oxford University Press, 1989] [hereafter, *OED*], s.v.).

I would not deny that interpreters of this passage in *Sabeth* like Märki, Döhl or myself equally tend to hear what we want. But without any reference to other literary illusions like the Echo myth, Märki writes,

> it becomes *immediately understandable* what is going on here: by imitating Elisabeth's name, Sabeth nevertheless preserves something of that silent unity found in all beings [. . .]. But at the same time, the raven, in assuming a name, steps out of the darkness of preindividual being and into the light of a unique person [emphasis and translation mine].⁷²

Märki clearly wants to understand that the birth of language arises from language itself, and that Sabeth breaks from the darkness of the preindividual into the "light of a distinct person." Märki claims, moreover, that all of this is *immediately* comprehensible, which as we have seen elsewhere marks the jettisoning of notions like medium or mediality *tout court*. That this scene is for Märki "immediately understandable" confirms Derrida's suggestion that Echo always *lets* us hear what we want, even if it is something other than what she seems to be uttering. Hearing what one wants to hear is to derive meaning from what might be called a *vouloir-entendre*.⁷³

Having taken a closer look at Derrida's reading of the Echo myth, we seem to have indeed travelled far from listening to the voices in this scene of Eich's *Sabeth*. But Derrida's reading is helpful in that it reveals how easily (and easily "immediate") both Elisabeth and Märki are deriving what they *want* to hear from what *is* heard. In opening up the possibility of Echo – and in this case, Sabeth – as uttering or pronouncing something other than what we (want to) hear, Derrida asks us to listen again, to hear perhaps something other. Might it be, for instance, that Sabeth also feigns the repetition of the last two syllables of Elisabeth's name "in order to proffer something else"? Listening both to the echoes of names and to the timbres of voices are two ways that help attune our ears beyond that which we might want to hear and instead to the acoustical marks and signs that reverberate at the threshold of a unified listening self.

The creation of Sabeth's name in this scene is unique since it illustrates a moment in which two acoustical marks or signs, "Sa" and "beth," are echoed to a point in which they become no longer echoes but fixed into a single sign, a name. While Derrida suggests that Echo feigns her repetition of Narcissus's last

---

72 Märki, *Günter Eichs Hörspielkunst*, 46.
73 I derive this from Derrida's correlate, *vouloir-dire* or "meaning (to say)" in Derrida's *Speech and Phenomena* (Jacques Derrida, *La voix et le phénomène* [Paris: Presses universitaires de France, 1967]). Both are related only in the sense that behind what is meant is always already a *desire*, a wanting-to-say or wanting-to-hear, which colors the meaning understood. Much more can be said about *vouloir-entendre*, since it points to the antinomy between conventional listening and the acoustical unconscious being pursued in this book.

syllables "in order to proffer something else," he then goes on to specify what that something might be: she feigns "actually in order to *sign* at that very instant her own name, and so to take back the initiative of answering or responding in a responsible way" (emphasis mine).[74] This is also the case with Sabeth, who inadvertently signs his own name in the act of echoing Elisabeth. Sabeth's signing of his name might have been unintentional, but it nevertheless becomes what is heard. Of course, long before Sabeth unwittingly signs his own name in Eich's play, there had long been another name assigned to the bird by the German speaker: "Rabe." What is interesting about this word is how similarly it too was apparently derived: the German word "Rabe" refers, as does the English word "raven," to "the harsh sound of the bird's call."[75] Apart from the Echo myth and Sabeth's scene, the creation of "Rabe" out of the sound of the raven's call is the unheard third scene of the play, what one might call the *Urszene* of humans encountering ravens. We may go one step further and read Sabeth's scene as a kind of reciprocal or antithesis to this imagined, impossible *Urszene*: instead of man deriving the name for this bird from hearing its harsh call, this giant raven in Eich's play derives its own name out of the utterances of man. In terms of Benjamin's theory of language, we can say that Sabeth's ears are attuned to the *Dingsprache* of man, to man's natural call. This reading flips the normal hierarchy of man giving a name to things and instead offers the possibility of things giving a name to themselves via man. It is not intended, therefore, that Sabeth signs his own name, although that turns out to be what we (want to) hear. Rather, Sabeth may very well be uttering the name *for man*. Until Elisabeth turns the tables on the raven and assigns him the name "Sabeth," it is the raven who has taken back "the initiative of answering or responding in a responsible way," which is the initiative of naming. The name for man that the raven assigns us is "sabeth."

We seem once again to have wandered far from listening to voices. What will turn us back to the voice is not necessarily how the bird, in listening to man, derives a name for man, but how Kurt Lieck's voice for Sabeth sounds less like the voice of a man and more like the sounds of a bird. In Lieck's performance of the name's first two enunciations, Sabeth's voice is still the guttural,

---

74 Derrida, *Voyous* 10; *Rogues* xii.
75 Here Duden's *Herkunftswörterbuch* echoes the *Oxford English Dictionary*: "Der Rabe ist also nach seinem heiseren Geschrei (als „Krächzer") genannt. Zu dieser lautnachahmenden Wurzel gehören z.B. aus anderen *ing.* Sprachen *griech.* krázein „krächzen, schreien", kórax „Rabe", *lat.* Crocire „krächzen", corvus „Rabe" und *russ.* krakat' „krächzen"" (*Das Herkunftswörterbuch, Etymologie der deutschen Sprache*, 2nd ed., ed. Günther Drowsdowski [Mannheim: Dudenverlag, 1989], 7:566).

harsh sounds of a raven, not the articulate language of man.[76] In this way, Lieck performs the language of man as it is turned back into a bird's call, into *Dingsprache*, the language of birds.[77] As we have already concluded, hearing the timbres of Sabeth and Elisabeth's voices certainly increases the dissymmetry between the two characters, allowing us at least one way to think of Sabeth's echo as not simply a reiteration of the same. Our subsequent reading of voices above serves to increase the importance of timbre, since it allows one to hear the dismantling of the language of man into a voice that is barely a human voice, perhaps even a *bare voice* that does not express a unified, individual self but rather enunciates – in the sense of putting forward, *proférer* – a series of sounds and acoustical marks not yet fixed to words or meanings. While this scene I would argue is not the birth of language from language itself, it nevertheless puts into play that sonically ambiguous threshold between the language of man and the language of things, where one language interpenetrates the other, and verbal mimesis occurs in both directions: from a bird's sound to man's word, but also from man's word to bird's sound.

The question that remains is whether Eich's penchant for the anthropomorphized animal, whose almost inhuman, other voice speaks the language of man, is also medially specific: was Eich considering the radiophonic medium when writing this scene? Or more to the point: did Eich need the radio apparatus to write the radio play, *Sabeth*? To answer the last question first: no, Eich did not need radio to have written *Sabeth*: one could easily imagine such a play performed in a darkened theater. But the radio play as a genre could not have developed without radio. As we have seen throughout the previous chapter and this one, radio plays were written, at least until the end of the 1950s, in such a way as to take full advantage of the intimate radio listener whose only recourse to the play is through the ear, and Eich was a master of this genre. While the radio itself might not necessarily be needed as the medium through which one listens to these, it cannot be said, following Siegert, that the medium of radio entirely disappears in Eich's plays. In both *Dreams* and *Sabeth*, Eich emphasizes certain words' unstable connections between their sounds and their meanings,

---

76 Although Sabeth eventually learns to conduct entire conversations in the language of man, his voice never loses the gravelly, deep tones of an alien voice throughout the radio play.

77 In the "Language" essay, Benjamin refers to the language of birds when he considers the use of attempting to grasp artistic forms as languages: "For an understanding of artistic forms, it is of value to attempt to grasp them all as languages and to seek their connection with natural languages. An example that is appropriate because it is derived from the acoustic sphere is the kinship between song and the language of birds [*die Verwandtschaft des Gesanges mit der Sprache der Vögel*]" (Benjamin, *GS* 2:156; *SW* 1:73).

connections that are made all the more vulnerable because of the words being only heard. Even though he does not take advantage of the world's material soundscape via radio, as Walter Ruttmann so famously did in *Weekend* (1927) or experimental radio artists accomplished with the Original-Ton in the 1960s, Eich nevertheless plays with language's own semantic vulnerability to its own tonal materiality. As he suggests in his short reflections and interviews on language and radio, Eich is concerned less with the receptivity of music and sounds than with the receptivity of language, the way it is heard and how meaning is derived from it through a particular mode of listening. In the last radio play that will be examined in this chapter, *The Year Lazertis*, Eich raises to a thematic level a particular mode of poetic listening that is not only rooted in philosophical discussions of the time but also has far-reaching implications for the German radio listener of the mid-twentieth century.

4.5 The Word in its Transformation: *The Year Lazertis*

Eich's *The Year Lazertis* was originally broadcast on 5 March 1954 by NWDR-Hamburg.[78] On the day of its premier, Heinz Schwitzke – at the time director of the radio play program for NWDR-Hamburg – was skeptical of the play's reception, fearing that it "will likely go far over the listener's heads."[79] *The Year Lazertis* is the story of a painter by the name of Paul who, while sleeping, thinks he overhears a conversation by a passing couple in the street in which a word that sounded something like "Lazertis" was uttered. He immediately begins to obsess over this word only barely heard, as if it isn't just any word but the Word that "resolves all secrets."[80] Starting out much like Poe's *The Man of the Crowd* – except that the sought-after object is an overheard word rather than a man – *The Year Lazertis* also hearkens back to one of Eich's earlier fragments, *An Hour with the Dictionary* (1933), as well as to his later comedic variation on the same motif, *Allah Has a Hundred Names* (*Allah hat hundert Namen*, 1957). In all three plays, words or names are obsessively sought but never found. On the one hand, the search for the word "Lazertis" as *Urwort* can be read as a mid-twentieth-century reincarnation of the Romanticist's blue flower, symbolizing the metaphyblsical yearning for that which is forever unattainable. Read in this way, it would indicate how much Eich relied on earlier, German Romantic notions of art and aesthetics. On the other hand,

---

[78] As of this publication, the NWDR 1954 broadcasting of "The Year Lazertis" ("Das Jahr Lazertis") can be accessed via this YouTube link: https://www.youtube.com/watch?v=IT66uu_XLLQ.
[79] Schwitzke, cited by Wagner, *Günter Eich und der Rundfunk*, 263.
[80] Eich, *GesW* 2:675.

recall the way Heidegger in "Poetically man dwells" explores two modes of measuring: as either "a curious excess [*ein seltsames Übermaß*] of frantic measuring and calculating," or an open taking-in, "a taking which never clutches [*an sich reißt*] at the measure but rather takes it in the collected perception that remains a listening."[81] I would argue that, in Eich's *The Year Lazertis*, both modes of measuring are raised to a thematic level as two very different *modes of listening*. In his mad search for confirming what he had heard, Paul never catches up to the couple who might have uttered the Word, but in pursuit he comes across a hunchback in the street by the name of Laparte. Paul thinks at first that he is just a beggar, but Laparte turns out to be a researcher who has written a book on lizards ("Eidechse"), whose Latin etymology Laparte explains is "Lazerte." What follows is a series of encounters with other words – from "Laertes" to "Lazarus" and "*la certitude*" – all of which have one thing in common: they all echo each other and are variations of "Lazertis," which itself has no meaning. In the end, Paul finds himself in a Brazilian insane asylum called La Certosa, and it remains unclear whether he will ever leave or whether he has simply imagined the whole story while there. The play is largely a narcissistic search for a word that, as mentioned in the previous section, has more to do with what the listener *wants* to hear than what was actually heard, if anything. But as we shall see at the very end of the play, Paul seems finally to give up the search and adopt an open receptivity "that remains a listening."

Early on it is established that Paul is an artist who paints only images of animals, which is described as lifelike or photographic (*naturgetreu*). This echoes *Sabeth*, when photographs are taken of the giant raven only to have no image of the bird once they are developed. By emphasizing the photographic or lifelike images of animals in a medium that has no access to visual images, Eich points to the unreliability and ultimately constructed nature of such images that attempt to measure reality accurately. While Eich's *Lazertis*, with its extended monologues and minimal use of sounds and music, appears to confirm Siegert's claim that the radio as a medium tends to disappear, Eich's explicit references to "lifelike" images in his plays serves nevertheless to remind listeners of their inability to see them, that certain measurements are simply inaccessible to the radio listener.

Paul's lifelike paintings of animals exemplify his untiring obsession to capture something real, whether it is the Word "Lazertis" or the animals he repeatedly paints. Early on Paul admits to Laparte that he keeps painting a fox: "A fox that steps out of the protected forest area [*Schonung*]. I paint him often,

---

[81] Heidegger, *GA* 7:201–202; *PLT* 223.

always the same. A beloved first prize for rifle clubs."⁸² Paul paints the fox "always the same" not to get it right, but in order to hunt it down. Like the fox in his painting, Paul also hunts obsessively for the single word, Lazertis, which is heard literally *in other words*. In attempting to fix Lazertis throughout the play, it is as if Paul is rehearsing his multiple attempts to paint lifelike foxes: he hunts for it everywhere, and it takes him to the jungles of Brazil and finally to an infirmary. Once again, the mad attempt to decipher the sounds of the conch shell heard by Nerval, the composer in Maurice Renard's "La mort et le coquillage" with which I began Chapter Two, resonates with Paul's desperate search for this single word, or the way Freud searches for the name "Signorelli" through his various *Ersatznamen*. And like Eckbert, Paul is left at the end riddled by its echoes and traces. Paul's untiring search, whether in painting or language, exemplifies the modern condition as described by Heidegger in "Poetically Man Dwells": Paul dwells unpoetically in his world because of his frantic attempt to measure something beyond all measure. Instead of "a letting come of what has been measured out,"⁸³ Paul clutches and grasps at the measuring stick, attempting to fix the word "Lazertis" like one of his lifelike foxes on canvas, which are themselves notoriously difficult to capture. Throughout the play, Eich thematizes Heidegger's description of frantic measuring, the frenetic search for meaning through that which is heard or what one thinks has been heard. This puts the listeners of radio play in a peculiar position: how should this radio play be listened to? One might say that just as Eich reminds his listeners of their reliance on the ear with explicit references to visual images that will never been seen, he also uses the acoustic medium to thematize the sonic displacement of a word from its utterance, its dissolution into its apparent sounds and the echoes of its phonetic parts, as we have previously examined in *Dreams*. One might even say that one of the linguistic principles that underlies Eich's *Lazertis* – and is a hallmark of Eich's radio language in general – is the word in its transformation, "das Wort in der Verwandlung."⁸⁴ His penchant for fantastic creatures and distant lands further acknowledges both the word and the voice that utters it as always underway, which in turn sends his radio listeners on acoustic journeys beyond their fixed place in front of the radio. In the case of *Lazertis*, Paul's search for the

---

82 Eich, *GesW* 2:677.
83 A "Kommen-lassen des Zu-Gemessenen" (Heidegger, *GA* 7:203; *PLT* 222).
84 I take this phrase from Benjamin's description of the linguistic principle that underlies the German *Trauerspiel*, which he calls "das Wort in der Verwandlung." See Benjamin's "Die Bedeutung der Sprache in Trauerspiel und Tragödie" (Benjamin, *GS* 2:138; *SW* 1:60). In comparison, see Schwitzke's title for his Eich chapter in his classic text, *Das Hörspiel*: "Günter Eich / Das Wort Unterwegs" (Schwitzke, *Das Hörspiel*, 409).

word, which leads him on an excursion to Brazil – his *Wanderung als Verwandlung* (trek as transformation) – thematizes how the listener of radio is "benommen," taken up and moved by the words and voices heard.

At the end of the radio play, another kind of listening comes to the fore. In the Brazilian infirmary, Paul has an extended conversation with Dr. Olivera about how he has been interned for over two years and now wishes to leave and return to Europe. After convincing his doctor that he be given a discharge certificate, he goes back to his room to pack his things. While packing, Paul realizes he would have to leave behind all the other patients that he has become acquainted with over the past two and a half years. "They could certainly all die without me," he muses to himself, "but I can't live without them."[85] Then the voice of Dr. Olivera is heard in the background, as if Paul is remembering what had just been said in their brief encounter: "They always think that going on a trip will get them further along. Here is the place where you could have arrived [*den Sie erreichen konnten*]."[86] Paul suddenly realizes that Dr. Olivera did not speak those words, but rather Paul himself did. This moment can be compared to Kasperl's hearing of his own recorded voice at the end of *Bustle about Kasperl*: both Kasperl and Paul recognize their own voice in a distorted playback of their own. The difference is that, whereas Kasperl's voice is "somewhat distorted in its tonal coloring,"[87] Dr. Oliviera's is a completely *other* voice than Paul's, or more specifically, it is his *as* an other. Paul's revelation is that of a *partages des voix*, a sharing and splitting of voices that comprise his own. With this insight, it becomes possible that *all* the voices heard from the beginning of the play were his own. One way to interpret this is that we have never left Paul's inner monologue, which would in turn further support the claim that Eich contributes significantly to the 1950s radio plays of inwardness. But another way to read Paul's realization is that, by hearing his voice as that of another – as hearing his own voice this way and otherwise – he awakens to a kind of self-recognition similar to Kasperl's, encountering a fragment of his own existence in the voice of another. A major difference, of course, is that at the end of *Bustle about Kasperl*, Benjamin stages a Brechtian situation in which Kasperl learns, through the playback of his own voice, what radio is ("wie Rundfunk ist"). What Paul learns is not medium-specific, but nevertheless involves a certain receptive condition or comportment of the listener in modernity: to no longer grasp for meaning or clutch at the measuring rod, but rather to take in

---

85 Eich, *GesW* 2:711.
86 Eich, *GesW* 2:711.
87 Benjamin, *GS* 4:695 [*WuN* 9.1:85]; *Radio Benjamin*, 219.

via a kind of collective perception that remains a listening. Indeed, Paul appears to give up his ongoing search for Lazertis in this moment, as the next lines seem to indicate: "Someone called to me, a women's voice. It was probably Manuela. I unpacked my bag."[88] What follows is a short inventory list reminiscent of Eich's most famous poem, *Inventur*. "It was not much," Paul reflects on his possessions, "but it was enough," as if the importance of the Word and its possession has now been replaced by the few objects already in his possession. The radio play ends with Paul hearing Manuela's call again, an interruption that we as listeners are not privy to, and he goes out of his room to ask what she wants.

This final scene is likely one of the reasons why Schwitzke had thought the play would go over the listeners' heads. But it reveals both Heidegger's influence on Eich's work, and Eich's own pedagogical impetus of instructing the listening public not just how to listen, but how to rediscover, as he said in 1953 prize speech, that intimacy (*Innigkeit*) with the world that has shrunken. Put another way, evoking Heidegger: in realizing it wasn't the doctor's words but his own, Paul finally decides to stop searching and start *dwelling*. In "Building – Dwelling – Thinking," Heidegger reminds us that part of dwelling means "to remain, to stay in a place," and to be at peace in this place.[89] Paul's revelation at the end of *The Year Lazertis* is to find safety from the excess of frantic measuring that otherwise leads to what both Heidegger and Eich in their respective essays refer to as a certain blindness. In foregoing any further attempt at measuring, Paul is able for the first time to *listen*, which is less a listening-for than a taking-in. It is important that the first thing Paul hears after his decision is someone calling him: "Someone calls out to me [*Jemand ruft nach mir*]."[90] Paul's very mode of listening changes in this final scene. In doing so, Eich also challenges his listeners to take up and hear perhaps what Paul has learned, so that they too could one day learn to listen, and dwell with listening, poetically.

As these three readings of Eich's radio plays have made clear, we have also not strayed very far from some of the elements of an acoustical unconscious elucidated in previous chapters. When analyzing Kraus's dictum repeatedly-cited by Benjamin – "The closer you look at a word, the more distantly it looks back at you" – Samuel Weber in *Mediauras* adds that the word "takes up and moves the beholder towards that which, though remote, is also closest-at-hand, in the sense of that 'optical' or 'tactical/tactile' (*taktish*) unconscious that

---

88 Benjamin, *GS* 4:695 [*WuN* 9.1:85]; *Radio Benjamin*, 219.
89 Heidegger, *GA* 7:203; *PLT* 147.
90 Eich, *GesW* 2:711.

Benjamin discerned in the most familiar, habitual gestures."[91] It is important to remember the situation in which Paul heard the word, apparently for the first time: "Someone who passed by my window must have said it while in conversation and incidentally."[92] Like the coaler Peter Munk hearing the apprentice's song as he awakens in Benjamin's *The Cold Heart*, Paul overhears the word while dozing and with only half an ear. This initial scene might not be as important if Paul's manner of hearing the word for the first time did not also reflect how radio as a medium was increasingly being "taken in" at the time, that is, as background, as incidental noise. Eich was aware that along with radio, certain ways of listening were becoming preferable to others. In the same way that habitual gestures are unconsciously performed, leading Benjamin to theorize the optical unconscious, listening to radio was expanding the acoustically habitual and familiar in ways that could not have been developed without it.[93]

The analyses of Eich's *Dreams*, *Sabeth* and *The Year Lazertis* presented in this chapter all attempt to come to terms with what, ironically, has not been listened too closely enough in Eich's radio plays: his search for ways in which modes of distracted listening or listening with half an ear could be further explored precisely through the ear and via the medium of radio. This includes not only the "comportment" of the voice, but also the disorientation of the listener and the repetition of words and their parts that disrupt their hearing as anything but a sure path to meaning, as thematized in *The Year Lazertis*. The tension of listening *for* possible meanings that is forever put off might be one of the reasons why Eich's plays have consistently been subjected to overinterpretation. By infusing his radio plays with the consequences of (mis)hearing at the linguistic, vocalic and thematic level, Eich does not simply employ tactics specific to radio as a medium, but also displaces and disrupts the radio "listener" who might otherwise take comfort in what is being *heard* as familiar. Just as he often denies his plays' characters of what they want to hear and see, so Eich tends in many of his radio plays to deny and problematize what radio listeners want to hear or what is most familiar to them, whether forcing them to listen to the consequences of having listened too complicitly (*Dreams*), confronting

---

91 Samuel Weber, *Mass Mediauras* (Stanford, CA: Stanford University Press, 1996), 107.
92 Eich, *GesW* 2:675.
93 While the advancement of sound recording technology, like film, offered for Benjamin, the possibility of greater critical analysis through repeated listenings, radio at the time did not allow for this. Radio distinguished itself from the phonograph, in that it not only made it impossible to go back and "listen again" to something that had just been broadcast, but it also generated new kinds of acoustic familiarity that triggered in their very ubiquity and nearness a certain remoteness of listening specific to the language of radio.

them with the very problem of what one wants to hear (*Sabeth*), or offering an alternative mode of listening akin to what Heidegger meant by collected perception (*Lazertis*). To awaken to and be disrupted out of our own comfortable and habitual modes of listening via the unique medium of radio – as this chapter has illustrated via Eich's radio plays specifically – is one way to trace the contours of the acoustical unconscious in the history of this medium's formal and technological developments.

5 Clatter in Kracauer and Kluge: Politicizing the Acoustical Unconscious

> Die Welt ist eine Glocke, die einen Riss hat: Sie klappert,
> aber klingt nicht. (The world is a bell that has a crack:
> it clatters but does not ring.) Goethe, *Maximen und Reflektionen*

Since at least his acceptance speech of the Fontane Prize for Literature in 1979, Alexander Kluge has pitted the idea of history and fiction against each other in productive ways.[1] The German title to one of his many collections of stories, *Cinema Stories* (*Geschichten vom Kino*, 2007), immediately draws attention to the fluid relation between stories and histories with the German word, *Geschichten*.[2] In the foreword to this collection, Kluge likens the power of cinema to that of music in that both are immortal and capable of "moving us inwardly":

> I would also like to make clear right away that for me these 120 stories deal with the "principle of cinema." I consider this "cinema" immortal and older than the art of film. This is because we impart [*mitteilen*] something in public with one another that "moves us inwardly." In that respect, film and music are related. Neither will die out. Even if the film projectors no longer clatter [*nicht mehr rattern*], there will be something – of this I firmly believe – "that functions like cinema."[3]

Just as Roland Barthes in *Camera Lucida* (*La chambre claire*, 1980) listens to the click of the camera when taking a photograph, admitting that there is "perhaps in me someone very old still [that] hears in the photographic mechanism the living

---

[1] On Kluge's early formulations about how historical issues are vital to his fiction, see Andrew Bowie, "New Histories: Aspects of the Prose of Alexander Kluge," in *Journal of European Studies* 12 (1982): 180–208. On Kluge's relation to "*histoire*" and "*discours*" as described by Emile Benveniste and extrapolated upon by Christian Metz, see Miriam Hansen, "The Stubborn Discourse: History and Story-Telling," in *Die Schrift an der Wand. Alexander Kluge: Rohstoffe und Materialien*, by Alexander Kluge (Osnabrück: Universitätsverlag Rasch, 2000), 119–132.

[2] While there are 120 stories in the German edition, the English translation by Martin Brady and Helen Hughes include only about a third of them (the German edition is 339 pages, while the English edition is 111 pages total). No reason is given for this reduction of material, other than the front matter stating that the English version was published "by arrangement with the author."

[3] Alexander Kluge, *Geschichten vom Kino* (Frankfurt a.M.: Suhrkamp, 2007) (hereafter, *GvK*), 7. The English translation here has been heavily modified, but I will nevertheless subsequently reference the pagination from Alexander Kluge, *Cinema Stories*, trans. Martin Brady and Helen Hughes (New York: New Directions, 2007) (hereafter, *CS*), whenever possible.

sound of the wood,"[4] so too for Kluge the clattering of the film projector is essential to something "that functions like cinema," something that reverberates beyond accepted Film History and is older than art. Long after the rattling of the film projector, what remains audible is more akin to the broken bell of Goethe's maxim in the epigraph above: Kluge's cinematic and literary worlds are filled with tears and cuts that make his cinematic worlds and texts clatter more than they chime.

Kluge's tendency toward the use of unsettling music and obstreperous sound can be traced back to early debates among contemporary film critics, perhaps most notably to those of Siegfried Kracauer, László Moholy-Nagy, Béla Balázs and Rudolf Arnheim. Of these, Kracauer wrote arguably the last of the so-called classical film theory texts, *Theory of Film: The Redemption of Physical Reality* (1960), which marked the end of an era of film theory that, as Miriam Hansen rightly posits, was "primarily concerned with questions of ontology and medium specificity."[5] While the book was published in 1960, with the German translation published four years later, it was originally conceived in the years 1940–1941 in Marseille, while Kracauer was awaiting papers in order to emigrate to the United States. Benjamin, who also arrived in Marseille in mid-August 1939 with similar hopes, witnessed Kracauer taking copious notes which "Benjamin, shrewdly if a bit ungenerously, interpreted as a single-minded strategy of survival."[6] But already then Kracauer was attuned to non-synchronous and disruptive uses of sound and music in film, which he later emphasized in chapters seven and eight of *Theory of Film*, entitled "Dialogue and Sound" and "Music," respectively. In the first section of the present chapter, I will focus on two examples from *Theory of Film*: the first is Kracauer's approval of Chaplin's corrosion of meaning in his first sound film, *Modern Times*. The second example involves Kracauer's recollection of a drunken piano accompanist during the silent era, whose total disregard for the projected image nevertheless led to random coincidences that were for Kracauer "perfect because of [their] accidental nature and indeterminacy."[7]

---

4 Roland Barthes, *Camera Lucida: Reflections on Photography*, trans. Richard Howard (New York: Hill and Wang, 1981), 15. The French is as follows: "peut-être en moi, quel qu'un très ancien entend encore dans l'appareil photographique le bruit vivant du bois." See Roland Barthes, *La chambre claire* (Paris: Gallimard, 1980), 33.
5 Miriam Hansen, *Cinema and Experience* (Berkeley: University of California Press, 2012), 254. While Kracauer's *Theory of Film: The Redemption of Physical Reality* was published in 1960, the German translation appeared four years later under the title *Theorie des Films. Die Errettung der äußeren Wirklichkeit* (1964).
6 Miriam Hansen, "Introduction," in *Theory of Film: The Redemption of Physical Reality*, by Siegfried Kracauer (Princeton, NJ: Princeton University Press, 1997), xiv.
7 Siegfried Kracauer, *Theory of Film: The Redemption of Physical Reality* (Princeton, NJ: Princeton University Press, 1997), 138.

Kracauer's emphasis on the asynchronous and non-mimetic of film sound and music also prepares us for Kluge's own reflections on the same.

Anyone who has watched even part of a film by Alexander Kluge is aware that he is dedicated more to the non-synchronous and disruptive combinations of sound, music and image than to any sense of linear continuity or conventional logic. The same kind of discontinuity is raised to a thematic level in much of his written work as well, which will be examined in later sections of this chapter. In a few of his short texts in *Cinema Stories* in particular, Kluge accentuates the non-diegetic sounds of artillery fire and bird calls that blend randomly with a film's soundtrack during a tent-film screening or open-air cinema. Kluge even has one of his characters conclude, while reflecting on the blurring of the soundtrack with random sounds beyond the screen, that cinema is "an in-itself impossible moment [*an sich unmöglicher Augenblick*]," one that could never have been conceived beforehand, and which could never be repeated again.[8]

As we shall see, both Kracauer and Kluge focus on these non-conformist and unconventional uses of sound and music in and around film because they lead the audience to find a deeper understanding of the accidental, the unexpected, and that which could not have otherwise been intended, which is to say, another way of hearing otherwise. For Kracauer and his ontological, media-specific agenda, this is cinema's *redemptive* function: its potential to redirect the audience's attention to the texture and grain of life that has otherwise been lost to abstract discourse. Kracauer deliberately chose the phrase, "the redemption of physical reality," for the subtitle of his book because of its theological connotations, which refer back specifically to the cabbalistic concept of *tikkun*, often translated as "repair."[9] For Kracauer, the intellectual's task was "to furnish an archive for the possibility, even if itself unrepresentable, of a utopian restoration of all things past and present," even that which has not yet been unnamed.[10] Kluge's overarching project for defining and doing cinema is similarly redemptive: Hansen calls it Kluge's interest in "the pragmatics of redemption."[11] This pragmatism is much more explicitly politically inclined than

---

8 Kluge, *GvK* 237; *CS* 65.
9 In a letter to Rudolph Arnheim, Kracauer defended his choice of the term, "redemption," whereas Arnheim had earlier proposed "recovery" or "reclamation" (the German word, "*Rückgewinnung*"). On this and a reference to *tikkun* in Scholem's reading of the messianic idea, see Hansen, *Cinema and Experience*, 291, n. 72.
10 Hansen, *Cinema and Experience*, 22.
11 Miriam Hansen, "Reinventing the Nickelodeon: Notes on Kluge and Early Cinema," *October* 46 (Fall 1988): 182.

Kracauer's, and leads Kluge to what he calls a cinema of emancipation. As we shall see, the emancipatory function of cinema for Kluge names the political outgrowth of a "storm of fantasy," a phrase Kluge employs to describe that which erupts out of an audience's experience of a cut or break in film: a point of interruption or shock that induces a radical shift of perspective that leads to a deeper, more critical understanding of what is being perceived.

Both Kracauer and Kluge's reflections on "cinematic" sound and music are thus inseparable from their own individual agendas of redemption and emancipation, which raises crucial questions when pursuing the concept of the acoustical unconscious in film: to what extent can it be infused with a politics of redemption? Is there perhaps something already inherently "redemptive" about Benjamin's concept of the optical unconscious, and by extrapolation the acoustical unconscious being explored here? Kracauer and Kluge's idiosyncratic reflections on sound and music in film will bring us closer to understanding the possible politicization of the acoustical unconscious and its consequences.

5.1 Something like an "Acoustic Unconscious"

Miriam Hansen was the one of the first film scholars in the English-speaking world to champion Kracauer's work, especially but not exclusively his work on film, placing him on par with such major figures as Benjamin and Adorno. She did so through not only her numerous articles on Kracauer but also her critical introduction to the first, 1997 reprint of his *Theory of Film*. The final chapter of her own posthumous book, *Cinema and Experience*, is, as she herself states, a "substantially revised version of my introduction to the reprint" of Kracauer's *Theory of Film*.[12] One of Hansen's additions is a footnote to an already parenthetical comment referring to Kracauer's "remarkably prescient chapter on 'dialogue and sound.'"[13] Having cited the footnote in my Introduction, I will only repeat here the first sentence: "Kracauer's reflections on film sound gesture toward something like an 'acoustic unconscious' and foreground experimental uses of sound ('anonymous noises,' multi-lingual speech, etc.) from Fritz Lang to René Claire and G. W. Pabst."[14] Important to note is Hansen's use of both the indefinite article and scare quotes, as if she was herself not sure of the legitimacy of the term. Since Hansen dedicates an earlier chapter heading entirely to

---

12 Hansen, *Cinema and Experience*, 350.
13 Hansen, *Cinema and Experience*, 261.
14 Hansen, *Cinema and Experience*, 352–353.

the optical unconscious, the question is no longer whether Hansen is thinking of Benjamin's optical unconscious when she refers "an 'acoustic unconscious,'" but to what extent Benjamin's optical unconscious and her proposed "acoustic unconscious" here in Kracauer differ.

While Hansen interprets Benjamin's concept of the optical unconscious in part as a derivation of his emphasis on the mimetic faculty, her reference above to an acoustic unconscious in Kracauer has little to do with Benjamin's notion of mimesis. In the paragraph where the above-cited footnote is found, Hansen is explaining what Kracauer meant by cinematic materiality:

> Kracauer's account of early cinema complicates the concept of the kind of reality that film is capable of engaging. [. . .] Kracauer aligns the virtually limitless range of filmable world with the multiplicity and heterogeneity of basic cinematic materials: "the whole world in every sense: from the beginning film strove toward sound, speech, color" (*W* 3:559). (Some of his early notes on sound – noise, speech, music – have made it into the final book, in particular the remarkably prescient chapter on "dialogue and sound.") [Hansen's footnote on "something like an 'acoustic unconscious'" is here – RGR]. Moreover, he understands cinematic materiality to include creations of fantasy: unlike the theater, "film mixes the *whole world* [emphasis original] into play, be that world real or imagined."[15]

Recognizing her parenthetical note on Kracauer's "dialogue and sound" chapter in context makes it clear that she is aligning Kracauer's references to sound with his definition of "cinematic materiality." Kracauer, for his part, is adamant that sound not only has a material dimension, but also that its materiality is inherently more cinematic.

As the title suggests, Kracauer's seventh chapter of *Theory of Film*, "Dialogue and Sound," is divided into two sections. In the second half, Kracauer emphasizes sound's materiality as having "cinematic interest": "Sounds share with visible phenomena two characteristics: they are recorded by a camera; and they belong to *material reality in a general sense*. This being so, camera explorations of the sound world itself can be said to lie, by extension, in a cinematic interest" (emphasis mine).[16] By "cinematic interest" Kracauer means the retention of and at the same time making transparent the "material reality" that only the camera has access to.[17] While Kracauer is referring to sound proper – that is, to "all

---

15 Hansen, *Cinema and Experience*, 261.
16 Kracauer, *Theory of Film*, 128. My emphasis.
17 As Kracauer states elsewhere in the book, "[w]hat accounts for the cinematic quality of films [. . .] is not so much their truth to our experience of reality or even to reality in a general sense as their absorption in camera-reality – visible physical existence" (Kracauer, *Theory of Film*, 116).

kinds of noises" – he begins the chapter by stating that sound could also be taken in the "loose" sense, in which case it "designates not only sound proper but the spoken word or dialogue as well."[18] This remark reveals how Kracauer already conceives of dialogue "loosely" as sound: like sound, dialogue also belongs, at least in part, to "material reality in a general sense." This does not mean he treats dialogue solely as sound; he recommends, for instance, that when "dealing with sound, it is best to treat dialogue – or speech, for that matter – and sound separately."[19] And yet, the further he gets into his first section on dialogue, the more Kracauer emphasizes dialogue *as* raw sound material.

After a fairly thorough historical and systematic overview of the Russian formalists' hopes for sound in film and the very unfortunate uses of dialogue in the first talkies, Kracauer runs through a list of what he calls non-cinematic and then "cinematic" (i.e., successful) uses of dialogue in film. Kracauer categorizes the "cinematic" uses of dialogue as follows: 1) *Speech deemphasized*; 2) *Speech is undermined from within*; and 3) *Shift of emphasis from the meanings of speech to its material qualities*. The film he singles out as exemplary of the third use of dialogue is Charlie Chaplin's 1936 classic, *Modern Times*, in particular the famous scene when Chaplin's voice is heard for the first time on screen.[20] As Kracauer writes of *Modern Times*, "when first incorporating the spoken word, Chaplin aimed at corroding it."[21] In this particular scene, Chaplin has landed a job as both waiter and singer in the café where his girlfriend works. He is nervous about his first performance singing in front of the crowd, and especially forgetting his lines. His girlfriend suggests that he write the lyrics of the song on his cuffs. What ensues, as Kracauer describes it, is a "hodge-podge of melodious, if incomprehensible, word formations [that] is both an attractive sound composition in its own right and an ingenious device for attuning the spectator perfectly to the pantomime which the involuntary rhapsodist is meanwhile performing."[22] While one would be hard-pressed to call what Chaplin mumbles "language," what remains are speech patterns that, along with Chaplin's pantomiming and body language, gesture to a kind of meaning, albeit nothing definitive.

---

18 Kracauer, *Theory of Film*, 103.
19 Kracauer, *Theory of Film*, 103.
20 While Chaplin had written dialogue for *City Lights* (1931) that was never used, and went as far as writing a complete script for *Modern Times*, he soon abandoned his attempts, reverting to a quasi-silent film format with synchronized sound effects. I say "quasi-silent film," since his playful use of sound and dialogue throughout the film is a testament to Chaplin's genius.
21 Kracauer, *Theory of Film*, 107.
22 Kracauer, *Theory of Film*, 110.

For Kracauer, this gesture toward but ultimate withholding of meaning heightens visual and sonic materiality, a process that emphasizes film's "cinematic quality." In his *Marseille Notebooks*, written twenty years earlier and the groundwork of *Theory of Film*, Kracauer is more emphatic on this point:

> Speech (*die Sprache*) itself has its material component as well. As with the actor, so is it possible with language to differentiate between being (*Sein*) and intention. Speech not only means something, it also has *a particular nature with which something is meant*. Since film roams the material dimension, one of its specific tasks is to expose the nature of speech (*Sprachnatur*) [emphasis original].[23]

Speech for Kracauer is distinguished between its being (*Sein*), which he aligns with its material dimension, and its intention, that is to say, the putative meaning it attempts to convey. Film's task is to expose the materiality of *Sprachnatur*, and in this context Kracauer refers in his *Marseille Notebooks* to Chaplin's wordy song without words:

> Chaplin wonderfully points out in *Modern Times* that the nature of language (*Sprachnatur*) in film may be more important than the intention of language (*Sprachintention*). Analysis of his *chanson*: it is a *reverse Volapük*, a mixture of words that appears to be *understood* by all but which in fact remains universally *not understood*.[24]

Kracauer's analysis of this scene in *Modern Times* echoes certain topics already examined in previous chapters. It is reminiscent, for instance, of Husserl's distinction between interpretation (*Deutung*) and meaning (*Bedeutung*) in section five of his *Logical Investigations*. But it also brings to mind Benjamin's emphasis on the comportment of the voice in radio, the difference being that Benjamin prefers another term to "materiality." Whereas Kracauer at times appears to play fast and loose with terms like "nature," "reality" and "materiality," Benjamin's notion of materiality is much more difficult to assess, due in large part because materiality for Benjamin can never be wholly severed from its historicity and

---

[23] Siegfried Kracauer, *Werke* (Frankfurt a.M.: Suhrkamp, 2004), 3:761–763. While I have chosen to translate "Sprache" here as "speech," with the understanding that Kracauer is undoubtedly thinking here of speech in film, "Sprache" should also be understood as language. In *Theory of Film* and these Marseille notes, he does not explicitly distinguish between *langue* and *parole*.

[24] Kracauer, *Werke*, 3:765. A nineteenth-century precursor to Esperanto, Volapück is a constructed language created by Johann Martin Schleyer, a Roman Catholic Priest from Baden who said that God had come to him in a dream and told him to create an international language that everyone would be able to understand and speak. For Kracauer, Chaplin's song functions like a Volapück in reverse: an international language we should all theoretically be able to understand, but which is in fact universally unable to be understood.

mnemonic associations. The historical materialist is intrigued primarily with dilapidated, forgotten objects that have been left behind, and engages or "activates" them via a certain open receptivity to the historical possibilities (which is decidedly not History) of the object at hand.[25] Kracauer, on the other hand, does not seem to limit himself to such objects; rather, what has been lost or forgotten is the material dimension of *all* objects, from the materiality of everyday things to what he calls *Sprachnatur*. Cinema's task for Kracauer is to expose and redeem such lost "materiality," and in this sense his film theory veers in the direction of early radio theorists' praise that radio brings about a renewed attention to the "materiality" of the voice and with it the Romanticist's impulse to return to that *Urzeit* when language was apparently more "musical."

The next chapter in Kracauer's *Theory of Film* is concerned with music in film. If Hansen recognized "something like an 'acoustic unconscious'" in Kracauer's attention to the material dimension of speech, might film music function similarly? The short answer is "no." For Kracauer, music in film is indispensable not because of its own material dimension but because of its organizational role: film music injects silent moving images with a necessary "aliveness" they would not otherwise have on their own, granting them "structured patterns where there were none before."[26] More importantly, film music for Kracauer also pulls the audience into the world of the film: "it is added to draw the spectator into the very center of the silent images and have him [sic] experience their photographic life."[27] This function is crucial, since the audience's now intimate relation to the image is what allows the latter's material dimension to be perceived. While Kracauer does not emphasize this point in *Theory of Film*, he does so explicitly in the Marseille notebooks: "*film music has the function of establishing contact between the image and the sensorium*, making the latter conductive to the currents emanating from the material images. Music *stimulates the sensory apparatus* and keeps it in vibration" (emphasis original).[28] Like film for Benjamin's optical unconscious or animals for Kafka's understanding of the forgotten, film music for Kracauer becomes a necessary conduit through which we learn about the material dimension experientially: we "learn about" or "get wind of" (*erfahren von*) the material dimension of cinema through film music because it opens up our

---

25 See Dan Mellamphy and Nandita Biswas Mellamphy's article, "What's the 'Matter' with Materialism? Walter Benjamin and the New Janitocracy," *Janus Head* 11, no. 1 (2009): 163–182; here, 164.
26 Kracauer, *Theory of Film*, 135.
27 Kracauer, *Theory of Film*, 135.
28 Kracauer, *Werke* 3:579.

sensorium to the images, allowing us to experience directly "their photographic life." Film music is certainly not the goal, nor is it the only conduit, but we cannot do without it.²⁹

Despite these functions, Kracauer was also fully conscious of the advantages of asynchronous music and its tendency to arouse unheard-of interpretations between the image and its musical accompaniment. Kracauer's most repeated anecdote on the role of music in silent film, which is found in *Theory of Film*, the Marseille notebooks, and even his quasi-autobiographical novel, *Georg*, is what Kracauer himself calls "the drunken pianist." In a book like *Theory of Film*, the main goal of which is to categorize systematically every aspect of the function of cinema, it is both curious and refreshing when Kracauer begins a section in the chapter on film music by recalling one of his own distant memories:

> I still remember, as if it were yesterday, an old movie house which was my favorite haunt in faraway days. [. . .] The music there was supplied by a gray-haired pianist as decrepit as the faded plush seats and the gilded plaster cupids. He too had seen better days. In his youth he had been a gifted artist with a brilliant future ahead of him, but then he had taken to the bottle, and all that now reminded one of those promising beginnings was his fluttering *lavallière*, a leftover from student life with its dream of glory. He was rarely what you would call sober. And whenever he performed, he was so completely immersed in himself that he did not waste a single glance on the screen. His music followed an unpredictable course of its own. [. . .] This lack of relation between the musical themes and the action they were supposed to sustain seemed very delightful indeed to me, for it made me see the story in a new and unexpected light or, more important, challenged me to lose myself in an uncharted wilderness opened up by allusive shots.³⁰

While this anecdote further supports Kracauer's claim that music functions like an acoustical lens through which the image is interpreted, it also illustrates the extent to which the drunken pianist's arbitrary accompaniment forces the audience to find their own interpretation "between the musical themes and the action they were supposed to sustain."³¹ Chaplin's corrosion of language that Kracauer champions in *Modern Times* is comparable here, since both Chaplin and the drunken pianist are not concerned with the imparting of meaning in

---

29 Film music is of course not the only interpretive medium that "colors" our view of the filmic world with emotions. Kracauer repeatedly compares the role of film music with the technique of "tinting" during the silent film era, which also acts like a conduit through which we perceive the material and therefore "cinematic" qualities of that which is presented: "The tints echoed music in the dimension of the visuals themselves" (Kracauer, *Theory of Film*, 137).
30 Kracauer, *Theory of Film*, 137–138.
31 Kracauer, *Theory of Film*, 137.

any conventional sense. Rather, they confront their audiences with the unexpected, forcing them to search for their own meaning while simultaneously gesturing toward the equally arbitrary construction of conventional meaning. In both cases, our ears prick up: what is Chaplin saying? Are those words? What does this piano music have to do with what's on the screen? Both examples redirect our attention away from conventional modes of meaning-making of speech and music in film and toward our capacity to interpret these image-sound combinations on our own.[32]

Just before his comments on the role of music in film, Kracauer writes in his Marseille notebooks that, "[w]hen emphasizing the material, film appeals in no way to understood meaning that in turn arouse emotions, it rather provokes *unconscious bodily reactions* out of which meaning may then grow" (emphasis mine).[33] As we have seen, one way of accessing cinematic materiality for Kracauer is through the paradoxically immaterial but nevertheless *vital* (in both senses of the term) component of film, its music. If music helps provoke in the viewer "unconscious bodily reactions" via the ear, this is perhaps another way to interpret a kind of acoustical unconscious in Kracauer's theory of film: as psychophysical reactions to unexpected coincidences – or in the case with Chaplin's *Volapük*, thwarted expectations – between what is heard and what is seen, which in turn impact how the audience interprets the scene's meaning.

Alexander Kluge is equally interested in these interpretive moments out of which meaning grows, and employs an additional term that helps him think

---

32 In the last paragraph of his anecdote, Kracauer further admits that "once in a while his music conformed to the dramatic events with an accuracy which struck me all the more as miraculous since it was entirely unintended. It was the same kind of sensation which I experienced when, walking the streets, I discovered that some painted clock dial outside a watchmaker's shop marked the exact hour as I was passing by. And these random coincidences [. . .] gave me the impression that there existed after all a relationship, however elusive, between the drunken pianist's soliloquies and the drama before my eyes – a relationship which I considered perfect because of its accidental nature and indeterminacy" (Kracauer, *Theory of Film*, 138). Kracauer's emphasis on the accidental and indeterminate is reminiscent both of Barthes' *punctum* and perhaps even Benjamin's aura that is famously constitutive of a "strange weave [*Gespinst*] of space and time: the unique appearance [*einmalige Erscheinung*] of a distance, however near it may be" (Walter Benjamin, *Gesammelte Schriften* [Frankfurt a.M.: Suhrkamp, 1972] [hereafter, *GS*], 7:355; Walter Benjamin, *Selected Writings*, ed. Michael W. Jennings, Marcus Bullock, Howard Eiland, and Gary Smith, trans. Rodney Livingstone and Edmund Jephcott [Cambridge: Harvard University Press, 1996–2003] [hereafter, *SW*], 3:104–105). For an excellent exploration of this trope throughout Kracauer's work but in *Theory of Film* in particular, see Janet Harbord, "Contingency's Work: Kracauer's *Theory of Film* and the Trope of the Accidental," *New Formations* 61 (Summer 2007): 90–103.
33 Kracauer, *Werke*, 3:577.

about what happens at this crucial moment: *Phantasie*. This term certainly does not come without its own baggage; Kluge had already appropriated this term from Freud and Marx when collaborating with Oskar Negt in *Public Sphere and Experience: Toward an Analysis of the Bourgeois and Proletarian Public Sphere* (*Öffentlichkeit und Erfahrung. Zur Organisationsanalyse von bürgerlicher und proletarischer Öffentlichkeit*, 1972).[34] When transferring fantasy's mediating function to the cinematic experience, Kluge attempts to explain that same curious process of meaning-formation that Kracauer describes above. For both Kracauer and Kluge, the function of music in film is strikingly similar. Still, whereas for Kracauer, film more generally *redeems* reality by redirecting our otherwise distracted attention to the materiality of things themselves, with music functioning as one unconscious sensory access point out of which meaning grows, Kluge emphasizes the *emancipatory*, and therefore political, dimension of the mediating capacity that he calls fantasy. Examining Kluge's role of fantasy and its political implications in film will reveal its relation both to Benjamin's notion of shock and the optical unconscious, both of which Kluge refers to explicitly.

5.2 Kluge's Fantasy in Film

As Miriam Hansen argues, Kluge's continued dependence on the aesthetics of early cinema, from the projector's loud rattling to the screen being dark for half the time, has long been familiar among "European avant-garde artists and intellectuals from the 1920s on: an enthusiasm for the cinema's anarchic beginnings, its aesthetic *and* political possibilities; a critique of its actual institutional development" (emphasis original).[35] One could say that Kluge's fascination with both fantasy as a concept and his avant-garde approach to early cinema is based on an overarching interest in discontinuity: fantasy involves, like the unconscious or dreams, the atemporal and an excess of multiplicity over unity, even if its

---

34 It was only in 1993 that the English translation of Negt and Kluge's *Public Sphere and Experience* was published. The North American reception of Kluge's work was therefore already anachronistic. While Kluge's notion of fantasy is well known among German film scholars, only a handful of other scholars, including Fredric Jameson and Richard Langston, have written on the term without immediate recourse to Kluge's notions of cinema. See Frederic Jameson, "On Negt and Kluge," *October* 46 (Fall 1988): 151–177, which I refer to in the following section, and Richard Langston, "Toward an Ethics of Fantasy: The Kantian Dialogues of Oskar Negt and Alexander Kluge," *The Germanic Review* 85, no. 4 (October–December 2010): 271–293.
35 Hansen, "Reinventing the Nickelodeon," 182.

main function is to mediate disparate "texts" such as the exterior world with consciousness and libidinal structures. Similarly, the intellectual history of European avant-garde film is above all a history whose *sine qua non* is the debunking of official Film History. As two traditions that stress the ruptures of (either conscious or historical) continuity and unity, it seems natural that fantasy and avant-garde film converges in Kluge's work.

In *Public Sphere and Experience*, Negt and Kluge recognize fantasy, "as it is commonly used in indicating dissociation [*in dem abgespaltenen Sinne*], is a product of the bourgeoisie."[36] A more productive definition of fantasy, they argue, would be as the organizer of mediation (*Vermittlung*), meaning that it should be left to organize according to its own laws of operation and its own means of production, both of which are invisible to and exceed bourgeois modes of operation. Negt and Kluge thus explicitly follow the mediating function of both Freud's and Marx's fantasy work (*Phantasiearbeit*) that, according to the authors in Germany circa 1972, was in danger of becoming obsolete. However, by recovering Freud's and Marx's *Phantasiearbeit* for the public sphere, the term "fantasy" necessarily takes on new characteristics. While Negt and Kluge readily admit to having adopted fantasy's mediating function and inherent temporal discontinuity from Freud, when applied to the public sphere, fantasy no longer refers to a purely subjective psychic category. In his 1988 article, "On Negt and Kluge," Fredric Jameson succinctly refers to how fantasy is developed beyond the individual by Negt and Kluge:

> As for desire and fantasy, their status in contemporary theory seems to result from the widespread feeling that narrative, image, fantasy, embodied symptom, are no longer mere subjective epiphenomena, but objective components of our social world, invested with all the ontological dignity of those hitherto "objective" social materials presented by economics, politics, and historiography. What is even more significant is that subjective or psychological phenomena are now increasingly seen as having epistemological and even practical functions. Fantasy is no longer felt to be a private and compensatory reaction against public situations, but rather *a way of reading* those situations, of thinking and mapping them, of intervening in them, albeit in a very different form from the abstract reflections of traditional philosophy or politics [emphasis mine].[37]

---

[36] Alexander Kluge and Oskar Negt, *Öffentlichkeit und Erfahrung. Zur Organisationsanalyse von bürgerlicher und proletarischer Öffentlichkeit* (Frankfurt a.M.: Suhrkamp, 1972) (hereafter, *ÖuE*), 72; Alexander Kluge and Oskar Negt, *Public Sphere and Experience: Toward an Analysis of the Bourgeois and Proletarian Public Sphere*, trans. Peter Labanyi, Jamie Owen Daniel, and Assenka Oksiloff (Minneapolis: University of Minnesota Press, 1993) (hereafter, *PSE*), 36.
[37] Jameson, "On Negt and Kluge," 171.

Writing in 1972, Negt and Kluge thus appear, for Jameson writing in the late 1980s, as precursors of the contemporaneous political and public status of fantasy, which becomes simultaneously a collective that reads and a reading of the collective.[38]

By the early 1980s, German film scholars were already interested in Kluge's reappropriation of fantasy for the public sphere and its function in cinema. In a "Special Double Issue on New German Cinema" of the *New German Critique* in the Fall of 1981, sections of Kluge's *Ulmer Dramaturgien. Reibungsverluste* (1980) were translated by Thomas Levine and Miriam Hansen. One section is called, "The Role of Fantasy [*Die Rolle der Phantasie*]," and it is to this section that many have turned in order to understand Kluge's definition of fantasy as it pertains to film, and specifically to film montage:

> Since every cut provokes phantasy, a storm of phantasy, you can even make a break in the film. It is exactly at such a point that information is conveyed. This is what Benjamin meant by the notion of shock. It would be wrong to say that a film should aim to shock the viewers – this would restrict their independence and powers of observation. The point here is the surprise which occurs when you suddenly – as if by subdominant thought processes [*nach einem nicht-aktuellen Konzept*] – understand something in depth and then, out of this deepened perspective redirect your phantasy to the real course of events.[39]

In appropriating Benjamin's notion of shock, Kluge makes sure it does not deprive the viewers of their "independence" and powers of observation. In this way, Kluge's use of fantasy in film is related less to Freud's notion of the mystical writing pad than to Brecht's *Verfremdungseffekt* and the shocks that Benjamin himself recognized specifically in Epic Theater:[40]

---

38 A good example of this is how Negt and Kluge extrapolate Freud's mode of analysis for reappropriating individual life history into the collective realm. See Kluge and Negt, *ÖuE* 74; *PSE* 37.

39 Alexander Kluge, "On Film and the Public Sphere," trans. Thomas Levin and Miriam Hansen, *New German Critique* 24/25 (Autumn–Winter, 1981–1983): 216. When citing from this translation, I honor Levin and Hansen's decision to translate Kluge's term, "Phantasie," as "phantasy." With all other references to the term, I follow Jameson, Langston and others' spelling of "fantasy."

40 In an otherwise insightful overview concerning Kluge's notion of montage, Michelle Langford writes that, "*Phantasie* is that which lies beneath the guarded exterior of the stimulus shield, and it is *Phantasie* that is set free when shock is able to break through the barrier." Although it is true that fantasy is both emancipated and emancipatory in Kluge, the analogy to Freud's writing pad appears misleading. Kluge's goal is not to traumatize his viewers but to surprise them into a deepened perspective and spark their critical faculties. See Michelle

Epic Theater advances, comparable to the pictures of a filmstrip, in jerks and jolts [*rückt* (. . .) *in Stößen vor*]. Its basic form is that of the shock with which the singular, clearly-demarcated situations of the play collide. The songs, legends, gestural conventions demarcate one situation from the others. In this way, intervals arise which tend rather to limit the illusions of the audience. They paralyze its readiness to identify [*zur Einfühlung*]. Such intervals are reserved for its critical disposition [*seiner kritischen Stellungnahme*].[41]

Kluge's project as a whole can be defined as accentuating the "jerks and jolts" of the filmstrip that for Benjamin remain a compelling, albeit technical comparison to the shock-form of epic theater. There are indeed multiple comparisons between Kluge's and Benjamin's passages above, not the least of which occurs between Benjamin's interval and Kluge's cut or *Schnittstelle*. Benjamin's interval is "the space in which events *take place*," which admirably mirrors the German word, *Schnittstelle*, or literally "cut-place."[42] For Kluge, the cut is precisely where the "storm of fantasy" takes place. Another similarity arises between the audience's reaction to that interval or cut. For Benjamin, it allows for a critical disposition while crippling the ease with which the audience empathizes. Kluge also makes clear how the viewers should not be shocked into paralysis, but shocked into a deeper understanding. Or more precisely: from the sudden moment of the cut and the storm of fantasy it produces we achieve a deepened perspective, out of which we redirect our fantasy to the physical, tangible or substantive course of events (*dem realen Vorgang zuwenden*). Whether this procedure is relatable or even practical, two things are clear: Kluge 1) emphasizes fantasy as a possessive ("your/our fantasy"), and 2) activates fantasy into a kind of critical function. The functional use of fantasy, moreover, involves the absence of all social norms and conventions. As Kluge explains:

> There is no social agreement [*keine gesellschaftliche Verständigung*] regulating the common use of fantasy. When you continue to speak after the other person has understood, then you exceed a social norm; [. . .] if you eat until you're full that's normal, but if you continue to eat, then that's for psychological reasons. This is to say that in all these cases there is a sense of proportion. But in the workings of fantasy [*Phantasietätigkeit*], there is no sense of proportion [*Maßverhältnisse*].[43]

Langford, "Alexander Kluge," *Senses of Cinema* 27 (July 2003): n.p., accessed 31 January 2021, http://sensesofcinema.com/2003/great-directors/kluge/.
41 Benjamin, *GS* 2:537–538; *SW* 4:306. Translation: Samuel Weber, *Benjamin's -abilities* (Cambridge: Harvard University Press, 2008), 106.
42 See Weber, *Benjamin's -abilities*, 106.
43 Alexander Kluge, *Ulmer Dramaturgien. Reibungsverluste* (Munich: Carl Hanser Verlag, 1980), 62; "Significance of Fantasy," in Kluge, "Kluge on Opera, Film, and Feelings," 215.

This definition of fantasy work echoes the more poetic measuring discussed by Heidegger and Eich in the previous chapter: without a measuring stick, one is left open to a crisis of proportion – neither near nor far, large nor small – which leads to a crisis of taking place, a "dis-position" in the way Weber translates *Stellungnahme*. The "storm of fantasy" provoked by the cut dispositions viewers who are in no position, so to speak, to rely on social norms or any other form of measurement.

Rather than forcing any predetermined meaning or response, Kluge's film editing style attempts to actualize the theoretical procedure described above: by presenting disparate images, sounds and music, he forces his viewers to make their own associations, which he hopes are constructed by critical and productive modes of fantasy that evolve out of displacement and crisis, a break from social norms, and a shifting of perspectives: "A continuous shifting of perspectives [*Perspektiven*] is typical of phantasy. In phantasy I can transport myself to Africa without effort or I can imagine myself involved in a love-scene in the middle of a desert – all this happens as in a dream."[44] Not unlike the dreamscapes found in Eich's radio plays, Kluge's description of fantasy here takes on the logic of the collective unconscious, accentuating unconscious wishes, blockages, and ephemeral details.

Miriam Hansen was the first and to my knowledge only scholar to link this psychic process in Kluge's film theory to Benjamin's optical unconscious. Hansen first cites a passage from Kluge's early collaborative text, *Stocktaking: Utopia Film* (*Bestandsaufnahme: Utopie Film*, 1983), in which he describes how singular traces of the public sphere that we all carry within us not only correspond to singular details in film, but that their subliminal complicity "presents at once a danger and a sensational opportunity for all utopian horizons."[45] Hansen then goes on to state that the correspondence between the details of a film and the singular traces of the public sphere we carry within us have "to do with Benjamin's 'optical unconscious.'"[46] Her reasoning is that Kluge is "interested in the pragmatics of redemption – gradations, distinctions, aesthetic valences of film that disappear with television, lost and new possibilities."[47] These qualities that for Hansen also characterize Benjamin's optical unconscious are important to recognize in Kluge's work, but this observation must be

---

44 Kluge, *Ulmer Dramaturgien* 62; Kluge, "Film and Public Sphere," 215.
45 Kluge, cited by Hansen, "Reinventing the Nickelodeon," 185.
46 Hansen, "Reinventing the Nickelodeon," 185.
47 Hansen, "Reinventing the Nickelodeon," 186. By accentuating Kluge's interest in the "pragmatics of redemption," Hansen is also gesturing here to Kracauer's subtitle to *Theory of Film*: "The Redemption of Physical Reality."

reconciled with Kluge's specific use of fantasy. For if Kluge is as interested in the optical unconscious as he is in the productive modes of an emancipatory fantasy, questions arise about whether the two are so easily discernable. Distinguishing between Kluge's productive procedure of fantasy and the Benjaminian optical unconscious will help, however, when considering the potential relevance of the acoustical unconscious in Kluge's work. One way to do this is to turn to a few stories in Kluge's *Cinema Stories*. Through his anecdotal, quasi-autobiographical literary style, Kluge communicates certain reflections on both Benjamin's film theory, the unconscious, fantasy and music.[48]

5.3 "An Observation on Walter Benjamin" by Kluge

In distinguishing between Kluge's fantasy and Benjamin's unconscious, we might say that the technical reality of film – the close-ups and slow motion, the cut, the "other nature" of the camera – comprises the optical unconscious, while Kluge's fantasy is the stuff of the spectator's "inner film." In other words, Kluge's fantasy derives from the spectator or group of spectators, while Benjamin's optical unconscious has less to do with the spectator than with the "lost and new possibilities" inherent to film as a medium. Following this, we may surmise the relation between Kluge's fantasy and Benjamin's optical unconscious as follows: the particular technical traits of film are what make structurally possible a film's interpenetration with what Kluge calls "our fantasy." This is not to say that the optical unconscious is synonymous simply with the "jerks and jolts" of cinema, nor is it quantifiable, allowing one to "measure" a particular film's use value for an alternative public sphere. But awakening to the optical unconscious – whether via the accentuation of hidden details or the "dynamite of the split second"[49] – might induce a certain feeling of shock, which for Kluge then dis-positions the spectator to experience a "storm of fantasy."

---

48 In *Cosmic Miniatures and the Future Sense: Alexander Kluge's 21st-Century Literary Experiments in German Cultural and Narrative Form* (Berlin: De Gruyter, 2017), Leslie Adelson pushes back against the "default assumption that Benjaminian motifs of fragmentation and montage figure only in non-narrative ways for Kluge" (31). By turning to Kluge's short prose pieces in *Cinema Stories*, I also wish to underscore how Kluge's literary experimentation is not mutually exclusive to his multifaceted film montage technique, which includes his use of music and sound. Although Adelson's focus is not on sense perception, she nevertheless highlights that "Kluge's cosmic miniatures are more centrally concerned with invisible rather than visible phenomena, as the recurring figure and problem of unseen extraterrestrials suggests" (Adelson, *Cosmic Miniatures and the Future Sense*, 48).
49 Benjamin, *GS* 1:499; *SW* 4:265.

When comparing Kluge's fantasy with Benjamin's optical unconscious, it is worth noting the parallels between this last phrase by Kluge and Benjamin's explanatory sentence of the camera's "other nature" in the artwork essay: the camera is "'[o]ther' above all in that a space [*Raum*] interwoven by the unconscious enters at the place [*an die Stelle*] where space is interwoven by human consciousness [translation modified]."[50] This *Stelle* is as much Kluge's *Schnittstelle* that provokes a storm of fantasy as it is, for Benjamin, the "giving way" of a space or room (*Raum*) of human consciousness to that of the unconscious. But there is a crucial difference between Benjamin's and Kluge's two "places": only *after* achieving a deepened perspective via an initial shock are we, according to Kluge, capable of redirecting our fantasy to the "tangible course of events." For Benjamin, that "space interwoven with the unconscious" appears to work *autonomously* from the spectator, working itself into human consciousness. Benjamin is not referring here to the *Phantasiearbeit* of any one person or even group of persons, but rather to *an* unconscious made accessible by the very existence of the camera, by its other nature that speaks differently, by the way it "sees otherwise." It is this convergence of an optically unconscious space with a space interwoven by human consciousness, the interpenetration of two *Räume* as Benjamin describes it, that opens up a place for Kluge's spectators to experience that "storm of fantasy." Crossmapping Benjamin's optical unconscious with Kluge's emancipatory fantasy makes clear that the latter appears as dependent on the optical unconscious as it is on the interval, cut, or initial shock.

And yet, Kluge prefers to limit his reading of the optical unconscious only to its political, and specifically emancipatory ramifications. This is nowhere better crystalized than in a short essay in *Cinema Stories* entitled "An Observation of Walter Benjamin" ("Eine Beobachtung von Walter Benjamin"), throughout which Kluge cites Benjamin's artwork essay. While it would be useful to examine all of Kluge's citations from the artwork essay and how he positions them in relation to one another (in footnotes, etc.), it should suffice to quote Kluge's summary of Benjamin's overall goal. After citing a few lines from the artwork essay's epilogue, in which Benjamin outlines ways in which fascism takes advantage of the masses through film, Kluge writes: "From this perspective, Benjamin develops a theory of film that would be useless to a cinema of fascism but useful for a cinema of emancipation."[51] Such is Kluge's understanding of the artwork essay's

---

50 Benjamin, *GS* 1:499; *SW* 4:265.
51 Kluge, *GvK*, 143; *CS* 42.

major achievement: Benjamin's essay is nothing more or less than a prolegomenon for the cinema of emancipation. What "emancipation" means for Kluge is revealed in dialogue form later in the same text:

- Isn't it difficult to base observations and formulations on the premise that they should be theoretically useless for fascists but especially useful for socialists (and workers in particular)?
- That is especially not easy with experiences in cinema practice [*Kinopraxis*]. Gersholm Scholem, who favored Benjamin, compares his method with the "elaborateness of the twelve-tone technique" in music. In the interests of the equality of all tones, a single tone may only reappear in a musical arc once all the other tones in the octave have had their chance.
- No simple process. Benjamin had to observe and check not only for its completeness, truth and formulatability [*Formulierbarkeit*], but also whether it conformed to the condition: useless for fascists while exclusively useful for socialists [translation modified].[52]

For Kluge, Benjamin writes the artwork essay in order to wrest cinema from fascist imperialism by discovering something about cinema that is useful exclusively for socialists but not for fascists. This emphasis on the political use-value of cinema is reminiscent of the way Negt and Kluge's definition of fantasy also functions politically: as long it is used "properly," it will achieve the goal of transforming "the experience bound up in fantasy into collective practical emancipation."[53] One can indeed draw a straight line from the emancipatory fantasy described by Negt and Kluge in 1972 to Kluge's own "cinema of emancipation" explored in *Cinema Stories* and specifically to his reading of Benjamin's artwork essay above. Whether we accept his interpretation as valid, one thing is clear: Kluge has no problem politicizing the artwork essay.

This rather one-sided interpretation of Benjamin's essay, moreover, confirms why Kluge would unsurprisingly read the use-value of Benjamin's optical unconscious as equally political:

In his essay [Benjamin] rigorously investigates the change in sense perception [*die Veränderung im sinnlichen Wahrnehmungsapparat*] that arose through the historical turning point of the twentieth century. The new perception occurs, he says, "in distraction," collectively, and "though force of habit." It corresponds, he claims, to a tactile reception ("without reflection"); this kind of reception (similar to the way in which one furnishes a home and knows, even in the dark, where the obstacles and pathways are) offers an

---

52 Kluge, *GvK*, 144; *CS* 43.
53 Negt and Kluge, *ÖuE* 67; *PSE* 33.

experience that is more immediate, revealing, and less easily misused by third parties than the work of the mind, which is always of utmost importance in traditional Enlightenment thought. All of this he studied via the praxis of movie theater audiences [translation modified].[54]

Kluge interprets Benjamin's critical examination of "the change in sense perception" as geared ultimately towards its use-value for a cinema of emancipation. It is clear that Kluge seems unwilling to work outside of the political implications of Benjamin's critical analysis: for Kluge, even the optical unconscious is a catalyst for how the cinema of emancipation generates gaps and fissures that are filled in by the spectator's fantasy, which Kluge measures politically. It should come as no surprise that the chapter in which "An Observation on Benjamin" is found in Kluge's section titled, "Films in War / Battle over Film" ("Filmen im Krieg / Kampf um den Film"). For Kluge, Benjamin's artwork essay is a major contribution to this battle over film.

5.4 Movement, Music and Film in *Cinema Stories*

In the foreword of *Cinema Stories* with which this chapter began, Kluge's notion of "Kino" is "immortal" and "older than film art": "This is because we impart [*mitteilen*] something in public with one another that 'moves us inwardly.' In that respect, film and music are related."[55] The idea of movement (*Bewegung*), both its physical and emotional connotations, is a central criterion that links music to Kluge's principle of cinema. Already as early as *Stocktaking: Utopia Film*, Kluge writes about the principle of cinema specifically in terms of movement, relying on the etymology of "Kino": "Translated from the Greek, the word 'Kino' means 'movement': the images are in motion, and the scenes put me in motion."[56] Kluge breaks down movement into what he deems its essential parts: the movement of images and the movement of the spectator's e-motion. But the movements of image and spectator also involve an essential *third* movement: being moved inwardly along with other spectators. Here we recognize the importance of Kluge's formulation, "a 'something' that moves *us* [emphasis mine] inwardly [das *uns* 'innerlich bewegt']": the addition of "us" accentuates the collective experience of film reception. "Inwardly" refers, in part, to subjectivity: Kluge emphasizes this point when he begins the foreword to

---

54 Kluge, *GvK* 143–44; *CS* 42–43.
55 Kluge, *GvK*, 7.
56 Alexander Kluge, *Bestandsaufnahme, Utopie Film: Zwanzig Jahre neuer deutscher Film* (Frankfurt a.M.: Zweitausendeins, 1983), 45. All translations of *Bestandsaufnahme* are mine.

5.4 Movement, Music and Film in *Cinema Stories*

Cinema Stories with the sentence, "[t]he stories in this book are subjective."[57] But equally important is a merging of the subject(ive) with others during a film screening. The spectator's "inner film" is therefore also always the "inner film" of the collective.[58] This collective movement, combined with its emotional and physical connotations, is for Kluge central to the experience of both cinema and music.

For Kluge, music has as much power as film to "move us inwardly," if not more so. In the same passage in *Stocktaking*, when he confirms the principle of cinema as movement, Kluge writes: "With the movement that music provokes, it is possible to circumvent place and position perhaps more freely and more detached."[59] The freer and more detached from any one fixed place or position, the more freely, it seems, that fantasy roams between film images and/or musical notes, all the while apparently merging with the fantasy of others. Free movement is a precondition for the provocation of emancipatory fantasy. If music is already so adept at and open to such movement, it is worth observing how Kluge describes and refers to the role of music in film. As we shall see, the phrase "in film" is precisely what music is not.

A number of stories in *Cinema* Stories, all of which are fictional despite being based on anecdotes or loosely connected to historical events, illustrate how the boundary between the film soundtrack and sounds from the surrounding world are at best fluid. In the first chapter, for instance, a one-page story entitled "Cinema in Crisis" ("Kino in der Not")[60] is about an old married couple who had run the Eldorado movie theater in Beirut for decades until it was razed to the ground by aerial bombing. With only the foundation of the building remaining, the couple cleared away the rubble and erected a tent in the center on the floor:

---

57 Kluge, *GvK* 7.
58 Kluge describes it thus: "I feel something, develop a perspective [*mache mir eine Perspektive*] by looking at it from another person's point of view [*Standpunkt*], and now I could communicate it even to third parties (although *my* nerves tell me *exactly what* I feel)" (emphasis original; Kluge, *Bestandsaufnahme*, 45). To create a perspective from the stand point of another involves the development of the collective I/eye and breaks down the fixed place of a single subject, despite the nervous system communicating to that subject "exactly what" it is feeling. In the next section, Kluge's particular notion of *Perspektiv* will be addressed in terms of sound specifically.
59 Kluge, *Bestandsaufnahme*, 45.
60 While this story is the seventh installment in the German edition's first chapter, it is the first story in the English edition.

> Under the tent stood the projectors, which had been rescued. In front of them, rows of makeshift seats (chairs from a café), and in front of those, the screen. The sound of battle, sometimes coming nearer, sometimes farther away, merged with the soundtrack of the films. The audience was somewhat safer under the tented roof than in the surviving buildings, since destroyed buildings were rarely attacked twice, and in this "cinema auditorium" [*Kinosaal*] there was no danger of being buried by falling masonry [translation modified].[61]

This opening description of the ruined Eldorado cinema describes not simply a tent in the middle of a ruined foundation, but a singular place that is both a safe haven and an enclosed space that nevertheless remains open to the external sonic environment. This is a concrete example that describes spatially how the soundtrack, like music, allows for the freeing up of and detachment from place. Even the term *Kinosaal*, aptly translated as "cinema auditorium" in the English edition, blends both music and cinema in a way that was already hinted at in the foreword.

The story also exemplifies a "double move" often found in Kluge's anecdotal style: an apparently history-specific (albeit fictional), unique circumstance is presented, almost as a kind of theatrical stage, upon which is played out what for Kluge are timeless, immortal ideas and emotions that themselves transcend the specific and detailed staging of them. In this case, the *Kinosaal* generates a particularly strong feeling of communal security, despite its cloth walls and the films having little to do with one another thematically. In a footnote to the story, Kluge emphasizes this point exactly: "the audience who visited this 'cinema in crisis' every night felt momentarily secure while the projectors rattled on. This corresponded to a strong emotion and was in this respect the program, in the sense of 'program cinema [*Programm Kino*]'" (translation modified).[62] The momentary sense of security, not the screening itself, was the program for the evening. The tent is of course little more than flimsy canvas, doubled by the thin screen upon which the films were projected. Neither layer protects the audience from any external sonic sensations, which corresponds to a third, thin layer not explicitly mentioned but relevant to our analysis: the tympanum of the ear or eardrum. The eardrum is a thin piece of skin-like tissue that transduces vibrations in the air in order to eventually send electric signals to the brain, informing it that sounds are being heard. Like the stretched canvas of the tent, the eardrum does nothing to protect us from the "sound of battle, sometimes coming

---

61 Kluge, *GvK* 23; *CS* 1.
62 Kluge, *GvK* 311; *CS* 95.

nearer, sometimes farther away."⁶³ And yet, the rattling of the film projector echoes Kluge's reference to the same in the foreword: it offers the audience a sense of security from the external noise to which they are vulnerable. The merging of the projector's secure rattling within the tent and the sounds of warfare from outside is what defines this cinema's crisis. Put another way, the projector's rattling is like the sonic equivalent of a small flame that keeps warm, if only momentarily, the shivering lives of those who have so far escaped the death that surrounds them.⁶⁴

A similar merging of film sound and external sounds with the accompanying feeling of communal security occurs in another fictional story, "The Final Film Screening in the Reich Chancellery" ("Die letzte Filmvorstellung in der Reichskanzlei"). In April 1945, Kluges accounts how a film screening was organized for those occupying the Führer's bunker under the Reich Chancellery.⁶⁵ The makeshift film screening was itself projected in one of the rooms of the Chancellery, the ceiling of which had been destroyed by recent air raids. Open to "the evening clouds above," this open-air cinema was also open to the natural sounds of the environment:

> From the garden of the Reich Chancellery, which had belonged earlier to Bismarck's seat of governance, birds sang. They had only recently returned to the besieged capital from their nesting places in the south. These strains of song [*Gesangsstrophen*], the background noises in the film soundtrack, and the artillery fire in the distance all blended with the overall diffuse light of evening [translation modified].⁶⁶

---

63 Kluge, *GvK* 23; *CS* 1. In *Eardrums: Literary Modernism as Sonic Warfare* (Evanston: Northwestern University Press, 2019), Tyler Whitney traces the genealogy of what he calls the "tympanic regime" by not only examining German literary and performative representations of the martial soundscape in the early twentieth century, but also focusing on the eardrum as "a site of corporeal vulnerability and a metaphor for the subject's often violent encounter with modern sound and the various social and cultural antagonisms with which it was inflected" (70). As he suggests in his conclusion, Whitney's interpretation of the eardrum could also be extrapolated to include artistic representations of sonic warfare in postwar German culture. A fruitful study would no doubt ensue between Whitney's historical and literary engagement with sonic warfare and the copious references to martial soundscapes in Kluge's written and filmic work.
64 This is a play on Benjamin's famous formulation about the reader of novels in his essay, "The Storyteller": "What draws the reader to a novel is the hope of warming his shivering life with a death he reads about" (Benjamin, *GS* 2:457; *SW* 3:156).
65 As far as I know, there is no historical record of this ever having taken place. Hitler apparently made his last trip to the surface on April 20, his fifty-sixth birthday, going to the ruined garden of the Reich Chancellery where he awarded the Iron Cross to boy soldiers of the Hitler Youth. That same night, Soviet artillery began firing on Berlin for the first time. See Antony Beevor, *Berlin: The Downfall 1945* (New York: Penguin, 2002).
66 Kluge, *GvK* 236; *CS* 64.

This time Kluge adds here the strains of birdsong to the combination of film sound and distant artillery fire. While this could certainly be read as a sonic extrapolation of the film's tragic love story that Kluge summarizes earlier in the text, the way Kluge reports the birds' migratory return to the garden of the Reich Chancellery is detached and cold, almost journalistic in tone. This situation is once again evidence of Kluge's double move mentioned above: Kluge stages a unique and apparently historically specific event in order to explore a much deeper, timeless experience that expresses, at least for Kluge, a guiding principle of cinema. Kluge ends the story with the reaction of a Nazi captain, present at the film screening, who admits that, while the film's plot was engaging,

> more compelling still was the sense of place [*Eindruck des Raums*] – a room that had lost its roof and could barely be further compromised by renewed bombardment. We were practically sitting in a scrap heap with our only consolation being the screen before us and an unobstructed view to the sky above. Those of us who had actively lived through the years 1926–1945, full of memories and longing for our wives, felt here enveloped in an "unrealizable moment [*unveräußerlichen Augenblick*]." In retrospect I would say that *that* is cinema, the captain continued. It has nothing to do with the concrete film that happens to be on screen (I'm no film critic, after all). Cinema is much more "an in-itself impossible moment [*an sich unmöglicher Augenblick*]," one that could never have been conceived beforehand, and which would never be repeated [translation modified].[67]

Just as the film program in the previous story was not the films themselves but the feeling of security shared by those in the tent, the captain similarly admits how it had less to do with the specific film and more with the place that gave them consolation. The "unrealizable moment" in which they felt enveloped (*eingeschlossen*), further blurs any demarcation between internal and external: the adjective "unveräußerlich," means both unrealizable and that which cannot be divested or put out, *ver-äußert*. Such an unpredictable and unrepeatable moment is both impossible to divest from and collectively shared, echoing Kluge's notion of cinema as that which "moves *us* inwardly." What moves us inwardly is not simply the film on the screen, but the unique cinematic experience that includes the image, the particular circumstances of the film screening and its viewers, as well as the latter's "sense of place" (*Eindruck des Raums*). The rattling projectors, the singing birds, and the distant sounds of war are all part of what "functions like cinema." While the "external" sounds are not part of the film per se, they nevertheless merge with the projected images, and in this way the film moves beyond the screen and merges with the world around it. These unique

---

[67] Kluge, *GvK* 237; *CS* 65.

and unrepeatable soundtracks, which might be called "interwoven soundtracks," exemplify acoustically the movements of film and spectators, of the "inner film" and external film sound images. They are for Kluge exemplary mementos that comprise the "histories" of cinema.

Kluge's story is reminiscent of Kracauer's own memento when describing the drunken pianist who completely ignored the images on the screen while playing music: "[p]recisely by disregarding the images on the screen, the old pianist caused them to yield many a secret."[68] Kracauer highlights the random coincidences that sometimes occurred between the screened images and the pianist's unintended music, giving him "the impression that there existed after all a relationship, however elusive, between the drunken pianist's soliloquies and the dramas before my eyes – a relationship I considered perfect because of its accidental nature and indeterminacy. I have never heard more fitting accompaniment."[69] This is high praise indeed, given the sheer number of films Kracauer watched and commented upon throughout his lifetime. Although Kracauer's anecdote is decisively subjective while Kluge emphasizes in his story a more communal experience, both are nevertheless gesturing toward an elusive, "in-itself impossible moment" that remains specific to the cinematic experience.

These unrealizable and unrepeatable moments, moreover, are what Kluge is referring to when he announces in his foreword to *Cinema Stories* that both music and cinema "will not go away [*gehen nicht unter*]." The immortality of cinema and music lies in these unrealizable moments' *iterability*, that is, the destiny of cinema and music to generate the *structural possibility* to repeat such unrepeatable, elusive moments. This does not mean that any one of these moments can be reproduced exactly again and in the same way, just as no "interwoven soundtrack" can be heard a second time. Rather, cinema and music generate the possibility that allows for these singular, unrepeatable moments to occur again and again, and their unintentionality appears to be a prerequisite for them to occur at all. Kluge stresses the singularity of the *cinematic* experience over any "filmic" experience, and in this way turns cinema into a kind of theater stage.

---

[68] Kracauer, *Theory of Film*, 137.
[69] Kracauer, *Theory of Film*, 137.

5.5 New Sound Perspectives and the Dissolution of *Götterdämmerung*

The specific backdrop of "The Final Film Screening in the Reich Chancellery," which may have been the main impetus for Kluge to write the story in the first place, is the immanent failure of the Third Reich. Given Kluge's own emphasis on how *Kino* is "immortal" and "older than film art," Kluge seems to argue here that fascism, faced with its own failure and mortality, attempts to appeal to the immortality of cinema, perhaps in order to prolong the inevitable and cheat fate. Or as a way to maintain the myth that it too would never die. But Kluge's deliberately theatrical final film screening in this text makes clear that even cinema's immortality has become useless to fascism. An even more explicit version of this theme is played out in "Götterdämmerung in Vienna" ("Götterdämmerung in Wien"), which was not included in the English edition of *Cinema Stories* but is nevertheless the final story in the fourth chapter of the original German edition.[70] The story is the longest of the three examined here, at just over six pages. Already within the first paragraph, however, the parallels to "The Final Film Screening in the Reich Chancellery" are obvious. The story begins in March 1945 in Vienna, when the city was already partly beset by Soviet forces. One of the last orders given by the gauleiter and defense commissioner for Vienna was a final festival performance of Wagner's *Götterdämmerung*, which was to be broadcast over all radio stations of the southeast that still remained under Nazi control. Kluge even quotes gauleiter Baldur von Schirach as saying, "Even if the Reich comes to an end, music must still remain for us."[71] Of course, Wagner's *Götterdämmerung* is not just any music:

---

[70] The likely reason for the story's exclusion from the English edition is because it appears in two other Kluge collections, *Chronik der Gefühle* (2000) and *Die Schrift an der Wand* (2000), neither of which have been translated. While it is not the case that all the stories excluded from the English edition originate from elsewhere (there are over 80 stories in *Geschichten vom Kino* that remain untranslated), every story that was reprinted (and often altered) for the 2007 publication of *Geschichten vom Kino* is absent from the English edition. Kluge's particular ordering of the stories, whether in the German or English version, are often thematic, as is the case with the observation on Benjamin. "Cinema in Distress" ("Kino in der Not"), for instance, is placed under the heading for chapter one, "A light that rattles loudly (*Ein Licht, das laut rattert*)," not because of any reference to early cinema but likely because of the story's emphasis on the projector's rattling. "The Final Film Screening in the Reich Chancellery" and "Götterdämmerung in Vienna" are both the last stories of their respective sections, likely due to their staging of a "final" film screening or performance.

[71] Kluge, *GvK* 153. No evidence suggests this story is historically accurate. In an article entitled, "Götterdämmerung, Führerdämmerung?" (*Opera Quarterly* 23, no. 2–3 [Spring–Summer 2007]: 184–198), Stephen McClatchie notes that *Götterdämmerung* was the last opera performed at the Wiener Staatsoper in 1944, but makes no reference to Kluge's claim about a final

5.5 New Sound Perspectives and the Dissolution of *Götterdämmerung* — 217

as Stephen McClatchie writes in "Götterdämmerung, *Führerdämmerung*?" it has "long been commonplace for historians and biographers to invoke the notion of Götterdämmerung – the twilight of the gods – when writing about the final days of Adolf Hitler and his monstrous Third Reich."[72] But beyond the hackneyed symbolism, which is mentioned only parenthetically in Kluge's story,[73] von Schirach's comment echoes Kluge's in the foreword: "Film and music are related. Neither will go away [*Beide gehen nicht unter*]."[74] For von Schirach, music must remain with the Reich, even if the Reich is doomed to fail. Both "The Final Film Screening in the Reich Chancellery" and "Götterdämmerung in Vienna" are thus short, fictional texts that perform Kluge's claim that even the immortality of cinema and music become useless to a fascism desperately holding on to the misguided belief in its own perpetuity.

Despite Kluge's claim that music will never "go under," the ironic twist in "Götterdämmerung in Vienna" is that the musical performance *literally* goes underground (*geht unter*). Because the Vienna opera house had been bombed, the orchestra is scattered into various groups and forced to rehearse in bomb shelters in and around central Vienna. Kluge explains:

> The left half of the orchestra, divided into five different groups, worked in cellars on the Ringstraße. The right half of the orchestra, including the tympani, were in four cellars under Kärtner Straße as well as in nearby streets. The singers were divided between the orchestra groups. [. . .] The music director, who sat initially disconnected in the wine cellar of an inn, was however soon connected to all the other cellars by way of a FIELD TELEPHONE. [. . .] The result was *a new kind of sound* [ein neuartiges Klangbild]. The noise of the final battles raging around Vienna could not be filtered out, and the orchestra fragments enacted no unified sound [italics added].[75]

In the two earlier stories, the merging of the soundtrack with external sounds – whether from nearby birds, distant artillery fire, or the projectors themselves – exemplify acoustically Kluge's ideas about the principle of cinema, and lead to the idea of an interwoven soundtrack. The description above, with artillery fire similarly intermingling with the underground music performance, certainly corroborates Kluge's continued fascination with a unique soundtrack made up

---

Viennese radio performance of *Götterdämmerung* on the order of Baldur von Schirach in March 1945. Kluge might have been inspired by the final concert of the Berlin Philharmonic on 12 April 1945, which included the finale from Wagner's *Götterdämmerung* but which did not take place in Berlin.

72 McClatchie, "Götterdämmerung," 184.
73 Kluge, *GvK* 153.
74 Kluge, *GvK* 7.
75 Kluge, *GvK* 154.

of disparate sound sources. To this is added the proposal to film the performance(s): later in the story, Lieutenant Colonel Gerd Jänicke decides to film the various bunker rehearsals, "and in fact without any regard to the noise of the cameras, given that a blimp was not available."[76] The end result is a film whose soundtrack includes "traces of authentic noise": what is recorded is "the technical camera noise and the impact of bombs and artillery fire."[77] This is certainly one distinction from the other stories, at least in terms of recorded film sound: instead of a single event of an interwoven yet unrepeatable soundtrack, the filming of the underground rehearsals of *Götterdämmerung* includes an interwoven soundtrack *as* its recorded soundtrack.

Another significant difference from the two other stories previously discussed is the unique fragmentation of the orchestral performance. One could say that Kluge stages an additional level of dissolution, in that the orchestra no longer has a single place – the stage – upon which to perform; rather, the orchestra is split into various groups underground in various cellars that are bound together only by the thin wire of a field telephone. This should be read, alongside Kluge's innumerable observations about music and opera in particular, as an ironic and literal, but also necessary fragmentation of Wagner's *Gesamtkunstwerke*, reminiscent of the fragmentary montage style so characteristic of Kluge's films and television work. Many scholars have studied Kluge's fragmentary use of music in film, and most agree with the general view that his use of "found" or preexisting music – that is to say, music not composed specifically for the film – splits associations between what is seen and what is heard, increasing the complexity of audio-visual readings. But few have isolated Kluge's vested interest in creating what he calls new "sound perspectives," an interest that he has developed in his written work since at least the 1980s. Because it is specific not simply to sound but to alternative ways sound is perceived, this notion comes closer to how the acoustical unconscious has been examined in this book than Kluge's particular version of fantasy. Indeed, one can say that the interwoven soundtrack exemplifies what Kluge calls new sound perspectives. Fantasy, which typically already involves a "constant shifting of perspectives," needed to be examined here precisely because it sets the stage upon which these perspectives are experienced.

---

[76] Kluge, *GvK* 154–155. Kluge defines "Blimp" in a footnote as a protective shield that would otherwise have muted the sound of the camera motor.
[77] Kluge, *GvK* 158.

5.5 New Sound Perspectives and the Dissolution of *Götterdämmerung* — 219

Although Kluge will not publish "Götterdämmerung in Vienna" until 1999,[78] a section of "Imaginary Opera Guide" in the *Yearbook of the Hamburg State Opera 1984–1988* (*Jahrbuch der Hamburgischen Staatsoper 1984–1988*, 1988) is written as if Kluge was already imagining the story:

> An [. . .] effect can be achieved for the musical parameters by creating *sound perspectives*: just as the individual musician seated in the midst of his or her colleagues does not hear the total sound of the orchestra but only those parts of the score played by the musicians in his or her vicinity, I can place microphones in such a manner that in a Wagner-orchestra, for instance, only the cello, contrabass, and bass drum, or, for that matter, any other group are extremely foregrounded. Such procedures seem to suggest an *artiste démoliseur*. However, by pushing the material to the verge of disintegration, one also opens up new qualities within it. Wagner's score now sounds like chamber music. It would be possible thus to create fragments and use them to adapt raw material of a second nature [emphasis mine].[79]

Kluge admits prior to this passage that these thoughts emerged from his reading of Adorno's "disintegration of materials" in his *Aesthetic Theory* (*Ästhetische Theorie*, 1970). Kluge's interpretation of this Adornian phrase is that "it refers to a newly awakened interest in precision, concentration, correlation, details, metamorphosis," all of which "open up new qualities within" the given (musical) work.[80] One is reminded of how even Adorno in later work embraced the increased analyzability of recorded music, which he likely picked up from Benjamin's own description of the analyzability of film when discussing the optical unconscious in the artwork essay.[81] Kluge's interpretation of Adorno led him to formulate the concept of *sound perspectives*, which would allow for the productive mode of disintegration in terms of music and sound. Kluge uses the German word *Perspektive* in a central passage that allowed us in the previous section to distinguish between fantasy and the Benjaminian unconscious: recall that a "deepened perspective" is, for Kluge, a precondition for the movement of

---

[78] As already mentioned, the story "Götterdämmerung in Wien" also appears in two other collections, *Chronik der Gefühle* and *Die Schrift an der Wand*, both published in 2000. A footnote in *Chronik der Gefühle* indicates that the story was first published in French in *Trafic Nr.31* (Paris 1999).
[79] See Alexander Kluge, "Ein imaginärer Opernführer," in *Jahrbuch der Hamburgischen Staatsoper 1984–1988* (Hamburg: Intendanz der Hamburgischen Staatsoper, 1988). Unfortunately, I have not had access to the original German text. The English citation is taken from Alexander Kluge, "Kluge on Opera, Film, and Feelings," ed. Miriam Hansen, trans. Miriam Hansen and Sara S. Poor, *New German Critique* 49 (Winter 1990): 89–138; here, 136.
[80] Kluge, "Kluge on Opera, Film, and Feelings," 135–136.
[81] See the first section of Chapter One for more about Adorno's increased interest in the analyzability of recorded music.

the spectator's (and spectators') fantasy.[82] Another clue in recognizing the importance of perspective in Kluge is the following, oft-quoted sentence from *History and Obstinacy* (*Geschichte und Eigensinn*, 1984): "At the beginning of each and every critical project one already finds a shift in perspective."[83] Finally, Kluge's description above of how sound perspectives open up "new qualities within" a given work appears to be the acoustical equivalent of Kluge's interest in the "lost and new possibilities" that Hansen aligns with Benjamin's optical unconscious. The way Kluge experiments with Wagnerian "chamber" music – disintegrating the musical material in order to allow for what could be called a "deepened sound perspective" – suggests how one can think the acoustical unconscious at work in Kluge's theoretical and fictional writing.

Nowhere does Kluge refer explicitly in "Götterdämmerung in Vienna" to the creation of sound perspectives, at least not theoretically as he does in "An Imaginary Opera Guide." He comes close, however, when describing the sounds from the underground orchestra divisions: "The result was *a new kind of sound* [ein neuartiges Klangbild]" (emphasis mine).[84] Near the end of the story, Kluge also approaches the notion of music fragmentation more critically: after the underground rehearsal was filmed by Lieutenant Colonel Gerd Jänicke and his team, Kluge goes on to describe how the film could not be successfully transported out of Vienna and fell into the hands of the Soviets. It was lost in one of their museum archives until it was rediscovered in 1991, subsequently developed in Hungary, and then sent to Venice with the intention of presenting it at the Venice Duomo on the tenth anniversary of Luigi Nono's death. An editing assistant of Jean-Luc Godard's became aware of this transfer and requested that the film

---

82 See Kluge, "On Film and the Public Sphere," 216, also cited in section 5.2 above. In *Bestandsaufnahme*, Kluge also refers to perspective and its role in fantasy a few pages later: "The constant shifting of perspectives is typical for fantasy" (Kluge, *Bestandsaufnahme*, 67).
83 Alexander Kluge and Oskar Negt, *Geschichte und Eigensinn* (Frankfurt a.M.: Zweitausendeins, 1985), 84. In the introduction to the recent English translation, Devin Fore emphasizes the importance of shifts in perspective throughout the book: "*History and Obstinacy* calls not for revelation, but for reconfiguration, for a shift in perspective that would demonstrate the motivated connections between seemingly unrelated particularities and incidents" (Devin Fore, "Introduction," in *History and Obstinacy*, by Alexander Kluge and Oskar Negt, ed. Devin Fore, trans. Richard Langston et al. [New York: Zone, 2014], 15–67; here, 54).
84 Kluge, GvK 154. Interestingly, a number of changes were made for the version of "Götterdämmerung in Vienna" found in *Geschichten von Kino*, including the sentence just quoted. In both German versions published seven years earlier, the sentence reads: "Es ergab sich auch ein anderes Klangbild." In replacing "ein anderes" with "ein neuartiges Klangbild," however minor an alteration, Kluge aligns his observations more consistently with the new as discussed by Adorno in *Ästhetische Theorie*.

be sent to Paris for restoration. An article was then apparently written about the film in the *Cahiers du cinéma* by one Antoine Bellot, and Kluge cites this article at the end of the story:

> The soundtrack shows, according to Bellot, a "gruesome beauty" or "something along the lines of moral fiber." One should *always* "fragment" Richard Wagner in this way. The trace of authentic noise registers the technical camera sound and the impact of bombs and artillery fire. This original tone, this "being in-the-middle" of things grants rhythm to the music of Wagner, turning it from a figure of the nineteenth century into the PROPERTY [EIGENTUM] of the twentieth century [emphasis original].[85]

Since Kluge attributes the article to a different author in each of the three published versions of "Götterdämmerung in Vienna,"[86] it is safe to say that the article is as fictional as the rest of the events recounted in the story. It is, however, yet another way for Kluge to inject his own critical interpretation of the fictional events within the story proper.[87]

There are two ways Kluge achieves an acoustically-oriented "pragmatics of redemption" in "Götterdämmerung in Vienna": by fragmenting the *Gesamt-* element of Wagner's *Gesamtkunstwerk*, and by interpenetrating or "rythmicizing" the disintegrated nineteenth-century music with twentieth-century background noise. Both methods offer new possibilities for listening to Wagner after the Nazi appropriation of the composer, "redeeming" Wagner by way of new sound perspectives. For Kluge, this is perhaps the only way to wrest Wagner from Nazi ownership: through the music's disintegration and interpenetration with the real soundtrack of the twentieth century.

It is precisely this move – from different sound perspectives in the film material to the redemption of Wagner's music – that spells out the relationship

---

85 Kluge, *GvK* 158.
86 All versions of "Götterdämmerung in Vienna" offer a different name for the journalist Kluge apparently cites from *Cahiers du cinéma*. In *Geschichten vom Kino*, the author's name is Antoine Bellot, but in *Chronik der Gefühle* it is Gerard Schlesinger, and in *Die Schrift an der Wand* the name is Gerard de Bontemps. Kluge is obviously having fun making up different authors' names for the same fictional article. One name that remains consistent throughout the versions, however, is Heiner Müller. The story itself is dedicated to Müller by Kluge in every version except the one in *Geschichten vom Kino*.
87 In this sense, Kluge plays the "In-Mitten-Sein" of his own story, disintegrating himself into multiple versions of (not quite) the same story. Kluge employs multiple quasi-narrative methods that allow him to enter into his stories and to pepper them with interpretation and critique. Another method is his considerable use of dialogue, typically between two anonymous speakers. The last three pages of "Götterdämmerung in Wien," for instance, is in this anonymous dialogue form, blocked off from the story with the subtitle, "Bildbeschreibung."

between the acoustical unconscious and Kluge's emancipatory fantasy that we have been pursuing throughout this chapter. It does not matter whether the story, "Götterdämmerung in Vienna," is wholly fabricated or not (it is). What matters is that Kluge not only describes a way of experiencing Wagner through a disunified, "new kind of sound (*neuartiges Klangbild*)" – less a *Gesamtkunstwerk* than the acoustical equivalent of a filmstrip's "jerks and jolts" – but he also imagines how such a new sound perspective provokes a "storm of fantasy" that allows for the redemption of Wagner from his fascistic appropriation. The irony is that the fictional film of *Götterdämmerung*, filmed by fascists, actually turns out to be a part of the cinema of emancipation, which adds yet another layer to Kluge's interpretation of Benjamin's artwork essay: if Benjamin is attempting, according to Kluge, to discover something about cinema that is useful for socialists but useless to fascists, Kluge adds with "Götterdämmerung in Vienna" that even fascist filmmaking, unbeknownst to the fascists themselves, turns out to be useful for socialists.

Since Kluge's audio-visual work will be analyzed in the following section, it is important to review our understanding of the acoustical unconscious in relation to Kluge as both theorist and storyteller thus far. First, since the acoustical unconscious, like the optical unconscious, is a precondition for the possibility of Kluge's particular form of emancipatory fantasy, it must be thought as strictly demarcated from the more general productive force of fantasy. This also means that the acoustical unconscious in Kluge's reflections on sound and music would in large part be related to his predilection for new sound perspectives, and in this way is closely aligned with how Hansen describes Kracauer as gesturing "toward something like an 'acoustic unconscious'" by foregrounding experimental uses of sound in his *Theory of Film*. The reception of different "sound perspectives" for Kluge involves a shock in the typical way we hear things, a shock that helps open the wellsprings of eruptive fantasy. A good example of this is the interpenetration and disintegration of sound material, be that "external" sound or a Wagnerian *Gesamtkunstwerk*. Such sound material is left by Kluge to sound out in its dissociation from any organic unity and in its own ambiguity of cinematic place. New sound perspectives are therefore not intended to shock the audience into a stupor or trauma, but rather to stimulate a mode of listening that "lies far below [*weit unterhalb*] the plane of so-called critical judgment, of self-critique and so-called personality."[88] This too is reminiscent of Kracauer's description of "unconscious bodily reactions out of which

---

[88] Kluge, *Bestandsaufnahme*, 95.

meaning may then grow."[89] For Kluge, new sound perspectives provoke a re-marking of sound materials, and fantasy is what helps reorganize the mediation of such sound material without any demand for unity or reunification, without any recourse to previous modes of measurement or convention. "Fantasy" for Kluge therefore names an instinctive mode of *reading* visual or auditory marks without recourse to any fixed place or position, which is at least one of the reasons why Kluge calls fantasy "emancipatory" and beyond subjectivity. In this way Kluge's cinema of emancipation becomes a communal space interwoven with the optico-acoustical unconscious.

This last point regarding fantasy's relation to the emancipatory and the public is indeed complex, for it invites the politicization of fantasy in the guise of its "redemptive" features. This is also what distinguishes Kluge from Kracauer's overarching project in *Theory of Film*, the goal of which was to redeem material reality by highlighting the cinematic, that is, the unique, media-specific functions of cinema. Kluge realizes the kind of experimental, unconventional use of sound and music that Kracauer described hypothetically, but redirects their redemptive possibilities away from the materiality of reality and toward its politicization. Kluge's emphasis on the redemptive qualities of an emancipatory fantasy that is freed from the self, from social norms and any sense of proportion allows us to read Kluge as gesturing toward the politicization of the acoustical unconscious in much the same way as he interprets Benjamin doing with the optical unconscious.

5.6 Fantasy in *Die Macht der Gefühle* and *Die Patriotin*

> The one thing that is missing when I read and write books is music. That is the intrinsic reason why I have made films, because film moves [*sich bewegen*] similarly to music.[90]

In his audio-visual work, Kluge exaggerates the disassembling of a musical event through image and sound montage. This is perhaps nowhere better recognized than in *The Power of Emotion* (*Die Macht der Gefühle*, 1984), a film that is impossible to avoid when discussing Kluge's particular use of music in film. Numerous articles have been written on this film and its music, some of the

---

89 Kracauer, *Werke*, 3:577.
90 Kluge, cited by Guntram Vogt, "'Ohne Musik ist alles Leben ein Irrtum'. Zu Alexander Kluges Musik-Magazinen," in *Die Schrift an der Wand – Alexander Kluge: Rohstoffe und Materialien*, ed. Christian Schulte (Osnabrück: Universitätsverlag Rasch, 2000), 254.

most extensive being the fourth chapter of Caryl Flinn's *New German Cinema: Music, History, and the Matter of Style* (2004). Although the plot of Kluge's *Power of Emotion* is difficult to summarize due to its "abbreviated, multiple story lines, scraps of film footage, photographs, paintings, old popular songs, and glimpsed opera performances,"[91] one can nevertheless succinctly encapsulate the role of opera in the film, as Gertrud Koch has done: opera "becomes for [Kluge] a pile of ruins left by the fatalistic course of history, which he sets out to rearrange. Once exploded into atomized details – ruins – the power of fate dissipates, as does the efficacy of any narrative closure. He [. . .] can now hunt for ways out and give recommendations."[92] This disintegration of opera in *The Power of Emotion* is reminiscent of the Viennese performance of *Götterdämmerung* explored in the previous section: it is not only set amidst the actual ruins of Vienna during the imminent ruins of the Third Reich, but also involves an orchestra similarly atomized into groups. Just as the imagined *Götterdämmerung* performance elicits "a new kind of sound image," Kluge goes out of his way to produce equally jarring *Klangbilder* of operatic episodes in *The Power of Emotion*. For instance, Flinn describes the way Kluge changes our seating arrangements:

> Ours is not a typical seat at the opera house. It is not the perspective of an audience member facing the stage, but rather is taken from behind the stage, where Kluge maintains the real labor is at work. [. . .] In addition to providing us with unusual seats at the opera, Kluge ensures that we arrive late or at the wrong time, denying us access to a stable position from which we might immerse ourselves in the proceedings.[93]

Flinn does not specifically cite Kluge's description of sound perspectives from "An Imaginary Opera Guide,"[94] but the passage above nevertheless indicates how alternate spatial and temporal perspectives open up new qualities within a given operatic work while simultaneously destabilizing our point-of-audition and denying us our "typical seat at the opera house." Once again, Kluge's goal is to strip away the familiarity of a "complete" musical event, calling that very

---

91 Caryl Flinn, *New German Cinema: Music, History, and the Matter of Style* (Berkeley and Los Angeles: University of California Press, 2004), 141.
92 Koch, cited by Flinn, *New German Cinema*, 142.
93 Flinn, *New German Cinema*, 152.
94 Flinn's only references to "Ein imaginärer Opernführer" are unfortunately oblique. Her first reference is in one of her two epigraphs: she cites Kluge saying, "We must work to develop an *imaginary opera*, to bring forward an alternative opera world" (Flinn, *New German Cinema*, 138). The second is in a footnote near the end of the chapter, informing the reader that "Kluge created a variety of what he called, after Adorno's proposal in 1964, 'imaginary operas' and 'imaginary opera guides'" (Flinn, *New German Cinema*, 301).

terminology into question. He does so by creating not another concert hall or opera house – which in this film he famously labels "the factory of emotions" – but rather a "meeting place for images," a *Versammlungsort für Bilder*.[95]

If we were to add the word "sound" to Kluge's following sentence: out of a "deepened [sound] perspective one redirects his fantasy to the real course of events,"[96] the consequence in the story, "Götterdämmerung in Vienna," would be that sound perspectives in particular, by redirecting fantasy, allow for the possibility of redeeming Wagner's opera: "One should *always* 'fragment' Richard Wagner in this way" (emphasis original).[97] The consequence for *The Power of Emotion* would be similar, although it involves another one of Wagner's operas: *Parsival*. As Flinn observes, references to *Parsival* abound throughout *The Power of Emotion*: Kluge borrows the opera's structure in order to apply its thematics of faith and redemption, while at the same time withholding "all dematerializing transcendence from Wagner's text."[98] Indeed, *The Power of Emotion* is Kluge's version of a twentieth-century *Parsival*, just as the fragmentary sound film imagined in "Götterdämmerung in Vienna" is what transforms Wagner's music "from a figure of the nineteenth century into the PROPERTY [EIGENTUM] of the twentieth century."[99] Despite major differences in media and scope, both Kluge's *Power of Emotion* and "Götterdämmerung in Vienna" contribute to the reappropriation and redemptive transformation of Wagner's music for a new century and history, achieved only by the fragmentation of

---

95 In the booklet that accompanies the fifteen DVD set of Kluge's *Sämtliche Kinofilme* (Alexander Kluge, *Neonröhren des Himmels: Filmalbum*, accompanying booklet to *Sämtliche Kinofilme* [Frankfurt a.M.: Zweitausendeins, 2007]), Kluge describes how a film program has nothing to do with whether the films relate to each other thematically, but rather with the surprising coincidences and differences that arise from watching them together. He then defines "public sphere" (*Öffentlichkeit*) in terms of this principle of programming: "Surprise, not concordance [*Einstimmung*] as a program principle. New public spheres therefore almost never emerge 'planned' because another difference belongs to them: the radical multiplication and dissemination of images via new media demands 'large projection' on the other hand, i.e. a MEETING PLACE FOR IMAGES [VERSAMMLUNGSORT FÜR BILDER]. It is a misconception that the public sphere requires only public spaces. Rather, it is the tension between isolation (where one has one's own experiences, discovers something on the computer, etc.) and prominent, shared spaces that we call public (chatting is one of them). Without such gathering places, experience remains without self-consciousness. Without singular experience, public places remain empty" (emphasis original; Kluge, *Neonröhren des Himmels*, 71).
96 Kluge, *Ulmer Dramaturgien*, 64.
97 Kluge, *GvK* 158.
98 Flinn, *New German Cinema*, 163.
99 Kluge, *GvK* 158.

sound material and the destabilization of the audience's sense of place and familiarity.

One problem accompanying this shared consequence, however, is that Kluge's "emancipatory fantasy" appears to become relegated to the emancipation of Wagner rather than to the emancipation of the workers. Perhaps it would be more accurate to say that Kluge wishes to redeem Wagner *for* the workers, for if Kluge follows his own interpretation of Benjamin's artwork essay, he would be attempting to develop a way to make Wagner's music of no use to fascists, while valuable for socialists and a cinema of emancipation. Film historian Roger Hillman also attempts to incorporate Kluge's definition of fantasy into an analysis of the music in the film, *The Patriot* (*Die Patriotin*, 1979).[100] When introducing a section on "Music and Dramaturgy," Hillman writes that, with "Kluge, the prior existence of nondiegetic music is not subsumed by the film's images. The immateriality of this music also releases the power of fantasy, deemed by Kluge to be nothing less than the most important form of human labor."[101] At another moment in the chapter, Hillman speaks more generally of *The Patriot*, its relation to fantasy and to its "corresponding musical form," the fantasia:

> Kluge's film [*Die Patriotin*] is a fantasy-driven essay on German history, from the narrative voice of the knee of a dead corporal through to a bit part in a World War I newsreel for an elephant called Jenny. It is simultaneously a roving approach to the history of fantasy, charting wishes and visions across the centuries. The corresponding musical form, the fantasia, emphasizes extemporization, and this characterizes the surface of Kluge's film far beyond the freewheeling musical examples themselves. Fantasy is not simply a balance to the chronicling side of historical documentation but a scattering of the trajectory of history, with past, present, and future coexisting. To attempt this in a narrative, let alone a visual narrative, is ambitious indeed.[102]

Hillman's attempt to implement Kluge's particular definition of fantasy his reading of *The Patriot* is admirable. Upon closer inspection, however, Hillman's reading of fantasy at work in *The Patriot* becomes less a capacity of the spectators or audience than it is the director's intent (discernable in part by Hillman's recourse to the fantasia[103]) and a quality of the film's narrative style. For Hillman,

---

100 See Roger Hillman, *Unsettling Scores: German Film, Music, and Ideology* (Bloomington, IN: Indiana University Press, 2005).
101 Hillman, *Unsettling Scores*, 97.
102 Hillman, *Unsettling Scores*, 90.
103 "Fantasia" is defined in *The New Grove Dictionary of Music and Musicians* as a term "adopted in the Renaissance for an instrumental composition whose form and invention spring 'solely from the fantasy and skill of the author who created it' (Luis de Milán, 1535–6).

the characteristic of fantasy to operate with "past, present, and future coexisting" is at least partly responsible for the film's lack of a "horizontal narrative."[104] What Hillman appears to be suggesting is that fantasy is incorporated into the way the film is edited, rather than it being solely derived from the spectators.

In neither Flinn's nor Hillman's analysis of music in *The Power of Emotion* and *The Patriot* is there much resembling Kluge's emphasis on emancipatory fantasy. Does Kluge's own definition of fantasy make it all but impossible to interpret one of his most central theories alongside his films and filmmaking? What has happened to this important tool "for any emancipatory practice," that "most important form of human labor"? Or is it not rather the case that Kluge offers up raw material, including unconventional sound perspectives, in order to release our own fantasy? Every scholar would likely agree that Kluge's overall project is to "represent an alternative version of history,"[105] and Flinn's and Hillman's analyses of Kluge are largely motivated by how much and how well these two films do so via music. What seems to be missing, however, is the role that the *audience's* fantasy plays in constructing this alternative history. Put another way: can critics of Kluge's film work discuss the role of fantasy without talking about themselves, or to those who have experienced Kluge's films?

Let us return briefly to the difference between fantasy and the optical and acoustical unconscious in order to understand why Kluge's emancipatory fantasy appears tangential to these otherwise insightful analyses. Fantasy for Kluge is never part of the film proper, but comes either before its inception – used theoretically and as a goal – or during its reception and on behalf of the audience. While it might not be deemed scholarly to explore my own flights of fantasy while listening, watching, or reading Kluge's work, what can and should be discussed in his films, for instance, are the techniques he uses in an attempt to provoke our "storm of fantasy," and whether or not these techniques succeed in doing so. Such techniques, furthermore, would be related to the

---

From the 16th century to the 19th the fantasia tended to retain this subjective license" (*The New Grove Dictionary of Music and Musicians*, 2nd ed., ed. Stanley Sadie [New York: Grove, 2000], 545). This definition does not coincide with the way Kluge defines fantasy's function in film as we have examined earlier in this chapter, though it could be said that Kluge is redeeming the fantasia for the twentieth century as well.

104 "Narrative drive is absent at the visual level in Kluge, with visuals accumulating within sequences rather than progressing horizontally. The same applies largely to the use of music, always preexisting music" (Hillman, *Unsettling Scores*, 90).

105 Hansen, "Reinventing the Nickelodeon," 129.

optical and acoustical unconscious in that they reveal, in the words of Hansen, the "pragmatics of redemption – gradations, distinctions, aesthetic valences of film [. . .], lost and new possibilities."[106] In terms of the acoustical unconscious, one of these lost and new possibilities is the creation of sound perspectives that disrupt the audience's familiarity with a musical work. In bringing the audience into a new relation with what it hears, it becomes conscious of an alternative mode of listening that not only blasts the music out of its familiar historicity, but also destabilizes the audience's usual position of listening, forcing us as the audience to reevaluate – ideally for Kluge, by means of fantasy – what it means to listen. Instead of attempting to integrate Kluge's version of fantasy into his analysis of music in *The Patriot*, it is necessary to discuss the film's use of music according to the Benjaminian theory of the optical unconscious and the acoustical unconscious that has been explored throughout this study.

One way to examine the breakdown of a familiar way of listening is to look at and listen to the last section of the film, *The Patriot*. The film loosely follows a history teacher by the name of Gabi Teichert (Hannelore Hoger) who finds it difficult "to set German history in a patriotic framework" (translation mine).[107] Dissatisfied with the teaching material German history has provided thus far, Gabi resorts to some rather unorthodox methods, including semi-illegal digging and the consumption of shredded history books. The final section of the film is headed, "New Year's Eve. 'Ode to Joy,'" and begins with Gabi and her female friends sitting around in her apartment kitchen drinking while they listen to the final movement of Beethoven's Ninth Symphony. Even though Kluge fragments the music, which sounds like it is coming from an off-screen radio, Gabi is having some success simultaneously writing out and singing along with the Schiller text that she and her friends only partly understand. This rather short kitchen scene, described by Flinn as more like "a karaoke singalong to scratchy, prerecorded accompaniment," is followed by a sequence of night shots showing New Year's Eve celebrations.[108] No longer fragmented, the Ninth continues "as acoustic backdrop"[109] through this montage of night scenes until they culminate rather suddenly with this intertitle on video blue (Fig. 5.1):

---

106 Hansen, "Reinventing the Nickelodeon," 186.
107 Alexander Kluge, *Die Patriotin: Texte, Bilder 1–6* (Frankfurt a.M.: Zweitausendeins, 1979), 23.
108 Caryl Flinn, "Strategies of Remembrance," in *Music and Cinema*, ed. James Buhler, Caryl Flinn, and David Neumeyer (Hanover, NH: University Press of New England for Wesleyan University Press, 2000), 123.
109 Hillman, *Unsettling Scores*, 107.

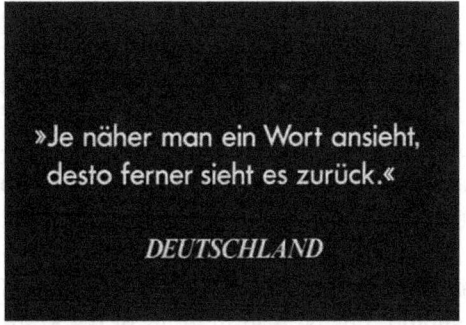

Fig. 5.1: Kraus quote in Kluge's *The Patriot*: "The closer you look at a word, the more distantly it looks back at you." GERMANY.

Although the word, "*DEUTSCHLAND*," appears a few seconds after the Kraus quote, Kluge's message appears clear enough: Teichert's search for a more "patriotic" history is caught up with the elusive word, GERMANY. Numerous scholars have commented on the importance of the Kraus intertitle, and even Kluge himself uses it as a "filmic experiment, freely adapted from Karl Kraus" in a 1983 lecture called, "Speech concerning one's own country: GERMANY [*Rede über das eigene Land: DEUTSCHLAND*]." In this 1983 lecture, Kluge uses the Kraus intertitle as if it were an optical illusion: he first invites the audience to read the Kraus text, and then to imagine writing the word "*DEUTSCHLAND*" under it and to stare at the word intensively for a moment. He then asks those in the audience for whom the word has receded from view to raise their hands: "Who is for farther? Who is for nearer? (Most of the audience members voted for farther)" (parentheses original).[110] But what even Kluge overlooks is what happens when a word looks back: it is not the case that it simply becomes either closer or more distant from the audience, for that would imply that the audience maintains their own fixed position. Rather, the word that looks back raises the possibility that the audience is moved along with it. Samuel Weber describes this movement as follows: "For what one 'sees' in the ever-more-distant word is not simply a reproduction of the same but something else, a distance that *takes up* and moves the beholder towards that which, though remote, is also closest at hand."[111] As discussed in the previous

---

[110] Alexander Kluge, *Fontane, Kleist, Deustschland, Büchner. Zur Grammatik der Zeit* (Berlin: Verlag Klaus Wagenbach, 2004), 57.
[111] Samuel Weber, *Mass Mediauras* (Stanford, CA: Stanford University Press, 1996), 107.

chapter, Paul's search for an ever-more-distant word in Eich's *The Year Lazertis* forces him to pursue it to distant lands, which eventually bring him to an infirmary. One can similarly imagine the word, "Germany," also forcing Gabi Teichert – as well as the spectators who watch her pursuit for a more "patriotic" history of Germany – to *be moved*, but differently than we have seen Kluge define movement according to cinema so far. What the Kraus quote adds to Kluge's "principle of cinema" is that the screen images (and sound images) not only "move us inwardly" but also set up a "scenario of inscription" that unsettles and disrupts any fixed position from which to read.[112] Kluge's description of "Kino" from *Stocktaking: Utopia Film* should thus be read in terms of the Kraus quote: "The images move [*bewegen sich*], the scenes put me in motion [*bringen mich in Bewegung*]."[113] Kluge is both moved (emotionally) by the scenes and put into motion, inscribed into the moving (sound) images.

The disruption of a fixed place of seeing and listening corresponds not only to Kluge's altered sound perspectives and unconventional seating arrangements at the opera house, but also how Gabi Teichert listens to Beethoven's Ninth Symphony in *The Patriot*. Kluge certainly makes it seem as if we are also sitting at the kitchen table listening to the Ninth from a scratchy, off-screen radio with Teichert and her friends. But Teichert's intense listening to Schiller's text also appears to literalize the Kraus dictum: by listening more closely to the words being sung, even Beethoven's Ninth "looks back more distantly." Hillman notes parenthetically that Teichert is working through stanzas of the "Ode to Joy" that is "not in common usage."[114] In fact, the stanza she reads was one that Beethoven cut out entirely. While listening to the Ninth Symphony, Teichert's friends – and by extension, the film's audience – is also listening to Teichert recite words of the "Ode to Joy" that have never been a part of the Ninth Symphony. This seventh verse of the "Ode to Joy," moreover, is commented upon by her friends as "gruesome":

---

112 Weber, *Mass Mediauras*, 106. This is also largely Miriam Hansen's argument. For Hansen, the Kraus intertitle reflects how Gabi Teichert's own gaze in the film "is rarely point-of-view constructions that would advance an illusionist continuity of diegetic space or unconscious identification for the viewer. Instead, the character's look emphasizes the disparity and incongruity of fictional and historical spaces, which in turn reinscribes the look with a desire that exceeds the closure of the merely visible" (Hansen, "Stubborn Discourse," 128). My reading supplements this line of thinking with an emphasis on what is heard.
113 Kluge, *Bestandsaufnahme*, 45.
114 Hillman, *Unsettling Scores*, 107.

Freude sprudelt in Pokalen,	Joy is bubbling in the goblets,
In der Traube goldnem Blut	Through the golden blood of grapes
Trinken Sanftmut Kannibalen,	Cannibals drink gentleness,
Die Verzweiflung Heldenmut –	Despair [drinks] courage –
Brueder, fliegt von euren Sitzen,	Brothers, fly from your seats,
Wenn der volle Römer kreist,	When the full wine glass circles 'round,
Lasst den Schaum zum Himmel sprützen:	Let the foam spray to the heavens:
Dieses Glas dem guten Geist.	This glass to the good spirit.

While Haun Saussy believes "Beethoven was perhaps wise to cut the poem's line about cannibals drinking gentleness [. . .] as all the reunited others imbibe the golden wine of joy," Kluge's highlighting of the deleted verse while the hyper-familiar Ninth Symphony music plays in the background suddenly has us all wondering whether we've listened closely enough to Beethoven's final movement of his last symphony, and whether there is more than "the general message of brotherhood and divinely assistant human unity."[115] Apart from any specific references that Schiller might have had to cannibals, this verse appears to sow seeds of doubt over whether all of humanity, including cannibals and those in despair, can be so easily united by the good Spirit. The verse also appears to celebrate "male homosocial and autoerotic exuberance,"[116] which puts into stark relief the group of women on screen who are only half-listening and certainly not taking up the call in this verse to fly up from their seats in jubilation. Juxtaposition and displacement abound so much that the comment "gruesome" may apply not simply to how Gabi's friend reacts to this particular verse of the "Ode to Joy," but to the scene as a whole.

While Kluge appears to succeed in making one of the most familiar musical works of all time less so, the question remains: are there political implications, and has he consciously primed his audience's eruptive fantasy? Who or what is being emancipated? An interesting gauge for this is the debate between Hillman and Flinn on the return of Beethoven's Ninth at the very end of *The Patriot*, near the end credits. The music is no longer fragmented as it is in the karaoke kitchen scene, but it is also no longer the choral section of the symphony either. As Hillman points out, the musical passage that Kluge excerpts for the end of the film is a critical moment in the Ninth Symphony, when "the central theme emerges in its least adorned form" in the cellos and double basses after various

---

[115] Haun Saussy, *Comparative Literature in an Age of Globalization* (Baltimore: Johns Hopkins University Press, 2006), 227.
[116] Katrin Pahl, *Tropes of Transport: Hegel and Emotion* (Evanston, IL: Northwestern University Press, 2012), 86.

orchestral combinations have attempted "a series of false starts and retracings of preceding material."[117] Both Hillman and Flinn explore the various implications of Kluge's musical choice, but with diverging results. Hillman's reading, which even Flinn admits is widely shared, falls into the category of resurrecting Beethoven's Ninth "into positivity." Hillman even invokes Benjamin's notion of aura and its relevance to the use of Beethoven's Ninth in *The Patriot*:

> In Benjaminian terms, Kluge tries to reinvest the aura of music that was subsequently ideologized. He does this not through a total depoliticization but through a return to a pre-Nazi era. [. . .] Politically, [Kluge] salvages Beethoven's Ninth from the bourgeois concert hall and the false socialism of the Nazis, regaining it for the "proletarian public sphere."[118]

This reading is of course reminiscent of the way Kluge attempts to redeem the music of Wagner in both "Götterdämmerung in Vienna" and *The Power of Emotion*. The problem with Hillman's recourse to Benjamin's concept of aura is that it apparently restores an "original impetus" that ultimately involves a "return to a pre-Nazi era." While the decline and resurgence of an aura may offer a distinct alternative to its fascist use, aura for Benjamin neither erases history nor returns the work of art to some "original impetus." Rather, Benjamin's concept of aura is intimately connected to the Kraus dictum above, for Kraus is describing nothing other than a word's aura. The distancing of the word embodies not only "the 'decline and fall of the aura,' its 'shrinking' and 'withering away,' but also its resurgence" or in terms of Kraus's word, its looking back.[119] Flinn's comments are much less idealistic than Hillman's, but rely on the same slight misreading of Kraus's dictum above.[120] Despite their otherwise informative and astute arguments, one may characterize Flinn and Hillman's debate by saying that, while the latter relies on the resurgence of the aura (the way "Deutschland"

---

117 Hillman, *Unsettling Scores*, 108.
118 Hillman, *Unsettling Scores*, 109. Flinn asks rhetorically, "might [Kluge] have considered the [Beethoven] movement so much a spent, allegorical ruin that [. . .] it could be 'resurrected into positivity'? This final reading is widely shared," (Flinn, *New German Cinema*, 136–137), but she goes on to offer a counter-argument, which will be considered presently.
119 Weber, *Mass Mediauras*, 107.
120 Flinn only grudgingly accepts that "'Germany' seems to be acoustically reinstated" through the Beethoven reference at the end of the film. Her counter-argument is supported by referring back to the Kraus intertitle in order to state that Germany "is rendered far more ephemeral and unstable in its visual presentation in the same final image, when the word 'Deutschland' fades from view" (Flinn, *New German Cinema*, 137). As we have seen, this argument is based on an interpretation of the Kraus quote that does not fully consider the equally unstable position of the audience.

appears in the intertitle), the former focuses on its decline (the word "Deutschland" disappearing from view).

The different interpretations also highlight the problem of determining whether Kluge uses Beethoven's Ninth "uncritically," that is to say, whether he depoliticizes the music in an attempt to revive or redeem its utopian potential.[121] It also leads one to ask more generally what the political stakes are in Kluge's project of redeeming the music of Beethoven and Wagner, especially by experimenting with them the way he does. Since we already know from the stories examined earlier how important it is not to listen simply to the music but also to the sounds in and around the filmic experience, let us listen more closely to the specific use of Beethoven's Ninth at the very end of *The Patriot* along with other elements of the soundtrack. The "Ode to Joy" melody enters at the end of the film "over a shot of an illuminated, snow-swept tree in the courtyard" of Gabi Teichert's apartment complex.[122] The panning shots of the snow-swept courtyard are intercut with shots of Gabi Teichert looking out her apartment window into the courtyard, suggesting a continuity of diegetic space that has largely been ruptured throughout the film. For Hillman, the visuals at the end of the film "reinforce the note of quiet hope" that echoes in the final musical statement.[123] In his accompanying voice-over, Kluge also adds to this quiet hope when he says, "Every year on New Year's, Eve Gabi Teichert sees 365 days ahead of her. So that there is hope to improve the introductory material in the history curriculum for the high schools in the coming year."[124]

However, neither Hillman nor Flinn comments on the sounds accompanying this final courtyard scene, which is anything but quiet. Kluge writes in the script: "Winter storm. Intensive, blowing snow. Thunder, lightning."[125] Kluge calls for thunder and lightning to accompany a snowstorm, which is rare indeed.[126] Such a unique sound-image combination once again recalls Kluge's often

---

121 Flinn concludes her chapter analysis of *The Patriot* with the observation that, in "the end, it may be impossible to resolve the film's uncritical use of Beethoven" (Flinn, *New German Cinema*, 137).
122 Hillman, *Unsettling Scores*, 109.
123 Hillman, *Unsettling Scores*, 108.
124 "Jedes Jahr wieder zu Silvester sieht Gabi Teichert 365 Tage vor sich. So, dass Hoffnung besteht, das Ausgangsmaterial für den Geschichtsunterricht für die Höheren Schülen im kommenden Jahr zu verbessern" (Kluge, *Die Patriotin*, 178). On the odd syntax structure that begins Kluge's second sentence, see Rainer Rother, *Die Gegenwart der Geschichte: ein Versuch über Film und zeitgenössische Literatur* (Stuttgart: Metzler, 1990), 94.
125 Kluge, *Die Patriotin*, 178.
126 The only snowstorms in which thunder and lightning occur are called "thundersnow." During such storms, the snowfall acts as an acoustic suppressor of the thunder. The thunder

forced and jarring convergences of sound/image or sound/sound that remain disjunctive. This is not simply some lightly falling snow that adds a "note of quiet hope," but an uncanny winter thunderstorm blowing in from Paradise.[127] Just before the snowstorm visuals and its unusual thunder fade, the instrumental excerpt from Beethoven's Ninth becomes audible. The last intertitle, furthermore, is just as jarring as the thunder snowstorm. For the final word, so to speak, is not given to Schiller – which would solidify beyond a doubt Germany's firm acoustical reinstatement – but to Brecht: "For a thousand years the dew fell. / Tomorrow there will be none. / The stars enter inexplicitly / into a new house."[128] Just as the snow swirls in the courtyard to the sound of thunder, Brecht's words serve to rhythmically unbalance the Beethoven melody. It would be too simple to suggest that Kluge seeks here to replace Brecht's verse with Schiller's "Ode to Joy." But it is also no longer the case that Kluge is using Beethoven's melody "uncritically," as Flinn claims. Perhaps it is best to hear Brecht's four lines in the same way as the original sounds of the bombing in Vienna are heard in "Götterdämmerung in Vienna": as "rhythmicizing" the music of Beethoven, fragmenting it "from a figure of the nineteenth century into the PROPERTY of the twentieth."[129]

While perhaps overpowering in its Germanness,[130] the Beethoven melody is nevertheless heard in stark disjunction with both the thundersnow storm

---

from a typical thunderstorm can be heard many kilometers away, while the thunder from thundersnow can usually be heard only within a two or three-kilometer radius from the lightning. Thundersnow storms usually also produce very heavy snowfalls. See Nikhil Swaminathan, "Thunder, Lighting and . . . Snow," *Scientific American*, 4 March 2009, https://www.scientificamerican.com/article/thundersnow-storm/.

127 I am referring to Benjamin's famous image of the *Angelus Novus* at the end of section nine of his posthumously published essay, "On the Concept of History." Miriam Hansen also compares Gabi Teichert to Benjamin's angel of history, albeit not in reference to the snowstorm at the end of the film. See Hansen, "The Stubborn Discourse," 129.

128 "Tausend Jahre fiel der Tau. / Morgen bleibt er aus. / Sterne treten ungenau / In ein neues Haus." Bertolt Brecht, *Werke. Große kommentierte Berliner und Frankfurter Ausgabe*, vol. 15 (Frankfurt a.M.: Suhrkamp, 1988), 89. For a highly detailed and informative examination of hope, futurity and the starry heavens in Kluge's cosmic miniatures, see Leslie Adelson, *Cosmic Miniatures and the Future Sense: Alexander Kluge's 21st-Century Literary Experiments in German Cultural and Narrative Form* (Berlin: De Gruyter, 2017).

129 Kluge, *GvK* 158.

130 Flinn's comment concerning Kluge's final use of Beethoven is almost scathing: "Perfectly recorded, it seems to correct the earlier, damaged version [Gabi Teichert] and her friends engaged with at the kitchen table. By withholding the lyrics, there is an additional sense that the women's attempts to understand the words are withdrawn as well. Unscratched, unscathed, "corrected," it is hard to detect much irony in this weighty sign of Germanness" (Flinn, *New German Cinema*, 136). Even Hillman cannot deny the Germanness of Beethoven at the end of

preceding it and the jarring counterpoint rhythm of Brecht's four silent lines. The Ninth Symphony's relation to these final accompanying sound and text images is one of tension and disruption, not conformity. In this way, the Beethoven melody is simultaneously closest to us – unscratched, unfragmented and heard "in its least adorned form"[131] – *and* more distant, since it is left at the end of the film suspended acoustically between the sounds of an uncanny winter thunderstorm and the Brecht poem that destabilizes the melody's rhythmic structure. By interrupting the thundersnow and being interrupted by Brecht, the Ninth Symphony "looks back" at us, asking us how we will reinscribe it into our century and the new year(s) to come.

When interpreting Benjamin's notion of the optical unconscious as offering "an experience that is more immediate, revealing, and less easily misused by third parties,"[132] Kluge is in the end most interested in its political function, in the use value of the optical unconscious for a cinema of emancipation. One might even say that Kluge superimposes a version of the political unconscious onto the Benjaminian optical unconscious, one that functions alongside Jameson's as attempting to both discover and recover a potentially repressed but alternative history of nationality and political appropriation. Fantasy, itself a runaway horse that Kluge nevertheless calls a political animal,[133] plays a role in such salvaging and reappropriation. And like fantasy, what Benjamin called the unique, "other nature" of the camera becomes similarly instrumentalized for both its visual and acoustic images. If Kluge's goal is ultimately to "salvage" Beethoven and Wagner, as Hillman writes, "from the bourgeois concert hall and the false socialism of the Nazis, regaining it for the 'proletarian public sphere,'"[134] Kluge's own project of the redemption of music is itself politically motivated. In his overarching project of redemption, culminating in conjunction with the audience's emancipatory fantasy, Kluge infuses the "gradations, distinctions, [and] aesthetic valences of film" sound with a "sound politics" of redemption, which is a practice unto itself.

---

the film: "It reestablishes the German core of a film which has examined what genuine patriotism might mean" (Hillman, *Unsettling Scores*, 107).
131 Hillman, *Unsettling Scores*, 108.
132 Kluge, GvK 143–144.
133 In *Kong's Finest Hour: A Chronicle of Connections* (Alexander Kluge, *Kongs große Stunde. Chronik des Zusammenhangs* [Frankfurt a.M.: Suhrkamp, 2015]), Kluge describes fantasy as "a POLITICAL ANIMAL and acts in the swarm [*Sie ist ein POLITISCHES TIER und verhält sich im Schwarm*]" (emphasis original, translation mine; Kluge, *Kongs große Stunde*, 253).
134 Hillman, *Unsettling Scores*, 108.

One may therefore conclude by posing two questions: 1) Is Kluge succeeding with his project of a cinema of emancipation? and 2) Can his work be interpreted as politicizing what this study has been calling the acoustical unconscious? Perhaps these questions should be left for the reader to decide. If the debate between Hillman and Flinn, two highly-informed and close readers of Kluge's work, has taught us anything, it is that widely disparate conclusions can be made from the same film sequence. Of course, it is one thing to convince a film scholar judging a film solely on the merits of its audio-visual associations, and another to provoke a "storm of fantasy" and to "move us inwardly," which as Kluge reminds us has more to do with surprise and wonder than conscious critical thought. Kluge himself argues that complete comprehension of a film would be "conceptual imperialism [*Begriffsimperialismus*] [. . .]. If I have understood everything, something has been emptied. We have to make films that are totally opposed to this colonization of consciousness."[135] Only that which remains beyond conventional understanding or conscious thought has the potential to create amazement and wonder, and therefore remains interesting.[136] In this sense, Kluge would likely be very satisfied with the debate between Hillman and Flinn, since the debate revolves around the functional ambiguity of Beethoven's Ninth Symphony at the end of *The Patriot*.

At the same time, Kluge's penchant for literalizations – from the fragmentation of the orchestra in "Götterdämmerung in Vienna" to Gabi Teichert's literal digging for German history – appears to problematize his claim above for making films that are "opposed to the colonization of consciousness." His literalizations, rather than suggesting an alternative way or mode of reading, tend to invite a certain "conceptual imperialism" of their own. How can we think, for instance, of Gabi's digging in the dirt to be anything other than literalizing the figurative language of uncovering the past? While he appears to obfuscate the understanding of every association, Kluge also makes certain associations *überdeutig*, to recall Freud's Signorelli parapraxis discussed in Chapter Two. Between these two extremes, one never quite knows what to think, which is perhaps the whole point.

---

135 Kluge, cited by Hillman, *Unsettling Scores*, 187. For the original German quote, see Kluge, *Die Patriotin*, 301.
136 Benjamin makes a similar comment about Brecht's epic theater: "Interest awakens in amazement (*Staunen*). In amazement alone is where interest finds its origin [. . .] Epic theatre is aimed at those who are interested and who 'do not think without reason' [*die "ohne Grund nicht denken"*]" (Benjamin, *GS* 2:522). As Weber notes, *Staunen* is not only a term "to describe the effect of what later will be called 'shock,'" but it is also integral to a certain learning process that does not lead "from ignorance to positive knowledge," but from a certain theatrical experimentation with the unknown that leads to "the singular, the incommensurable, the irreducibly different" (Weber, *Benjamin's -abilities*, 107–108).

One thing is clear: whether or not he succeeds in a cinema of emancipation and the resurgence of music's aura in the midst of its decline, Kluge's work repeatedly shows an unfaltering dedication to the "unseen" and "unheard" image that only film and cinema can offer. There are two levels in which Kluge claims such images can be interpreted. First, unseen and unheard images are essential to Kluge's theory of fantasy, in that they are produced *between* two images. This process can be thought of either as classic film montage (the third unseen image between two images), which Kluge is well aware of,[137] or what might be called Kluge's own peculiar version of *cinema* montage – that is, the unexpected "third" event that occurs between screen and spectators and in his so-called "meeting place for images" (*Versammlungsort für Bilder*). But another group of unseen and unheard images are privy to the optical and acoustical unconscious, at least in the way Kluge understands Benjamin. The optical unconscious involves for Kluge "unseen images" that "become visible once the camera reveals them."[138] This chapter has argued that, despite not formulating it explicitly in any of his theoretical or fictional work, Kluge is at least as interested in the acoustical unconscious as he is in the optical unconscious, if not more so: he appears as attuned to unseen images as he is to what might be called previously "unheard sound images," that is to say, sound images that become audible only through such methods as the creation of new sound perspectives, interwoven soundtracks, and the disintegration of sound material.[139] Like Eisenstein, Kluge

---

137 In the booklet that accompanies his film project, *Nachrichten aus der ideologischen Antike. Marx – Eisenstein – Das Kapital* (Frankfurt a.M.: Suhrkamp, 2008), Alexander Kluge describes "Eisenstein's theory of the 'third image,' the EPIPHANY. One sees contrasts (for example, two opposing images), and in the process a third (invisible) image arises spontaneously in the mind" (translation mine; Kluge, *Nachrichten*, 21). The way Kluge formulates Eisenstein's theory parallels his own theory of fantasy in *Public Sphere and Experience.*
138 Kluge, Nachrichten, 21.
139 Since well before Claudia Gorbman's *Unheard Melodies: Narrative Film Music* (Indianapolis: Indiana University Press, 1987), the role of music in film was thought to be fulfilled, to quote Kracauer who is referencing Epstein and Balàzs, "if it is not heard at all but gears our senses so completely to the film shots that they impress us as self-contained entities in the manner of photographs" (Kracauer, *Theory of Film*, 135). As Hoeckner and Nusbaum suggest, Gorbman's and early film theorists' claims "that musical underscoring is 'unheard' rests on the assumption that so-called non-diegetic film music (whose invisible source is lodged outside of the world of the filmic narration) is not consciously attended to, or at least perceived at a lower level of attention than the pictures or other elements of filmic narration, especially dialogue" (Berthold Hoeckner and Howard C. Nusbaum, "Music and Memory in Film and Other Multimedia: The Casablanca Effect," in *The Psychology of Music in Multimedia*, ed. Siu-Lan Tan, Annabel J. Cohen, Scott D. Lipscomb, and Roger A. Kendall, 235–263 [Oxford: Oxford University Press, 2013]; published to Oxford Scholarship Online, September 2013). But recent

wants to arrange these unheard and unseen images, in his words, "like serial music did with tones. Images that are different from each other, plus the irreconcilable, autonomous gap that emerges by being next to each other, yield a new correlation."[140] To keep an ear open to the acoustical unconscious in Kluge means to open our fantasy to new acoustical correlations that "overtake us by surprise and leave us wondering in their wake," as much of Kluge's material so often does.[141]

---

scientific studies show that an audience's attention to the visual elements of a film make it easier to examine the stimulating effects of its auditory components, an interdependent relationship that Berthold Hoeckner pays special attention to in his book, *Film, Music, Memory* (Chicago: University of Chicago Press, 2019). As I hope to have made clear throughout this study, I do not align any so-called "unheard image" to the acoustical unconscious per se but rather, following Benjamin and Derrida, nevertheless wish to accentuate the unrepresentable, unconventional or "unheard-of" connotations of the term.
140 Kluge, *Nachrichten*, 21–22.
141 Weber, *Benjamin's -abilities*, 114.

Conclusion: Toward a Genealogy of the Acoustical Unconscious

> As a historical object, sound cannot furnish a good story or consistent cast of characters nor can it validate any ersatz notion of progress or generational maturity. The history is scattered, fleeting, and highly mediated – it is as poor an object in any respect as sound itself.[1]
>
> Instead of adding faith to metaphysics, if the genealogist listens to history [*prend soin d'écouter l'histoire plutôt que d'ajouter foi à la métaphysique*], he finds that there is "something altogether other [*tout autre chose*]" behind things: not a timeless and essential secret, but the secret that they have no essence or that their essence was fabricated in a piecemeal fashion from foreign forms.[2]

No single author examined in this study explicitly refers to the acoustical unconscious, and Walter Benjamin, more than most others examined here, is almost never referred to as a thinker of music, sound or the auditory experience. Like Foucault after him, Benjamin can be equally criticized as "someone who either wholly neglected, or explicitly downplayed, the role of auditory perception and sound in his analyses."[3] While it has become hackneyed, as Hansen reminds us, "to blame Adorno for the mutilation of the artwork essay,"[4] there is likely some truth to the notion that Benjamin may have shied away from writing more on music and sound in part because of Adorno's dominating presence in the field. Other scholars point to Benjamin's own self-professed misunderstanding of music in his letters, or to Adorno's characterization of Benjamin as someone for whom music was evidently far from his thoughts.[5] So while the acoustical

---

1 Douglas Kahn and Gregory Whitehead, eds., *Wireless Imagination: Sound, Radio, and the Avant-Garde* (Cambridge: MIT Press, 1994), 2.
2 Michel Foucault, "Nietzsche, Genealogy, History," in *The Foucault Reader*, trans. Donald F. Bouchard and Sherry Simon (New York: Pantheon Books, 1984), 78. The original French can be found in Michel Foucault, "Nietzsche, la généalogie, l'histoire," in *Hommage à Jean Hyppolite*, by Suzanne Bachelard (Paris: Presses universitaires de France, 1971), 148.
3 See Lauri Siisiäinen, *Foucault and the Politics of Hearing* (New York: Routledge, 2012), esp. 1–5, where she outlines the criticism heaped upon Foucault for his apparently reductive-essentialist conception of audition, which her book aims to contest.
4 Miriam Hansen, *Cinema and Experience* (Berkeley: University of California Press, 2012), 161.
5 In separate letters, Benjamin professes not to follow Adorno's reflections on Wagner (to Horkheimer on 6 January 1938, in Walter Benjamin, *Briefe 2*, edited by Gershom Scholem and Theodor W. Adorno [Frankfurt a.M.: Suhrkamp, 1978], 741) and Mahler (to Adorno on 9 December 1938, in Benjamin, *Briefe 2*, 798; see also Walter Benjamin, *Selected Writings*, ed. Michael W. Jennings, Marcus Bullock, Howard Eiland, and Gary Smith, trans. Rodney Livingstone and Edmund Jephcott [Cambridge: Harvard University Press, 1996–2003] [hereafter, *SW*], 4:110) due to a self-proclaimed inability to comprehend the composers' music. In both cases, claiming to not understand music,

unconscious might already be a challenging enough term to examine, it becomes all the more so when confronted with the general bias that Benjamin had little to say about music, tone or sound compared to his interests in color and vision.[6]

When a concept like the acoustical unconscious does surface in more recent scholarship, as briefly outlined in the introduction, its various names – acoustic(al) unconscious, sonic unconscious, the audible or auditory unconscious – already belies the problem of any fixed determination. But even the question concerning the term's (various) definition(s) avoids more difficult ones: what might such a concept mean *for us*, as both a collective and in the present age? If the optical unconscious could not be thought before film, what can be thought "now" that could not have been before an acoustical unconscious?

The degree and scope of the term certainly awaits its full determination by those scholars who, in various fields of study, are most intrigued by its multifaceted implications. The present study originally began with a more modest proposal: to think the acoustical unconscious as a corollary or supplement to Benjamin's optical unconscious. Despite its extrapolation through Tieck, Eich and Kluge, the term as it is employed always harkens back, however distantly, to an acoustical variant of the Benjaminian optical unconscious rather than, say, to Leibniz's *petites perceptions*, Wordsworth's dysphemism, D. H. Lawrence's audible unconscious or Hermann von Helmholtz's physiological acoustics.[7] The acoustical

---

however, appears to be a convenient way to abstain from any sustained critique of Adorno's theories. For his part, Adorno seems to have accepted Benjamin's self-assessment: in his monograph, *Alban Berg – Der Meister des kleinsten Übergangs* (*Alban Berg – Master of the Smallest Link*, 1968), Adorno writes that music was far from Benjamin's thinking, and that during his youth, Benjamin even harbored a "certain animosity" toward musicians (Theodor Adorno, *Gesammelte Schriften* [Berlin: Directmedia, 2003] [hereafter, *GesS*], 13:356). Asmus Trautsch writes in *Klang und Musik*, "[i]n view of his distance from music and musicians, as stated by himself and Adorno, the reason for this seemingly auditorily insensitive attitude seems to lie simply in individual disinterest" (Asmus Trautsch, "Die abgelauschte Stadt und der Rhythmus des Glücks," in *Klang und Musik bei Walter Benjamin*, ed. Tobias Robert Klein and Asmus Trautsch [Munich: Wilhelm Fink, 2013], 18). Trautsch nevertheless goes on to dispel this notion with an astonishing collection of references to music and sound in Benjamin's oeuvre.

6 So far, the only major collection of essays that addresses specifically Benjamin's myriad references to sound and music is the one mentioned in the previous footnote.

7 In his *Psychoanalysis and the Unconscious* (1921), D. H. Lawrence wrote: "We know where is life, where is pulp. We have seen blind puppies, blind kittens crawling. They give strange little cries. Whence these cries? Are they mental exclamations? As in a ventriloquist, they come from the stomach. There lies the wakeful center. There speaks the first consciousness, the audible unconscious, in the squeak of these infantile things, which is so curiously and indescribably moving, reacting direct upon the great abdominal center, the preconscious mind in

unconscious outlined in this study gestures less toward any ontology or grounding of the term as such than "toward something like an 'acoustic unconscious'" inflected foremost via Benjamin's existent work,[8] including the media about and for which he wrote (radio and film), as well as his reflections on literature and the problems of psychology, perception and the sociology of language.

At the same time, since the acoustical unconscious is entwined with Benjamin's reflections on language and literature, upon which this study is founded, the concept is in some ways even more complex than his optical unconscious. For it calls into question the very limitation that Benjamin attributes to the optical unconscious: namely, that the latter could be neither thought nor theorized before the advent of the photograph. With the reading of the Mummerehlen fragment in Chapter One, the limitation of the acoustical unconscious as relating solely to technological reproducibility already becomes untenable.[9] The question thus remains: What are the limits of the acoustical unconscious if it can also be thought in terms of words on a page? What about the role of an acoustical unconscious in *Lautpoesie*, or in the rhythm of poetry more generally? What about other German authors whose work has been consistently read in terms of music or the acoustical, such as Eichendorff, Hoffmann, or Thomas Mann, to name but a few? Rather than attempting to answer these and myriad other questions concerning the limits of a general theory of the acoustical unconscious, I have limited this study to what a Benjaminian version of the acoustical unconscious might be, which includes its relevance beyond technological reproducibility, and how this singular concept can be thought alongside the written word, radio, and film.

As examined in the introduction and throughout this book, one of the more all-encompassing definitions of a Benjaminian acoustical unconscious is its relationship to a particular mode of reading, or more precisely, to a particular mode of legibility that emerges out of a disjunctive encounter between the "reader" and the language of the medium being "read" (for which the dilemma

---

man." See D. H. Lawrence, *Psychoanalysis and the Unconscious and Fantasia of the Unconscious* (Cambridge: Cambridge University Press, 2006), 20. For a discussion of Helmholtz's physiological acoustics, see Viet Erlmann, *Reason and Resonance: A History of Modern Aurality* (New York: Zone Books, 2010), and especially Benjamin Steege, *Helmholtz and the Modern Listener* (Cambridge University Press, 2012). For the references to Leibniz and Wordsworth, see the Introduction.

8 Hansen, *Cinema and Experience*, 352.

9 To be sure, Rosalind Krauss also parts from Benjamin's optical unconscious as limited to technological reproducibility when she applies the term, for instance, to the artworks of Ruskin and Mondrain.

is always, in light of the Karl Kraus quote and the analyses pursued in this book: who or what is reading whom?). There are two, seemingly disparate ways of approaching the acoustical unconscious's affiliation with legibility via Benjamin: by way of the optical unconscious, and via Benjamin's specific references to legibility, especially in terms of the dialectical image. These paths are not as divergent as one might assume.

Let us begin with the optical unconscious, which has traditionally not been interpreted as heralding a particular mode of reading. And yet, in *Cinema and Experience* Hansen describes the optical unconscious as being "lodged at the level of inscription and individual reception": while she is referring here to the images on a screen or details in a photograph, it is not difficult to read this and Hansen's fuller description of the optical unconscious as constitutive of a particular *reading* process:

> The mimetic, cognitive capacity of photographic inscription rests, to varying degrees, with the element of chance and contingency inherent in machinic vision, however carefully the image may be constructed. The camera's otherness – one might say its track with the look of the other – translates into an affinity with the normally unseen and indeterminate, the unintended or repressed. Like Roland Barthes's *punctum*, such moments of contingency and alterity may act as a hook that arrests, attracts, and jolts the later beholder. The optical unconscious thus as much refers to the psychic projection and involuntary memory triggered in the beholder as it assumes something encrypted in the image that nobody was aware of at the time of exposure. In other words, the technological disjunction between storage and release entails an unconscious element at two levels: the (fixed) moment of inscription and the (variable) time of reception.[10]

Reading words on a page can similarly be described as a "technological disjunction between [. . .] the (fixed) moment of inscription and the (variable) time of reception," and the "element of chance or contingency" is inherent not only to machinic vision, but can also be read into the most well-wrought prose by any astute, "close reader," however carefully the text may have been constructed. In pursuit of the acoustical unconscious that constitutes a particular mode of reading, it should not be overlooked that the optical unconscious equally allows for a certain legibility of that which could not have been read before. As a term that helps illustrate the shifting threshold between conscious and unconscious optical apperception, Benjamin's optical unconscious points to fundamental shifts of "optical readability" specific to photography and film. And just as the optical unconscious helps name the emergence of an optical readability particular to new media in Benjamin's lifetime, so should the

---

10 Hansen, *Cinema and Experience*, 156.

introduction of a Benjaminian acoustical unconscious be considered an investigation into the "disjunction between storage and release" of acoustical marks, including both sound recording and the non-discursive sonority of the printed word.

For all her insightful work on the trajectory between innervation and the mimetic faculty as they pertain to the optical unconscious in *Cinema and Experience*, Hansen does not read it as a specifically optical mode of reading. Furthermore, she continues to label the optical unconscious "rather elusive": "While I think there is still purchase to Benjamin's claim, we should bear in mind that the optical unconscious is obviously not a philosophical concept but rather an experimental metaphor, and, like all complex tropes, has multiple and shifting meanings."[11] She does not go on to say precisely for what the optical unconscious is an "experimental metaphor," though following her description of the optical unconscious above, perhaps it could be read as a metaphor for a certain mode of reading. However, reading for Benjamin cannot be thought in any conventional sense, as that which makes meaning possible and knowable. As Samuel Weber reminds us, "Benjamin never forgot that reading, far from being simply the reassuring recognition of the familiar, involved the taking of risks and the exposure to danger."[12] Reading for Benjamin is a "critical, dangerous moment" that disrupts what is otherwise thought as known, established, or having meaning. This important characterization of reading is found in N1,3 of his *Arcades Project*, where Benjamin expounds on the readability (*Lesbarkeit*) of the dialectical image, of "dialectics at a standstill." In describing this image, Benjamin writes: "It is not so much that what has gone by [*das Vergangene*] casts its light upon the present, or that the present casts its light upon what is gone; rather, the image is the constellation that ensues when what has been [*das Gewesene*] converges with the Now in a flash" (translation Weber's).[13] Weber calls this ensuing constellation a "disjunctive convergence" that generates "a different sort of space," a constellation "defined by the *potentiality* of *Zerspringen*, of breaking

---

11 Hansen, *Cinema and Experience*, 156. While Hansen writes "there is still purchase in Benjamin's claim" of the optical unconscious, she compromises its relevance by labeling it an "experimental metaphor" and complex trope. Viet Erlmann is even more severe in his assessment of the term's relevance today: "Of course, few today share Benjamin's messianic fervor and confidence in technology as a key to 'another nature' (current scholarship tends to stress the reverse notion that technology 'inscribes' nature before it becomes recognized as Nature)" (Erlmann, *Reason and Resonance*, 272).
12 Samuel Weber, *Benjamin's -abilities* (Cambridge: Harvard University Press, 2008), 229.
13 Benjamin, cited by Weber, *Benjamin's -abilities*, 229.

apart" (italics original).¹⁴ Reading for Benjamin is the articulation of this convergence, which is anything but stable, hence his reference to that "critical, dangerous moment that underlies all reading" (translation Weber's).¹⁵

Without intending to relativize the precise terms that Benjamin employs in this key passage – the "Now of Knowability," for instance, or the tension that emerges between the extreme instance of the lightning flash and the extreme stasis of the constellation¹⁶ – it is nevertheless useful to align the structure of convergence here with how Benjamin describes the encounter with the optical unconscious in the artwork essay: "Clearly, it is an other nature that speaks to the camera rather than to the eye. 'Other' above all in that a space interwoven with the unconscious takes the place [*an die Stelle . . . tritt*] of a space interwoven with human consciousness" (translation modified).¹⁷ Whether it takes the place of human consciousness or whether the latter "gives way" to a space interwoven by the unconscious,¹⁸ a similar kind of disjunctive convergence is taking place here. It relies more heavily on psychoanalytic terminology, to be sure; but again, Benjamin's use of these terms beyond their established definitions in Freudian psychology already invites, as we have seen, a certain "elusiveness" or precariousness about what is meant. Furthermore, we should not overlook Benjamin's description of how cinema has exploded the spectators' relation to their otherwise habitualized spaces, which in the first version of the essay almost immediately precedes the sentence cited above: "Our bars and city streets, our offices and furnished rooms, our railroad stations and our factories seemed to close relentlessly around us. Then came film and exploded this prison-world

---

14 Weber, *Benjamin's -abilities*, 230.
15 Benjamin, cited by Weber, *Benjamin's -abilities*, 229.
16 Weber, *Benjamin's -abilities*, 230.
17 Walter Benjamin, *Gesammelte Schriften* (Frankfurt a.M.: Suhrkamp, 1972) (hereafter, *GS*), 1:500 [Walter Benjamin, *Werke und Nachlass: Kritische Gesamtausgabe* (Frankfurt a.M.: Suhrkamp, 2008–) (hereafter, *WuN*), 16:240]; Benjamin, *SW*, 4:266.
18 The verb phrase used here, *an die Stelle treten*, is idiomatic for taking the place of something, though it could also mean stepping into or coming up to something. The English translators avoid these spatial problems and, in an attempt to keep the sentence structure mainly intact, write "that a space informed by the human consciousness gives way to a space informed by the unconscious" (Benjamin, *GS* 1:500 [*WuN* 16:240]; *SW* 4:266). What is lost in translation here is agency, that which is being acted upon. Does human consciousness "give way," allowing an unconscious space to move in, or does the latter take the former's place, rushing in like a flash and with no warning? The phrase "gives way" suggests a reciprocating relationship, while the original German suggests more of the disjunctive convergence being addressed here.

with the dynamite of the split second, so that now we can set off calmly on journeys of adventure among its far-flung debris" (translation modified).[19] Benjamin's reference to the explosive power of cinema recalls the lightening flash convergence of the Now with what has been (*das Gewesene*) that occurs in that dangerous moment of reading the dialectical image. This is not to say that going to the movies for Benjamin amounts to an act of reading the dialectical image, but what is consistent between the two is the framework of a disjunctive convergence described in similarly spatial terms. Despite using different terminology to describe what at first appear to be quite different experiences, the disjunctive nature of the convergence between the *space* of human consciousness and that of the optical unconscious appears concomitant with the specific notion of legibility that Benjamin attributes to the dialectical image.

Reading the optical unconscious as an "experimental metaphor" for a specifically Benjaminian notion of legibility, which itself breaks with what is traditionally meant by reading, lends further credence to the acoustical unconscious as implicating its own particular mode of reading.[20] Throughout this study, the pursuit of an acoustical unconscious has consistently been accompanied by chronic and synchronic disjunctiveness, whether that refers to the meaning of words as they break down into paronymic associations, the eruptive displacement of the seeing self as experienced by Bertha in Tieck's "Eckbert," the voice that dissociates from Kasperl or, for that matter, from any sense of unified identity in Eich's radio plays, or even Kluge's interpenetrated soundtracks examined in the final chapter. Articulating not identity and synthesis but rather "a disjunctive bringing-together and keeping-apart" is a key theoretical and

---

19 Benjamin, *GS* 1:500 [*WuN* 16:240]; *SW* 4:265–266.
20 Another reason for interpreting both the optical and acoustical unconscious as indicative of different modes of reading is the way Benjamin, in a few highly condensed notes he wrote around 1917, defines perception specifically *as* reading. In a fragment called "On Perception in itself [*Über die Wahrnehmung in sich*]," Benjamin's first line is: "Perception is reading [*Die Wahrnehmung ist Lesen*]" (*GS* 6, 32). In a footnote addressing these fragments, Peter Fenves suggests that "[s]ometimes, however, perception is equivalent to 'pure seeing,' as it is discussed in the studies on color (*GS* 6, 65). The difference between the two concepts of perception seems to lie in the context in which they emerge: perception per se is comparable to 'pure seeing,' whereas perception is understood as 'interpretation' when it is distinguished from experience, which is essentially continuous" (Peter Fenves, *The Messianic Reduction: Walter Benjamin and the Shape of Time* [Stanford, CA: Stanford University Press, 2010], 281). It would be worthwhile to compare "pure seeing" with the possibility of a "pure listening," whether they would be structurally or contextually similar, whether the latter could be related to the *Urvernehmen* ("primal listening") found in the "Epistemo-Critical Preface," and the extent to which either is relatable to the optical and acoustical unconscious, respectively.

performative gesture that Benjamin employs repeatedly throughout his work.[21] With the acoustical unconscious being constitutive of a certain mode of legibility, one can say that this Benjaminian gesture both migrates into the realm of acoustic media and their aesthetic possibilities, while simultaneously, and no doubt disjunctively, becomes equally relevant to that non-discursive sonority of language with which Derrida was so intrigued.

The task of reading genealogically is not unrelated to the disjunctive convergence being examined here. The title of this conclusion, "Toward a Genealogy of the Acoustical Unconscious," suggests that the turn toward such a genealogy, while proposed at the end of this study, has only just begun. Despite the so-called conclusion you are currently reading, such a project remains necessarily unfinished and incomplete, and will require a number of future turns and re-turns. According to Peter Szendy, for whom "the history of the notion of the work *conditions* the history of listening, *and vice versa*" (emphasis original), his own working out of a "history of listening" constantly has him listening in on and turning back to his own listening experiences, rereading and questioning his own conclusions.[22]

Any "genealogy" of the acoustical unconscious will necessarily forever be a long way off, sounding out as if from a great distance, however close it may seem. This study has pricked its ears in this general direction, with the aim of contributing to the so-called "auditory turn" in the humanities. But "toward" has another meaning not unrelated to how Jean-Luc Nancy defines listening (*écouter*): "to listen is to be straining *toward* a possible meaning, and consequently one that is not immediately accessible" (emphasis mine).[23] To be "toward" a genealogy is to tend toward it, that is to say, to stretch like ears do when listening. This is certainly one way to think of the methodology contained in the present work: to turn toward one possible sense of the acoustical unconscious, as listening in on its potential resonances and historical plasticity.

---

21 Weber, *Benjamin's -abilities*, 230.
22 Peter Szendy, *Listen: A History of Our Ears*, trans. Charlotte Mandell (New York: Fordham University Press, 2008), 102. Szendy is explicit about the need to turn back to and re-read his own work. In his contribution to *Thresholds of Listening* (Fordham 2015), he also repeats this gesture: "It is always a weird experience to re-read something that one wrote many years earlier. Words about listening, for example, written when no one much thought about an 'auditory turn in the humanities,' nor talked about 'sound studies.'" See Peter Szendy, "The Auditory Re-Turn (The Point of Listening)," in *Thresholds of Listening: Sound, Technics, Space*, ed. Sander van Maas (New York: Fordham University Press, 2015), 18.
23 Jean-Luc Nancy, *Listening*, trans. Charlotte Mandell (New York: Fordham University Press, 2007), 6. See also the original French in Jean-Luc Nancy, *À l'écoute* (Paris: Éditions Galilée 2002), 19.

The point of approaching the acoustical unconscious genealogically is therefore not to construct a historically informed, theoretical framework that is first extrapolated from the optical unconscious and subsequently applied to various readings set in chronological order. The individual readings of Benjamin, Tieck, Eich, and Kluge are not meant to be pieces of a puzzle such that, when they are linked together, the result is a crystal-clear theory of the acoustical unconscious. Rather, each chapter stages a critical problem relevant to issues of the acoustical unconscious, and the singularity of that problem, elaborated upon through close readings, is to be kept in disjunctive synthesis with the one that came before it. The acoustical unconscious explored in these pages is not meant to be a commanding force that determines how things are read, but rather a theoretical nexus around which orbit issues concerning hearing and listening, self and knowledge, which in turn help to orient particular interpretations while offering neither an origin nor definitive conclusions.

When thinking of the acoustical unconscious, let me suggest in conclusion the image of what might be called the "genealogical ear." On the one hand, genealogy by definition recognizes and accentuates figures of disfiguration, the breakdown of memory, self and other, and questions the motivations behind meaning and knowledge. On the other hand, our anatomical inner ear – more precisely, the vestibular system within the inner ear – helps to maintain balance and equilibrium when we turn our bodies in one direction or another, allowing us to stay erect while standing and informing us of where we are in relation to gravity. It does so via three semicircular canals, each one on a different plane at right angles from the other two, and each one dealing with a different movement: up and down, side to side, and tilting from one side to the other. The vestibular system of the genealogical ear, however, would involve entirely different modes of orientation. In the last section of his essay on genealogy, Foucault offers three uses of history: genealogy as directed *against* reality, identity, and truth.[24] Such would be the three axes of the genealogical ear's vestibular system: far from bringing equilibrium and balance, it upsets fixed notions of history as recognizable or representational, as having any sense of temporal continuity, and as being factually accurate.

---

24 "Le sens historique comporte trois usages qui s'opposent terme à terme eux trois modalités platoniciennes de l'histoire. L'un, c'est l'usage parodique et destructeur de réalité, qui s'oppose au thème de l'histoire – réminiscence ou reconnaissance; l'autre c'est l'usage dissociatif et destructeur d'identité qui s'oppose à l'histoire – continuité ou tradition; le troisième, c'est l'usage sacrificiel, et destructeur de vérité qui s'oppose à l'histoire – connaissance" (Foucault, "Nietzsche, la généalogie, l'histoire," 167).

The acoustical unconscious could be read as stepping into, figuratively speaking of course, these canals of the vestibular system of the genealogical ear, which like forgetting, is never simply our own. Rather than orienting us physically in relation to gravity and the objects around us like our inner ear does, the genealogical ear destabilizes and reorients us, converging disjunctively with a space interwoven with the acoustical unconscious. Only a genealogical ear would be able to listen to these scattered and fleeting acousmatic "objects" of study; only the genealogical ear knows of its own stretching towards a possible sense while simultaneously being aware and even celebrating the futility of synthesizing such objects. In the pursuit of a Benjaminian acoustical unconscious, what has been amplified is a disequilibrium about the knowledge of our selves and our relation to the apparently "external" world: words are no longer what they were, meanings and identifiable voices give way to sounds and phonemes, and what we thought we heard – *Mummerehlen, Strohmian,* the word *Lazertis* or Beethoven's Ninth Symphony – disrupts our sense of history, memory and identity, while also opening us up both to possible reinterpretations of ourselves, and to other possible modes of knowing, which may include non-knowing or a knowing to come. Or to ventriloquize Derrida: when hearing otherwise, we no longer know.[25]

---

25 Jacques Derrida, *La voix et le phénomène* (Paris: Presses universitaires de France, 1967), 115–116; *Speech and Phenomena*, trans. David B. Allison (Evanston, IL: Northwestern University Press, 1973), 103. See also the first part of the Introduction.

Works Cited

Adelson, Leslie. *Cosmic Miniatures and the Future Sense: Alexander Kluge's 21st-Century Literary Experiments in German Cultural and Narrative Form*. Berlin: De Gruyter, 2017.
Adorno, Theodor. *The Intellectual Migration: Europe and America, 1930–1960*. Edited by Donald Fleming and Bernard Bailyn. Cambridge, MA: Belknap Press, 1969.
Adorno, Theodor. *Introduction to the Sociology of Music*. Translated by E. B. Ashton. New York: Continuum, [1976] 1988.
Adorno, Theodor. *Notes to Literature*. Translated by Shierry Weber Nicholsen. New York: Columbia University Press, 1992.
Adorno, Theodor. *Prismen*. Frankfurt a.M.: Suhrkamp, 1955.
Adorno, Theodor. *Prisms*. Translated by Samuel and Shierry Weber. Cambridge: MIT Press, 1967.
Alter, Nora M. "Screening Out Sound: Arnheim and Cinema's Silence." In *Arnheim for Film and Media Studies*, edited by Scott Higgins, 70–87. New York: Routledge, 2011.
Arnheim, Rudolph. *Film as Art*. Berkeley: University of California Press, 1969.
Arnheim, Rudolph. *Film als Kunst*. Berlin: Rowohlt, 1932.
Arnheim, Rudolph. "Function to Expression." In *Toward a Psychology of Art: Collected Essays*, by Rudolph Arnheim, 192–213. Berkeley: University of California Press, 1994.
Arnheim, Rudolph. "On the Nature of Photography." In *New Essays on the Psychology of Art*, by Rudolph Arnheim, 102–114. Berkeley: University of California Press, 1986.
Arnheim, Rudolph. *New Essays on the Psychology of Art*. Berkeley: University of California Press, 1986.
Arnheim, Rudolph. *Radio*. Translated by Margaret Ludwig and Herbert Read. London: Faber & Faber, 1933.
Arnheim, Rudolph. *Rundfunk als Hörkunst und weitere Aufsätze zum Hörfunk*. Frankfurt a.M.: Suhrkamp, 2001.
Arnheim, Rudolph. *Toward a Psychology of Art: Collected Essays*. Berkeley: University of California Press, 1994.
Arnheim, Rudolph. "Why Words are Needed." *Journal of Aesthetic Education* 32, no. 2 (Summer 1998): 21–25.
Arnheim, Rudolph. "The World of the Daytime Serial." In *Radio Research, 1942–1943*, edited by Paul Lazarsfeld and Frank Stanton, 34–85. New York: Duell, Sloan & Pearce, 1944.
Balázs, Béla. *Der Geist des Films*. Frankfurt a.M.: Suhrkamp, 2001.
Barthes, Roland. *Camera Lucida: Reflections on Photography*. Translated by Richard Howard. New York: Hill and Wang, 1981.
Barthes, Roland. *La chambre Claire*. Paris: Gallimard, 1980.
Beevor, Antony. *Berlin: The Downfall 1945*. New York: Penguin, 2002.
Benjamin, Walter. *The Arcades Project*. Translated by Howard Eiland and Kevin McLaughlin. Cambridge: Harvard University Press, 2002.
Benjamin, Walter. *Briefe 2*. Edited by Gershom Scholem and Theodor W. Adorno. Frankfurt a.M.: Suhrkamp, 1978.
Benjamin, Walter. *Gesammelte Schriften*. Frankfurt a.M.: Suhrkamp, 1972.
Benjamin, Walter. *The Origin of German Tragic Drama*. Translated by John Osborne. London: New Left Books, 1977.
Benjamin, Walter. *Origin of the German Trauerspiel*. Translated by Howard Eiland. Cambridge: Harvard University Press, 2019.

Benjamin, Walter. *Radio Benjamin*. Edited by Lecia Rosenthal. Translated by Jonathan Lutes. London/New York: Verso, 2014.
Benjamin, Walter. *Selected Writings*. Edited by Michael W. Jennings, Marcus Bullock, Howard Eiland, and Gary Smith. Translated by Rodney Livingstone and Edmund Jephcott. Cambridge: Harvard University Press, 1996–2003.
Benjamin, Walter. *Werke und Nachlass: Kritische Gesamtausgabe*. Frankfurt a.M.: Suhrkamp, 2008–.
Benjamin, Walter, and Theodor Adorno. *Adorno & Benjamin: The Complete Correspondence, 1928–1940*. Translated by N. Walker. Cambridge: Harvard University Press, 1999.
Benjamin, Walter, and Theodor Adorno. *Briefwechsel 1928–1940*. Frankfurt a.M.: Suhrkamp, 1995.
Bernstein, Susan. "The Other Synaesthesia." In *Points of Departure: Samuel Weber between Spectrality and Writing*, edited by Peter Fenves, Kevin McLaughlin, and Marc Redfield (Evanston, IL: Northwestern University Press, 2016), 131–147.
Bloch, Ernst. *The Principle of Hope*. Vol. 1. Translated by Neville Plaice, Stephen Plaice, and Paul Knight. Cambridge: MIT Press, 1986.
Bloch, Ernst. *Das Prinzip Hoffnung*. Frankfurt a.M.: Suhrkamp, 1959.
Bloch, Ernst. *Verfremdungen*. Frankfurt a.M.: Suhrkamp, 1965.
Bordwell, David. "Rudolf Arnheim: Clarity, Simplicity, Balance." In *Arnheim for Film and Media Studies*, edited by Scott Higgins, 20–29. New York: Routledge, 2011.
Bowie, Andrew. "New Histories: Aspects of the Prose of Alexander Kluge." *Journal of European Studies* 12 (1982): 180–208.
Bowie, Andrew. *From Romanticism to Critical Theory: The Philosophy of German Literary Theory*. New York: Routledge, 1996.
Brecht, Bertolt. *Brecht on Film and Radio*. Edited by Marc Silberman. London: Methuen, 2000.
Brecht, Bertolt. "Der Rundfunk als Kommunikationsapparat." In *Bertolt Brecht: Gesammelte Werke*, by Bertolt Brecht, *8.2*: 127–134. Frankfurt a. M.: Suhrkamp, 1967.
Brecht, Bertolt. *Werke. Grosse kommentierte Berliner und Frankfurter Ausgabe*. Vol. 5. Frankfurt a.M.: Suhrkamp, 1988.
Brown, Alan S. *The Déjà Vu Experience*. New York: Psychology Press, 2004.
Brunette, Peter, and David Wells. *Screen/Play: Derrida and Film Theory*. Princeton, NJ: Princeton University Press, 1989.
Buschman, Christel, Alexander Kluge, and Willi Segler. *Die Patriotin*. Directed by Alexander Kluge. Performed by Hannelore Hoger. Kairos-Film, 1979. DVD.
Cadava, Eduardo. *Words of Light: Theses on the Photography of History*. Princeton, NJ: Princeton University Press, 1997.
Carroll, Noël. *Philosophical Problems of Classical Film Theory*. Princeton, NJ: Princeton University Press, 1988.
Caygill, Howard. *Walter Benjamin: The Colour of Experience*. New York: Routledge, 1998.
Chion, Michel. *Audio-Vision*. New York: Columbia University Press, 1994.
Chion, Michel. *The Voice in Cinema*. Translated by Claudia Gorbman. New York: Columbia University Press, 1999.
Chow, Rey. "Walter Benjamin's Love Affair with Death." *New German Critique* no. 48 (Autumn 1989), 63–86.
Cleary, Anne M., and Alan S. Brown. *The Déjà Vu Experience: Essays in Cognitive Psychology*. New York: Routledge, 2021.

Cobussen, Marcel. "Music and Network: The Becoming Insect of Music." In *Music and Networking*, edited by T. Markovic and V. Mikic, 19–27. Belgrade: University of the Arts, 2005.
Cory, Mark E. "Soundplay: The Polyphonous Tradition of German Radio Art." In *Wireless Imagination: Sound, Radio, and the avant-garde*, edited by Douglas Kahn and Gregory Whitehead, 331–372. Cambridge: MIT Press, 1992.
Cox, Christoph. "Sound Art and the Sonic Unconscious." *Organised Sound* 14, no.1 (2009): 19–26.
Crary, Jonathan. *Suspensions of Perception: Attention, Spectacle, and Modern Culture.* Cambridge: MIT Press, 2001.
Cuomo, Glenn R. *Career at the Cost of Compromise: Günter Eich's Life and Work in the Years 1933–1945.* Amsterdam: Rodopi, 1989.
Currid, Brian. *A National Acoustics: Music and Mass Publicity in Weimar and Nazi Germany.* Minneapolis: University of Minnesota Press, 2006.
Deleuze, Gilles, and Félix Guattari. *Anti-Oedipus: Capitalism and Schizophrenia.* Translated by Robert Hurley, Mark Seem, and Helen R. Lane. Minneapolis: University of Minnesota Press, 1983.
Deleuze, Gilles, and Félix Guattari. *A Thousand Plateaus: Capitalism and Schizophrenia.* Translated by Brian Massumi. Minneapolis: University of Minnesota Press, 1987.
Derrida, Jacques. *L'animal que donc je suis.* Paris: Éditions Galilée, 2006.
Derrida, Jacques. *The Animal that Therefore I Am.* Translated by David Wills. New York: Fordham University Press, 2008.
Derrida, Jacques. *Rogues: Two Essays on Reason.* Translated by Pascale-Anne Brault and Michael Naas. Stanford, CA: Stanford University Press, 2005.
Derrida, Jacques. *Speech and Phenomena.* Translated by David B. Allison. Evanston, IL: Northwestern University Press, 1973.
Derrida, Jacques. *La voix et le phénomène.* Paris: Presses universitaires de France, 1967.
Derrida, Jacques. *Voyous.* Paris: Éditions Galilée, 2003.
Derrida, Jacques. *Writing and Difference.* Translated by Alan Bass. Chicago: University of Chicago Press, 1978.
Das deutsche Wörterbuch von Jacob und Wilhelm Grimm auf CD-Rom und im Internet. Digitized version in Wörterbuchnetz des Trier Center for Digital Humanities, version 01/21. https://www.woerterbuchnetz.de/DWB.
Das Herkunftswörterbuch, Etymologie der deutschen Sprache. Vol. 7. 2nd ed. Edited by Günther Drowsdowski. Mannheim: Dudenverlag, 1989.
Dick, Philip K. *Ubik.* New York: First Vintage Books, 1991.
Diederichs, Helmut. "Nachwort." In *Rundfunk als Hörkunst und weitere Aufsätze zum Hörfunk*, by Rudolf Arnheim, 217–236. Frankfurt a.M.: Suhrkamp, 2001.
Döhl, Richard. "Zum Hörspielwerk Günter Eichs." WDR 3, 13 December 1976. Accessed 22 August 2021. https://www.reinhard-doehl.de/eich1.htm.
Dolan, Emily I. *Orchestral Revolution: Haydn and the Technologies of Timbre.* Cambridge: Cambridge University Press, 2013.
Dolar, Mladen. *A Voice and Nothing More.* Cambridge: MIT Press, 2006.
Eich, Günter. "Abgekürzte Dramaturgie des Hörspiels [1968]." In *Gesammelte Werke in vier Bänden*, Bd. 4, rev. ed., edited by Axel Vieregg, 511–512. Frankfurt a.M.: Suhrkamp, 1991.
Eich, Günter. *Angina Days: Selected Poems of Günter Eich.* Translated by Michael Hoffmann. Princeton, NJ: Princeton University Press, 2011.

Eich, Günter. *Gesammelte Werke*. Frankfurt a.M.: Suhrkamp, 1973.
Eich, Günter. *Journeys: Two Radio Plays*. London: Cape, 1968.
Eich, Günter. "Der Schriftsteller vor der Realität." In *Über Günter Eich*, edited by Susanne Müller-Hanpft, 19–20. Frankfurt a.M.: Suhrkamp, 1970.
Eiland, Howard. "Reception in Distraction." *Boundary 2* 30, no. 1 (Spring 2003): 51–66.
Ellis, John M. "Tieck: 'Der blonde Eckbert.'" In *Narration in the German Novelle: Theory and Interpretation*, by John M. Ellis, 77–93. London: Cambridge University Press, 1974.
Emerson, Ralph Waldo. *The Complete Works of Ralph Waldo Emerson*. Vol. 9. Cambridge, MA: Riverside Press, 1904.
Emerson, Ralph Waldo. "Waldeinsamkeit." In *The Complete Works of Ralph Waldo Emerson: Poems*, vol. 9, by Ralph Waldo Emerson, 183–184. Cambridge, MA: Riverside Press, 1904.
Enn, Anthony. "Telepathie – Telefon – Terror. Ausweitung und Verstümmelungen des Körpers." In *Hörstürze: Akustik und Gewalt im 20. Jahrhundert*, edited by Nicola Gess, Florian Schreiner, and Manuela K. Schulz, 89–112. Würzburg: Königshausen & Neumann, 2005.
Erlmann, Veit. "'Acoustic Space' – Marshall McLuhan Defended Against Himself." *The Senses & Society* 11, no.1 (2016): 36–49.
Erlmann, Veit. *Reasonand Resonance: A History of Modern Aurality*. New York: Zone Books, 2010.
Feld, Steven. "Waterfalls of Song: An Acoustemology of Place Resounding in Bosavi, Papua New Guinea." In *Senses of Place*, edited by Steven Feld and Keith H. Basso, 91–136. Santa Fe, NM: School of American Research Press, 1996.
Fenves, Peter. *The Messianic Reduction: Walter Benjamin and the Shape of Time*. Stanford, CA: Stanford University Press, 2010.
Fetscher, Justus. "Blindness and 'Showside': Non-Visual Aspects of German Radio and Radio Plays in the 1950s." *Monatshefte* 98, no. 2 (Summer 2006): 244–266.
Fickert, Kurt. "The Relevance of the Incest Motif in 'Der blonde Eckbert.'" *Germanic Notes* 13, no. 3 (1982): 33–35.
Flinn, Caryl. *New German Cinema: Music, History, and the Matter of Style*. Berkeley and Los Angeles: University of California Press, 2004.
Flinn, Caryl. "Strategies of Remembrance." In *Music and Cinema*, edited by James Buhler, Caryl Flinn, and David Neumeyer, 118–141. Hanover, NH: University Press of New England for Wesleyan University Press, 2000.
Fore, Devin. "Introduction." In *History and Obstinacy*, by Alexander Kluge and Oskar Negt, edited by Devin Fore, translated by Richard Langston et al., 15–67. New York: Zone, 2014.
Foucault, Michel. "Nietzsche, la genealogie, l'histoire." In *Hommage à Jean Hyppolite*, by Suzanne Bachelard, 145–172. Paris: Presses universitaires de France, 1971.
Foucault, Michel. "Nietzsche, Genealogy, History." In *The Foucault Reader*, translated by Donald F. Bouchard and Sherry Simon, 76–100. New York: Pantheon Books, 1984.
Freud, Sigmund. *Aus den Anfängen der Psychoanalyse; Briefe an Wilhelm Fliess, Abhandlungen und Notizen aus den Jahren 1887–1902*. London: Imago, 1950.
Freud, Sigmund. *The Complete Letters of Sigmund Freud to Wilhelm Fliess 1887–1904*. Translated by Jeffrey Moussaieff Masson. Cambridge, MA: Belknap Press, 1985.
Freud, Sigmund. *Gesammelte Werke*. London: Imago, 1940–1952.
Freud, Sigmund. *Jenseits des Lustprinzips*. Leipzig/Wien/Zürich: Internationaler Psychoanalytischer Verlag, 1921.

Freud, Sigmund. *The Standard Edition of the Complete Psychological Works of Sigmund Freud*. Translated by James Strachey. London: Hogarth Press, 1953–1974.

Friedlander, Eli. "Farben und Laute in der *Berliner Kindheit um neunzehnhundert*." In *Klang und Musik bei Walter Benjamin*, edited by Tobias Robert Klein and Asmus Trautsch, 54–67. Munich: Wilhelm Fink, 2013.

Fries, Thomas. "'Ein romantisches Märchen: Der Blonde Eckbert' von Ludwig Tieck." *MLN* 88, no. 6 (December 1973): 1180–1211.

Frost, Everett, and Margaret Herzfeld-Sander, eds. *German Radio Plays*. The German Library 86. New York: Continuum, 1991.

Ganos, Christos, Timo Ogrzal, Alfons Schnitzler, and Alexander Münchau. "The pathophysiology of echopraxia/echolalia: Relevance to Gilles de la Tourette syndrome." *Movement Disorders* 27, no. 10 (September 2012): 1222–1229.

Gellen, Kata. *Kafka and Noise: The Discovery of Cinematic Sound in Literary Modernism*. Evanston, IL: Northwestern University Press, 2019.

Gelso, Charles, and Jeffrey Hayes. *Countertransference and the Therapist's Inner Experience: Perils and Possibilities*. Mahwah, NJ: Lawrence Erlbaum Associates, 2007.

Goodman, Kevis. *Georgic Modernity and British Romanticism: Poetry and the Mediation of History*. Cambridge: Cambridge University Press, 2004.

Goodman, Nelson, and Catherine Z. Elgin. *Reconceptions in Philosophy & Other Arts & Sciences*. Indianapolis: Hackett Publishing Company Inc., 1988.

Gorbman, Claudia. *Unheard Melodies: Narrative Film Music*. Indianapolis: Indiana University Press, 1987.

Hagen, Wolfgang. *Das Radio: Zur Geschichte und Theorie des Hörfunks – Deutschland, USA*. Munich: Wilhelm Fink, 2005.

Hamacher, Werner. "Intensive Sprache." In *Übersetzen: Walter Benjamin*, by Christiaan L. Hart Nibbrig, 174–235. Frankfurt a.M.: Suhrkamp, 2001.

Hamacher, Werner. "The Word 'Wolke' – If It Is One." In *Benjamin's Ground: New Readings of Walter Benjamin*, translated by P. Fenves, 147–176. Detroit: Wayne State University Press, 1988.

Hamilton, John. *Music, Madness, and the Unworking of Language*. New York: Columbia University Press, 2008.

Hansen, Miriam. "Benjamin and Cinema: Not a One-Way Street." In *Benjamin's Ghosts: Interventions in Contemporary Literary and Cultural Theory*, edited by Gerhard Richter, 41–73. Stanford, CA: Stanford University Press, 2002.

Hansen, Miriam. *Cinema and Experience*. Berkeley: University of California Press, 2012.

Hansen, Miriam. "Introduction." In *Theory of Film: The Redemption of Physical Reality*, by Siegfried Kracauer, vii–xlvi. Princeton, NJ: Princeton University Press, 1997.

Hansen, Miriam. "Of Mice and Ducks: Benjamin and Adorno on Disney." *South Atlantic Quarterly* 92, no. 1 (Winter 1993): 27–61.

Hansen, Miriam. "Reinventing the Nickelodeon: Notes on Kluge and Early Cinema." *October* 46 (Fall 1988): 179–198.

Hansen, Miriam. "The Stubborn Discourse: History and Story-Telling." In *Die Schrift an der Wand. Alexander Kluge: Rohstoffe und Materialien*, by Alexander Kluge, 119–132. Osnabrück: Universitätsverlag Rasch, 2000.

Harbord, Janet. "Contingency's Work: Kracauer's *Theory of Film* and the Trope of the Accidental." *New Formations* 61 (Summer 2007): 90–103.

Hauff, Wilhelm. *Das kalte Herz: Ein Märchen*. Berlin: Holzinger, 2016.

Heidegger, Martin. *Gesamtausgabe*. Frankfurt a.M.: Klostermann, 2000.
Heidegger, Martin. *Poetry Language Thought*. Translated by Albert Hofstadter. New York: Perennial Classics, 2001.
Heller-Roazen, Daniel. *Echolalias: On the Forgetting of Language*. New York: Zone Books, 2005.
Heydenreich, Maria. *Wachstafel und Weltformel. Erinnerungspoetik und Wissenschaftskritik in Günter Eichs "Maulwürfen."* Göttingen: Vandhoeck & Ruprecht, 2007.
Hillman, Roger. *Unsettling Scores: German Film, Music, and Ideology*. Bloomington, IN: Indiana University Press, 2005.
Hoeckner, Berthold. *Film, Music, Memory*. Chicago: University of Chicago Press, 2019.
Hoeckner, Berthold and Howard C. Nusbaum. "Music and Memory in Film and Other Multimedia: The Casablanca Effect." In *The Psychology of Music in Multimedia*, edited by Siu-Lan Tan, Annabel J. Cohen, Scott D. Lipscomb, and Roger A. Kendall, 235–263. Oxford: Oxford University Press, 2013. Published to Oxford Scholarship Online, September 2013.
Hölderlin, Friedrich. "In lieblicher Bläue . . ." (1823)/"In lovely blueness . . . ." In *Poems and Fragments*, by Friedrich Hölderlin, 792–793. Bilingual ed. Translated by Michael Hamburger. London: Anvil Press Poetry, 2004.
Hubbs, Valentine C. "Tieck, Eckbert und das kollektive Unbewußte." *PMLA: Publications of the Modern Language Association of America* 71, no. 4 (September 1956): 686–693.
Hunt, F. V. "Acoustical vs Acoustical." *The Journal of the Acoustical Society of America* 27, no. 5 (1955). Published online 29 June 2005, https://doi.org/10.1121/1.1908102.
Ihde, Don. *Listening and Voice: A Phenomenology of Sound*. Athens, OH: Ohio University Press, 1976.
Jameson, Frederic. "On Negt and Kluge." *October 46* (Fall 1988): 151–177.
Jameson, Frederic. *The Political Unconscious: Narrative as a Socially Symbolic Act*. Ithaca, NY: Cornell University Press, 1981.
Kahn, Douglas, and Gregory Whitehead, eds. *Wireless Imagination: Sound, Radio, and the Avant-Garde*. Cambridge: MIT Press, 1994.
Keskinen, Mikko. "Hearing Voices in Dreams: Freud's Tossing and Turning with Speech and Writing." *PSYART: A Hyperlink Journal for the Psychological Study of the Arts*. Accessed 28 January 2021. http://psyartjournal.com/article/show/keskinen-hearing_voices_in_dreams_freuds_tossing_.
Kittler, Friedrich. *Grammophon. Film. Typewriter*. Berlin: Brinkman & Bose, 1986.
Kittler, Friedrich. *Gramophone, Film, Typewriter*. Translated by Geoffrey Winthrop-Young and Michael Wutz. Stanford, CA: Stanford University Press, 1999.
Klein, Tobias Robert, and Asmus Trautsch, eds. *Klang und Musik bei Walter Benjamin*. Munich: Wilhelm Fink, 2013.
Kluge, Alexander. *Bestandsaufnahme, Utopie Film: Zwanzig Jahre neuer deutscher Film*. Frankfurt a.M.: Zweitausendeins, 1983.
Kluge, Alexander. *Cinema Stories*. Translated by Martin Brady and Helen Hughes. New York: New Directions, 2007.
Kluge, Alexander. *Eigentum am Lebenslauf. Das Gesamte im Werk des Alexander Kluge*. Interviewed and directed by Andreas Ammer. Bayerischer Rundfunk, 2007. CD.
Kluge, Alexander. *Fontane, Kleist, Deustschland, Büchner. Zur Grammatik der Zeit*. Berlin: Verlag Klaus Wagenbach, 2004.
Kluge, Alexander. *Geschichten vom Kino*. Frankfurt a.M.: Suhrkamp, 2007.

Kluge, Alexander. "Ein imaginärer Opernführer." In *Jahrbuch der Hamburgischen Staatsoper 1984–1988*. Hamburg: Intendanz der Hamburgischen Staatsoper, 1988.
Kluge, Alexander. "Kluge on Opera, Film, and Feelings." Edited by Miriam Hansen. Translated by Miriam Hansen and Sara S. Poor. *New German Critique* 49 (Winter 1990): 89–138.
Kluge, Alexander. *Kongs große Stunde. Chronik des Zusammenhangs*. Frankfurt a.M.: Suhrkamp, 2015.
Kluge, Alexander. *Die Macht der Gefühle*. Frankfurt a.M.: Zweitausendeins, 1984.
Kluge, Alexander. *Die Macht der Gefühle*. Directed by Alexander Kluge. Performed by Hannelore Hoger. Kairos-Film, 1984. DVD.
Kluge, Alexander. *Nachrichten aus der ideologischen Antike. Marx – Eisenstein – Das Kapital*. Frankfurt a.M.: Suhrkamp, 2008. Booklet.
Kluge, Alexander. *Neonröhren des Himmels: Filmalbum. Beibuch zu Sämtliche Kinofilme*. Frankfurt a.M.: Zweitausendeins, 2007.
Kluge, Alexander. *Die Patriotin: Texte, Bilder 1–6*. Frankfurt a.M.: Zweitausendeins, 1979.
Kluge, Alexander. *Ulmer Dramaturgien. Reibungsverluste*. Munich: Carl Hanser Verlag, 1980.
Kluge, Alexander. "On Film and the Public Sphere." Translated by Thomas Y. Levin and Miriam B. Hansen. *New German Critique* 24/25 (Autumn-Winter, 1981–1983): 206–220.
Kluge, Alexander, and Oskar Negt. *Geschichte und Eigensinn*. Frankfurt a.M.: Zweitausendeins, 1985.
Kluge, Alexander, and Oskar Negt. *Öffentlichkeit und Erfahrung. Zur Organisationsanalyse von bürgerlicher und proletarischer Öffentlichkeit*. Frankfurt a.M.: Suhrkamp, 1972.
Kluge, Alexander, and Oskar Negt. *Die Patriotin*. Frankfurt a.M.: Zweitausendeins, 1980. Film.
Kluge, Alexander, and Oskar Negt. *Public Sphere and Experience: Toward an Analysis of the Bourgeois and Proletarian Public Sphere*. Translated by Peter Labanyi, Jamie Owen Daniel, and Assenka Oksiloff. Minneapolis: University of Minnesota Press, 1993.
Koch, Gertrud. "Rudolf Arnheim: The Materialist of Aesthetic Illusion: Gestalt Theory and Reviewer's Practice." *New German Critique* 51 (Fall 1990): 164–178.
Koepnick, Lutz. "Benjamin's Silence." In *Sound Matters: Essays on the Acoustics of Modern German Culture*, edited by Nora M. Alter and Lutz Koepnick, 117–129. New York: Berghahn Books, 2004.
Kolb, Richard. *Das Horoskop des Hörspiels*. Berlin: Max Hesse Verlag, 1932.
Koschorke, Albrecht. "Imaginationen der Kulturgrenze. Zu Ludwig Tiecks Erzählung 'Der blonde Eckbert.'" In *Kultur-Schreiben als romantisches Projekt: Romantische Ethnographie im Spannungsfeld zwischen Imagination und Wissenschaft*, edited by David Wellbery, 135–153. Würzburg: Königshausen & Neumann, 2012.
Kracauer, Siegfried. *Theory of Film: The Redemption of Physical Reality*. Princeton, NJ: Princeton University Press, 1997.
Kracauer, Siegfried. *Werke*. Frankfurt a.M.: Suhrkamp, 2004.
Krapp, Peter. *Déjà Vu: Aberrations of Cultural Memory*. Minneapolis: University of Minnesota Press, 2004.
Krauss, Rosalind E. *The Optical Unconscious*. Cambridge: MIT Press, 1993.
Krug, Hans-Jürgen. *Kleine Geschichte des Hörspiels*. Konstanz: UVK Verlagsgesellschaft mbH, 2008.
Kühn, Walter. "Das alte Buch. Eichs Beitrag zur Festschrift von Martin Heidegger." *Berliner Hefte zur Geschichte des literarischen Lebens*, vol. 7, 152–171. Berlin: Institut für deutsche Literatur, 2005.

Kühn, Walter. *Vermischte Zustände. Heidegger im literarisch-philosophischen Leben der fünfziger Jahre des zwanzigsten Jahrhunderts*. Würzburg: Königshausen & Neumann, 2015.
Lacoue-Labarthe, Philippe. *Typography: Mimesis, Philosophy, Politics*. Cambridge: Harvard University Press, 1989.
Langford, Michelle. "Alexander Kluge." *Senses of Cinema 27* (July 2003): n.p. Accessed 31 January 2021. http://sensesofcinema.com/2003/great-directors/kluge/.
Langston, Richard. "Toward an Ethics of Fantasy: The Kantian Dialogues of Oskar Negt and Alexander Kluge." *The Germanic Review* 85, no. 4 (October–December 2010): 271–293.
Lawrence, D. H. *Psychoanalysis and the Unconscious and Fantasia of the Unconscious*. Cambridge: Cambridge University Press, 2006.
Lecourt, Edith. *Freud et l'univers sonore: le tic-tac du désir*. Paris: L'Harmattan, 1992.
Levin, Thomas. "For the Record: Adorno on Music in the Age of Its Technological Reproducibility." *October* 55 (Winter 1990): 23–47.
Märki, Peter. *Günter Eichs Hörspielkunst*. Frankfurt a.M.: Akademische Verlagsgesellschaft, 1974.
Mathis, Donald R. *Melodic Sculpturing: The Art and Science of Singing*. Bloomington, IN: Arthur House, 2009.
McArthur, Emily. "The iPhone *Erfahrung*: Siri, the Auditory Unconscious, and Walter Benjamin's 'Aura.'" In *Design, Mediation, and the Posthuman*, edited by Dennis M. Weiss, Amy D. Propen, and Colbey Emmerson Reid, 113–128. Lanham, MD: Lexington Books, 2014.
McClatchie, Stephen. "Götterdämmerung, *Führerdämmerung*?" *Opera Quarterly* 23, no. 2–3 (Spring–Summer 2007): 184–198.
Mellamphy, Dan, and Nandita Biswas Mellamphy. "What's the 'Matter' with Materialism? Walter Benjamin and the New Janitocracy." *Janus Head* 11, no. 1 (2009): 163–182.
Menke, Bettine. "'However One Calls Into the Forest . . .': Echoes of Translation." In *Walter Benjamin and Romanticism*, edited by Andrew E. Benjamin and Beatrice Hanssen, 83–97. New York: Continuum, 2002.
Molnar, Michael. "Reading the Look." In *Reading Freud's Reading*, edited by Sander L. Gilman, 77–90. New York: New York University Press, 1994.
Mowitt, John. "Whistle." In *Sounds: The Ambient Humanities*, by John Mowitt, 40–57. Berkeley: University of California Press, 2014.
Nägele, Rainer. *Echoes of Translation: Reading Between Texts*. Baltimore: Johns Hopkins University Press, 1997.
Nancy, Jean-Luc. *À l'écoute*. Paris: Éditions Galilée, 2002.
Nancy, Jean-Luc. *Listening*. Translated by Charlotte Mandell. New York: Fordham University Press, 2007.
Napolin, Julie Beth. "The Fact of Resonance: An Acoustics of Determination in Faulkner and Benjamin." *Symploke* 23, no. 1–2 (2015): 171–186.
Napolin, Julie Beth. *The Fact of Resonance: Modernist Acoustics and Narrative Form*. New York: Fordham University Press, 2020.
Nietzsche, Friedrich. *Sämtliche Werke*. Berlin/New York: De Gruyter, 1999.
Nietzsche, Friedrich. *Thus Spoke Zarathustra*. Translated by Adrian del Caro. Cambridge: Cambridge University Press, 2006.
North, Paul. *The Problem of Distraction*. Stanford, CA: Stanford University Press, 2012.

Oxford English Dictionary. 2nd ed. 20 vols. Oxford: Oxford University Press, 1989. Continually updated at http://www.oed.com/.
Pahl, Katrin. *Tropes of Transport: Hegel and Emotion*. Evanston, IL: Northwestern University Press, 2012.
Petersson, Dag. *The Art of Reconciliation: Photography and the Conception of Dialectics in Benjamin, Hegel, and Derrida*. Hampshire: Palgrave, 2013.
Philpotts, Matthew. *The Margins of Dictatorship: Assent and Dissent in the Work of Günter Eich and Bertolt Brecht*. Oxford: Peter Lang, 2003.
Philpotts, Matthew. "Surrendering the Author-function: Günter Eich and the National Socialist System." In *Modes of Censorship: National Contexts and Diverse Media*, edited by Francesca Billiani, 257–278. New York: Routledge, 2014.
Ponge, Francis. "Anthracite, or Coal Par Excellence [*L'anthracite, ou le charbon par excellence*]." In *Francis Ponge: Selected Poems*, edited by Margaret Guiton, 134–137. Winston-Salem, NC: Wake Forest University Press, 1994.
Ponge, Francis. *Francis Ponge: Selected Poems*. Edited by Margaret Guiton. Winston-Salem, NC: Wake Forest University Press, 1994.
Ponge, Francis. "Notes on a shell [*Notes pour un coquillage*]." In *Francis Ponge: Selected Poems*, edited by Margaret Guiton, 62. Winston-Salem, NC: Wake Forest University Press, 1994.
Rank, Otto. *Das Inzest-Motiv in Dichtung und Sage*. 2nd ed. Leipzig and Vienna: Franz Deuticke, [1912] 1926.
Reik, Theodor. *Listening with the Third Ear*. New York: Farrar, Strauss & Giroux, [1948] 1983.
Renard, Maurice. "La mort et le coquillage." In *Le voyage immobile, suivi d'autres histoires singuliéres*, by Maurice Renard, 101–109. Paris: Georges Crès, 1922.
Renard, Maurice. *Le voyage immobile, suivi d'autres histoires singuliéres*. Paris: Georges Crès, 1922.
Rentschler, Eric. "Rudolf Arnheim's Early Passage between Social and Aesthetic Film Criticism." In *Arnheim for Film and Media Studies*, edited by Scott Higgins, 52–68. New York: Routledge, 2011.
Richter, Gerhard. *Inheriting Walter Benjamin*. London: Bloomsbury, 2016.
Richter, Gerhard. *Walter Benjamin and the Corpus of Autobiography*. Detroit: Wayne State University Press, 2000.
Rickels, Laurence A. *Aberrations of Mourning*. Minneapolis: University of Minnesota Press, 2011.
Rippere, Victoria L. "Ludwig Tieck's 'Der blonde Eckbert': A Psychological Reading." *PMLA: Publications of the Modern Language Association of America* 85, no. 3 (May 1970): 473–486.
Ritter, Johann Wilhelm. *Fragmente aus dem Nachlasse eines jungen Physikers*. Leipzig: Kiepenhauer Verlag, 1984.
Ronell, Avital. *The Telephone Book: Technology, Schizophrenia, Electric Speech*. Lincoln: University of Nebraska Press, 1989.
Rrenban, Monad. *Wild, Unforgettable Philosophy in Early Works of Walter Benjamin*. Lanham, MD: Lexington Books, 2004.
Ryder, Robert. "Innervation." In *Fueling Culture: 101 Words for Energy and Environment*, edited by Jennifer Wenzel, Patricia Yaeger, and Imre Szeman, 202–205. New York: Fordham University Press, 2017.
Ryder, Robert. "On the Minute – Out of Time: Reading the Misreading of Time in Walter Benjamin's 'Auf die Minute' (1934)." *Germanic Review* 91, no. 3 (2016): 217–235.

Ryder, Robert. "Shell-Shock: Sounding the Acoustical Unconscious." *The New Review of Film and Television Studies* 5, no. 2 (August 2007): 135–155.

Saussy, Haun. *Comparative Literature in an Age of Globalization*. Baltimore: Johns Hopkins University Press, 2006.

Schäfer, Klaus. "Sprachliche Analyse zu 'Muschel.'" Accessed 11 August 2021. https://www.schaefer-sac.de/klaus/sdc/z-pdf/MUSCHEL.PDF.

Schafer, R. Murray. "Open Ears." In *Auditory Culture Reader*, edited by Michael Bull and Les Back, 25–40. New York: Berg, 2003.

Schiller-Lerg, Sabine. *Walter Benjamin und der Rundfunk*. Munich: K. G. Saur, 1984.

Schwartz, David. *Listening Subjects: Music, Psychoanalysis, Culture*. Durham, NC: Duke University Press, 1997.

Schwitzke, Heinz. *Das Hörspiel: Dramaturgie und Geschichte*. Köln: Kiepenheuer und Witsch, 1963.

Schwitzke, Heinz. *Über Günter Eich*. Frankfurt a.M.: Suhrkamp, 1970.

Sellner, Timothy F. "Jungian Psychology and the Romantic Fairy Tale: A New Look at Tieck's Der blonde Eckbert." *Germanic Review* 55 (1980): 89–97.

Siegert, Bernard. "1953, March 26: The Bayrische Rundfunk broadcasts Max Frisch's radio play *Herr Biedermann und die Brandstifter*." In *A New History of German Literature*, edited by David Wellbery, 861–866. Cambridge: Harvard University Press, 2004.

Siegert, Bernhard. "Hold me in your arms, Ma Bell. Telefonie und Literatur." In *Telefonie und Gesellschaft. Beiträge zu einer Soziologie des Telefons*, edited by Ulrich Lange and Klaus Beck, 330–347. Berlin: Spiess, 1989.

Siisiäinen, Lauri. *Foucault and the Politics of Hearing*. New York: Routledge, 2012.

Smith, David Livingston. *Approaching Psychoanalysis: An Introductory Course*. London: Karnac Books, [1999] 2005.

Stanley, Robert. "Tieck's Der blonde Eckbert and Flaubert's Saint Julien: Blood and Guilt in Two Tales." *Journal of Evolutionary Psychology* 5, no. 3–4 (August 1984): 245–253.

Smith, Steven C. *A Heart at Fire's Center: The Life and Music of Bernard Herrmann*. Berkeley/Los Angeles/London: University of California Press, 2002.

Steege, Benjamin. *Helmholtz and the Modern Listener*. Cambridge: Cambridge University Press, 2012.

Sterne, Jonathan. *The Audible Past: Cultural Origins of Sound Reproduction*. Durham, NC: Duke University Press, 2003.

Sterne, Jonathan. *Sound Studies Reader*. New York: Routledge, 2012.

Strässle, Thomas. "'Das Hören ist ein Sehen von und durch innen': Johann Wilhelm Ritter and the Aesthetics of Music." In *Music and Literature in German Romanticism*, edited by Siobhán Donovan and Robin Elliott, 27–41. Rochester, NY: Camden House, 2004.

Swaminathan, Nikhil. "Thunder, Lighting and . . . Snow." *Scientific American*, 4 March 2009. https://www.scientificamerican.com/article/thundersnow-storm/.

Szendy, Peter. "The Auditory Re-Turn (The Point of Listening)." In *Thresholds of Listening: Sound, Technics, Space*, edited by Sander van Maas, 18–29. New York: Fordham University Press, 2015.

Szendy, Peter. *Listen: A History of Our Ears*. Translated by Charlotte Mandell. New York: Fordham University Press, 2008.

Tagliacozzo, Tamara. *Experience and Infinite Task: Knowledge, Language and Messianism in the Philosophy of Walter Benjamin*. Lanham, MD: Rowman & Littlefield, 2018.

Tartar, Maria. "Unholy Alliances: Narrative Ambiguity in Tieck's 'Der blonde Eckbert.'" *MLN* 102, no. 3 (April 1987): 608–626.
The New Grove Dictionary of Music and Musicians. 2nd ed. Edited by Stanley Sadie. New York: Grove, 2000.
Tieck, Ludwig. "Eckbert the Fair." In *Six German Romantic Tales*, translated by Ronald Taylor, 16–33. London: Angel Books, 1985.
Tieck, Ludwig. *Schriften in zwölf Bänden*. Frankfurt: Deutscher Klassiker Verlag, 1985.
Trautsch, Asmus. "Die abgelauschte Stadt und der Rhythmus des Glücks." In *Klang und Musik bei Walter Benjamin*, edited by Tobias Robert Klein and Asmus Trautsch, 17–46. Munich: Wilhelm Fink, 2013.
Turvey, Malcolm. "Arnheim and Modernism." In *Arnheim for Film and Media Studies*, edited by Scott Higgins, 31–49. New York: Routledge, 2011.
Vancour, Shawn. "Arnheim on Radio: *Materialtheorie* and Beyond." In *Arnheim for Film and Media Studies*, edited by Scott Higgins, 178–194. New York: Routledge, 2011.
Vieregg, Axel. *Der eigenen Fehlbarkeit begegnet. Günter Eichs Realitäten 1933–1945*. Eggingen: Edition Isele, 1993.
Vieregg, Axel. "The Spanner in the Works." In *The Berlin Review of Books*, 30 March 2011. http://berlinbooks.org/brb/2011/03/the-spanner-in-the-works/.
Vieregg, Axel, ed. *"Unsere Sünden sind Maulwürfe." Die Günter-Eich-Debatte*. Amsterdam: Rodopi, 1996.
Vogt, Guntram. "»Ohne Musik ist alles Leben ein Irrtum«. Zu Alexander Kluges Musik-Magazinen." In *Die Schrift an der Wand – Alexander Kluge: Rohstoffe und Materialien*, edited by Christian Schulte, 253–270. Osnabrück: Universitätsverlag Rasch, 2000.
Wagner, Hans-Ulrich. "'Den Feldzug gegen den Rundfunk fortsetzen.' Günter Eich und der Rundfunk 1928–1940." In *Günter Eich 1907–1972. Nach dem Ende der Biographie*, edited by Peter Walther, 49–60. Berlin: Lukas Verlag, 2000.
Wagner, Hans-Ulrich. *Günter Eich und der Rundfunk. Essay und Dokumentation*. Potsdam: Verlag für Berlin-Brandenburg, 1999.
Weber, Samuel. "Anxiety – Borderlines in/of Psychoanalysis." *Zeitschrift für Medien- und Kulturforschung* 0 (2009): 73–86.
Weber, Samuel. "Anxiety: The Uncanny Borderline of Psychoanalysis?" *Konturen* 3 (2010): 45–62.
Weber, Samuel. *Benjamin's -abilities*. Cambridge: Harvard University Press, 2008.
Weber, Samuel. *Legend of Freud*. Stanford, CA: Stanford University Press, 2000.
Weber, Samuel. *Mass Mediauras*. Stanford, CA: Stanford University Press, 1996.
Weber, Samuel. *Theatricality as Medium*. New York: Fordham University Press, 2005.
Weber, Samuel. "The Visible, Invisible and Divisible: Thoughts on the Acoustic and Literary Image." *Belgrade Journal of Media and Communications* 1 (2009): 31–50.
Weissberg, Liliane. "Wiederholungen." In *Erinnern und Vergessen in der Europäischen Romantik*, edited by Günter Oesterle, 177–191. Würzburg: Königshausen & Neumann, 2001.
Whitney, Tyler. *Eardrums: Literary Modernism as Sonic Warfare*. Evanston, IL: Northwestern University Press, 2019.
Wordsworth, William. *The Excursion*. London: Macmillan, 1935.
Zimmermann, Harro. "Kult der Anschauung – Blinder Funk. Nachbemerkungen zur Radiotheorie von Rudolf Arnheim." *Jahrbuch zur Kultur und Literatur der Weimarer Republik* 9 (2004): 223–248.
Zipes, Jack. *Spells of Enchantment*. New York: Penguin Group, 1991.

Index

acoustical unconscious 7–27, 28–41, 47, 61–64, 85, 99–100, 124–27, 131–32, 150, 157, 195–202, 220–23, 227–28, 236–38, 239–49. See also optical unconscious; unconscious
Adorno, Theodor 18–19, 29, 43, 68, 121–22, 219, 239–40
alarm 69, 85, 88, 96. See also bird song; interruption
animals 3, 87–94, 184, 186, 199. See also Kafka, Franz
Arnheim, Rudolph 34, 36, 100, 102–10, 111–28, 137–338, 150–51, 162, 193. See also gesture
– art of listening/not listening 117–127, 132
– "Psychology of the Radio Listener" 107, 118–19, 122–23, 127
– *Film as Art* 32, 107, 109, 113–14
– materiality 108–17, 149–50
– *Radio as Aural Art* 107–9, 113, 116, 118
attention
– free-floating 124–27, 166–67. See also Freud, Sigmund
– as searchlight 124–25. See also Reik, Theodor
awakening 20–21, 63, 69, 83–85, 88, 94, 102–3, 106–8, 152–54, 156, 167–72, 176–80, 190–91, 207. See also forgetting; remembering

Barthes, Roland 192–93, 242
Baudelaire 26, 43
Beethoven, Ludwig van 228, 231–36, 248
Benjamin, Walter 13–14, 16–17, 19–21, 24, 28–37, 63–65, 67–69, 71, 82–85, 87–88, 90, 100–6, 108–9, 118–19, 124, 126–30, 132–35, 139–40, 145–51, 155–56, 177–78, 193, 195–96, 202, 203–5, 207–8, 220, 222–23, 226, 232, 235, 239–41, 144–45
– *Arcades Project* 43n43, 68, 243
– *Berlin Childhood around 1900* 6, 19, 28–29, 40–41, 49–51, 55, 60, 67, 148, 153. See also Walter, Benjamin: "Mummerehlen"

– *Berlin Chronicle* 8, 19, 28, 35–37, 39–40, 51, 53, 63, 84–85, 99–100, 153
– *Bustle about Kasperl* 101, 108, 134, 140–54, 157
– *The Cold Heart* 101, 108, 134–39, 141–42, 144, 151, 157, 190
– comportment of voice 107, 110, 113, 116, 128, 198–99. See also voice
– "Doctrine of the Similar" 1, 31, 55
– forgetting 65, 68–69, 85. See also memory; remembering
– "Franz Kafka" 68, 152
– "Kasperl and the Radio" 140–41, 151. See also Benjamin, Walter: *Bustle about Kasperl*
– "Little History of Photography" 37, 39
– "The Lamp" 1, 54–56, 58–61
– "Mummerehlen" 50–54, 58–59, 75, 106, 141. See also Benjamin, Walter: *Berlin Childhood*
– "On the Mimetic Faculty" 1, 31, 54–55
– *Origin of the German Trauerspiel* 1–3, 10, 13, 104–5, 167
– *Problems in the Sociology of Language* 129, 132–33
– "Reflections on Radio" 23, 102
– *Reflections on Radio* 105–6, 152–53
– shell 1, 3–4, 6–7, 9, 18, 28–29, 40–41, 50–66, 66–68, 85, 88, 101, 172, 187. See also telephone
– "The Telephone" 44, 46–47, 51, 53, 148. See also Benjamin, Walter: *Berlin Childhood*
– "Theater and Radio" 151–52
– voice and gesture 103–5, 108, 115, 119, 127–34, 143, 246. See also gesture; voice
– *Work of Art in the Age of its Technological Reproducibility* 19–20, 25, 28–36, 39–40, 44–45, 57, 61–62, 71, 126–27, 131, 149–50, 208–10, 219, 222, 226, 239, 244
bird song 18, 33–34, 67–69, 79–80, 85, 92–99, 183–84, 186, 194, 213–14, 217. See also alarm; interruption

Bloch, Ernst 84–87, 89–91, 99–100, 103. See also *déjà entendu/déjà vu*
body 21, 65, 103, 128–29, 138, 148, 172, 176–78, 197
Brecht, Bertolt 111, 118–19, 127, 133, 135, 151–52, 188, 204–5, 234–35. See also gesture

camera 20, 24, 27, 33–34, 36, 42, 45–47, 57, 61, 65, 83, 131, 192–93, 196, 218, 221, 235, 237, 244
– other nature of 40, 56, 101, 207–8
Chaplin, Charlie *Modern Times* 193, 197, 200–1
childhood 1, 3, 41, 43–44, 51–55, 63–64, 67, 70, 78, 82, 84, 88–89, 92–93, 96–97, 99–100, 132–34, 153, 179
Chion, Michel 146–47, 176
cinema 9, 14–17, 19–20, 24–26, 28–35, 44, 102–4, 109–10, 112–14, 117, 131, 149–52, 179–80, 192–28, 230, 233, 235–37, 240–42, 244–45
– of emancipation 194–95, 208–10, 222–23, 235–36. See also Kluge, Alexander
conch shell. See Benjamin, Walter: shell
consciousness 21–22, 27, 35–36, 46, 61, 65, 77, 83, 90, 100–1, 103–4, 112–13, 123–25, 127, 131–32, 145, 150, 167, 177, 208, 236, 244–45. See also unconsciousness
Cordava, Eduardo 51–52
Cory, Mark E. 168

darkness 36, 85, 90–91, 99–100, 182. See also Bloch, Ernst
déjà entendu/déjà vu 28–30, 35–40, 51, 53, 63, 84–86, 91, 99, 179. See also echo; memory
Deleuze and Guattari 24–25, 111
Derrida, Jacques 4–7, 21, 23, 46, 69n12, 96, 181, 183, 246, 248

ear
– listening with half 117–18, 121–24, 190. See also hearing; listening

– listening with third 117, 125n80, 127. See also hearing; listening
echo 35n25, 36–37, 40, 42, 62, 64, 84, 144–47, 180–83, 186–87. See also *déjà entendu/déjà vu*
Eich, Günter 153–66, 159–66, 178–80, 187–89, 206, 240, 245
– *An Hour with the Dictionary* 173, 185
– *Dreams* 150, 156, 167–78, 181, 184–85, 187, 190
– *Rebellion in Gold City* 158–60
– *Sabeth* 144, 178–86, 190–91. See also Sabeth (raven)
– *The Year Lazertis* 185–191, 230, 248
emancipation. See cinema of emancipation; fantasy, emancipatory
Erlmann, Viet 14–18

fantasy 201–7, 218–19, 223–39
– emancipatory 222–23, 227–28. See also cinema of emancipation
– storm of. See Kluge, Alexander: storm of fantasy
fascism 30, 151, 209, 217, 222, 226, 232
Faulkner, William 16–17
film. See cinema
Flinn, Caryl 224, 227–28, 232–34, 236
forgetting 20, 26, 43, 49, 65, 68–72, 77–78, 81–94, 96, 137, 139, 178–79, 247. See also awakening; memory; remembering
Foucault, Michel 239
Freud, Sigmund 7, 13, 18–21, 30–31, 43, 64–65, 100, 115, 121–27, 144–45, 166–67, 170–71, 202–4, 244
– *Interpretation of Dreams* 144, 170
– *Psychopathology of Everyday Life* 20, 31, 69–71, 75–77, 81, 131
– Signorelli parapraxis 70–87, 81–82, 84, 86, 92–93, 187, 236
Fries, Thomas 81, 84n52, 99
future 37–40, 47–49, 52–53, 63–64, 69–70, 138, 226–27. See also *déjà entendu/déjà vu*

gesture 5–6, 8, 37–38, 53, 104–5, 115–16, 119, 127–31, 138, 143, 190, 195, 245–46. See also voice

Godard, Jean-Luc 220–21
glove 37–38, 52–53, 64–65, 69, 84, 101, 138
guilt 81, 87, 93, 136

Hamacher, Werner 58–60
Hansen, Miriam 16, 18, 34, 39–40, 149–152, 193, 195–96, 199, 202–3, 206, 220, 222, 227–29, 239
– *Cinema and Experience* 14, 31, 195, 242–43
hearing 2–7, 9, 15, 18, 21–22, 26, 29, 34, 40, 44, 62–63, 68, 70, 90–92, 96, 99, 101, 106, 117, 127, 140, 147, 150, 171, 176–78, 183–84, 188–90, 194, 247–48. See also ear; listening
– otherwise 4, 10, 194, 248
Heidegger, Martin 89, 153, 158–66, 191, 206
– "Building—Dwelling—Thinking" 173, 189
– "Poetically Man Dwells" 164, 166, 186–87
Herder 104, 113, 129, 162
Hillman, Roger 226–27, 232–36
Hölderlin, Friedrich 117, 164
Husserl 5–6, 198

Ihde, Don 53, 169
interruption 115–16, 125, 128, 132–34, 137–39, 141, 151–52, 189, 195, 235. See also alarm; bird song

Jameson, Frederic 25, 178, 203–4, 235
Jung, Karl 18–19, 80

Kafka, Franz 3, 45–46, 50n60, 65, 87–88, 101, 127, 152, 157, 199. See also animals
Kittler, Friedrich 66–67
Koch, Gertrud 110, 224
Kluge, Alexander 24, 192–94, 195, 201–211, 222–233, 240, 245. See also fantasy, emancipatory
– *Cinema Stories* 192, 194, 207–23, 225, 246
– *The Patriot* 226–28, 232, 236
– *The Power of Emotions* 223–25, 227
– *Stocktaking Utopia Film* 206, 210–11
– storm of fantasy 195, 205–6,
Kracauer, Siegfried 16, 192–221
– *Marseille Notebooks* 198–201

– *Theory of Film* 14–15, 193, 195–96, 198–99, 222–23
Kraus, Karl 77, 127–29, 189, 229–30, 242
Krauss, Rosalind 25

Lacan, Jacques 46
– "Position of the Unconscious" 96
lamp. See Benjamin, Walter: shell
language 50–51, 64–65, 103–4, 109, 133–34, 139, 141, 157, 161–62, 165, 184–85, 241
– sonority of 8, 10, 23, 64, 113, 246. See also Derrida, Jacques
listening 2–3, 23, 53, 67–68, 101, 106, 112, 117–23, 169, 183–84, 186, 188–89, 246 See also ear, hearing
– distracted 125–27, 190. See also Arnheim, Rudolph; ear; hearing; receptivity
– with half an ear 117–18, 121–23, 190
– passive 118–20, 122
– primal 4, 7, 167

Marki, Peter 178, 180–82
Marx, Karl 202–3. See also fantasy
McLuhan, Marshal 17, 27
measuring 13, 113, 117, 153, 162–66, 186–89, 206–7, 210. See also Eich, Günter; Heidegger, Martin
memory 9, 16, 38, 41–43, 52, 68–70, 76–78, 83, 86, 91, 93, 136, 148, 247–48. See also childhood; forgetting; remembering
Mickey Mouse 30n6, 140–54
microphone 34, 40, 131, 138, 147–48, 175, 219
mimesis 1, 31, 56, 113, 129–31, 141, 193, 196. See also voice
Molnar, Michael 72–73
music 1–9, 17–19, 29, 55–57, 61–62, 108–12, 117, 120–21, 135–36, 185–86, 192–96, 199–202, 206–15, 216–38, 239–41

name 69–70, 78, 82, 183. See also forgetting; remembering
Nancy, Jean-Luc 113, 146–47
– *Listening* 112, 246
Napolin, Julie Beth 14–18, 20, 181

National Socialism 100, 153–54, 156–61, 163, 216–17, 224
Nietzsche, Friedrich 91, 117, 124, 125n80
– *Zarathustra* 88–91, 94
North, Paul 126
Novalis 104, 109, 162

optical unconscious 10, 12, 14, 19–20, 24, 28, 31–32, 36–37, 39–40, 47, 83, 127, 131, 145, 150, 190, 195–96, 199, 208–10, 223, 227–28, 235, 240–42, 244. See also see also acoustical unconscious; *déjà entendu/déjà vu*; unconscious

perception 5, 18–22, 26, 43, 50, 110, 112–13, 126–27, 162–63, 166–67, 176, 186, 189, 191, 209–10, 239–41, 245n20
phenomenology 104, 110, 113, 149–50, 169
phonetics 9, 22, 29, 60–63, 74, 130–31, 187
photography 19, 28, 32–33, 36–37, 39–40, 59, 243
Piaget, Jean 132–33
poetry 154–55, 160–61, 163–66, 241. See also Eich, Günter
Proust 3, 21, 29, 43–44, 47, 49–50, 84, 103, 136

radio 9–10, 23, 26, 100–16, 118–27, 131–54, 155–62, 167–71, 172–80, 184–91, 241, 245
rebus 70, 72, 75, 77–78, 81–82, 85–86, 93, 100, 113. See also Freud, Sigmund
receptivity 2, 7, 107, 121, 125, 139, 154, 166–67, 185–86, 199. See also listening
redemption 194–95, 206, 221–22, 225, 228, 235
Reik, Theodor 117, 124–27
remembering 3, 78, 82, 106, 139, 173, 188. See also awakening; forgetting; name; memory
Renard, Maurice 66, 68, 172–73, 187
repetition 22, 44, 69, 91, 93, 97–100, 143, 145, 181–82, 190
Rickels, Laurence 45–46
Ritter, Johann Wilhelm 34n19, 55–56
Romanticism 104, 109, 156–57, 160–62, 185, 199

Ronell, Avital 46, 48
Rousseau 104, 162
Ruttmann, Walter 185

Sabeth (raven) 178–85. See also Eich, Günter: *Sabeth*
Saussy, Haun 231
Schoen, Ernst 107–8, 134, 136, 139
Scholem, Gershom 68, 107–8, 129, 209
Schwitzke, Heins 156, 172, 185, 189
senses 16n35, 43–46, 49, 132, 166, 169. See also hearing; synesthesia
shell. See Benjamin, Walter: shell
shock 36–37, 136, 195, 202, 204–5, 207–8, 222
Siegert, Bernhard 45n48, 156–57, 171, 178, 184, 186
signification 2, 8, 113–16, 174, 138
Signorelli, Luca. See Freud: Signorelli parapraxis
slow motion 32–36, 106–7, 150–51, 207. See also cinema
sound 17, 25, 60–61, 67–68, 100, 113, 133–34, 139, 149, 157, 169, 193–94, 196, 218–20, 222. See also hearing
Sterne, Jonathan 17, 25
stranger 37–38, 64–65, 69–70, 82, 84, 89, 101, 136–37, 151
synesthesia 56, 175. See also senses
Szendy, Peter 246

telephone 9–10, 28, 40–50, 53, 63–65, 67–104, 122–23, 131, 144. See also Benjamin: shell
Tieck, Johann Ludwig 9, 26, 78–94, 103, 158, 240, 245, 247
– "Eckbert the Fair" 47, 67–81, 80–89, 91–100, 136, 147–48, 178–79, 187, 245, 248. See also bird song
timbre 23, 111–13, 116–17, 153, 182, 184. See also voice

uncanny 45, 52
unconscious 7, 13, 20–21, 24–25, 29, 43, 45–46, 49–50, 64–65, 69, 71–72, 82–84, 100–1, 122–23, 176, 201, 208, 222–23. See also acoustical

unconscious; consciousness; Freud, Sigmund; optical unconscious
– collective 17, 84n52, 150–51

voice 23, 45, 103–5, 108–13, 115–16, 119, 125, 128–31, 145–47, 149–50, 153, 167, 171, 175, 183–84, 197. See also echo; gesture; timbre
– comportment of 104–5, 107, 110, 113, 115–16, 125, 128–29, 139, 125, 153, 167, 198–99. See also Benjamin, Walter
– gesticulating 113, 127–134

Vygotsky, Lev 132–33, 151

Wagner 218, 220–22, 225–26, 232, 235
Weber, Samuel 2, 11, 43–44, 90, 105–6, 115, 128–29, 138, 145, 189–90, 206, 243–44
Weimar Republic 101, 153, 157, 168
Weissberg, Liliane 81, 97–99
wireless 108, 118–20
word-as-symbol 105–6, 116n50, 139
Wordsworth, William 57–58
WWII 88, 153, 155, 157, 160–61

www.ingramcontent.com/pod-product-compliance
Lightning Source LLC
Chambersburg PA
CBHW050519170426
43201CB00013B/2011